Fellowship and Freedom

Fellowship and Freedom

The Merchant Adventurers and
the Restructuring of English
Commerce, 1582–1700

THOMAS LENG

OXFORD

UNIVERSITY PRESS

OXFORD
UNIVERSITY PRESS

Great Clarendon Street, Oxford, OX2 6DP,
United Kingdom

Oxford University Press is a department of the University of Oxford.
It furthers the University's objective of excellence in research, scholarship,
and education by publishing worldwide. Oxford is a registered trade mark of
Oxford University Press in the UK and in certain other countries

First Edition published in 2020

Impression: 1

Published in the United States of America by Oxford University Press
198 Madison Avenue, New York, NY 10016, United States of America

British Library Cataloguing in Publication Data

Data available

Library of Congress Control Number: 2019954818

ISBN 978-0-19-879447-9

Printed and bound in Great Britain by
Clays Ltd, Elcograf S.p.A.

Links to third party websites are provided by Oxford in good faith and
for information only. Oxford disclaims any responsibility for the materials
contained in any third party website referenced in this work.

Contents

Acknowledgements

Many scholars have helped in the course of the researching and writing of this book. I would particularly like to thank my colleagues and students at the University of Sheffield, especially Mike Braddick, James Shaw, and Phil Withington, and my SCEMS co-director Tom Rutter. The organizers and audiences of research seminars at the Institute of Historical Research, London, and the University of Warwick, who heard parts of the book in progress, were very helpful. David Ormrod, Patrick Wallis, and Nuala Zahedieh have been particularly hospitable and encouraging, as have Will Pettigrew and his project team, including Edmond Smith, Aske Brock, Tristan Stein, and Liam Haydon. The anonymous readers for Oxford University Press made constructive and useful comments, and Cathryn Steele has been an excellent editor. The staff at the different archives and libraries listed in the bibliography have also been extremely helpful. Finally, Miriam Dobson has offered her support and advice throughout. This book is dedicated to her, Zoe, and Adam.

Abbreviations

Add.	Additional Manuscripts
APC	*Acts of the Privy Council of England*, 46 vols (London, 1890–1946)
BL	British Library
Bodl. Lib.	Bodleian Library
Bradshaw Letters	'The Manuscripts of Miss Farrington of Worden Hall, Co. Lancaster', in *Sixth Report of The Royal Commission on Historical Manuscripts* (London, 1877), pp. 426–44
CJ	Journals of the House of Commons
Coventry Papers	*Coventry Papers from the Archives of the Marquess of Bath at Longleat*, microfilm edition (1969)
CP	*Cecil Papers Online*
Hamburg Register	Register book of the Church of the English Court, Hamburg, Staatsarchiv Hamburg, 521–1
HL	Huntington Library
HMC	Historical Manuscripts Commission (for details of particular volumes, see Bibliography)
HMC Sackville I	*Calendar of the Manuscripts of Major-General Lord Sackville... Preserved at Knole, Sevenoaks, Kent. Volume I. Cranfield Papers 1551–1612*, ed. A. P. Newton (London, 1942)
HMC Sackville II	*Calendar of the Manuscripts of The Right Honourable Lord Sackville of Knole, Sevenoaks, Kent. Volume II. Papers Relating to Lionel Cranfield's Business Overseas, 1597–1612*, ed. F. J. Fisher (London, 1966).
HP	Hartlib Papers
KHLC	Kent History and Library Centre
Laws	W. E. Lingelbach (ed.), *The Merchant Adventurers of England: Their Laws and Ordinances with Other Documents* (1902)
Misselden, 'Discourse'	Edward Misselden, 'A Discourse, shewing the Necessity of the Restoringe of the Marchaunts Aduenturers Priviledges & Government in their Mart Towne in Germany', BL, Sloane MS 1453
NLW	National Library of Wales
NRO	Northamptonshire Record Office

ODNB	*Oxford Dictionary of National Biography*, electronic edition, Oxford University Press, 2004
SP	State Papers
SRO	Somerset Record Office
Thurloe State Papers	Thomas Birch (ed.), *A Collection of the State Papers of John Thurloe*, 7 vols (London, 1742)
TNA	The National Archives
Whitelocke Papers	*Whitelocke Papers from the Archives of the Marquess of Bath*, microfilm edition (1972)
WSA	Wiltshire and Swindon Archives

Conventions for Dating, Transcriptions, and Money

Dates are given old style, with the exception that the new year is dated from 1 January. The original spelling has been retained in manuscript transcriptions, with the exception that abbreviations and contractions have been silently expanded. Both Hamburg and the Netherlands used a similar money of account to England, based on pond/pfund, schelling/schilling and groot/grot: amounts of money in these currencies are followed by the abbreviation vls, short for vlamische (i.e. Flemish), following the practice in John J. McCusker, *Money and Exchange in Europe and America, 1600–1775: A Handbook* (Chapel Hill, 1978). All other amounts of money are in sterling.

Introduction

The Fellowship of Merchant Adventurers
after Antwerp

The governed trade of the Merchants Adventurers, is kept beyond the Seas and maintayned there by the privelidges of forrayne Princes, and of some one or more certayne Townes, where the said Merchants made their residence; Whereunto all forreyn Merchants desiring to buy English Cloth muste resorte, where they must either buy at such prices as the sellers reasonably impose, or return home unfurnished, loosing their charges; And in the opinyon of best experienced Merchants, there is Five in the hundreth in proffitt difference betwixt will you buy when a marchant offred his comodities to sell, and will you sell? when the Comoditie is sought after to be bought;...For an unskilfull multitude is a disturbance to skilfull traffique, in that an unnecessary multitude of Sellers, doe alwayes abase the price of the wares they sell, and likewise advance the Comodities theye buye.

Discourse of the Merchant Adventurers in response to the
free trade bill of 1604 (BL, Harleian 36, fol. 32v)

For the restreyninge of our Trade to our Mart Towne is the fundamental Statute of our Fellowship, upon which all the rest of our Lawes & Ordinances & consequently our Government have their dependence: And those many great priviledges which we enjoy from this Cittie are grounded & granted us upone noe other consideration, then the reciprocall advantage they have proposed to themselves, by haveinge our Trade confined unto their Cittie the place of our Residence; And therefore if we meane to continue our Governmement, or preserve our priviledges, We must of necessity hold strictly to that Law which is the foundacion of them both...

Petition of the Deputy, Assistants and Fellowship of Merchant
Adventurers of England residing at Hamburg to Lord Arlington,
18 October 1672 (Coventry Papers, 39, fol. 27v)

The seventeenth century has long been recognized as a turning point in England's commercial history. From a place on the margins of Europe in 1600, having

Fellowship and Freedom: The Merchant Adventurers and the Restructuring of English Commerce, 1582–1700.
Thomas Leng, Oxford University Press (2020). © Thomas Leng. DOI: 10.1093/oso/9780198794479.001.0001

recently lost the last remnant of its continental empire, by the close of the seventeenth century England had become a major European and rising global power with an established north American and Caribbean empire fuelled by the African slave trade, a growing commercial and naval presence in the Mediterranean, and (thanks to the East India Company) increasingly territorial ambitions in the far east.[1] From a position summed up by Christopher Clay as 'not many degrees removed from that of the colonial economy, dependent upon sales of primary products to more advanced regions and purchasing manufactures and services from them', England in 1700 was on the verge of reversing this relationship, not just with its colonial dependencies, but with parts of Europe too.[2]

Within this story, the dynamic zones have usually been presented as the new markets of the south, the far east, and especially the Atlantic. But throughout the seventeenth century, England's most important trading partners, statistically speaking, lay much closer to home. To be sure, seventeenth-century England's turbulent relationship with the United Provinces of the Netherlands has always attracted attention.[3] But the more prosaic aspects of England's commerce across the channel, and the textiles that continued to dominate it, have tended to be obscured by the new areas of enterprise. The rise of England's extra-European, multilateral trades, fuelled by imports and re-exports, has been framed against the decline of an earlier system: the bilateral export of semi-manufactured woollen cloth, often in return for more highly manufactured goods, a model destined to be supplanted in the early modern period. It is a narrative that draws our attention away from English trade with north-west Europe, where most of those cloths were destined to be sold in 1600, although it has been estimated that 41.9 per cent of English exports by value were still sent to those parts at the close of the century.[4] Woollen textiles still made up around 68.7 per cent of English domestic exports by that point, although by now the old draperies that were the traditional product of the cloth industry had been overtaken by the new draperies that had emerged in the late sixteenth century.[5] England's trade with its near neighbours, and its textile exports, were thus by no means rendered insignificant by the rise of colonial and long-distance commerce; indeed, David Ormrod has argued that the commercial pre-eminence acquired by England in the early eighteenth century was to a large extent dependent on the prior restructuring of its relationship

[1]   Classic overviews include G. D. Ramsay, *English Overseas Trade during the Centuries of Emergence* (London, 1957); Charles Wilson, *England's Apprenticeship 1603–1763* (London, 1965); Ralph Davis, 'English foreign trade, 1660–1700', in W. E. Minchington (ed.), *The Growth of English Trade in the Seventeenth and Eighteenth Centuries* (London, 1969), pp. 78–98; C. G. A. Clay, *Economic Expansion and Social Change: England 1500–1700. II. Industry, Trade and Government* (Cambridge, 1984).
[2]   Clay, *Economic Expansion*, II, p. 103.
[3]   Charles Wilson, *Profit and Power: A Study of England and the Dutch Wars* (London, 1978).
[4]   Clay, *Economic Expansion*, II, p. 142.   [5]   Ibid., p. 144.

with its closest trading partner, the United Provinces, as London supplanted Amsterdam as the hub of European commerce.[6]

For much of the seventeenth century, England's trade to the Netherlands was encompassed by the privileges of the trading company known as the Fellowship of Merchant Adventurers of England. That the names of its theatres of operation—Germany and the Low Countries—did not appear in its corporate title reflects the fact that, in the sixteenth century, this was England's primary trading company. The names of other corporations, like the Spanish or the Barbary companies, were regionally specific, but the title Merchant Adventurer signified to everyone a merchant involved in England's most substantial trade, the export of woollen cloth to 'Holland, Zealand, Brabant and Flanders, East Friezland, West Friezland, Hamburg and the territories of the same', as the Company's 1564 charter put it.[7] Its members were amongst Tudor London's commercial princes— Sir Thomas Gresham the most famous—and they dominated City government. Only in the second half of the seventeenth century did the Merchant Adventurers begin to be known as the Hamburg Company, a reflection of its diminished status and the contraction of its effective monopoly.

This book tells the story of this trading company as it fell from its late-sixteenth-century position at the pinnacle of England's trading elite, weakened by a series of commercial and political blows across the following century, before finally losing the last vestiges of its English privileges following the Glorious Revolution. Relative to other corporations and its free-trading rivals, the Company of Merchant Adventurers was destined to be a loser in the commercial and political changes of the era, but the decline of the Merchant Adventurers, and what it represented, is as much a part of the story of the transformation of English commerce as is the rise of the East India Company or the triangular trades of the Atlantic world. This is not just because of the continued importance of the cloth trade and trade to north-west Europe in general; it is also because of the approach to the regulation of commerce that the Company epitomized. The Fellowship of Merchant Adventurers was the major representative of a type of trading company that dominated England's overseas trade for much of the period 1500–1700: the 'regulated' company, whose members traded on their own accounts but according to a set of shared regulations, and whose status was upheld by regionally defined monopolistic privileges enshrined in a royal charter. Although it only received a charter granting full legal rights of incorporation from the crown in 1564, by then the Merchant Adventurers could claim an existence dating back over 250 years, during which it had perfected a distinctive regime for the government of trade

---

[6] David Ormrod, *The Rise of Commercial Empires: England and the Netherlands in the Age of Mercantilism, 1650–1770* (Cambridge, 2003).
[7] W. E. Lingelbach (ed.), *The Merchant Adventurers of England: Their Laws and Ordinances with Other Documents* (1902), p. 233 (hereafter *Laws*).

which is aptly summed up by the two epigraphs opening this book. The Company's regulations were fashioned to bring order to the marketplace, through restraining trade to 'certayne Townes' and to specialist 'mere' merchants possessed of the skill necessary to conduct commerce profitably. Freedom to participate in this market was exclusive, reserved for those with the appropriate training and so a source of 'privilege and exclusion'.[8] This was not simply for their own profit, however: because of the skilful Merchant Adventurer's ability to uphold the price of his major export, cloth, the true advantage was to the commonwealth. More than any other commodity, cloth was integral to the sixteenth-century understanding of commonwealth as the shared values that bound together English society.[9] The production of cloth was the nation's first real national industry, woven from the warp of husbandry and the weft of industry. The commercial regime that the Company purported to uphold—sometimes referred to in this book as the 'mart-trading system'—was therefore intended to do more than simply protect the interests of Company members: it was invested with moral intent, resting on a social vision in which the collective good was paramount, and individual profit merely the proper reward for pursuing one's allotted place in the commonwealth.

As something of an extension of the domestic guild system to the realm of overseas trade, the regulated company has generally been cast as more primitive than the joint stock corporation which was at the forefront of England's cross-continental trade in this period, remnant of a fading medieval moral order and its restrictive social division of labour.[10] In this interpretation, the geographical and occupational boundaries which defined the Merchant Adventurers' mart-trading system were doomed to break down under the onslaught of emerging capitalism, and the entrepreneurial energies it unleashed. In a more competitive and dynamic environment, joint stock corporations, with their economies of scale and institutional hierarchies, not to mention their capacity to deploy violence, possessed a will to survive that was lacking in the regulated companies, burdened as they were by an obsolete vision of brotherhood and equity in trade. The ideal of fellowship amongst brethren, in this sense, could not survive the growing demands for commercial freedom that accompanied the growth of English trade. Indeed, the similarity between the two quotations reproduced above, separated by almost seven decades of commercial expansion, might suggest a static moral vision,

---

[8] S. R. Epstein, *Freedom and Growth: The Rise of States and Markets in Europe, 1300–1750* (London and New York, 2000), p. 15.

[9] Rose Hentschell, *The Culture of Cloth in Early Modern England* (Aldershot, 2008); David Rollinson, *A Commonwealth of the People: Popular Politics and England's Long Social Revolution, 1066–1649* (Cambridge, 2010), pp. 301–38.

[10] See for instance P. W. Klein's association of the Company with 'medieval instruments for regulating trade'. '"Little London": British merchants in Rotterdam during the seventeenth and eighteenth centuries', in D. C. Coleman and Peter Mathias (eds), *Enterprise and History: Essays in Honour of Charles Wilson* (Cambridge, 1984), p. 121.

reflected also in the defensive language deployed in both, with the Company's trade needing to be 'kept' from its rivals and 'maintayned' against the harmful effects of change. Both statements were written to defend the Company against threats associated with these widening commercial horizons, the first in response to the famous 1604 parliamentary free trade bill which intended to open the market up to new entrants and break down the barriers erected by company privileges. The second of these two extracts, however, was a defence not against external attack, but rather, the actions of an insider with expansive commercial interests, John Banckes, who had transgressed the mart-trading system, symptom of the Company's failure to tame the baser instincts of its own members when confronted with the temptations of the market.[11]

The capacity of Merchant Adventurers like Banckes to undermine the Company's orderly marketplace, and the response of the Company and its membership, will be at the heart of this book. Whereas much literature has presented the Company of Merchant Adventurers as a passive victim of factors outside of its control (notably structural changes to the European economy and the English polity), this account reveals a much more dynamic organization and community of merchants, capable of responding to changes at a collective and individual level, although these responses had the potential to create division and conflict with the Company, as with the case of John Banckes. The existence of 'disorderly brethren' like him raises questions about how corporate affiliation shaped the behaviour of individual Merchant Adventurers, how far the Company was able to sustain its moral vision in the face of external and internal challenges, as well as how the Company and its members were able to adapt to the commercial and political changes that this period witnessed, and at what price. This book will argue that these questions are at the heart of our understanding of how and why the Fellowship of Merchant Adventurers eventually came to lose its status over the course of the seventeenth century, but they are ones that can be equally asked of other merchant companies.

* * *

This book contributes to a flourishing recent literature on premodern merchant corporations which has re-evaluated their importance in spreading markets and laying the foundations of modern European empires. These themes have emerged from two distinct scholarly trends, each of which has tended to focus on different periods and forms of mercantile organization. First, an institutional turn in economic history has led to debate over the role of merchant guilds in establishing markets during medieval Europe's 'commercial revolution', as well as the importance of early modern joint stock companies in providing solutions for the

---

[11] For more on this case, see Chapters 4 and 8.

challenges facing transoceanic commerce.[12] Second, early modernists largely interested in processes of globalization and empire building have reconsidered the role of trading companies traditionally seen as profit-driven organizations, particularly England's novel joint stock companies, instead identifying them as deeply political bodies preoccupied with the government of people and territory as well as trade.[13] Though in general these two scholarly strands ask different questions, they share an interest in how corporate forms of organization were capable of overcoming the challenges facing commercial and colonial expansion, making new forms of economic and political cooperation and domination possible. This emphasis on expansion and novelty, as well as success, perhaps explains why early modern England's regulated companies have, with the partial exception of the Levant Company, been largely absent from this literature.[14] Although the Merchant Adventurers did move into new territories in the late sixteenth century, the Company cannot be associated with the opening of novel trade routes in the same way as the Russia, Turkey, Levant or East India companies can be. However, despite this recent neglect, the Merchant Adventurers occupied a significant place for an earlier generation of economic historians who considered the early modern period as a dramatic turning point in the transition from feudalism to capitalism, and the regulated trading company as a chief casualty of this shift.

This was the case with one of the pioneering figures of economic history in Britain, George Unwin, who devoted a 1913 lecture to 'the place of the Merchant

---

[12] For different perspectives in this debate, see A. Greif, P. Milgrom, and B. R. Weingast, 'Coordination, commitment, and enforcement: the case of the merchant guild', *Journal of Political Economy* 102 (1994), pp. 745–76; Oliver Volckart and Antje Mangels, 'Are the roots of the modern *Lex Mercatoria* really medieval?', *Southern Economic Journal* 65 (1999), pp. 427–50; Avner Greif, *Institutions and the Path to the Modern Economy: Lessons from Medieval Trade* (Cambridge, 2006); M. Boldory, 'Socio-economic institutions and transaction costs: merchant guilds and rural trade in eighteenth-century Lower Silesia', *European Review of Economic History* 13 (2009), pp. 173–98; E. Lindberg, 'Club goods and inefficient institutions: why Danzig and Lübeck failed in the early modern period', *Economic History Review* 62, 3 (2009), pp. 604–28; Sheilagh Ogilvie, *Institutions and European Trade: Merchant Guilds, 1000–1800* (Cambridge, 2011). For joint stocks, see A. M. Carlos and S. Nicholas, ' "Giants of an earlier capitalism": the chartered trading companies as modern multinationals', *Business History Review* 62 (1988), pp. 398–419; 'Agency problems in early chartered companies: the case of the Hudson's Bay Company', *Journal of Economic History* 50, 4 (1990), pp. 853–75; 'Theory and history: seventeenth-century joint-stock chartered trading companies', *Journal of Economic History* 56, 4 (1996), pp. 916–24.

[13] For instance P. J. Stern, *The Company-State: Corporate Sovereignty and the Early Modern Foundations of the British Empire in India* (Oxford, 2011); William A. Pettigrew, *Freedom's Debt: The Royal African Company and the Politics of the Atlantic Slave Trade, 1672–1752* (Chapel Hill, 2013); Felicity Stout, *Exploring Russia in the Elizabethan Commonwealth: The Muscovy Company and Giles Fletcher, the Elder (1546–1611)* (Manchester, 2015); William A. Pettigrew, 'Corporate constitutionalism and the dialogue between the global and local in seventeenth-century English history', *Itinerario* 39 (2015), pp. 487–501.

[14] The Levant Company's trade to Venice is considered in Maria Fusaro, *Political Economies of Empire in the Early Modern Mediterranean: The Decline of Venice and the Rise of England, 1450–1700* (Cambridge, 2015).

Adventurers in English History'.[15] Unwin was responding to a picture that had emerged in certain recent works by German economic historians, for whom the Company was at the forefront of a nationalistic drive to wrest control of English trade from the hands of foreigners, notably its long-term rivals the Hanseatic League. Writing in the aftermath of German unification, these authors found something to admire in Elizabethan England's apparently strong central government and unified national character, which manifested themselves in a clear economic policy—'far-sighted, determined, consistent, unscrupulous; in short, a Bismarckian policy'—that had been sadly lacking in the fragmented Holy Roman Empire.[16] A similarly positive account had been presented by a Canadian historian, William Ezra Lingelbach, who had recently published an edition of the Merchant Adventurers' early-seventeenth-century manuscript 'Lawes, Customes and Ordinances', which, together with the recently calendared state papers and published acts of the Privy Council, had opened the subject up to scholarly investigation.[17] Instead, and in contrast to his positive view of the role of voluntary associations elsewhere in late medieval social and economic life, Unwin painted an unflattering portrait of a Company which tended to restrict rather than expand trade, a poor contrast to those 'interlopers' willing to adventure beyond the protected environs of the mart towns, particularly after the Company's temporary banishment from the Holy Roman Empire in 1598.[18] Unwin's discussion stopped at the turn of the seventeenth century, but his damning account of an organization lazily depending on its privileges and thus depressing the growth of trade firmly situated the Company within an antiquated commercial order. Although rather more sympathetic to the Company's attempts to stabilize the market, Ephraim Lipson also presented the Company as destined to be out-competed by interlopers once royal protection was gradually withdrawn and 'the logic of economic facts' came into play; a more competitive commercial environment characterized by the growth of continental cloth industry discredited the

---

[15] George Unwin, *Studies in Economic History: The Collected Papers of George Unwin*, ed. R. H. Tawney, second edition (London, 1958), pp. 133–220.

[16] Ibid., p. 215. The work Unwin singled out was on Emden, which briefly hosted the Company in the late sixteenth century, Bernhard Hagedorn, *Ostfrieslands Handel und Schiffart vom ausgang des 16. Jahrhunderts bis zum Westfälischen Frieden (1580–1648)* (Berlin, 1912), but he also cited Georg Schanz, *Englische Handelspolitik gegen Ende des Mittelalters* (Leipzig, 1881), and Richard Ehrenberg, *Hamburg und England im Zeitalter der Königin Elisabeth* (Jena, 1896), though largely for factual purposes.

[17] As well as his 1902 edition of *The Merchant Adventurers of England: Their Laws and Ordinances with Other Documents*, Lingelbach published two important articles on the Company: 'The internal organisation of the Merchant Adventurers of England', *Transactions of the Royal Historical Society* new series, 16 (1902), pp. 19–67, and 'The Merchant Adventurers at Hamburg', *The American Historical Review*, 9, 2 (1904), pp. 265–87. For Unwin's views on corporations, see Phil Withington, *Society in Early Modern England: The Vernacular Origins of Some Powerful Ideas* (Cambridge, 2010), pp. 132–3.

[18] Unwin, *Studies in Economic History*, pp. 217–20.

Merchant Adventurers' policy of upholding prices, and favoured the greater flexibility of interlopers.[19]

Amongst these pioneers of English economic history, a more favourable verdict was given by Astrid Friis, who lauded the Company not only for 'ousting the foreign merchants from the market', but also for mitigating against the full force of 'capitalism' (taken to mean the tendency of capital to concentrate in fewer and fewer hands).[20] Thanks to her exhaustive study of the port books, Friis was able to assess the distribution of trade between the Company and its rivals. Although this revealed the unequal division of trade within Company ranks, Friis suggested that this did not preclude the existence of a large stratum of middling traders who benefited from the Company's managed trade.[21] Given the Company's ability to sustain a fairly broadly based trade, interlopers had little need to operate outside of its regulative framework, and indeed Friis found no significant trace of their involvement in the cloth trade from the port books.[22] To Friis, political intervention rather than domestic competition was the only serious challenge to the Jacobean Company, notably in the form of the Cokayne Project, whereby the Company lost its privileges in 1614 to a rival society. Although restored in 1617, the Company was weakened enough that it struggled to withstand the attacks that came in the wake of the depression in the cloth trade of the early 1620s.[23] In this account the decline of the Company, when it came, was triggered by external attacks rather than any intrinsic problems in its system of trade, but even so Friis conceded that it ultimately struggled to keep up with changing patterns of continental demand, especially the turn away from broadcloth to the new draperies. Barry Supple also stressed how continental competition undermined the Company doctrine of holding high prices, emphasizing how the more adaptable and lower-quality new draperies were difficult to engross into corporate hands.[24] Ultimately these new products were part of a larger story, the broadening horizons of English trade and the turn to new markets, from the Mediterranean to the Atlantic and far east.[25]

The tendency to identify the Merchant Adventurers with a pre-capitalist form of commercial organization rendered obsolete by the expansion of English trade found its fullest form in the work of the Marxist historian Robert Brenner.[26] For Brenner the early modern transition from feudalism to capitalism was axiomatic,

---

[19] Ephraim Lipson, *The Economic History of England. II. The Age of Mercantilism* (London, 1931), p. 262.

[20] Astrid Friis, *Alderman Cockayne's Project and the Cloth Trade: The Commercial Policy of England in Its Main Aspects, 1603–1625* (London and Copenhagen, 1927), p. 47.

[21] Ibid., pp. 78–82, 99–100.   [22] Ibid., pp. 76, 110–14.   [23] Ibid., pp. 382–3, 429–31.

[24] Barry Supple, *Commercial Crisis and Change in England, 1600–4: A Study in the Instability of a Mercantile Economy* (Cambridge, 1959), pp. 147–8.

[25] Ibid., pp. 152–62.

[26] Robert Brenner, *Merchants and Revolution: Commercial Change, Political Conflict, and London Overseas Traders, 1550–1653* (Cambridge, 1993).

and could be charted via changing forms of mercantile organization. The Merchant Adventurers exemplified the premodern (and non-capitalist) merchant corporation, reliant on a politically constituted form of property derived from its monopoly.[27] Complacently basking in false security behind their walls of privilege, Merchant Adventurers largely failed to participate in the first stage of import-led commercial revolution focused on the Levant and East Indies, let alone in the colonial trades that followed in their wake. Fitting in with his larger arguments that located the emergence of capitalism in changing social relations in the English countryside, Brenner posited England as the exception to a general trend of economic downturn across Europe which depressed the Merchant Adventurers' traditional markets.[28] Left behind by changing economic forces, the Merchant Adventurers were bypassed by the political struggle to reconstitute commercial government in a capitalist manner during the English Revolution, at most the passive victims of a free trade movement whose key battlegrounds Brenner located elsewhere.

Brenner's work was predicated on an essential distinction between the company merchant and the free trading 'new merchants' who were the ultimate winners of the English Revolution. These differences were charted in terms of their background, their style of business management, their relationship with the state, and most importantly how they fitted into the larger economic system: whereas the rentier company merchants were dependent on protection by the feudal monarchy, the new merchants were associated with the open markets of capitalism.[29] These new merchants were the antonym of the 'mere merchant' locked into a politically constituted market, their ability to cross occupational and geographical boundaries enabling new synergies between different forms of economic activity, including the reinvestment of commercial profit in production, the colonial plantation economies acting as harbinger of the capitalist processes that would transform the world. This distinction, however, can be criticized on several points, including the existence of considerable overlaps between company and colonial merchants; the continued willingness of the latter to adopt corporate forms of commercial government when it suited them; and perhaps most fundamentally,

---

[27] Ibid., pp. 52–61.
[28] See T. H. Aston and C. H. E. Philpin (eds), *The Brenner Debate: Agrarian Class Structure and Economic Development in Pre-Industrial Europe* (Cambridge, 1985).
[29] Brenner's work should be understood in terms of debates within Marxism surrounding the origins of capitalism, and particularly the role of medieval towns and their burghers as possible 'incubators' of a capitalism that emerged from the division of labour, a view associated by Brenner with Marx's early, Adam Smith-influenced, thought. Brenner rejected this view in favour of what he saw as Marx's later emphasis on revolutions in the mode of production which were rooted in agrarian social change. Robert Brenner, 'Bourgeois revolution and transition to capitalism', in A. L Beier, David Cannadine, and James M. Rosenheim (eds), *The First Modern Society: Essays in Honour of Lawrence Stone* (Cambridge, 1989), pp. 271–304. See also Ellen Meiksins Wood, 'Capitalism, merchants and bourgeois revolution: reflections on the Brenner debate and its sequel', *International Review of Social History* 41 (1996), pp. 209–32.

their enthusiasm for calling on state protection to advance their interests, even to the extent of resurrecting monopolistic devices intended to defend their profits. Even so, Brenner's grand narrative remains an essential starting point, particularly thanks to his recognition that merchants are not ahistorical character types performing essentially the same role throughout time, but are embedded within larger economic, social, and political configurations that are subject to change. Although corporations were not a straightforward victim of the global expansion of English commerce or the beginnings of the navigation system, the ways in which merchants interacted with trading companies were not static, and the companies themselves came to perform different roles.

Brenner's insight that the merchants of late seventeenth century England represented something different from their equivalents a century earlier continues to warrant attention, then, but there his prosopographical approach undoubtedly simplified the complexity of these changes by classifying merchants according to their corporate or business affiliations. In the case of the Merchant Adventurers, it is tempting to identify members with the qualities emphasized in Company publicity—order, fellowship, and stability—thereby representing them as passive vehicles of internalized corporate norms rather than agents capable of strategic behaviour, 'oversocialized' as opposed to the 'undersocialized' self-interested rational actor found in neoclassical economic thought.[30] The existence of internal fissures in the edifice of corporate unity has occasionally been noticed by historians, and as early as 1959 T. S. Willan concluded that companies including the Merchant Adventurers 'were much less monolithic in structure and much less monopolistic in practice than their charters and ordinances imply', a conclusion that W.-R. Baumann's investigations into the Company's trade into Germany amply supported.[31] However, much more needs to be done in order to understand how corporate affiliation shaped the business lives of particular merchants, and how this shifted as the place of these companies within the larger economic system changed. This book takes the interactions between the Company and its membership as its starting point, looking at the Company from within rather than from without. This is a particularly valuable perspective because of the regulated form of the Company, which was by its very nature decentred and pluralistic. But this approach raises the complex question of where we are to draw the line between the Company and the membership who governed it, in short, how the Company existed as a political community.

One feature of recent scholarship on trading companies has been to situate them within, as Philip J. Stern has put it, 'an early modern world filled with a

---

[30] See Mark Granovetter, 'Economic action and social structure: the problem of embeddedness', *American Journal of Sociology* 91 (1985), pp. 481–510.

[31] T. S. Willan, *Studies in Elizabethan Foreign Trade* (Manchester, 1959), p. 64; W.-R. Baumann, *The Merchants Adventurers and the Continental Cloth-Trade (1560s–1620s)* (Berlin, 1990).

variety of corporate bodies politic and hyphenated, hybrid, overlapping, and composite forms of sovereignty.[32] This has involved taking seriously the political claims found in company charters, letters, petitions and so on, which maintained these were political bodies involved in the government of people and places, as well as goods. It has also entailed a recovery of the social dimension of corporate organization, recognising the corporate cultures which were intended to bind members into a larger whole, though this process did not happen automatically. As with other corporations, trading companies were characterized by internal debates and contests over the behaviour expected of members, corporate govern-ance, and the broader purposes that this government was intended to achieve. Such internal contests, as well as criticism from excluded outsiders, often drew on the same 'commonwealth' values that informed the existence of these corpor-ations: company regulation was an outcome of negotiation.[33] This was equally the case with the domestic equivalents of trading companies, such as urban corpor-ations and craft guilds. Studies of the latter, for instance, have emphasized the flexibility of their regulatory regimes, the limits of which were continually tested by members; guild government tended to focus on persuasion and accommoda-tion rather than rigid enforcement of rules, meaning they were much more adapt-able to change than has traditionally been considered.[34] As we will see, similar conclusions can be drawn regarding the Merchant Adventurers. Overseas trading companies, however, did depart from most other corporations in significant ways, notably due to the distances that separated members from one another. This is significant because, as Phil Withington has discussed, the concept of place was integral to the notion of the civic commonwealth, whether this was conceived of socially, as something signified by calling, occupation or institutional role, or spatially, as vested in particular sites such as the household, neighbourhood or civic building.[35] Clearly this was different for trading companies and their mem-bers, for whom 'place' was established as much through associations that were spatially extended—one's place within a commercial network—as through institutional affiliation or residence. In fact the question of distance has been a significant theme of studies of premodern trade, where it is usually cast as the 'principal–agent problem': how to effectively coordinate decision making and maintain trust across space and time in an era of unreliable communications

---

[32] Stern, *Company-State*, p. 3.
[33] Stout, *Exploring Russia*, chapter 1.
[34] See e.g. J. P. Ward, *Metropolitan Communities: Trade Guilds, Identity, and Change in Early Modern London* (Stanford, 1997); Ian Anders Gadd and Patrick Wallis (eds), *Guilds, Society and Economy in London 1450–1800* (London, 2002); S. R. Epstein and Maarten Praak (eds), *Guilds, Innovation, and the European Economy, 1400–1800* (Cambridge, 2008).
[35] Phil Withington, *The Politics of Commonwealth: Citizens and Freemen in Early Modern England* (Cambridge, 2005), pp. 85–123.

and weak legal enforcement mechanisms defending property rights.[36] One contribution of the new scholarship on trading companies has been to frame this as a political as well as economic issue, a problem of authority and order. Miles Ogborn, for instance, has discussed the writing technologies deployed by the East India Company to convey power and authority at a distance.[37] The Company's London governors developed sophisticated institutional arrangements in order to monitor the conduct of employees in factories overseas, to incentivize good behaviour and engineer consent in order to ensure that corporate interests were maintained, although in practice this was balanced by a pragmatic willingness to tacitly endorse agents' independence.[38] Such solutions were the product of negotiations that were highly political, and centred on the distribution and exercise of power within the corporation. Employees overseas were able to exploit their positionality in order to win concessions from the board of directors in London, where power theoretically resided. In many corporations, such tensions between centre and periphery were complicated by relations between the company and the state, which also had a stake in monitoring English subjects overseas.[39]

For trading companies, the problem of distance was not just one of coordination and control, however. Chartered companies were entrusted with the power to govern themselves, but civic government entailed deliberation and participation as well as the exercise of authority.[40] In the urban civic commonwealth, the town hall acted not only as a projection of oligarchic authority: this was a space where the urban community could be bought together as a self-governing whole, a place of integration.[41] Overseas trading companies faced the challenge of how to integrate its dispersed membership, to enable the deliberation and participation on which self-government depended. The constitutions of different trading companies varied in this respect: joint stock companies differentiated between managers, shareholders, and employees, allowing for the creation of institutional hierarchies and chains of command. Regulated companies were theoretically more egalitarian, with all freemen having a stake in the decision-making process and the election of officers. Even amongst regulated companies there was diversity, however. In the case of the more recently founded companies, such as the

---

[36] For an overview in relation to corporations, see Ogilvie, *Institutions and European Trade*, chapter 8.

[37] Miles Ogborn, *Indian Ink: Script and Print in the Making of the English East India Company* (Chicago and London, 2007).

[38] Emily Erikson, *Between Monopoly and Free Trade: The English East India Company, 1600–1757* (Princeton and Oxford, 2014).

[39] Stern, *Company State*; Rupali Mishra, 'Diplomacy at the edge: split interests in the Roe embassy to the Mughal Court', *Journal of British Studies* 53 (2014), pp. 5–28; Jason Cameron White, 'Royal authority versus corporate sovereignty: the Levant Company and the ambiguities of early Stuart statecraft', *The Seventeenth Century* 32 (2017), pp. 231–55.

[40] Withington, *Politics of Commonwealth*, p. 96.

[41] Ibid. See also Robert Tittler, *Architecture and Power: The Town Hall and the English Urban Community c.1500–1640* (Oxford, 1991).

Eastland and Levant companies, power was centred on the company courts and governors in London, with the generally more junior members who staffed the companies' overseas residences distanced from the decision-making process, although the heads of these factories could often attain importance, frequently serving diplomatic functions.[42]

In the case of the Merchant Adventurers, too, the mart towns were generally home to the younger generation of members, at least at the start of the period. However, this Company differed from most others by virtue of its head court being located overseas. Although by the sixteenth century the Company's governor resided in London, he was elected in the chief mart town, along with the Company's other officers. This was a legacy of the Company's origins which, as Anne F. Sutton has demonstrated, should be located on the continent rather than in any English grant, in the form of privileges secured by merchants at the close of the thirteenth century from the Duke of Brabant recognizing the prior existence of an English community trading in his territories. These merchants, who soon became known collectively as 'Merchant Adventurers', represented 'a complicated and disparate "body" with branches in London and many provincial cities, with many different trading interests, and with different establishments in several foreign countries'.[43] Only later did the Company acquire formal recognition from the English crown, though its institutional development was shaped by interested parties in England, notably the Mercers Company of London, whose members secured the election of a governor at Antwerp in 1421.[44] The Company began to house the first meetings of a 'general court of adventurers' at London later in the century. Formal royal recognition, beginning with a grant in 1407, tended to be sought in the context of inter-corporate rivalries over control of the Company in London, as well as contests between Londoners and merchants of the outports. Pressure from the latter was responsible for a parliamentary statute of 1497 lowering the entry fine to the Company to 10 marks. In response to this the London merchants secured the permanent establishment of a general court in the city in 1506, and further extended their control over the Company.[45] However, London's dominance continued to be challenged by the outports, many of which (including York, Hull, and Newcastle) possessed their own local merchant guilds intended to regulate trade passing through the city in the interests of inhabitants, which acted

---

[42] Henryk Zins, *England and the Baltic in the Elizabethan era* (Manchester, 1972), pp. 120–1; Alfred Wood, *A History of the Levant Company* (Oxford, 1935).

[43] Anne F. Sutton, 'The Merchant Adventurers of England: their origins and the Mercers' Company of London', *Historical Research* 75, 1 (2002), p. 33.

[44] Ibid.; E. M. Carus-Wilson, 'The origins and early development of the Merchant Adventurers' organization in London as shown in their own mediaeval records', *Economic History Review* 4, 2 (1933), pp. 147–76. See also Douglas R. Bison, *The Merchant Adventurers of England: The Company and the Crown, 1474–1564* (Newark, 1993).

[45] Friis, *Alderman Cockayne's Project*, pp. 29–31.

as a rival source of corporate allegiance.[46] Power was more dispersed in the Company of Merchant Adventurers than the other trading companies, meaning if anything that the potential for division between its different residences was greater.

For all the influence that the London membership had won over the Company's government, it was still the case that the bulk of its administration was concentrated overseas. Company discipline weighed much more heavily on Merchant Adventurers in the mart towns than those in London, but equally their experience of belonging to a distinctive community of merchants was more intense. Although the subject of this book is the Fellowship of Merchant Adventurers as a whole, the focus will generally be on the Company's mart towns. These were far from static social environments, and indeed changing relations between the mart towns and the Company in England will be a major theme. In the earlier part of our period, the structural problem of distance was to an extent mitigated by features of the merchant life-cycle which bridged the geographical divide, ensuring that the interests of the members at home and those in the mart towns did not diverge too dangerously. For in the Company's trade, a member's place within the merchant life-cycle and thereby the social order coincided with their geographical location, at least in a normative sense: aspiring Merchant Adventurers were expected to serve the earlier part of their careers overseas, acquiring the experience and assets necessary to assume economic independence, before returning home to enjoy this status in their own households. By no means all Merchant Adventurers followed this path, but it appears to have been common enough to inform expectations about career progression. It also acted as a tie between the membership in the mart towns and England. Junior Merchant Adventurers in the former could look forward to assuming their place amongst the latter, giving them a stake in the reproduction of the Company's existing commercial regime. Merchant Adventurers in London were afforded a voice in the government of the Company in the mart towns via their agents, who were often in a dependent position and therefore susceptible to influence. Shared experiences of the mart towns, shared acquaintances, and shared expectations were the social glue which helped to bind the Company together.

Over time, however, these relationships changed. As noticed by Elisabeth Karin Newman in an unpublished study which remains the best account of the Company in its final years, by the Restoration the Hamburg residence was home

---

[46] For Newcastle, see 'Extracts from the records of the Merchant Adventurers of Newcastle-upon-Tyne. Vol I', *The Publications of the Surtees Society* 93 (1895), 'Vol II' 101 (1899); for York, see Maud Sellers (ed.), 'The York Merchants and Merchant Adventurers 1356–1917', *The Publications of the Surtees Society* 129 (1918). A powerful study of the institutional culture of such local merchant guilds (though not in this case one whose members tended to trade to Germany and the Netherlands) is David Harris Sacks, *The Widening Gate: Bristol and the Atlantic Economy, 1450–1700* (Berkeley and London, 1993).

to a class of long-term residents who were essentially independent commission agents rather than apprentices or salaried servants.[47] Because they were not tied by bonds of deference to their English principals, these merchants were much more willing to assert their independence. This shift in the social and commercial ties connecting the Company had important implications for how it was able to function as a self-governing corporation, which came to a head at the point that the Company finally lost its domestic privileges following the Glorious Revolution. The divergence between the Company's membership in Hamburg and London, as well as the outports, became the chief structural challenge to corporate unity, which the Company's constitution ultimately proved unable to sustain. Well before then, however, other potential fissures had opened within the Company's ranks. Many of these emerged during the closing decades of the sixteenth century, and the departure of the Merchant Adventurers from its sixteenth-century mart town, Antwerp.

*   *   *

Most of the fundamental features of the mart-trading system associated with the Merchant Adventurers emerged during the sixteenth-century, at a time when the Company was largely based in the city of Antwerp. It was in the first half of the century that the export of undyed and undressed English broadcloth to Antwerp expanded at the expense of its Flemish competitor, before peaking mid-century. The membership at London were able to respond to the ensuing fall, however, by consolidating their authority with royal support, for example by increasing the fine for entry by redemption to 100 marks, restricting membership to 'mere merchants', and introducing the 'stint' system of stipulated maximum exports per merchant. The Company's alliance with the crown was cemented by its acquiescing to an increase in customs on exported broadcloth in 1558, with higher rates imposed on exports by non-English merchants (14s. 6d. per cloth as compared to 6s. 8d. for Company members). Although the Company's major continental rivals, the merchants of the Hanseatic League, were initially rated at the same level as Englishmen, further measures weakening Hanse franchises helped the Merchant Adventurers to capture a greater share of the export trade, allowing them to maintain the volume of their trade at a stable level even as overall exports fell.[48] Thus the Company had begun to secure its domination over English cloth exports at the expense of English and foreign rivals whilst based at Antwerp, the unparalleled entrepôt of sixteenth-century northern Europe.

---

[47] Elisabeth Karin Newman, 'Anglo-Hamburg trade in the late seventeenth and early eighteenth centuries', PhD thesis, LSE (1979), p. 266.

[48] Anne F. Sutton, *The Mercery of London: Trade, Goods and People, 1130–1578* (Aldershot, 2005), pp. 411–31; Brenner, *Merchants and Revolution*, pp. 7–8, 52–61; G. D. Ramsay, *The City of London in International Politics at the Accession of Elizabeth Tudor* (Manchester, 1975), pp. 65–70; T. H. Lloyd, *England and the German Hanse, 1157–1611: A Study of Their Trade and Commercial Diplomacy* (Cambridge, 1991), chapter 6.

In Antwerp exported English cloth was sent for dyeing and finishing to Brabant and from there distributed to markets throughout Europe, whilst English merchants were able to access a variety of goods from across the world for import: it was a natural staple for the English cloth trade.[49] An essentially bilateral trade concentrated on a single location was readily susceptible to corporate regulation, allowing the Merchant Adventurers to control the volume and rhythm of exports in order to maintain prices. Despite occasional tensions with the Antwerp merchant community, the Merchant Adventurers were best served by peace and cooperation between England and the Low Countries, the 'ancient amity' symbolized by the treaty of 1496 known as 'Magnus Intercursus': to a large extent they belonged to a regional community of interests whose membership crossed national boundaries.[50] This was to change in the 1560s, when diplomatic tensions between the English and Spanish crowns unsettled the position of the Merchant Adventurers at Antwerp, a situation which worsened with the outbreak of the Dutch revolt. Displacement from Antwerp forced the Company to look for new homes away from the troubled Low Countries, first Emden, and then Hamburg. Antwerp continued to attract English trade, but the prospect of resurrecting a permanent mart there ended with its fall to the Prince of Parma in 1585. By then, the Company had formally chosen Protestant Middelburg as a new mart town to serve the Low Countries, in 1582.

With the adoption of a permanent dual-mart system in 1582, the post-Antwerp era in the history of the Merchant Adventurers really begins. To be sure, the Company had rarely been tied to a single continental base, occasionally withdrawing to Calais in support of royal diplomacy, and cultivating towns like Bergen-op-Zoom as a rival to Antwerp in order to ensure that its presence was not taken for granted. But these alternatives were effectively intended to provide a direct replacement for Antwerp, indicative of its dominant role as the great entrepôt of northern Europe up to the 1560s. In the decades that followed, the Merchant Adventurers had to adapt to an emerging multi-polar northern European trading world lacking a single distributive centre.[51] The establishment of a German mart town opened up access into northern Germany, whilst Middelburg provided avenues to furnish both the Low Countries and southern Germany, with displaced merchants from Antwerp and the southern Low Countries initially moving in to perform these distributive services in the transit trade. But the coexistence of two mart towns complicated the system that the Merchant Adventurers had settled into at Antwerp, whilst the partition of its trade did not end there. During the unsettled 1560s and 1570s English merchants had been forced to look for new markets beyond the mart towns. Indeed the

---

[49] Ramsay, *City of London*, pp. 22–5.   [50] Ormrod, *Rise of Commercial Empires*, p. 35.
[51] Oscar Gelderblom, *Cities of Commerce: The Institutional Foundations of International Trade in the Low Countries, 1250–1650* (Princeton and Oxford, 2013).

Company had sanctioned attendance at the Frankfurt fair as early as 1564, after cloth sales at Emden had failed, and thereafter Company members continued to ply the markets of inner Germany.[52] The centrifugal forces unleashed by the decline of Antwerp would prove to be a challenge to the corporate unity of the Merchant Adventurers over the following century. The year 1582 therefore serves as a convenient starting point for this book.

The move from Antwerp also had important implications for the Company's relationship with the state. As Ramsay demonstrated, the Company's royal charter of 18 July 1564 was a by-product of the frenetic commercial diplomacy which followed the publishing of an edict in 1563 by the Habsburg Regent of the Netherlands banning English imports, a symptom of a cooling of the 'ancient amity' between England and the Low Countries in an age of confessional conflict.[53] As well as religious divisions, commercial grievances played a part in the issuing of this edict, including the prejudicial customs rates imposed on non-English merchants in 1558. Although this measure was largely driven by the crown's financial needs, it also reflected an increasingly nationalistic spirit in commercial policy, fed by resentment at the presence of wealthy alien merchants in London apparently prospering at the expense of English consumers and producers. Underlying this was a growing desire to overcome the dependent position that the English economy seemed to be in, in relation both to foreign merchants and to the Antwerp entrepôt in general. From a diplomatic perspective, over-reliance on Antwerp meant that England was vulnerable to strong-arming by its political masters the Habsburgs, particularly following the loss of Calais as an alternative market. But the presence of sympathetic co-religionists in ports such as Hamburg, Bremen, and Emden, all of which were keen to emulate Antwerp by drawing English trade to themselves, presented a different option: not just another way to access the great stream of trade that ran from northern to southern Europe via the Low Countries, but a new channel that would lead direct to the vast central European market, the chief destination for most English cloths. Ramsay recognized the significance of the Company's move to Emden in East Friesland in 1564, a watershed moment as England began to extricate itself from the gravitational pull of Antwerp.[54] Although this was a politically driven project, some Merchant Adventurers recognized this as an opportunity for the Company to augment its power. Arguing that any seepage of trade back into the Netherlands would be a fatal blow to the Emden experiment, the Company called for an enhancement of its powers over interlopers.[55] The move eastwards also demanded that the Company's territorial rights were redefined to include not just Emden but potential competitors such as Hamburg. As well as confirming its enlarged territorial claims, the 1564 charter thus focused on buttressing the authority of the Company's

---

[52] Baumann, *Merchants Adventurers*, pp. 166–88.
[53] Ramsay, *City of London*.   [54] Ibid., p. 283.   [55] Ibid., p. 235.

governing structures, particularly that of the London governor, in recognition of the likelihood that many members comfortably ensconced at Antwerp would be reluctant to relocate to Emden.[56]

By posing as chief conduit of royal diplomacy, the Company had achieved a new level of authority. When its chief English corporate rival, the wool-exporting Staplers Company, secured an invite to return to Bruges in May 1564, the Merchant Adventurers successfully protested that this would be to the advantage of Flemish cloth making.[57] Thereafter, the interests of cloth- over wool exporters would consistently win out. But these triumphs were not without their costs. The Company's essential dependency on royal support was never clearer, making it all the more vulnerable to any loss of political favour, whilst the victory of a political economy based on the export of manufactured goods could be exploited by other interested parties in order to attack the Company for failing to export enough cloths, or at least enough which had been dyed and dressed domestically (an allegation frequently made by the London Clothworkers' Company).[58] Another enduring challenge that surfaced with the Company's move to Emden was that of controlling the behaviour of its own members. When sales proved to be disappointing, many Merchant Adventurers responded by travelling to the Frankfurt mart with their cloths, and restraining this instinct to 'straggle' beyond the mart towns would continue to be a problem.[59] This reflects a dilemma which would loom over the Company for the rest of its history: whether to uphold its monopoly by concentrating trade on one mart town, or to follow the opportunities that emerged following the collapse of the Antwerp entrepôt. In the short term the former instinct won out: once the alarmed rulers of Antwerp secured a reversal of government policy, the Company took up their offer to return, although in 1569 it once again decided to withdraw, this time to Hamburg.[60] Middelburg was as close as the Company would come to resurrecting its mart on the Scheldt.

The non-renewal of the Company's privileges at Hamburg in 1579 (under Hanseatic pressure) led to a return to Emden which lasted till 1587, when the Company moved to the small town of Stade on the Elbe, essentially due to its proximity to Hamburg, now recognized as the gateway to inland Germany.[61] The Company eventually achieved its goal of returning to Hamburg in 1612, and remained there for the rest of its history. By contrast its fortunes in the United Provinces became increasingly unsettled, as it struggled to position itself in

---

[56]   Ibid., pp. 257–8.   [57]   Ibid., p. 274.

[58]   G. D. Ramsay, 'Industrial discontent in early Elizabethan London: clothworkers and Merchant Adventurers in conflict', *London Journal* 1 (1975), pp. 227–39.

[59]   Ramsay, *City of London*, p. 265; Baumann, *Merchants Adventurers*.

[60]   Ramsay, *City of London*, pp. 282–3; G. D. Ramsay, *The Queen's Merchants and the Revolt of the Netherlands* (Manchester, 1986).

[61]   G. D. Ramsay, 'The settlement of the Merchant Adventurers at Stade, 1587–1611', in Tom Scott and E. I. Kouri (eds), *Politics and Society in Reformation Europe: Essays for Sir Geoffrey Elton on his Sixty-Fifth Birthday* (London, 1987), pp. 452–72.

relation to the emerging entrepôt of Amsterdam, meaning that as the period went on the Company was increasingly identified with Hamburg. This was an ironic reversal from the situation in the early seventeenth century, when the Netherlands were still seen as the Company's natural home and the new German markets a potential distraction from the mart-trading system. Why this reversal occurred is to a large extent explained by factors which were largely beyond the Company's control. Premodern merchant companies such as the Merchant Adventurers acted as mediators between the political economies of different states, and recent studies have emphasized that companies had to negotiate their privileges overseas as well as at home. This was a delicate balancing act. As the Company put it in its response to the 1604 free trade bill (quoted above), its governed trade in the mart towns was 'maintayned…by the privelidges of forrayne Princes'. In the case of the Merchant Adventurers, this situation was complicated by the close diplomatic relations between England and the regions where its privileges extended: treaties tended to include clauses guaranteeing reciprocal market access, which could interfere with corporate privileges.[62] The economies of England and the Low Countries had co-evolved over centuries, and commercial relationships between the two encompassed many different interests involved in the production and distribution of woollen cloth. For convenience it is useful to distinguish between two key stages of cloth production: the manufacture of the basic product (cloth making), and its dyeing and dressing, or finishing.[63] Each stage involved a range of processes, but in general took place under distinct regimes organized by different people. Cloth making in England was the responsibility of clothiers, entrepreneurs who bought up the raw materials and put them out locally to be made up into pieces which were then sold to merchants, who were responsible for conveying them to the centres which had the capacity to turn the basic product into something suitable to be transmitted to retailers. These two stages of production could be undertaken in different locations: the assumption of Tudor Englishmen that the pre-eminence of domestic wool supplies ensured a comparative advantage in cloth making was shaken by the growth of wool exports from other regions such as Spain in the seventeenth century. Equally, the responsibility of transporting undressed cloth to the finishing centres and then to its final markets could be undertaken by merchants of different nationalities, operating under different institutional constraints. The organization of the European cloth trade was shaped by the various industrial and commercial interests implicated in it, and

---

[62] A. F. Sutton and L. Visser-Fuchs (eds), *The Book of Privileges of the Merchant Adventurers of England, 1296–1483* (Oxford, 2009).
[63] General studies of the cloth industry include G. D. Ramsay, *The Wiltshire Woollen Industry in the Sixteenth and Seventeenth Centuries* (London, 1965); G. D. Ramsay, *The English Woollen Industry, 1500–1750* (London and Basingstoke, 1982); Eric Kerridge, *Textile Manufactures in Early Modern England* (Manchester, 1985); Michael Zell, *Industry in the Countryside: Wealden Society in the Sixteenth Century* (Cambridge, 1994).

their relative successes in winning the support of states that also had a significant fiscal interest in the size and organization of the trade itself.

The particularly strong position that the Merchant Adventurers acquired in the late sixteenth century was the product of a fortuitous alignment of English political economy, the economic and diplomatic priorities of the emerging Dutch state, and the commercial ambitions of the German cities which competed to attract the Company to them. The basic division of labour in the cloth trade between England and the Low Countries was already well established by then, with the former focusing on cloth production, and the latter cloth finishing. The decision of the English crown to favour English merchants in the conveyance of the semi-manufactured product between these two centres was a more recent one, which soured relations with the Antwerp merchant community as well as the Hanseatic League. However, enough parties in the United Provinces had something to gain from the finishing and distribution of English cloth to overcome any resentment about the Company's privileged status, which ensured that it could regain a foothold in this market, its entrance eased by Dutch dependence of on English military aid. The Company would continue to receive invitations to take up residency from Dutch towns for decades to come, product of the competitive urban environment of this federal state.[64] Something similar was true in the cases of Emden, Stade, and Hamburg, which were equally inspired by the example of Antwerp to seek to become regional entrepôts and centres of cloth finishing, in the case of the latter two at the expense of their Hanseatic loyalties.[65] These constellations of interest were in delicate balance, however. Others with a stake in the cloth industry—English clothiers hoping for a more competitive market, London clothworkers resentful at the Company exporting their product in an unfinished state, and cloth makers in the Netherlands—had good reasons to resent the status quo. Rival merchant interests, English and foreign, continued to jealously eye the lucrative trade route that the Merchant Adventurers had come to monopolize. In the second half of the seventeenth century the city of Hamburg began to have second thoughts about whether it was benefiting from the relationship as it was currently configured. However, it was in the Netherlands that a much more fundamental realignment of trading interests and priorities took place, with catastrophic effects on the Company's ability to sustain its privileged position in that market. This was all the more the case because it coincided with a larger restructuring of Anglo-Dutch commercial relations, associated with the passing of the Navigation Acts and the Anglo-Dutch wars.

---

[64] Gelderblom, *Cities of Commerce*.
[65] For Hamburg, see E. Lindberg, 'Merchant guilds in Hamburg and Konigsberg: a comparative study of urban institutions and economic development in the early-modern period', *Journal of European Economic History* (2010), pp. 33–65.

This has been the theme of the most recent major work to consider the Merchant Adventurers in this period, David Ormrod's account of the rise of England as a 'national entrepôt' in the era of Anglo-Dutch rivalry.[66] This process was partly dependent on 'the dismantling of privileged corporate access to the mart towns of Holland and the creation of new frameworks for conducting trade with nearby Europe'.[67] The increasing tendency of the English state to dilute the Company's privileges from the 1620s onwards reflected the growing weight of industrial interests, which resulted in the ending of prejudicial customs rates on aliens in 1672, reversing a century of policy intended to keep cloth exports in English hands. The liberalization of exports was accompanied by tightened control of imports as well as colonial trade, the purposes of the Navigation Acts passed from 1651 onwards, and the Company's status in the United Provinces suffered due to the conflicts that followed.[68] Well before then, however, the Company had found the Netherlands to be an increasingly inhospitable environment. The prohibition of coloured cloth imports during the Cokayne Project was a sign of the preparedness of the Dutch state to defend cloth-finishing interests, but increasingly Dutch cloth production was on the rise. The well-organized cloth buyers of Holland meanwhile were able to thwart the Company's efforts to restrain trade to its mart town, which was always difficult given the competitive urban environment of the United Provinces.[69] Interlopers benefited in the short term, but in the longer term many English merchants withdrew from the cloth export trade, their place taken by foreign buyers who were drawn into the orbit of the English entrepôt much as English merchants had been drawn to Antwerp a century earlier.[70]

Shifts in Anglo-Dutch relations were unquestionably critical to the Company's eventual loss of privilege. Equally important was the dramatic decline in demand for English cloth in the Company's chief markets which set in during the 1620s, leaving it in possession of a much less valuable monopoly. Supple estimated that the Company's members accounted for about three-quarters of London's old drapery exports at the start of the century, around 100,000 notional shortcloths in a normal year.[71] By 1640 exports of the old draperies to Germany and the Netherlands from London by English merchants had more than halved, and they would continue to fall, dwindling to around 15,000 in 1678 (although the value of exports of new draperies was rising, along with exports from such places as Exeter and Hull).[72] At the same time the active membership of the Company was shrinking. In Hamburg, the merchant community fell from over a hundred

---

[66] Ormrod, *Rise of Commercial Empires*.
[67] Ibid., p. 27.   [68] Ibid., pp. 35–9.
[69] N. M. Posthumus, *De Nationale Organisatie der Lakenkoopers Tijdens de Republiek* (Utrecht, 1927), pp. xxi–xxii.
[70] Ormrod, *Rise of Commercial Empires*, pp. 134–40.   [71] Supple, *Commercial Crisis*, p. 24.
[72] Newman, 'Anglo-Hamburg trade', pp. 107–9. For details, see Chapter 2 of this book.

resident merchants at any one time at the start of the seventeenth century to about forty at its close, though these figures are rough estimates.[73] The size of the membership in England is harder still to identify: the Company secretary John Wheeler's 1601 figure of some 3,500 Merchant Adventurers dispersed across the nation was intended to counter claims that the Company was a narrow monopoly, and certainly misrepresented the distribution of trade within its ranks.[74] Ramsay's analysis of London's port books for 1565 revealed 246 merchants shipping cloth to Antwerp.[75] Friis' figures for the early seventeenth century suggested similar numbers, with 219 London Merchant Adventurers active in 1606.[76] By comparison, in 1609 twenty-nine merchants were sending goods from York and Hull to the Company's mart towns, for instance.[77] By 1677, the number exporting old draperies from London to Hamburg (the Netherlands by now being effectively beyond the Company's control) was thirty, although much of the trade was dominated by just eight merchants.[78] As this decline in numbers was not so sharp in provincial ports like Hull, London's traditional dominance of the Company was being eroded.[79] These figures, however, can only give a very rough sense of the approximate size of the Company, and as we shall see, those merchants who appear in the port books were surrounded by a range of partners, dependants, agents, and others who were implicated in the trade.

Even so, the diminution of the Company's exports and membership had a clear impact on its political importance, particularly in relation to the representative of the more buoyant areas of English trade. In this light the Company struggled to counter those who argued in favour of opening up the market. Having said that, it was at least theoretically possible to combine the key elements of the mart-trading system with open-access membership, and as we will see this was essentially the strategy the Company was following by the Restoration. The ultimate failure of this strategy had many causes, but particularly significant was the growing difficulty of coordinating decision making amongst a membership that was increasingly diverging in its interests. The focus of this book will be on these internal changes, the endogenous factors behind the Company's decline rather than the exogenous ones—falling demand for broadcloth, deteriorating Anglo-Dutch relations, the navigation system—which have generally been emphasized in the literature (although these will be important contexts). The Company's ability to sustain its position depended in part on how willing merchants were to sacrifice aspects of their commercial independence and delegate their decision making in

---

[73] Ibid., p. 35.   [74] Lingelbach, 'Internal organisation', p. 36.
[75] Ramsay, *Queen's Merchants*, p. 63.
[76] Friis, *Alderman Cockayne's Project*, p. 77.   [77] Ibid., pp. 120–1.
[78] TNA, E190/67/2. For more details, see Chapter 2.
[79] Newman, 'Anglo-Hamburg trade', pp. 136–7. These figures are discussed in Chapter 2.

return for a share in its trade and an opportunity to participate in its government. By the end of our period, this was decreasingly the case.

* * *

Although much writing about merchant corporations has focused on their achievements, whether that be (as with neo-institutional economic history) the reduction of transaction costs and the spread of markets, or (in the case of much recent history of English corporations) the extension of English political authority and commercial activity to new parts of the world, the question of decline is also important to these debates.[80] One proposition is that merchant guilds were likely to decline once the services they offered to members were superseded by more open-access institutional arrangements, often provided for by states, whereupon surviving corporations assumed the role of monopolistic and thus growth-retardant rent seekers.[81] Central to this question is how individual merchants deployed different institutional solutions to the challenges they faced. However, as Sheilagh Ogilvie has argued, the emphasis on the commercial services which merchant guilds offered to members entails a narrow reading of the meaning of corporate affiliation which prioritizes modern concepts of efficiency and, on the macro-level, economic growth, over alternative measures of value and well-being.[82] Such treatments also tend to depoliticize these institutions, failing to acknowledge the harmful distributional effects of their monopolies on the excluded, as well as on the economy at large, which could be an explanation for survival as well as decline.[83] Equally, the tendency to treat merchant guilds in isolation from the 'interconnected system of institutions' in which they were embedded, including 'the family, the legal system, the urban community, the church, the state', can lead to their roles in supporting commercial activity being overestimated.[84] Whether or not the merchant guilds of the medieval commercial revolution were acting in absence of alternative public-order legal regimes securing property rights, for the Merchant Adventurers 'trade ran in channels that were politically predetermined',

---

[80] Oscar Gelderblom and Regina Grafe, 'The rise and fall of the merchant guilds: re-thinking the comparative study of commercial institutions in premodern Europe', *Journal of Interdisciplinary History* 40, 4 (2010), pp. 477–511.

[81] Greif, Milgrom, and Weingast, 'Coordination, commitment, and enforcement', p. 773. This argument has some similarities with R. W. K. Hinton's explanation for the decline of trading company privileges, in his case the Eastland Company, which he associated with the emergence of the navigation system, whereby the state took over some of the functions of trading company government. *The Eastland Trade and the Common Weal in the Seventeenth Century* (Cambridge, 1959). See also Michael J. Braddick, *State Formation in Early Modern England c.1550–1700* (Cambridge, 2000), pp. 411–13.

[82] Sheilagh Ogilvie, 'Whatever is, is right? Economic institutions in pre-industrial Europe', *Economic History Review* 60, 4 (2007), p. 665.

[83] Ibid., p. 662.   [84] Ogilvie, *Institutions and European Trade*, p. 286.

and the Company was deeply engaged with those states and cities through which these channels passed.[85]

This book will follow the 'multivariate approach' recommended by Ogilvie, considering the Company of Merchant Adventurers as but one institution which shaped the business lives and choices of its members.[86] The question of what it meant to be a member of this particular trading Company will be central, but it is important to recognize that the Company was more than just a set of regulations and governing structures protecting a monopolized market; it also represented a community of merchants bound by their corporate affiliation, as well as other commercial and social ties. Fellowship, in this sense, entailed not only the formal obligations that came with Company membership, but also the sociability through which Merchant Adventurers fashioned bonds with their brethren.[87] Just as membership of the Company demanded that individual Merchant Adventurers follow certain rules in the conduct of their business, so participation and success in this community required a degree of conformity to normalized practices. Although there was a relationship between these two standards of conduct, they were not identical: breaking the Company's regulations might lead to ostracism, but not always.

Part One of this book seeks to identify the standards of conduct expected of Merchant Adventurers, as well as how these were changing over time. It considers the extent to which this was a distinctive community of merchants possessing a clear sense of identity and boundaries distinguishing insiders from outsiders. This entails situating the Company and its members within a larger mercantile world, or, as Richard Grassby put it, a 'business community' that (in his interpretation) was relatively homogeneous. Although they might have shared certain distinctive values, for Grassby merchants, like other businessmen, did not possess a clear mentality at odds with the values of contemporary society; they belonged to a 'symbiotic culture' characterized by continual mobility between land and trade, which gradually changed the character of English society without revolutionizing it.[88] Perry Gauci's study of the period 1660–1720 did treat overseas traders as a distinct caste and laid more emphasis on the traditional distrust of commerce amongst the landed classes, but he still downplayed the differences between company merchants and 'free traders', both of whom were equally enmeshed in the same associational and institutional world which sustained the networks necessary for overseas trade.[89] In light of such accounts, we might expect to find little

---

[85] Ramsay, *Queen's Merchants*, p. 198.   [86] Ogilvie, 'Whatever is, is right?', p. 667.

[87] For the ideal of good fellowship, see Mark Hailwood, *Alehouses and Good Fellowship in Early Modern England* (Woodbridge, 2014), pp. 134–52.

[88] Richard Grassby, *The Business Community of Seventeenth-Century England* (Cambridge, 1995), pp. 364–94.

[89] Perry Gauci, *The Politics of Trade: The Overseas Merchant in State and Society, 1660–1720* (Oxford, 2001), p. 172.

to distinguish the lives and values of Merchant Adventurers from those of the landowners, professionals, and domestic businessmen who comprised the bulk of England's 'middling sort', let alone the broader English merchant community.

Certainly, we should not be under the illusion that Merchant Adventurers saw the world purely through the lens of Company membership. Many of the recurring challenges of conducting overseas trade in this period were common to merchants in general, whether or not they belonged to a trading company. However, as we will see in Part One, the business lives of Merchant Adventurers did possess certain distinctive features, associated with such things as the Company's admission and regulatory regime, the commodities that members traded in, the trade routes they plied, and the Company's relatively decentralized governing structures. Indeed, it was in the mart towns rather than London that Company membership was felt most strongly. As Justyna Wubs-Mrozewicz has noted with regard to the medieval Hanse, whose federal structure somewhat mirrors that of the Merchant Adventurers, it was in the Hanseatic residences overseas—the *Kontore*—that the boundaries defining the community were sharpest, reinforced by rites of passage and common experiences as mundane as shared eating.[90] Whereas in London established Merchant Adventurers might be absorbed into a broader business community and the opportunities to diversify that came with it, in the mart towns the boundaries of the merchant community were sharper, and opportunities arguably more constricted. Indeed, this book will argue that as these opportunities broadened for the former, with the expansion of English trade into new regions, the divergence between members in England and the mart towns grew wider, and the boundaries defining membership of this community became harder to locate.

Cutting across these geographical divides, however, were social ties which connected Merchant Adventurers in different locations. Company membership and the group affiliation that came from it was but one form of association which shaped the business lives of Merchant Adventurers, which were entangled in the informal networks that were necessary for the practical management of overseas trade in the premodern period.[91] These alternative affiliations could be in tension: loyalty to one's own network might come before loyalty to the Company, whilst

---

[90] Justyna Wubs-Mrozewicz, 'Rules of inclusion, rules of exclusion: the Hanseatic *Kontor* in Bergen in the late Middle Ages and its normative boundaries', *German History* 29 (2011), pp. 1–22. See also Donatella Calabi and Derek Keene, 'Merchants' lodgings and cultural exchange', in Donatella Calabi and Stephen Turk Christensen (eds), *Cultural Exchange in Early Modern Europe. Volume 2. Cities and Cultural Exchange in Europe, 1400–1700* (Cambridge and New York, 2007), pp. 315–48.

[91] Studies of British commercial networks include David Hancock, *Citizens of the World: London Merchants and the Integration of the British Atlantic Community, 1735–1785* (Cambridge, 1995); Nuala Zahedieh, *The Capital and the Colonies: London and the Atlantic Economy 1660–1700* (Cambridge, 2010); Sheryllyne Haggerty, *'Merely for Money'? Business Culture in the British Atlantic, 1750–1815* (Liverpool, 2012).

networks commonly extended beyond the bounds of the Company.[92] On the other hand, these networks were constitutive of the social structure of the Company as a community of merchants. Indeed, the Company might be conceived of as a 'whole network' comprised of multiple overlapping ties, which provided Merchant Adventurers seeking to fashion their own business networks with a large pool of potential partners, whose reputations were to an extent accredited by other members.[93] Though this study will not adopt formal network analysis, the metaphorical understanding of networks is useful in conceiving of the relationships that made business possible, as well as the overall shape of the merchant community. As we will see, commonalities in mercantile experience such as time spent in the mart towns created a high degree of density within the overall network in the earlier part of our period, although the dual-mart system compromised this somewhat. Even so, the multitude of 'strong ties' within the network ensured that information about the market and the individuals operating within it circulated widely, and even if much of this information might be repeated, this could increase a merchant's confidence in its security, particularly in the case of crucial decisions such as the choice of a partner.[94] Network participation could thus serve to generate a degree of loyalty to a particular market that was derived from the depth and extent of one's social connections within it, complementing any loyalty and commitment engendered by corporate affiliation. Over time, the shape of this network did change, however, as the Company's German and Dutch mart towns followed different paths, and in some senses it was those who could exploit their position in order to access new opportunities outside of the Company's traditional markets who were able to fare best from the commercial changes of the period. In order to understand how Company membership shaped the business lives and decisions of particular Merchant Adventurers, we need to take this social 'embeddedness' of the market into account.

Fortunately, the sources that merchants from this period have tended to leave behind offer a window into the wider social worlds they were a part of, particularly correspondence, which was often preserved as legally admissible evidence of business relationships in the absence of formal contracts. In the premodern era letters were critical to the management of a merchant's business; they were a

[92] For the relationship between the group and the network, see Justyna Wubs-Mrozewicz, 'The medieval Hanse: groups and networks of traders. The case of the Bergen *Kontor* (Norway)', in J. A. Solórzano Telechea, M. Bochaca, and A. Aguiar Andrade (eds), *Gentes de Mar en la Cuidad Atlántica Medieval* (Logroño, 2012), pp. 213–33.

[93] For a discussion of the Hanseatic League in these terms, see Ulf Christian Ewert and Stephan Selzer, *Institutions of Hanseatic Trade: Studies on the Political Economy of a Medieval Network Organization* (Frankfurt am Main and New York, 2016). See also Justyna Wubs-Mrozewicz, 'The Hanse in medieval and early modern Europe: an introduction', in Justyna Wubs-Mrozewicz and Stuart Jenks (eds), *The Hanse in Medieval and Early Modern Europe* (Leiden and Boston, 2013), p. 10.

[94] Emily Erikson and Sampsa Samilia, 'Social networks and port traffic in early modern overseas trade', *Social Science History* 39 (2015), p. 155.

means for principals to convey instructions to their agents, but also to negotiate relationships and the expectations on which these relations rested. Letters communicated commercial information but also news about the conduct of other members of the business community, knowledge that was critical in a credit-based economy.[95] They are thus excellent evidence not only for commercial practices, but also for attitudes and expectations.[96] Given the non-survival of the Company's own archive, merchant letters are invaluable in understanding how the Company's governing structures and regulatory system functioned in practice. They can also provide some evidence for the structure of the whole network of the Company's membership, recording information about relationships, for instance in bills of exchange which are also often recorded in account books. This information can be used alongside records such as port books (recording custom entries), and the surviving register of the Company's church at Hamburg (discussed in Chapter 1, below), to provide details about the size of the merchant community, the distribution of trade within it, and the careers of and connections between at least some of its membership. Part One will draw on the letters and papers of six Merchant Adventurers, who came of age during three successive eras in the Company's history: the Company's late-sixteenth-century heyday, the period of readjustment following the Cokayne Project and 1620s depression, and the post-Restoration contraction of the Company's authority to Hamburg. As these individuals figure so prominently in Part One, they warrant introduction here.

Chronologically the first is John Quarles junior, the son of a London Merchant Adventurer, who specialized in the export of quality dyed and dressed cloths. Evidence for his business largely comes from letters sent from his agents and apprentices in the 1590s, George Lowe in Stade and John Kendrick in Middelburg. But Quarles' interests extended beyond the Company's mart towns, and he was deeply engaged with the notorious interloper Thomas Jackson, who was pursuing opportunities to trade into the heart of the Holy Roman Empire, ventures which eventually contributed to Quarles' insolvency in 1608. Quarles' slightly younger contemporary was the best-known and well-studied Merchant Adventurer of the seventeenth century, Lionel Cranfield. Cranfield was also the scion of an established family of Merchant Adventurers, and he thrived in the early years of the seventeenth century, as evidenced by his correspondence with his Stade factor Richard Rawstorm, his friend and sometime Middelburg agent Daniel Cooper, and his broader network. Cranfield's ascendancy was momentarily endangered by the failure of his former master and father-in-law Richard Sheppard, a painful

---

[95] Craig Muldrew, *The Economy of Obligation: The Culture of Credit and Social Relations in Early Modern England* (Basingstoke, 1998).

[96] Francesca Trivellato, *The Familiarity of Strangers: The Sephardic Diaspora, Livorno, and Cross-Cultural Trade in the Early Modern Period* (New Haven and London, 2009). For a similar attempt to use letters to understand the Merchant Adventurers, see Ormrod, *Rise of Merchant Empires*, p. 125.

story discussed in Chapter 3. Cranfield's papers thus represent the two extremes of the fortunes of Merchant Adventurers: his own dizzying rise to success and eventually political office, and Sheppard's even more rapid fall into failure.

George Warner seems not to have experienced quite so dramatic a career as either Quarles or Cranfield, though the times he lived through were certainly turbulent. The child of Warwickshire gentry, Warner became active in business in the 1630s, an unpropitious time to become a Merchant Adventurer. His papers, including many letters to and from his Hamburg agent Pearce Starkie, cover the period 1638–43, and thus the disruptions caused by the outbreak of civil war. Warner's ultimate fate is unknown, but given the difficulties he was evidently already beginning to experience in this period and his family's royalism, it is unlikely to have been a particularly happy one. William Attwood, a rough contemporary of Warner, enjoyed a more successful civil war. Whilst Warner managed his trade from London, Attwood was reflective of a growing trend for certain Merchant Adventurers to spend the bulk of their careers overseas, in his case acting as the Hamburg representative of a partnership with his father-in-law Walter Pell, residing in Hamburg from 1626 to the early 1650s, when he returned to London and gradually retired from trade. Most of his voluminous papers cover this stage of his life, but he continued to correspond with former Hamburg associates, giving much evidence about the evolving social world of the Company's mart town.

John Sanford also enjoyed a prosperous career, although he was active at a time of decline for the Company. A second son of a Somerset gentleman, Sanford was in Hamburg by 1662, though he returned to England in 1665, perhaps to take up the inheritance that had come to him thanks to his elder brother's death. By 1675 he was prominent enough to serve as London treasurer to the Merchant Adventurers, and later in life he was Member of Parliament for Taunton, a steadfast Tory. Sanford's success was a contrast to our final case, Matthew Ashton, who differed from the other five by virtue of his origins in the north of England. His surviving papers—letters and accounts from 1678 to the end of the century— cover the period when he was seeking to navigate the transition from servitude to independence, as he attempted to establish himself as a factor in Hamburg, acting for a range of Hull, Leeds, and London merchants. As well as showing how the mart towns served to integrate the different branches of the Company socially and commercially, Ashton's papers demonstrate the process whereby aspiring Merchant Adventurers established themselves within the Company's ranks, or, in his case, failed to do so, for his fortunes ended in insolvency, rescued only by a fortunate inheritance.

Between them these six merchants span the century following the Company's departure from Antwerp, and encompass different aspects of the Company's trade and the divergent fortunes of its members. Their papers also introduce a much larger cast of characters, allowing us to piece together an impressionistic picture of the merchant community as it evolved over time. This is the task of Part One, though the approach is structural rather than chronological, with each chapter

considering themes and challenges that were common to all members of the Company. Chapter 1, 'Becoming a Merchant Adventurer', considers the process of establishing oneself within this community, particularly through apprenticeship, but also through the sociability that was a feature of life in the mart towns. Chapter 2, 'Show Days', looks at the regular management of trade by established Merchant Adventurers, considering the networks they assembled and the strategies they deployed in order to profit from the export of cloth. Chapter 3, 'Running on the Exchange', examines how merchants responded to the risks and shocks which characterized this period. Chapter 4, 'Disorderly Brethren?', concludes Part One by considering the role of the Company itself in the day-to-day affairs of its members, in terms of both commercial regulation and participation in decision making.

As Part One shows, the Merchant Adventurers were a more dynamic and variegated community of merchants than is often appreciated, and the cloth trade was more challenging than is suggested by the common image of the Company's members as complacent rent-seekers. Mastery of this particular commodity, as well as the social world of the mart towns where it was marketed, was not easily acquired. Membership of the Company entailed more than simply the purchase of a share in a protected trade. The significant investment of time and resources necessary to establish oneself in this trade perhaps explains why Merchant Adventurers could struggle when seeking to diversify into newer, more dynamic regions, although the extent to which they participated in newer trades has almost certainly been underestimated by historians such as Brenner. Even within the relatively limited boundaries of their own trade, there was capacity for innovation and expansion, however, sometimes (as with the import of linen or the re-export of colonial goods) associated with the emerging long-distance trades, although this could strain the mart-trading system to its limits. Merchant Adventurers participated in the new opportunities of the period, but not evenly, and this accentuated other divisions within the Company's ranks, notably the growing divergence between the Company's continental mart towns and its English membership. Whilst the Company struggled to maintain its foothold in the Netherlands, its trade there eventually becoming absorbed into a pluralistic mercantile world, in Hamburg the social ties binding the merchant community together coalesced as it became home to an increasingly settled class of long-term residents. In the process, the Fellowship of Merchant Adventurers came to represent different things to different constituencies within its membership.

Part Two will explore how these changes were experienced at the level of the corporation. Given the absence of most of the Company's corporate records, these chapters will draw on a range of different sources, including the merchant papers discussed in Part One as well as petitions, treatises, correspondence, and so on preserved in the state papers and the private collections of public figures. Each of the chapters considers a different moment of internal division in the century following the Company's departure from Antwerp, when the conventions of

corporate secrecy momentarily failed, and Company politics burst forth into a public arena. Chapter 5 assesses the aftermath of the Company's expulsion from the Holy Roman Empire following the imperial mandate of 1597. This prompted a contest between those members who were reluctant to lose their German markets, even at the price of abandoning certain key aspects of the mart-trading system, and those who sought to maintain it. The demand for commercial liberty, usually associated with external attacks on the Company such as the 1604 free trade bill, could come from within. This contest was not principally between members in England and those in the mart towns, but the potential for such a divergence can be seen in Chapter 6, which considers the effects of the Cokayne Project on the Company's members. It was in the mart towns, and particularly Hamburg, that the threat that the Cokayne Project posed not just to the Merchant Adventurers as a corporation, but to the trading system that it sustained, was felt most strongly. The growing willingness of members in the mart towns to identify their collective interests as distinct from those of the membership in England is apparent in the political contests that shook the Company in the middle decades of the century, the subject of Chapter 7. Although on one level Merchant Adventurers were divided over the same religious and political issues which led to civil war in England, in their case these contests turned into a series of power struggles between the membership and its deputy governors in the mart towns, which hinged on the question of where authority resided within the Company. The final chapter considers the Company's attempts to maintain its privileges from external attacks, focusing on the Restoration, and especially the 1680s, when the Company experienced an unexpected revival in its political fortunes. That this coincided with the most divided era in the Company's recent history, with the membership in Hamburg and London pitted against each other, is a sign of how deeply the two residences had diverged from each other by that point.

As we will see, neither the Company as an institution, nor its members, were static in this era of dramatic commercial and political change, but adaptation came at a price. External factors may have been the root causes of the Company's failure to retain its privileged status, but it was also the case that the Company was failing to reproduce itself as a merchant community characterized by shared norms and values, and especially, a distinctive mercantile identity that was associated with the mart-trading system.[97] Critical to this was a collapse of the traditional means by which new members were recruited to the Company and trained in its ways, thereby becoming endowed with the 'mere merchant' status which was central to the Company's claims to privilege. It is here, with the ways that new members came to enter into the ranks of the Fellowship of Merchant Adventurers as both a corporation and a community, that Part One begins.

---

[97] For similar points about how the Antwerp craft guilds failed to reproduce themselves in the eighteenth century, see Bert De Munck, 'Skills, trust, and changing consumer preferences: the decline of Antwerp's craft guilds from the perspective of the product market, c.1500–c.1800', *International Review of Social History* 53 (2008), pp. 197–233.

PART ONE

1

Becoming a Merchant Adventurer

The root and spring of all this almost incredible Trade and Traffique, hath had his increase and proceeding from the politike gouernement, lawes, and orders deuised, and obserued of olde time in the said Companie, ... one day still being a Schoole-master vnto the other, and men by experience, vse and knowledge of forreigne people, and their fashions, orders, and kind of dealing growing dayly and from time to time to an exacter course and greater perfection of matters, and vnderstanding of their owne estate, and what is fittest for the vphold-ing, and maintenance therof: These said ordinances containe in them all kind of good discipline, instruction and rules to bring vp youth in, and to keep them in order: so that the Merchants Aduenturers dwell-ing in the aboue mentioned Cities and Townes of the Realme of England, send their yong men, sonnes, and seruants, or Apprentises, who for the most part are Gentlemens sonnes, and mens children of good means or qualitie, to the Mart Townes beyond the seas, there to learne good fashions, and to gaine experience and knowledge in trade, and the maners of strange Nations, thereby the better to know the world betimes, and to be able to go through with the same, to the honor and seruice of their prince and countrie, and their owne wel-fare, and aduancement in the Common-wealth, whereof a very great number haue shewed themselues, and at this day many are very not-able and beneficiall members.

John Wheeler, *A Treatise of Commerce* (London, 1601), p. 24

To its secretary John Wheeler, the success of the Merchant Adventurers rested above all on the collective experience accumulated by generations of its members, and embodied in the Company's laws and ordinances. This wisdom was transmit-ted to young men who were sent from all parts of the kingdom to learn the art of merchandise directly from its leading practitioners, making the Company 'a plenti-full Nurserie', from which 'haue sprung and proceeded almost all the principall Marchants of this Realme'.[1] In this account, the mart towns were schools of civil-ity, experience, and discipline, breeding grounds for those skilful merchants who would conduct trade in the orderly manner that the Company prided itself on.

---

[1] John Wheeler, *A Treatise of Commerce* (London, 1601), p. 9.

Fellowship and Freedom: The Merchant Adventurers and the Restructuring of English Commerce, 1582–1700.
Thomas Leng, Oxford University Press (2020). © Thomas Leng. DOI: 10.1093/oso/9780198794479.001.0001

The prominence accorded to recruitment in Wheeler's apologetic *Treatise* was no accident. Central to the Company's defence against the charge of monopoly was its supposed ability to create new merchants, drawn from across the nation and the social spectrum (though with a bias towards the landed elites), countering those who presented it as a narrow clique conspiring against the commonwealth. So far from restricting commerce into members' hands, the Company was responsible for making merchants, that most socially useful of occupations. This chapter will evaluate such claims, examining how merchants came to be recruited into the Company's ranks and how they gained the experience necessary to succeed in trade, particularly through the institution of apprenticeship. Apprenticeship was not just the main means to join the privileged ranks of the Company and gain knowledge of its trade; it was also an opportunity to accumulate the other assets crucial for success—reputation, contacts (social capital), and the 'stock' which would enable a merchant to achieve commercial independence. For the established merchant, apprenticeship was an additional source of capital, and often a means to consolidate social relations with their peers. Apprenticeship was also deployed in the managing of businesses, with apprentices serving as a workforce bound by ties of patriarchal discipline within a household unit, but potentially extending far beyond its physical site. Apprenticeship was thus a means through which merchants created, consolidated, and managed those networks on which their businesses relied.[2]

Apprenticeship supplemented the authority of a principal over his agent with that of a master over his servant, a form of business management redolent of a household economy. For the majority of aspiring Merchant Adventurers, then, the formative relationship in their career would have been that with their master. As we will see, masters exercised a high degree of influence over their apprentices' prospects, and this could also be a means by which certain values and norms were transmitted through the Company's ranks. Needing to earn their masters' trust in order to access the most valuable opportunities open to them, servants had an incentive to conform to expectations, to dutifully perform prescribed roles, a deterrence perhaps to more innovative behaviour. The experience of arriving in the mart town as a young merchant would have been replicated across the generations, and such shared experiences could be generative of a sense of group identity and solidarity that could translate into social capital.[3] However, any such 'bounded solidarity' which might have emerged from consciousness of belonging

---

[2] For the roles that apprentices played in the businesses of an early Elizabethan Merchant Adventurer, see G. D. Ramsay (ed.), *John Isham Mercer and Merchant Adventurer: Two Account Books of a London Merchant in the Reign of Elizabeth I*, Publications of the Northamptonshire Record Society 21 (1962), pp. xcvi–xcviii.

[3] A useful introduction to debates over the concept of social capital is Alejandro Portes, *Economic Sociology: A Systematic Enquiry* (Princeton and Oxford, 2010), chapter 3. See also Ogilvie, *Institutions and European Trade*, pp. 427–33.

to a group could have its downsides: a heightened awareness of the distinction between insiders and outsiders might blind members to the opportunities presented through interaction with the latter.[4] Masters, though, were not the only influences that shaped the career-paths of aspiring Merchant Adventurers. Service in the distant mart towns could loosen the ties of household discipline, whilst servants' aspirations to achieve household independence could be at odds with their masters' designs. Thus the breakdown of social discipline in the mart towns was a common source of anxiety in Company discourse. In 1611, the Merchant Adventurer Edward Misselden portrayed the German mart town of Stade as a place where government had failed amongst the 'factors & yonger sort' who predominated there, leading to 'the miscarraige of their persons' and 'the misordering of their trade'.[5] Masters fretted about servants squandering their estate on mismatched deals, or being led astray by boisterous youths. Frequently these concerns were underlain by anxieties about the coming-of-age of their apprentices, whose transition to independence could create dangerous discontinuities in business management, and see former servants become rivals privy to a merchant's deepest secrets. For the established Merchant Adventurer, an apprentice was an investment, a potentially valuable future source of support, but like all investments, they could go bad.

Entrance into the ranks of the Company of Merchant Adventurers was more complex than simply purchasing a share in a privileged trade. This was a social journey through which merchants constructed their reputations and fashioned the ties that would sustain their future businesses. This meant that the merchant community was ever changing, as new merchants rose within the Company's ranks whilst others fell, and new alliances were forged. Such generational turnover opened the space for change: newcomers could be innovators, accessing new opportunities, fashioning new sorts of relationships, or fulfilling new roles. Over time, such changes would transform the nature of those ties which bound together the disparate branches of the Company, contributing to the growing challenge of maintaining corporate unity across a geographically dispersed membership.

The Beginnings of Service

For an organization such as the Fellowship of Merchant Adventurers, policing admission was essential to upholding the value of its privileges to members. The Company accordingly devoted the entire second chapter of its 'Laws, Customes

---

[4] For bounded solidarity, see Portes, *Economic Sociology*, pp. 42–3.
[5] Edward Misselden, 'A Discourse, shewing the Necessity of the Restoringe of the Marchaunts Aduenturers Priviledges & Government in their Mart Towne in Germany', BL, Sloane 1453, fol. 10v.

and Ordinances' to procedures for admission into the Fellowship.[6] As was commonly the case with such corporations, entrance could come through patrimony, service with a free brother, or the payment of a redemption fine, set at a costly £200 at the start of our period. Another barrier to 'Redemptioners' was the payment of double Company impositions for their first seven years of trade, whilst any apprentices whose indenture predated their master's redemption would have to pay a £50 fine to acquire their own freedom.[7] Apprentices and sons bound after a redemptioner's freedom could be admitted for the lesser fine of 10 marks (£6 13s. 4d.), but this still demarcated them as members of the so-called 'new Hanse', distinct from the 'old Hanse' who paid the traditional fine of 6s. 8d. These terms were a legacy of the 1497 parliamentary act opening up membership for those willing to pay a fine, and although they were rather antiquated by the seventeenth century, it is possible that certain privileges (such as access to the Company's free licence to export 30,000 undressed cloths) were reserved for those who acquired the freedom through patrimony or apprenticeship.

The Company further ensured the purity of its ranks by specifically excluding certain trades ('Artificer, Husbandman or Handycraftsman'), bankrupts, and those of non-English parentage, although with exceptions for children of freemen born of foreign women. Lineage was important: the sons and apprentices of bankrupts and disenfranchised members were also excluded, although exceptions could be made. Admission to the freedom took place overseas, in whichever mart town was then home to the Company's principal court, at which time the apprentice took his Company oath. These provisions ensured that, at the start of the period at least, admission to the Company was largely reserved for those who were either sons or apprentices of existing freemen, or potentially both. Other measures were intended to limit the number of new entrants into the trade. Only active merchants or Company officers could be masters, and members were barred from making free more than a single apprentice for the first seven years of their own freedom; thereafter, they could take on another servant until their twentieth year, and three in total thereafter. However, merchants were allowed to take on one additional apprentice if they qualified by patrimony, or were the former servant of a master who had died or retired from trade.

The printed indenture preserved by William Attwood, who was apprenticed to the Mercer and Merchant Adventurer Nicholas Backhouse in 1625, spelled out the typical expectations of apprenticeship, binding him to serve his master faithfully, to keep his secrets and preserve his goods, and commanding him not to

---

[6] *Laws*, pp. 34–52. For a discussion of the provenance of this document, see Chapter 4.
[7] The level of impositions was 8d. per shortcloth and 12d. per long/fine cloth. These were raised to 12d./18d. in 1618 in order to raise money to pay off the debts the Company had accrued following the Cokayne Project. An additional charge of 2s. 8d. per shortcloth and 4s. per longcloth was also introduced as a loan to the Company known as 'impressed money', which was then raised to 4s./6s., though cloths dyed out of the whites were shortly after exempted. Ibid., pp. 178–9, 188.

'haunt Taverns or Playhouses' or stray from the household at night-time, or to commit fornication or contract marriage. In return, Attwood could expect to be instructed 'with due correction', housed, fed, and clothed: by the contract, both parties agreed to 'bindeth himselfe vnto the other'.[8]

Apprentice Merchant Adventurers, particularly in London, belonged to a large class of young men whose formative years were spent in service, subject to the same sorts of disciplining efforts intended to socialize them to adult life, directed both from their masters and from other sources of authority, such as the church.[9] But in some respects the experience of training to be a Merchant Adventurer was distinctive. First, the socialization process was intended to raise young men to join the ranks of a specialist caste, the overseas merchant, and to induct them into the relatively bounded social world of the Merchant Adventurers. Knowledge of the personalities within this community, as well as the normative values and practices which were current within it, was important for success in trade. And this knowledge could not be acquired by remaining in a master's household; service overseas was generally seen as an essential stage of training, an experience that distinguished apprentice merchants from their peers.[10] Indeed, the Company's regulations for apprentices paid particular attention to service overseas, forbidding them from lodging in 'a suspected house or place of yll rule', inn, tavern or victualling house, and monitoring their place of residence.[11] They were fined 40s. for dining outside of the Company's house without special leave, whilst excessive drinking, playing cards, gambling, 'dancinge, mumminge or walkinge abroad in the night seasone', quarrelling, carrying arms, and dressing beyond their station were all subject to punishment.[12] Finally, apprentices were permitted to 'bee in pack house vnder a ffreeman', but were forbidden from trading on their own account until the last year of their term, although masters could employ their apprentices' stock on their behalf.[13]

The value of apprenticeship as a source of training can be seen by the fact that many freemen of the Company bound their sons to another merchant in spite of them qualifying for the freedom through patrimony. This was the case with Lionel Cranfield, whose father Thomas was a London-based Merchant Adventurer. Lionel himself was apprenticed to his uncle William's partner, Richard Sheppard, in 1590, aged 15. Although Sheppard was a Grocer, Cranfield became free of his father's company, the Mercers, in 1597, by which time his merchant career was already well under way.[14] John Quarles' father, a Merchant Adventurer and

[8] TNA, C109/19.
[9] Paul Griffiths, *Youth and Authority: Formative Experiences in England, 1560–1640* (Oxford, 1996).
[10] Perry Gauci, *Emporium of the World: The Merchants of London 1660–1800* (London and New York, 2007), p. 115.
[11] *Laws*, p. 46.   [12] Ibid., p. 47.
[13] Ibid., p. 43.   [14] HMC Sackville I, p. 23.

Draper also called John, included a similar arrangement in his will of 1577, placing his youngest son (born in 1563) in the custody of his former apprentice, Richard Bowdler, until the age of 21, although it is unclear whether he was formally bound as an apprentice.[15] Bowdler was entrusted with £500 of the £1,250 portion which had been left to Quarles, the remainder being deployed by a number of his father's former servants.

Quarles and Cranfield's careers were no doubt boosted by their status as internal recruits to the Company, but they drew their own apprentices from a range of backgrounds. Quarles' agents in Middelburg and Stade in the mid-1590s were his apprentices William Calley and George Lowe, the children of provincial gentlemen from Wiltshire and Shrewsbury respectively (though Calley had at least one ancestor who had been a London merchant).[16] Calley's replacement in Middelburg was John Kendrick, son of a Reading clothier. All three went on to have largely successful mercantile careers, Kendrick spectacularly so. Cranfield's first apprentice was Richard Perrott of Hereford, whose uncle's widow had married Cranfield's former master Richard Sheppard.[17] The four other Merchant Adventurers to be discussed in Part One were also provincial recruits to the Company's ranks. George Warner was the son of a Warwickshire gentleman, and was apprenticed to the Grocer John Chamberlen in 1630, though he would later describe another Grocer, Sir George Clerke, as his master.[18] William Attwood's family originated in Essex, and he entered the household of Nicholas Backhouse in 1625 shortly after the death of his father, whilst John Sanford was originally from Somerset, and began his service with the Mercer Lucy Knightley in 1656, aged about 16. Finally Matthew Ashton was born in 1655, the younger son of one Edward Ashton of Clubcliffe, Methley, near Leeds. In 1672 he was apprenticed to the Merchant Adventurer Alderman Godfrey Lawson of Leeds.

These examples illustrate the geographical and, to an extent, social range of backgrounds from which apprentice Merchant Adventurers were drawn, reflecting the relative openness of the apprenticeship market to those who could afford it, although it is likely that social contacts were deployed to help locate an appropriate master (Attwood and perhaps Sanford had pre-existent family ties within the Company).[19] Merchants in need of an apprentice could deploy their

---

[15] TNA, PROB 11/60/37.

[16] 'The Society's MSS. Chiseldon, &c', *The Wiltshire Magazine*, Dec. 1900, pp. 140–1.

[17] R. K. Turvey, 'NLW, roll 135: a seventeenth-century pedigree roll from Herefordshire', *Cylchgrawn Llyfrgell Genedlaethol Cymru* 30, 4 (1998), pp. 380–1. In 1606, Cranfield was charging £50 as his premium for taking on an apprentice. HMC Sackville I, p. 125.

[18] Warner referred to Clerke as his master in entries from 1638 in his ledger, TNA, SP 46/85/3.

[19] Tim Leunig, Chris Minns, and Patrick Wallis, 'Networks in the premodern economy: the market for London apprenticeships, 1600–1749', *Journal of Economic History* 71, 2 (2011), pp. 413–43. Attwood was executor to his kinsman Edward Attwood, whose will was made in Hamburg in 1627 (TNA, PROB 11/153/574). A Thomas Santford was recorded in the Hamburg church register in the 1620s and 1630s: Hamburg Register.

correspondents to scout for suitable candidates: 'a good doer and of good government', or 'one of good Civill education & that writes & Ciphers well & that is entred in Bookekeeping'.[20] Provincial gentlemen were reliant on acquiring good advice from insiders. For example, Sir John Wynn of Gwydir in north Wales enlisted the Merchant Adventurer Robert Geoffreys when looking to place his son Owen with a merchant.[21] If this suggests that prospective apprentices had little say in the choice of their master, in this example at least this was not the case. Owen was placed with this merchant for a trial period in order to see whether 'they like each other', and in fact this proved not to be the case. Fortunately Owen had 'heard of a marchante of good sorte and Credit, that wanted a servant' (Richard Cox, member of the Muscovy and Levant Companies as well as a Merchant Adventurer), and was 'resolved to serve him or none', indicative of the degree of agency that apprentices could often exercise over the terms of their service.[22]

In 1614 Sir John also deployed Geoffreys to place his 17-year-old son Maurice with the Merchant Adventurer Rowland Backhouse.[23] This time Sir John insisted on a lengthy trial period before paying the £150 fee, having some doubts about his son's health—'if the master should finger the money and he prove sicklie then all were lost'.[24] Fortunately Maurice thrived in his new environment (his brother later reported that 'he is much altered in my mynde of all a weaklinge is like to proove the hardiest of us all'), and so was bound to Backhouse for nine years, with a promise to be free to trade for himself for the final two.[25]

Like hundreds of others, Maurice Wynn's induction into the world of the Merchant Adventurers began in the household of his master. In an era before the emergence of the modern business firm, business and domestic life happened side-by-side.[26] Evidence for this earliest stage of apprenticeship is scarce, but scattered references can give some impression of what household service involved. Schooling evidently encompassed the rudiments of accounting. George Warner asked his Hamburg factor Pearce Starkie to send monthly copies of his journal 'As well to make a yonge youth which I have perfect in Accompts as to know more

---

[20] Richard Sheppard–Thomas Wotton, 30 Jan. 1602, HMC Sackville II, p. 110; Richard Twyford–William Attwood, 15 Jan. 1667, TNA, C109/19.

[21] Robert Lewys–Sir John Wynn, 12 Dec. 1608, NLW, 9053E/489.

[22] Robert Geoffreys and John Williams–Sir John Wynn, 8 Mar. 1609, NLW, 9053E/494. Patrick Wallis, 'Apprenticeship and training in premodern England', *Journal of Economic History* 68, 3 (2008), pp. 832–61.

[23] Richard Wynn–Sir John Wynn, 14 Feb. 1615, NLW, 9055E/684.

[24] Sir John Wynn–John Powell, 3 Jan. 1615, NLW, 9055E/681.

[25] Robert Wynn–Sir John Wynn, 14 Nov. 1615, NLW, 9055E/706; Maurice Wynn, London–Sir John Wynn, 22 May 1615, NLW, 9055E/696.

[26] Richard Grassby, *Kinship and Capitalism: Marriage, Family, and Business in the English-Speaking World, 1580–1740* (Cambridge, 2001), p. 296.

Exactly how my Estate stands there'.[27] Servants could be entrusted with paying out 'petty Charges'.[28] Much was probably learned by observing a master at close quarters, whether that be in their counting house, when purchasing cloths at Blackwell Hall, or at the custom house and the wharfside. Proximity to their master at work would expose a servant to those commonplaces that comprised the proverbial wisdom of merchants, and which occasionally resurfaced in correspondence, as when George Lowe cited his master Quarles' 'ould precept that yt is ill adventuring on any comodytye when yt is at an extreame high & unwonted price'.[29]

Training thus involved absorbing a combination of specialized skills, knowledge, and practical wisdom, but the apprentice was also expected to contribute to the regular running of the household. The vast majority of this day-to-day labour left no evidence, but merchants' daybooks give some impression of the range of activities apprentices performed. One unusual incident recorded in Richard Sheppard's daybook also highlights another aspect of apprenticeship which is rarely recorded: the opportunities for sociability that could exist even in the context of household service. On 7 December 1595 Sheppard's servant Robert Swaddon had been sent to pay a debt to Randal Cranfield, but having done so Cranfield refused to deliver to Swaddon the bond in question, and withheld £100 of the money he had received. Swaddon wrote a lengthy account in his master's daybook, calling on his 'fellows' Lionel Cranfield and Thomas Wotton (Sheppard's current apprentices), who had also been present, to add their signatures as witnesses.[30] Such fellowship amongst members of a household meant that apprenticeship was not quite so socially isolating an experience as we might imagine; as well as securing the trust of masters, household service could enable youths to begin to fashion the ties amongst their peers that would later be crucial to mercantile success. The social world of apprentices did not necessarily end at their master's door, therefore. Arriving in London from the north Welsh countryside, Maurice Wynn could rely on support from expatriate Welshmen associated with his family. Nor was he cut adrift from his relations in distant Gwydir. He regularly wrote to his parents to request that they send him money for clothing and other things, reciprocating by sending them goods only available in London (for his mother, a beaver-fur hat), the modest first steps of a commercial career.[31]

Further opportunities to extend their experience and contacts were presented to apprentices on those occasions when their masters were called away from home. On one visit to the continent, Lionel Cranfield entrusted the management

---

[27] Warner–Pearce Starkie, 3 Apr. 1640, TNA, SP 46/85/1, fol. 23v. See also Grassby, *Business Community*, p. 195.
[28] William Attwood's petty cash book, TNA, C109/20.
[29] Lowe–Quarles, 26 Nov. 1593, TNA, SP 46/176, fol. 16r. See also Grassby, *Business Community*, p. 196.
[30] HMC Sackville, I, pp. 10–11.
[31] Maurice Wynn–Lady Sydney Wynn, 2 June 1617, NLW, 9056E/789.

of his affairs to Richard Perrott, and he took care to instil in him an awareness of the responsibilities this entailed, advising Perrott that his 'carefulness, pains, diligence be such in my absence as may rather increase the good liking I have already conceived of you'.[32] The household itself was to be governed by Cranfield's mother, and Perrott was given clear orders to treat her 'reverently', and ensure that his 'fellows' did likewise, confirming his status within the domestic hierarchy. In 1603 Perrott was again entrusted with Cranfield's London household whilst his master sought refuge from the plague. However, when Cranfield reprimanded his servant for some minor failing, Perrott replied that 'if you are fearful of me you may be severed when you have please', his patience evidently tested by having to cope with business in the pestilential city.[33] Meanwhile Perrott was struggling to collect payments from his master's debtors, leading him to complain that 'Here is great want of you'.[34] As temporary custodians of a master's credit, it was vital to ensure that apprentices were equipped to make payments on their master's behalf, and Cranfield gave careful instructions to ensure that his debts were 'royally discharged in such sort as may be for my credit'.[35] But when merchants failed to provide a sufficiently well-regarded servant to act in their stead, their own reputation could be damaged. In 1641 George Warner complained to Edward Knightlie, who was then visiting Hamburg, that he had left his business with an apprentice who is 'but rawe, & not too farre to bee trusted'. When another merchant refused to present Knightlie's bill of exchange to this servant for payment, Warner was forced to accept it his stead, and consequently complained to Knightlie about leaving his business 'heare unsettled'.[36]

Household service, then, introduced apprentices to the essentials of running a business, including accounting, handling wares, making and collecting payments, and upholding the reputation of the household, as well as presenting opportunities to begin to fashion their own. However, this only exposed them to one side of the business of a Merchant Adventurer. In order to establish that 'knowledge of forreigne people' which John Wheeler emphasized as central to his Company's success, it was necessary for servants to depart from their master's immediate supervision, and experience the trading worlds of the mart towns.

In the Mart Town

It is impossible to know how many aspiring Merchant Adventurers spent time in the mart towns, at what stage in their careers, and for how long, but a sample of thirty-four new communicants in the Merchant Adventurers' church at Hamburg

---

[32] Cranfield–Richard Perrott, 2 Mar. 1600, HMC Sackville I, p. 29.
[33] Perrott–Cranfield, Nov. 1603, HMC Sackville II, p. 142.
[34] Perrott–Cranfield, 11 Nov. 1603, HMC Sackville II, p. 142.
[35] Cranfield–Perrott, 2 Mar. 1600, HMC Sackville I, p. 30.
[36] Warner–Knightlie, 16 Apr. 1641, TNA, SP 46/85/1, fol. 55v.

for whom it has been possible to identify the start of their apprenticeship shows that, on average, they joined the Company church during their fourth year of apprenticeship, although this varied considerably.[37] Leaving their masters' household may have felt like a moment of liberation, and a chance for them to begin the journey to independence in earnest, but in practice initial experiences in the mart towns often entailed swapping one master for another, as apprentices were sent to 'stand in packhouse' with one of their master's factors. These early visits could be short: having already earned the good will of his master Lionel Cranfield at home, Richard Perrott was sent to Emden in autumn 1600 to stand with Cranfield's factor Richard Rawstorm, before visiting Stade two years later.[38] In April 1603 he was sent to Middelburg, to stand with Cranfield's sometime agent Daniel Cooper, and in June travelled back to Stade, although the outbreak of plague that year led to him being called home.[39]

Such visits gave young merchants a taste of the social worlds of the mart towns, and the lives of the factors who resided there. Maurice Wynn arrived in Hamburg on his master's business in 1619, four years into his apprenticeship. He soon became acquainted with the communal life of the English community, characterized by collective meals in the Company's house and thrice weekly sermons.[40] Despite the harsh climate, Wynn boasted that 'this ayer doth very well agree with me', and seems to have wasted no time in seeking to establish himself within this particularly masculine social environment. As he explained to his father when requesting a supplement to his regular annual allowance of £10, 'heere a man must goe merchantlike and weare better apparell [than] wee are use to doe in London, beside divers other necessary expences'.[41] Aspiring merchants had to make their presence known amongst their peers, as well as customers. John Sanford advised his brother-in-law Lucy Knightley, who was set for Hamburg, to make every effort to 'appear in the world and putt your self forward in busines', as well as to 'be cheerfull & merry which is for your health and will take with most dutch humours'.[42] This needed to be balanced by circumspection, however; Sanford advised Knightley to 'study & observe the humers of the Dutch for

---

[37] This piece of data was created by locating apprentice records for new communicants registered in the Hamburg Register, using the open access online database Records of London's Livery Companies Online (https://www.londonroll.org/home; Drapers, Mercers, Clothworkers), and the genealogical subscription access site Find My Past (http://www.findmypast.com; Haberdashers). The arithmetical mean and median were 3.8 and 3 years, although the data only give the year when apprenticeships began. Joining the church does not straightforwardly equate with arrival in the mart town, but is the best available indicator in the absence of other information.

[38] Rawstorm–Cranfield, 24 Sept. 1600, HMC Sackville II, p. 38; Perrott–Cranfield, 22 Oct. 1602, ibid., p. 127.

[39] Perrott–Cranfield, 19 Apr. 1603, HMC Sackville II, p. 130; Perrott–Cranfield, 23 June 1603, ibid, p. 134.

[40] Maurice Wynn–Sir John Wynn, 31 May 1619, NLW, 9056E/865.   [41] Ibid.

[42] Sanford–Lucy Knightley Jr, 13 Mar. and 10 Apr. 1674, SRO, DD\SF/7/2/1.

without that yow will never com to Rights with them'.[43] Two decades earlier, William Lowther had advised his brother Christopher to conduct himself carefully when arriving in Hamburg, and in 'the first yeare to say little and onely to see the passage of business and to observe the nature and the disposition of all men'. Above all, it was necessary to have the measure of his customers, and William promised to give further information on those 'who are good and who not', although he promised that his brother would find 'better direction' from an acquaintance in Hamburg, one Mr [Henry?] Crisp, who would 'tell yow whose bill will sell, and whose not, and whose debts we must ride out'.[44]

Aspiring Merchant Adventurers sent to the mart towns did not arrive as isolated individuals, then, but were inaugurated into pre-existent commercial networks which were a source of support and information, but also a means for masters to monitor conduct. Sanford also advised that Knightley would find an ally in Hamburg in the form of his factor John Ayshford, who would 'advise you in all things, with home, be free; have all wayes a cherfull hart & goe merely about your business, and be sure to shune & avoide all Idle company following JA advice in all thinges'. Young men like Knightley who were placed in the custody of an experienced factor were able to learn the fundamentals of business in the mart town: transferring cloth from the Company's ships to the packhouse, organizing the display of goods on show days, bargaining with customers, arranging the shipping home of wares, and so on. In July 1641 George Warner sent his servant Edward Halford to stand with his Hamburg factor Pearce Starkie, promising the latter that he would acquire a useful assistant in routine tasks such as writing up sales and pursuing debtors beyond the mart town.[45] Warner promised to write to the Company at Hamburg to secure his freedom as soon as his servant had proven himself.[46] Similarly in 1659 William Attwood sent his servant William Palmer to stand with his Hamburg factor, coincidentally also called Edward Halford (probably a kinsman of Warner's former apprentice).[47] Palmer was also due to receive his freedom, but Halford was commanded to keep him in his service, and 'in all affaires of Packhouse and Countinghouse & Burse keepe noethinge from his knowledge, if his deportment bee accordingly'.[48] Soon Palmer was dispatched to nearby Lubeck for schooling in the language and arithmetic.[49]

[43] Sanford-Lucy Knightley Jr, 29 June 1671, ibid.
[44] D. R. Hainsworth (ed.), *Commercial Papers of Sir Christopher Lowther 1611-1644*, Publications of the Surtees Society 189 (1974), p. 205.
[45] Warner–Pearce Starkie, 16 July 1641, TNA, SP 46/85/1, fol. 66r.
[46] Warner–Pearce Starkie, 10 Dec. 1641, TNA, SP 46/85/1, fol. 74v.
[47] Halford–Attwood, 22 Mar. 1659, TNA, C109/24.
[48] Halford–Attwood, 12 Apr. 1659, TNA, C109/24.
[49] Halford–Attwood, 31 May 1659, TNA, C109/24. Such expenses were to be borne by their master: Matthew Ashton accounted his four months of language schooling at 4s. 8d. vls, with a further 8s. paid to his 'writeing Mr'. Ashton-Godfrey Lawson, 20 Jan. 1679, Bodl. Lib., Eng. misc. c602, fol. 4v.

Attwood was evidently anxious to ensure that Palmer was not enjoying his greater independence too much, and Halford reassured him that he was not keeping 'badd Company'.[50] Other masters, too, fretted about servants being misled whilst beyond the reach of their disciplining hands. In 1641 Warner instructed Starkie to keep a close watch on his apprentice: 'by noe meanes I desire you to keepe him idle, for of that cometh noe goodnesse, and I know att his first Cominge there will be Company enough to leade him away to drinkinge &c if he be not the more Carefull of himselfe which I hope he will, but if not pray take account of him how hee spends his tyme & if he doth anythinge that is not fitting spare not to tell him of it'.[51] Even after he had ceased to be his apprentice, Richard Sheppard still deigned to advise Thomas Wotton about how to behave on arrival in a new town, where men will 'look deeply into your usage, behaviour and carriage, and in your manner of going in your apparel'.[52] Wotton should thus 'abolish drunkenness, pride, lechery, unseemly behaviour and keep company with the best of credit', or else fall prey to the machinations of Dutch merchants, 'a subtle crew of people such as will over-reach you with bad commodities'.[53] The notoriety of a city like Hamburg could give parents a cause to worry, too: Maurice Wynn's mother advised him to 'have a speciall Care that yow be not seduced by any to yeeld to that vice of drunkenes which that Countrey is most subiect unto of any other nation'.[54]

Masters had good cause to be wary, for wayward apprentices could be a costly burden. In January 1596 John Quarles dispatched his servant William Gresham to Stade to fill in for George Lowe, who was due to visit England. Prior to this Gresham had spent time in Middelburg, where he had already acquired a reputation as a spendthrift, having reportedly 'outrunne himself' there.[55] Lowe was entrusted with bringing the wayward youth to heel, and promised that 'this place will quickly break hym both of his [gameing] & Ryotous expence, for neyther shall he fynde such company here to followe them nor if he did could yt be concealed longe from the deputy or treasorer & then should he be forced to leave them if good counsell would not prevayle with him'.[56] However, sustaining this level of discipline whilst providing Gresham with the experience necessary to complete his training was difficult. Although he had been advised not to trust Gresham with handling money, Lowe feared that 'I cannot possibly keepe my self soe cleare out of his daunger unlesse I should wholly discourage hym and bringe a bad report upon my self for hard usage towardes hym'.[57] Normal practice in such arrangements was for an apprentice to have full sight of his master's letters,

[50] Halford–Attwood, 20 Mar. 1660, TNA, C109/24.
[51] Warner–Starkie, 16 July 1641, TNA, SP 46/85/1, fol. 66r.
[52] Sheppard–Wotton, 30 Jan. 1601, HMC Sackville II, p. 110.   [53] Ibid., p. 111.
[54] Lady Sydney Wynn–Maurice Wynn, 4 Mar. 1620, NLW, 9056E/895.
[55] Lowe–Quarles, 18 Feb. 1596, TNA, SP 46/19, fol. 157r.   [56] Ibid.
[57] Lowe–Quarles, 18 Feb. 1596, TNA, SP 46/19, fol. 157v.

but Quarles sent secret instructions for how to deal with Gresham 'in such sort as he shall neyther suspect or perceive' that he was being treated differently.[58] Despite Lowe's promises to treat Gresham 'kyndly & instructe hym the best I may', he had little success in mending the young man's character, which was described as 'very sad & dampishe'.[59] Gresham's unwillingness to survive on the 'ordynary allowance of 50s a monthe', meant that Lowe ultimately entrusted his packhouse to another merchant when he eventually did visit England.[60]

Although Gresham was ultimately not trusted to perform this role, many examples survive of apprentices taking temporary care of business overseas, or managing it on a longer-term basis. During his 1603 visit to Stade, Richard Perrott was given joint commission with Richard Rawstorm to handle Cranfield's business, with the intention of eventually taking the business into his own hands. This handover had to be performed carefully so as to avoid upsetting Rawstorm whilst he still had control of Cranfield's business.[61] Although the outbreak of plague in London brought this visit to an early end, Perrott found himself in a similar position in the following year when he was entrusted with taking over Cranfield's Middelburg business from Thomas Wright, with whom he initially lodged. When Perrott attempted to take possession of Cranfield's effects, Wright responded by furiously turning him out of his residence, though not before Perrott had taken the opportunity to peruse his books and report back to Cranfield. Thus, merchants might use their apprentices to monitor the actions of their agents overseas, as well as vice versa. Despite this, Cranfield still suspected that Perrott had been corrupted by residing with this notoriously drunken merchant, leading his hard-pressed servant to protest that 'I never would be his guest at the English House, nor dinner nor supper nor any man else's', preferring to sup privately 'that I would not be over-seen with drink whereby he or any man else might undermine me'.[62]

It is unclear when Richard Perrott completed his apprenticeship. Certainly he continued in Cranfield's service for several years after 1604, jointly managing affairs in Stade with Rawstorm from 1607 to 1608, and thereafter handling Cranfield's business in Danzig, but as it was common for former apprentices to continue to serve their former masters, his indenture may well have expired by then. Merchants did deploy their apprentices as agents overseas for longer periods, however, and there were clear advantages in doing so. Principals needed to delegate a degree of agency to their agents, but also exercise some control over their decisions. Apprentices had the advantage of being subject to a degree of household discipline, albeit at a distance. One means to convey authority was

[58] Lowe–Quarles, 15 Mar. 1596, TNA, SP 46/176, fol. 128r.   [59] Ibid.
[60] Lowe–Quarles, 8 June 1596, TNA, SP 46/176, fol. 130r; 15 June 1596, TNA, SP 46/176, fol. 132r.
[61] Perrott–Cranfield, 23 June 1603, HMC Sackville II, p. 134.
[62] Perrott–Cranfield, 17 Aug. 1604, HMC Sackville, II, p. 149.

through letters, and correspondence between masters and servants overseas illustrates the negotiation of their relationships, as apprentices sought to retain their masters' goodwill, whilst steering a course that would allow them to assume independence. George Lowe's letters to John Quarles give a particularly detailed picture of how such a relationship developed over time. Lowe probably entered Quarles' service in about 1589, aged 19. By 1593, when his extant correspondence begins, he was handling Quarles' business in Stade, and continued to do so until 1598, having become free of the Company in 1597. Although none of Quarles' letters to him survive, Lowe's replies show how his master used correspondence to guide his servant's actions, sending continual 'advice' about prices to buy and sell at, commissions to purchase particular goods, and reprimands when his servant failed to fulfil his expectations. In his own letters Lowe presented himself as an able, trustworthy and dutiful servant, sending Quarles detailed intelligence about market conditions, 'as by duety I am bounde to give yowe intelligence & of all thinges which may further the welfare of your busynesse'.[63]

Letters were thus a means for young merchants to construct their reputations, but often they were forced to justify their actions to anxious or grumbling masters. This was a kind of bargaining process, as masters and servants bickered over the quality of consignments, with Lowe using this as an excuse for his failure to achieve Quarles' 'wonted price'. In autumn 1594 Lowe wrote his master that 'throughe yor comission tyinge me not to sell any under 20li hosowever I am as a stole to other men to make their marketts', and complained that 'yt hath not bene heretofore yor custome to tye me to prices but rather to give me order to sell with the first therby to prevent others in sale'.[64] Deploying an apprentice or servant as agent gave a merchant more authority over their conduct than would be the case with a factor acting on commission, but potentially at the price of the flexibility that allowed commission agents to capitalize on opportunities based on their own judgement. Quarles' strict instructions about purchasing wares for import were a particular source of frustration.[65] Whereas there was a degree of predictability in the market for English cloth in Stade, the import trade was more volatile. Lowe was often frustrated by having to secure prior approval for purchases from his master, and when Quarles commissioned the purchase of certain goods, Lowe often found them to be unavailable at the prices specified.[66] In late 1594 Quarles sent commission for fustians and other fabrics, but the order arrived too late and 'they were before disbersed into many mens handes'.[67] Lowe wrote that 'would I not alwayes be tyed to your comissions, but have liberty somtymes to buy that I should of my self thinke

[63] Lowe–Quarles, 17 Apr. 1594, TNA, SP 46/176, fol. 37r–v.
[64] Lowe–Quarles, 14 Nov. 1594, TNA, SP 46/176, fol. 66r.
[65] Lowe–Quarles, 28 Oct. 1593, TNA, SP 46/176, fol. 8r.
[66] Lowe–Quarles, 18 Nov. 1593, TNA, SP 46/176, fol. 12v; 1 Jan. 1595, TNA, SP 46/176, fol. 71r.
[67] Lowe–Quarles, 28 Nov. 1594, TNA, SP 46/176, fol. 69r.

most advantageable for somtymes all comissions are not to be followed, but accordinge to the quantyty & price of the comodytye Requested'.[68]

The purchase of goods for import, even more than the sale of cloth, thus required a degree of independence which masters were reluctant to grant young merchants. Lowe complained that his master believed him to 'lacke both skill & experience to chuse the comodytye', and was keen to prove otherwise.[69] Only once a purchase of silks sold unexpectedly well did Quarles begin to allow his servant 'liberty...to buy somtymes althoe without comission such thinges as I shall see likelyhood of advantage', and Lowe promised 'not to be ventrous on such thinges wherin I have noe Iudgement/ nor overbould on knewe comodytyes without circumspection & good advise'.[70]

Lowe used such deals to construct his own independent mercantile personality, therefore, presenting himself as someone possessed of the knowledge and experience necessary in a merchant. Also important were the contacts which Lowe had accrued during his residence in the mart town, which provided him with the information necessary to adventure on goods with confidence. Although masters often registered concern about the 'company' which their servants were likely to fall into on arrival in the mart towns, such sociability was an important part of their transition to independence, enabling them to broaden their associations and assemble the networks that were critical to future success. Lowe acquired a useful correspondent in the form of the London merchant John Cornelius, who was 'very dilligent & forward in givinge me advise of the allterations of tyme there in wares which is a principall helpe to any man that hath here his Residence'.[71] But his master was not entirely comfortable with Lowe receiving intelligence from another source, which practice he termed 'saylinge after another mans compasse'.[72] As was commonly the case amongst agents, Lowe supplemented the business of his principal Quarles with other commissions. However, Quarles became uneasy about his servant disclosing the secrets of his business to potential rivals, forcing Lowe to defend his relationship with Cornelius, who was 'soe Redy in givinge lardge & sounde advise of many thinges to be formerly unknowne, that I can be contented to take paynes for him without Requytall'.[73] Quarles could thus rest assured that Cornelius had no intention to move into his specialized area of coloured cloth.

Quarles' concerns here were arguably not just about losing valuable trade secrets. As his servant accumulated his own contacts, his dependence on his

[68] Lowe–Quarles, 18 Dec. 1594, TNA, SP 46/176, fol. 127r.
[69] Lowe–Quarles, 28 Nov. 1594, TNA, SP 46/176, fol. 69v.
[70] Lowe–Quarles, 2 Feb. 1595, TNA, SP 46/176, fol. 411v.
[71] Lowe–Quarles, 8 Nov. 1594, TNA, SP 46/19, fol. 123v.
[72] Lowe–Quarles, 1 Jan. 1595, TNA, SP 46/176, fol. 71v.
[73] Lowe–Quarles, undated (Nov. 1594?), TNA, SP 46/176, fol. 405r.

master was diminished. Negotiating the transition to economic independence was a fraught task for masters and servants alike.

Transitions to Independence

An aspiring merchant's first few years spent overseas were critical for the establishment of economic independence. Those not fortunate enough to have a large inheritance needed to accumulate a stock with which to commence trade on their own account; as George Lowe complained to his master, 'my patrimony as yowe knowe is very small & yet I finde my frendes such as I doubt whether I shall ever obtayne that or noe from them. Soe as service must be my refuge & therfore my greatest hope in your favour'.[74] But all merchants had to use this time productively by accumulating the other assets necessary for success.

The conditions under which apprentices served their masters overseas are often unclear. 'Petty charges' such as rent, food, and apparel were paid for by masters; some may have been paid an allowance.[75] However, apprentice-servants do not seem to have generally received commission from sales and purchases, as was usually the case with factors. Accumulating a stock was thus a challenge, and explains why apprentices like George Lowe were so keen to take on commissions from other merchants, although Lowe was scrupulous in showing that they would not prejudice his master's trade. When offered temporary custody of the business of Robert Clive, the servant of Sir Thomas Lawrence, Lowe wrote that this would be 'rather helpfull then disadvantageous to me in your busynesse'.[76] Lowe shared his packhouse with Clive, and because his main trade was in packcloth rather than Quarles' speciality of coloured cloth, their businesses were complementary. This was also the case with the trade of Robert Burleigh, which had been offered to Lowe after the death of his factor John Greene, and Lowe took this as a chance to complain to Quarles about the lack of trade coming his way: 'your owne busynesse beinge not great in this place I could well accomplishe an other mans doinges here, & bycawse I knowe noe other meanes I would be glad by any industry to helpe my self'.[77] Eventually Quarles consented to speak to Burleigh on Lowe's behalf, though ultimately Burleigh preferred to send his own servant.

Apprentices might supplement any income they earned from commissions by borrowing from the Company, which was custodian of several charitable bequests intended to aid young merchants. Sometimes masters were entrusted with the use of part of their apprentices' inheritance, which was destined to be their starting

---

[74] Lowe–Quarles, 9 Sept. 1593, TNA, SP 46/19, fol. 105v.
[75] John Kendrick–Quarles, 25 Jan. 1600, TNA, SP 46/176, fol. 286v.
[76] Lowe–Quarles, 13 Dec. 1593, TNA, SP 176, fol. 410v.
[77] Lowe–Quarles, 9 Sept. 1593, TNA, SP 46/19, fol. 105v.

capital. When Robert Swaddon began his apprenticeship in 1590, his clothier father entrusted 100 marks to his master Richard Sheppard to employ on his son's behalf until the end of his service; later on he delivered twenty cloths for his son's disposal.[78] Maurice Wynn frequently entreated his father to send him money to supplement his meagre allowance.[79] Wynn had the misfortune of arriving in Hamburg at the outset of the Thirty Years War and struggled to establish himself in the midst of the depression of the early 1620s. To his father he complained that 'The ordinary trade of marchaundaize is now soe very bad that a man had better keepe sheepe then to follow the same', a contrast to 'former times' when 'a man dureing his aprenticeshipp might get soe much money as hee might well live upon the same heer after'.[80] Wynn eventually cajoled his father to send him a consignment of lead from his mines in north Wales, which he hoped to find a market for if not in Hamburg, then in the Mediterranean; he also hoped to establish a trade in Welsh butter, 'for by the owld trades ther is nothing got, therfore yt behooveth us to looke out for new'.[81] For the son of a wealthy landowner, to be forced to beg for such favours in this manner was hard to accept:

> yt stickes something in my stomack to see all my brethren both younger & elder, seetled in such a course to live all like gentlemen, & my selfe not able to live like a poore man. I am one borne out of dew time, yt seemes, as St Paule saith, and Dutie ties mee from saying I am searved as the Itallian marchantes doe when they have a great many sonns, they are put in a monnestary & soe they are noe more troubled with them, thought is Free.[82]

Maurice's dilemma was that of many younger gentry sons who had been apprenticed with a merchant, and thus straddled two worlds: 'either to follow marchaundize or beetake myselfe to a contrie life'.[83] Although his father arranged a marriage with a gentlewoman with land worth £200 per annum, Wynn preferred to extend his apprenticeship for a year in order to 'get a prettie some of monney together that heerafter I may imploy it in trade in the contrie ... by this meanes I shall have two stringes to my bow, that in case Tenannts make bad payment, I may supplie my selfe out of the profit of my trade ther'.

Matthew Ashton found himself in a somewhat similar position to Wynn as his own apprenticeship came to an end in 1680, at which point he was standing in packhouse with the factor Richard Twyford at Hamburg, waiting impatiently for

---

[78] Exemplification of William Swaddon versus Richard Sheppard, 14 Feb. 1598, TNA, C78/112, no. 15.

[79] Maurice Wynn–Sir John Wynn, 31 May 1619, NLW, 9056E/865.

[80] Maurice Wynn–Sir John Wynn, 30 June 1621, NLW, 9057E/964.

[81] Maurice Wynn–Sir John Wynn, 20 Mar. 1622, NLW, 9058E/1013. See also letters of 3 June 1622, NLW, 9058E/1023; 31 Aug. 1622, NLW, 9058E/1031; 1 Jan. 1623, NLW, 9058E/1060; Maurice Wynn–Sir John Wynn, 31 Mar. 1624, NLW, 9059E/1205.

[82] Maurice Wynn–Sir John Wynn, 23 Aug. 1623, NLW, 9058E/1132.

[83] Maurice Wynn–Sir John Wynn, 19 Apr. 1623, NLW, 9058E/1088.

his master to release him from his service. Ashton was also the younger son of landed gentry and his father had recently died, leaving him lands including the family estate at Clubcliffe. Here was an ideal initial stock which might allow Ashton to commence in trade, and he claimed that several merchants had approached him about entering into a partnership on the basis of the £500 that he anticipated receiving.[84] However, Ashton's elder brother Edward tarried at selling the land, against Ashton's wishes. To add to Ashton's frustration, Edward had the good fortune to inherit the lands of his childless uncle Richard Frank at Campsall, apparently a much more valuable manor than Clubcliffe (he went so far as to change his surname to Frank to fit his new condition). Although since arriving in Hamburg he had found that 'business doth not fall out according to my expectations', Ashton still hoped to continue in trade, if not in Hamburg then in some other parts, rather than 'live like a begger at home'.[85] Although Ashton eventually secured a loan from his brother, this fell short of expectations, and so in 1681 he was forced to take up the arduous life of the full-time factor, slowly building up his commissions whilst using whatever he could spare from his factorage to drive his own ventures.

Having scraped together a modest sum by such means, young merchants could commence trading on their own account. Wynn received £100 from his father which he planned to use in his private trade, 'hugger mugger, privatelie being ashamed to put yt into my master's handes, to Imploy in trade, beecawse yt is soe smale a some'.[86] In any case by now Wynn believed his master Backhouse to be 'well stepped in yeers' and without 'that Judgment in bying his commodities as others have', another incentive for him to keep his stock out of his master's hands. As we have seen, Company orders prohibited such private trading before the final year of an apprentice's term. However, according to John Kendrick it was common practice, although one Kendrick claimed to have abstained from:

I have heatherto forborne to followe the course of other men by undertradinge (howebeit I knowe you have wincked therat in all your former servants) & purpose by gods grace soe to continue, hoping (as you have alwaies promised) when time searveth I shall finde a good Master of you: It showld seeme by your wrightinge you conceave otherwise of me & that you thincke I have by undirect cources gott allreadie good store of money in your service, wherin I protest I am guiltlesse, for unlesse it be some small matter by Factory I have not (as I hope to be saved) benefitted my sealf one pennie since my first comminge over.[87]

[84] Ashton–Edward Frank, 26 Aug. 1679, Bodl. Lib., Eng. misc. c602, fol. 7r.
[85] Ashton–Edward Frank, 8 July 1679, Bodl. Lib., Eng. misc. c602, fol. 6r; 5 Oct. 1680, ibid., fol. 21v.
[86] Maurice Wynn–Sir John Wynn, 18 Oct. 1623, NLW, 9059E/1154.
[87] Kendrick–Quarles, 23 Feb. 1600, TNA, SP 46/176, fol. 293v.

This quotation shows that whilst 'undertradinge' by servants could be a source of concern, such behaviour was sometimes tacitly 'wincked' at. The reasons for the former are clear. As well as violating the Company's orders, apprentices engaged in independent trade could neglect their master's business, or disclose valuable secrets. These were the issues which troubled William Calley in March 1601, when he discovered that his Antwerp servant John Chandler had been selling cloth for a rival merchant, James Monger (actually a Merchant of the Staple).[88] When Calley observed Monger buying a particular sort of 'azured' coloured cloth which Chandler had recently advised Calley to send, he deduced that Monger 'had advise for azures before us which is a monstrous villanie'. He proceeded to berate his 'wicked Servaunte' for this 'abominable and horrible deceipte', at length. Calley's principal fear was that his servant had disclosed the 'secretts' of his trade, which would lead to his certain 'overthrow'. Furthermore Chandler's inability to provide useful 'weekelye advise what passeth in our busines' could now be explained by the fact that he was 'growne alreadye up to the eares' in his own. Such 'hugger mugger' trade could only be profitable if a servant did 'one waie or other wronge theire master'. Calley explained that he had planned to allow Chandler to commence independent trade having completed his seven years' service, in accordance with Company orders, but his servant's impatience threatened to cost him his freedom. All this deceit would be for nothing, however, as Chandler's partners would gain at his expense, safe in the knowledge that he would not dare to complain. Chandler was thus the latest in a long line of 'forwarde fellowes' deluded by the 'overweeninge of theire owne witts and of theire presumynge of theire owne cappacities', who had been 'drawne away with the unlawfull desier of uniuste gaine before theire times'.

In spite of his anger, Calley promised Chandler not to 'caste you of or seeke your undoinge', on the provision that he disclosed 'the whole and plaine truth of all youre dealinges'. Rather than risk losing his services entirely, Calley evidently preferred the option of retaining a suitably repentant servant, particularly as Chandler's 'discreddittinge' would reflect badly on his own business management. Although his reply to this offer does not survive, Chandler did remain in Calley's service until August 1601. However, when his master summoned him home, Chandler resisted any humiliating return to 'kitchen or shoe house employment' in Calley's household.[89] Accordingly he requested that if Calley had no more employment for him overseas, then he free him from service, which would be no more than that 'which both moral honesty and a good conscience will bind you unto and which the good and loyal service I have done you in these parts hath deserved at your hands'. Apprentices who had tasted independence might be

[88] Calley–Chandler, 19 Mar. 1601, WSA, 1178/332/2.
[89] Chandler–Calley, Aug. 1601, WSA, 1178/332/2.

reluctant to return to the confines of their masters' households, and in fact Chandler was still in Antwerp fifteen years later.[90]

Given the difficulty of suppressing an apprentice's desire for independence, it was perhaps wise to indulge these inclinations. By doing so, a master might earn his servant's gratitude: after Quarles had agreed to sell a consignment of copper on his behalf and return the proceeds in cloth, Lowe gave thanks 'for yower favourable consideratyon of me as well therin as in the Rest, besechynge yowe to vouchsafe the contynuance therof, & what my uttermost indevours in yor affayres cannot deserve, my prayers for yowe shall I trust supply'.[91] This example illustrates how masters could permit private trade as a means to strengthen bonds with their apprentices, ties which often persisted after they became free: Lowe was not unusual in continuing to serve Quarles after the expiration of his indenture. This meant that frequently young merchants continued in a state of dependence on their former master even after they had completed their service, often under similar conditions.[92] Richard Sheppard offered to pay his former servant Thomas Wotton's charges of rent and lodging in order to retain his service overseas; Wotton in turn was permitted to use his own stock to purchase goods, as long as they were consigned to Sheppard or his son John.[93] In 1617, shortly after the expiry of his service, Thomas Barker agreed to serve as Hamburg factor for his former master Thomas Sheppard and his partner John Ferrar for seven years, on a salary of £100 a year, but with the condition that he should not trade for himself or others without express permission (an agreement which ended in legal action following Sheppard and Ferrar's insolvency).[94]

For recently freed merchants without the means to trade independently, continued service for their master could be a lifeline. At the outset of his career John Ramm wrote to his former master Attwood that he had turned down all offers of partnership, 'being more desirous of tendering my servis to yor Imployment', in either Hamburg or England.[95] Unfortunately for Ramm, Attwood was then retiring from trade. Sometimes a master's departure from commerce could present an opportunity, however; Richard Perrott remained in Lionel Cranfield's service as he moved into custom farming and office holding, eventually securing a position in the custom house.[96]

The ending of apprenticeship was therefore not necessarily the watershed that we might expect, and was often followed by a 'journeyman' phase when merchants commonly continued in the service of their former master overseas, their income supplemented by other commissions, before they were able to accumulate enough

---

[90] See his letters to the diplomat William Trumbull, HMC Downshire III–V.
[91] Lowe–Quarles, 22 Oct. 1596, TNA, SP 46/176, fol. 168v.
[92] For examples from the early Elizabethan period, see Ramsay (ed.), *John Isham*, pp. xcvi–xcvii.
[93] Wotton–Sheppard, 11 Mar. 1601, HMC Sackville II, p. 233.
[94] Final decree in *Thomas Barker v. Thomas Sheppard and John Ferrar*, TNA, C78/270, no. 10.
[95] Ramm–Attwood, 9 Nov. 1658, TNA, C109/20.   [96] Turvey, 'NLW, roll 135', p. 380.

stock to establish their own household. The bonds of apprenticeship could endure long into a merchant's career, therefore, perhaps culminating in formal partnerships between erstwhile servants and their masters, who thereby ensured continuity in business management. John Quarles entered into a partnership with his former servant William Calley in 1594, when he was still in Middelburg, partly 'in respect of his skill in the Trade in forreigne partes', lending him half of his £2,000 stock; after he broke with Calley acrimoniously, Quarles entered into a new partnership with John Kendrick.[97] George Warner's former master Sir George Clerke also helped establish him with two loans in 1638, some of which Warner used to purchase a large consignment of cloth from Clerke.[98] To masters, apprentices were an investment which was expected to pay dividends even after the expiry of their indenture: William Calley's sense of betrayal at his servant John Chandler's actions was partly because he did 'make a conscience of your estate and woulde bee gladde that you shoulde doe well, wherebye (if it soe pleased God) I mighte have comforte and credditte of you heerafter'.[99] If not an actual partner, a suitably loyal ex-apprentice might become a valuable ally: John Sanford wrote to his partner Lucy Knightley's apprentice Thomas Biggs of Hamburg that 'I would have you eminent and bring you in esteeme with marchants', and recommended him as a partner to another correspondent on the basis that he 'was our servant these 8 years so you may judge we have reason to know him'.[100]

If all went to plan, merchants could use these early years as a springboard for future success, accumulating enough stock to trade independently, making enduring contacts amongst fellow members of the Company and customers, and establishing their reputation. However, there were many obstacles standing in the way of the achievement of economic independence, which might leave aspiring Merchant Adventurers in a condition of constantly frustrated or deferred manhood, at least according to prevailing patriarchal norms.[101] A comparison between one of the most precocious members of the Company in the earlier part of the period, Lionel Cranfield, and his peers, indicates some of those factors that shaped the fortunes of young merchants. Cranfield commenced his apprenticeship under Richard Sheppard in 1590, aged 15, and was based in Stade for some months in 1594 and again from 1596–7, serving both his master and Sheppard's partner, Cranfield's uncle William. By then Cranfield's father was dead, and Cranfield was able to deploy his inheritance of over £500 at the outset of his mercantile career.[102] Cranfield's transition to independence appears to have been

[97] Exemplification of chancery decree in suit of William Calley versus John Quarles, WSA, 1178/333.
[98] See Warner's ledger, TNA, SP 46/85/3.
[99] Calley–Chandler, 19 Mar. 1601, WSA, 1178/332/2.
[100] Sanford–Thomas Biggs, 25 July 1673; Sanford–Samuel Sykes, 10 Jan. 1674, SRO, DD\SF/7/2/1.
[101] Alexandra Shepard, 'Manhood, credit and patriarchy in early modern England c.1580–1640', Past and Present 167, 1 (2000), pp. 75–106.
[102] HMC Sackville, I, p. 17.

fairly seamless, perhaps too much so for the liking of his master, who grieved at the loss of such a capable servant.[103] This coincided with the disruption caused by the Company's expulsion from Stade following the imperial mandate of 1597 (discussed in Chapter 5), and Cranfield's rise may have been aided by his willingness to keep a foothold in the German market by trading to Hamburg, drawing on recent acquaintances in the mart town as his agents. Cranfield continued to share his time between London and the mart towns, and used Sheppard as his London agent when overseas; in return, he continued to do Sheppard's business when in Stade.[104] In March 1599 Cranfield computed the net value of his estate as £2,628 6s.[105] Little wonder, then, that Sheppard consented to Cranfield's desire to wed his daughter.[106] At the age of 24, Cranfield was fully established in his own household in London, and his business went on to thrive.

Cranfield's fellow apprentice under Sheppard, Thomas Wotton, fared rather differently. Having entered Sheppard's service around 1593, it was Wotton who took up responsibility of keeping his master's day book when Cranfield went to Stade in 1594, and thereafter Wotton was always been a step behind his more favoured predecessor. He apparently had to wait until 1600 for his first significant commission overseas, being sent to Emden to pick up the language and learn the essentials of trade. Even then, half his charges were borne by Cranfield. Sheppard had promised to send Wotton to either Amsterdam or Middelburg once this arrangement ceased, but when he was instead summoned home to London, Wotton claimed that the news had 'driven me into that astonishment, as I may well say at this præsent am not my selfe'.[107] This, he explained, was not so much due to his own disappointment, as that of his mother and friends, who had hoped that 'after 7 or 8 yeares time spent in your service, it pleased God to put it in your mind at last to send me over, wherby I might learne to live in the world, but as my voyage was dawngerous at first, so in the end it falls out for me I may well saye most infortunate and unluckye'. Even though Cranfield had by then left Sheppard's service, Wotton complained that his master preferred to advance his son John as his Emden agent, meaning 'I am scarcely made acquainted with any sales, or barter which he makes.'[108] This was particularly hard to take given John Sheppard's evident incapability as a merchant: having briefly attended Cambridge University in 1595, John had been brought home to attend to his father's business, but as late as 1599 Richard Sheppard preferred to rely on Cranfield, writing that John 'lacks experience, and therefore is not of much use'.[109] Wotton was thus being starved of the opportunities that would allow him to establish independence, leaving him to

---

[103] Sheppard–Daniel Cooper, 4 Jan. 1597, HMC Sackville I, p. 22.
[104] Cranfield–Sheppard, 29 Aug. 1597, HMC Sackville I, pp. 22–3; Sheppard–Cranfield, 10 Mar. 1598, ibid., p. 27.
[105] Ibid., p. 28.   [106] Sheppard–Cranfield, 2 Feb. 1599, ibid., pp. 26–7.
[107] Wotton–Sheppard, 12 May 1600, KHLC, U269/1/CB352 (HMC Sackville II, p. 231).
[108] Ibid.   [109] Sheppard–Cranfield, 10 Mar. 1599, HMC Sackville I, p. 27.

plead that 'yf you send for me home, becawse I am raw & unexperienced, I know you do consider, that everyone must have a beginning & learning which throwgh time wilbe better perfitted'.[110]

This evidence suggests the existence of a 'pecking order' amongst servants within a master's household, with Wotton suffering by being behind the precocious Cranfield as well as Sheppard's son.[111] Masters were able to distribute the opportunities necessary to success to their favoured servants, making their judgements on the basis of perceptions of ability and honesty, but also the social value that these servants may already have possessed by virtue of their birth: this was no meritocracy. Ultimately Wotton did persuade his master to send him to Amsterdam, but with the bulk of his master's trade going to the Company's official mart towns, Wotton struggled to establish a reputation amongst local merchants. Thus he continued to fall behind his contemporaries, complaining that 'It doth not a little towch me to see since my coming over so many here raysed up to great busines, and creditt, whome since my first coming into your service I have knowne my selfe to be equall or no way inferiour vnto'.[112] Even once he became free of the Company in February 1601, Wotton continued to be closely bound to his former master, assuring him later that year that 'as I am your servant so I am to be disposed of by you at your own pleasure', and promising to be obedient to his 'absolute command'.[113] But with his career failing to take off, Wotton was open to the idea of starting again as a factor in the Levant.[114] However, Wotton failed to make his break before Sheppard's bankruptcy (as will be discussed in Chapter 3), and his own credit seems to have suffered an enduring blemish. According to Gerard Malynes, a servant had 'no other credit but his Masters', a lesson Wotton learned from experience; as he wrote to Sheppard, 'whatsoever tendeth to the impairing of your credit also wholly diminishes mine'.[115]

Another of Cranfield's contemporaries who experienced a protracted transition to independence was his friend, Daniel Cooper, a fellow apprentice at Stade. Cranfield and Cooper acted as agents for each other for much of the duration of Cranfield's mercantile career, and in contrast to the studied, if brittle, politeness usually found in mercantile correspondence, Cooper was unafraid to berate Cranfield about his character blemishes, surely the legacy of their youthful friendship.[116] Cooper was already handling Cranfield's cloths in Stade in July 1597, at which time he was struggling to pay some large debts of his own, probably accrued in his independent trading. Cooper had an unhappy relationship with his

[110] Wotton–Sheppard, 12 May 1600, KHLC, U269/1/CB352 (HMC Sackville II, p. 232).
[111] Griffiths, *Youth and Authority*, p. 294.
[112] Wotton–Sheppard, 19 Feb. 1601, KHLC, U269/1/CB352 (HMC Sackville II, p. 56).
[113] Wotton–Sheppard, 22 Sept. 1601, HMC Sackville II, p. 234; 28 Sept. 1601, ibid., p. 89.
[114] Wotton–Sheppard, 27 Oct. 1601, HMC Sackville II, pp. 92–3.
[115] Gerard Malynes, *Consuetudo, vel lex mercatoria, or The Ancient Law-Merchant* (London, 1622), p. 108; Wotton–Sheppard, 27 Oct. 1601, HMC Sackville II, p. 92.
[116] For instance Cooper–Cranfield, 7 Mar. 1601, HMC Sackville II, pp. 56–7.

master Alderman Robert Hampson, whom he termed the 'old dog', and relied on friends including Cranfield to maintain his credit.[117] When in the following month he fell out with his master's brother—'a drunken beast'—over accounts, Cooper was called home to explain himself.[118]

Cooper was in Stade again in February 1599, but by the following January he was based at Middelburg, where he acted as Cranfield's agent for the following decade. In Middelburg Cooper sustained a substantial, though secretive, trade on his own account. In January 1600 he made a significant adventure on goods including pepper, and intended to give Cranfield details of to whom they were consigned, but not before enquiring 'wether my Master Can by the lawe heare or the orders of our Companye, foerse you toe declare uppon yor othe what is in yor knowledge'.[119] In June 1601 Cooper reported that his master was lately 'verye suspitious' about his dealings.[120] Cooper suspected that Hampson would soon send his son over 'toe bee poeringe intoe my busynes', though he purported to be untroubled by this intrusion: 'hee is fytter for other matters & will never hurte merchante'.[121] Cooper's efforts to establish himself were continually undermined by Hampson's plans to relocate him to another town, and he complained that his master's desire was that 'I shall in my olde dayes become A traveller'.[122] But with his own business to take care of, Cooper vowed to resist any such designs:

> yf hee will not bee Contente I shoulde thrive lett hyme sende whome hee will toe have the Charge of his bussynes with my bondes & Indentewrs and I will geve hyme his owne and healpe annye suche servante for 2 years which hee shall send as willinglie as yf hee gave me all my charges & wages and will demande butt 20li starling per anno of hyme...yf hee will nott yealde toe this I will hoeld hyme att the staffes ende for I meane nott Come for Englande this 2 years & ½: God willinge but keape this toe yor selfe my playne exkews toe hyme shall bee yf I come for Englande I muste marrye which will bee A greatt hynderans untoe me, & to hyme which boen I will geve hyme toe knawe uppon. I will doe noethinge withoute your good advis and Counsell, and otherwayes then an onnest man I will never doe...[123]

Cooper was still grumbling about his master in January 1602, but by then he accounted himself worth £750, good payment of his debts permitting, plus more in household stuff and apparel, and £100 which he was due to receive following

[117] Cooper–Cranfield, 19 July 1597, HMC Sackville II, pp. 2–3.
[118] Cooper–Cranfield, 22 Aug. 1597, HMC Sackville II, p. 3.
[119] Cooper–Cranfield, 5 Jan. 1600, KHLC, U269/1/CB49 (HMC Sackville II, p. 10).
[120] Cooper–Cranfield, 13 June 1601, KHLC, U269/1/CB49 (HMC Sackville II, p. 76).
[121] Ibid. (HMC Sackville II, p. 77).
[122] Cooper–Cranfield, 31 Jan. 1601, HMC Sackville II, p. 53.
[123] Cooper–Cranfield, 13 June 1601, KHLC, U269/1/CB49 (HMC Sackville II, p. 77).

marriage.[124] But he was still in Middelburg in May 1603, receiving consignments of cloth from Hampson as well as on his own account.[125]

Eventually Cooper did establish himself as an independent merchant, but he lagged behind Cranfield, which perhaps explains why he was driven to chase after several risky speculations which often left his fingers burnt, souring relations with the man he still called his master.[126] Cooper often turned to friends such as Cranfield for assistance when his deals got out of hand. In return for Cranfield's help he promised to 'bee bounde durynge my lyvfe to bee servyssable vnto you, or annye of yours that shall pleas toe Commaunde me': the price of freeing himself from one relationship of service was to enter into another.[127] Such occasions thus bought out his lingering resentment at their varying fortunes:

> Freind Lyonell I have byn somewhat troblsome unto you and more chargable then I coulde wishe I weare...I am ashamed to enlardge muche uppon theis matters, tyme maye with your good favour and countenans bringe me in part oute of yor debte / in the meane whyle accompt that you have paid deare for A trew servessable Freind to you or any Freind of yors duringe my lyvfe....I have in 11 yeare byn beholdinge to noe man butt God & everie man hathe byn beholdinge to me well the wheel is turned & God hathe raised me good friendes yor selfe beinge the prinsipauell otherwayes I had not byn heare nowe, I Cannot maeke you amendes butt I wishe yf yt woulde doe you good the best blood in my harte.[128]

Like Wotton, Cooper had to suffer the indignity of watching the ascent of his peers whilst his own youth slipped away: 'Such poer yonge ould mens caesses as myne is toe bee lamented that woulde fayne thrive, and doe Fynde suche darke cloudes as happen in my labours when I am butt...seackinge toe reap my feirst smaell parcell of ffrewtes.'[129]

Unsurprisingly such frustrations could push young merchants into desperate acts. One servant who according to George Lowe had 'almost undon' his master, Sir Thomas Lawrence, was Nicholas Goldsmith. Following Lawrence's suicide, Goldsmith was sued in Chancery by his family, who alleged Goldsmith had been 'very Improvident & simple' in his master's affairs.[130] Another merchant to suffer from the misbehaviour of his servant overseas was Alderman Henry Rowe, whose

[124] Cooper–Cranfield, 4 Jan. 1602, HMC Sackville II, p. 107.
[125] Cooper–Cranfield, 14 May 1603, HMC Sackville II, p. 132.
[126] R. H. Tawney, *Business and Politics under James I: Lionel Cranfield as Merchant and Minister* (Cambridge, 1958), pp. 39–40; Cooper–Cranfield, 5 Jan. 1600, HMC Sackville II, pp. 10–11; 2 Aug. 1600, ibid., p. 32.
[127] Cooper–Cranfield, 19 July 1597, KHLC, U269/1/CB49 (HMC Sackville II, p. 2).
[128] Cooper–Cranfield, 15 Feb. 1599, KHLC, U269/1/CB49 (HMC Sackville II, p. 4).
[129] Cooper–Cranfield, 7 Mar. 1601, KHLC, U269/1/CB49 (HMC Sackville II, p. 56).
[130] TNA, C2/Eliz/B2/36.

Middelburg servant was Anthony Wright. In December 1600 Daniel Cooper warned Cranfield that 'thinges ar monsterous yll' with Wright, and prophesied that 'thear will burste oute A vylle soer & I feare oulde wrighte and alderman Roe will Ringe for yt'.[131] Wright was likely to 'prove a knave', and Cooper was concerned that 'his faell will maecke oulde foelkes suspitious/ & peradventewre my master will goe toe shifte me agayne which woulde Come me yll toe pass in respeckte I have somuche Clothe uppon my handes att Embden'.[132] Eventually Wright took the usual course for insolvent factors, and ran away, leading his master to petition the Privy Council to ensure the recovery of any goods he had left behind.[133]

Most extreme was the case of another of Cranfield's contemporaries, Robert Swaddon. Shortly after the incident recounted in Richard Sheppard's daybook and discussed above, Swaddon absconded from his master's household with a large sum of money, setting on a journey that took him to France and across England: Cranfield's uncle William reported that 'the vyllaine ryde frome place to place spending frankly with other mens money'.[134] He was eventually captured and delivered back to Sheppard, only to escape and go on to have a career forging bills of exchange.[135] For Robert Tittler, 'Swaddon the swindler' appeared to be a case of a criminal by inclination rather than circumstance, and certainly contemporary judgements of the young man were harsh. After a second recapture, William Cranfield reported to Lionel that 'he Leys in the conter & I thinke will come to be hangd in the ende for he hath no fear of god in him/ he had his wyne before him when they tok him/ [& said] he would drink his wyne afor he repent'.[136] But the story may not have been so straightforward: in 1598 Swaddon's father sued Richard Sheppard for allegedly appropriating the money and cloths which had been entrusted him on Swaddon's behalf. Although the court found that Sheppard had been 'muche damnyfyed' by his apprentice, if there was any truth in the allegation then it would go some way to explaining Swaddon's initial transgression, perhaps believing that the money he took from his master was rightfully his.[137]

Whatever his motivations, Swaddon blamed his increasingly desperate actions on those family and friends who had deserted him: 'the chif thinge that mad him goe away as he alleges was that he understode that his mother & frindes would do nothing for him'.[138] Social support amongst their peers was critical to those, like

---

[131] Cooper–Cranfield, 6 Dec. 1600, KHLC, U269/1/CB49 (HMC Sackville II, p. 46).

[132] Cooper–Cranfield, 13 & 18 Dec. 1600, ibid. (HMC Sackville II, pp. 47–8).

[133] Cooper–Cranfield, 27 Dec. 1600, HMC Sackville II, p. 48; APC 1600–1, pp. 117–19.

[134] William–Lionel Cranfield, 23 Oct. 1596, KHLC, U269/1/CB59.

[135] Robert Tittler, *Townspeople and Nation: English Urban Experiences, 1540–1640* (Stanford, 2001), pp. 156–63.

[136] William–Lionel Cranfield, 21 Mar. 1597, KHLC, U269/1/CB59.

[137] Exemplification of *William Swaddon v. Richard Sheppard*, 14 Feb. 1598, TNA, C78/112, no. 15.

[138] William–Lionel Cranfield, 21 Mar. 1597, KHLC, U269/1/CB59.

Daniel Cooper, who could not rely on the support of their family or master at home. But friendships sealed through youthful exuberance and the 'present-centred prodigality' of 'good fellowship' could become problematic once young men sought to establish their reputations as reliable, sober merchants.[139] When Cranfield agreed to deploy Cooper as his agent in Middelburg, Cooper promised that he was 'much altered in one good poynte for I groe neare when yt is too laett, and I thanke God lyve in good order & moderatelie all exces of good felloshipp hoellie left asyde'.[140] But when he attempted to place his brother in Cranfield's service, Cranfield refused, and Cooper suspected his friend was 'rather affeared he would prove a wag like me his brother'.[141] Cooper's jealousy at Cranfield's rise to established householder came out when the two had a falling out over accounts: 'I repente noe kyndnes I have don you & expeckte the lycke from you. what wee weare when good fellowshipp rayned att Stoad I knowe and feall & doe leave you toe yor good fortewne, & Content my selfe with the Clipte winges of myne one forttewne.'[142]

Resentment about young upstarts such as Cranfield was not limited to their less successful peers. Cranfield's own father Thomas had enjoyed a similarly rapid rise to fortune, which evidently perturbed as well as astonished his former master Vincent Randall: 'for you begane to occupy for your sellfe 6 yerys sonner than ever I doud & I do not mystrust yf you do tacke my symple cunsell you shall do well better than ye do loucke for at my hand I do thynke'.[143] Half a century later Lionel's own 'ample trayde' was attracting similar attention: Cooper reported that his rivals did 'Carpe mightelie', with Alderman Roe reported to have muttered that 'you drove as greatt A trayed as an alderman butt the son would not shyne alwayes'.[144]

For established merchants, the prospect of being outstripped by their former servant must have been an alarming one. Randall warned Thomas Cranfield about proud youths who disdained their 'elders & betters', but ended up bankrupt.[145] However, he claimed his intent was not to discourage his former servant; on the contrary, 'I wold have you so to occupy that I with other maye Jugge you to be a gaynner & no losser & spare not that for I wolbe veri lowthe to se you goo backe word & specialli under my handes but to se you to cum forward & to do full well.'[146] There was much to be gained from keeping a successful former servant close by: Thomas Cranfield married his former master's daughter, just as Lionel Cranfield would do decades later. But the latter's fraught relationship with

---

[139] Hailwood, *Alehouses and Good Fellowship*, p. 149.
[140] Cooper–Cranfield, 14 Jan. 1600, KHLC, U269/1/CB49 (HMC Sackville II, p. 11).
[141] Cooper–Cranfield, 1 Nov. 1600, HMC Sackville II, p. 43.
[142] Cooper–Cranfield, 31 Jan. 1601, KHLC, U269/1/CB49 (HMC Sackville II, p. 53).
[143] Randall–Thomas Cranfield, Antwerp, 13 Apr. 1551, HMC Sackville I, p. 3.
[144] Cooper–Cranfield, 11 Apr. 1601, KHLC, U269/1/CB49 (HMC Sackville II, p. 64).
[145] Randall–Thomas Cranfield, Antwerp, 13 Apr. 1551, HMC Sackville I, p. 2.
[146] Ibid., p. 3.

Richard Sheppard, to be discussed in Chapter 3, suggests a residual resentment on the part of the latter that kinship did not extinguish.

Establishing a Household

Having traversed the state of dependency that apprenticeship entailed, economic independence was generally associated with the establishment of a household. As well as sustaining the management of their business, a merchant's household gave him access to a broader associational world which enabled the pursuit of social, as well as business, goals, and in these respects, London offered opportunities lacking in the mart towns, meaning that economic maturity for most Merchant Adventurers coincided with a return to England.[147] In terms of business management, proximity to core markets was one advantage; Blackwell Hall for cloth, the Royal Exchange, perhaps livery company halls, were all attractions of a City residence. Opportunities for interaction with their peers spilled out from these formal institutional sites, though; the City was an arena for sociability which allowed a merchant to form relationships within the community of Merchant Adventurers and beyond it, potentially opening doors to other opportunities. This is a side of a merchant's life which rarely emerges from business letters, though the extensive surviving papers of Lionel Cranfield give some impression of the huge range of associates with which commercial life brought a merchant into contact, ranging from partners in bowling and betting to money lending and custom farming.[148]

The other typical purpose of the household was of course reproductive, and access to the London marriage market was one incentive to setting up household in the capital. As well as providing a dowry, marriage could be a means to cement relations within the ranks of the Company. This was the case with several of our examples: along with Cranfield, John Quarles, William Calley, and George Lowe all married into notable Merchant Adventurer families.[149] Both Calley and Lowe delayed marriage until they were able to return home, although Lowe had left Quarles' service in Stade a decade before he married. John Kendrick spent a longer part of his career in the mart town of Middelburg, where he was based in 1611 having arrived there in Quarles' service in 1596, but he died a bachelor. This was also the case with one of the most successful Merchant Adventurers of the early seventeenth century, William Jones, who was based in Stade as partner of

---

[147] For London, see Gauci, *Politics of Trade*; *Emporium of the World*; Zahedieh, *Capital and the Colonies*.

[148] HMC Sackville I, pp. 38, 48.

[149] Quarles married the daughter of Sir Henry Billingsley, William Calley married Judith, daughter of the Richard Bowdler who had raised Quarles after his father's death, and George Lowe wed Anne Duncomb, the widowed daughter of Sir Thomas Bennett. Marrying a widow of a Company member was one means for Merchant Adventurers without a large inheritance to acquire capital: see Ramsay (ed.), *John Isham*, p. xxxvi.

Richard Beale of London, and left a huge fortune in his will, which reads as a who's who of the social world of the Merchant Adventurers in Germany.[150] Fortunes could clearly be made overseas, but in the earlier part of the period at least, they were largely enjoyed in England.

In fact Company rules actively discouraged the formation of households overseas by forbidding marriage to women born outside of England, even those who had been endenized or naturalized, on pain of disenfranchisement.[151] Alongside this rule, members were forbidden from purchasing or obtaining (for instance through marriage) lands or property overseas. These requirements had been included in the 1564 royal charter, apparently in order to weaken any objections to the move to Emden that might have been raised by the small number of English merchants with established households in Antwerp.[152] Clearly the intention was to ensure that Merchant Adventurers overseas did not become absorbed into their host societies and so forget their responsibilities to their principals in London, as well as the English crown. However, the Company did allow members to request licence to sue for letters patent from the crown for remission from these requirements, with readmission coming in 'open Generall Court' on repayment of their initial entry fine, plus a discretionary gratification.[153] Even so, the member in question was required to sell any foreign lands or property, and to remove with wife and family to England, though Company officers were spared the latter requirement.

These rules thus restricted the supply of potential wives in the mart towns. A marriage market did exist in Stade in the late sixteenth century, and it was evidently a competitive one. George Lowe reported that his friend Harry Billingsley was 'in the way of marryage with Mr Thomsons daughter & lykely to speede, but in Regard the mayd hath bene sought by many whoe could not...obtayne her he doubteth he shalbe crossed in yt by the yll wylles of many'.[154] In these circumstances it is unsurprising that most Merchant Adventurers at the start of the period seem to have postponed marriage until they were able to return to England. But later generations were apparently more willing to marry and raise households overseas, at least in Hamburg. This might have been linked to a relaxation of rules regarding marriage in an act of the Company court at Middelburg from December 1609. Although this act repeated the clause against marrying foreign-born women, it made exception for those who had first obtained permission from the Company court, alongside those who had acquired letters patent, whilst making no mention of the requirement about having to then depart to England.[155] However, despite the Company seeking legal clarification on the matter in 1620, these rules remained ambiguous, and some merchants continued to

---

[150] For this, see Chapter 6 of this book.   [151] *Laws*, p. 189.
[152] Ramsay, *City of London*, p. 257.   [153] *Laws*, pp. 190–1.
[154] Lowe–Quarles, 8 July 1596, TNA, SP 46/176, fol. 140r.   [155] *Laws*, p. 194.

suffer disenfranchisement on grounds of their marriages, including John Quarles' nephew, also called John, who was deprived of his freedom by the Delft court in the 1630s.[156]

We have relatively little information for how the demographic basis of the Company's Dutch residences changed over the course of this period, but in the case of Hamburg, the survival of the Company churches register from 1620, recording communicants, births, and marriages, offers some indication.[157] The book commenced with a comprehensive list of the communicating population, which totalled 201 individuals. Thirty were residents of the Company house, including the deputy governor Richard Gore, pastors William Loe and Thomas Young, secretary Joseph Avery, the concierge George Shepham and three other officers, with twelve servants and ten family members shared between them. Forty of the remaining male population were listed as married. The wives of some of this group were not named, and others cohabited, so these were not necessarily as extensive households as might have been the case in England: few had adult children or servants listed as part of their household, though they may have hired locals. Even so these were probably relatively well established Merchant Adventurers, acting as either partners of or commission agents for their English equivalents, and thus the leading members of the community (seven of them were identified as elders of the church). Alongside this group were eighty-five bachelors, presumably a mixture of apprentices and 'journeymen' making their first steps as Merchant Adventurers (amongst them were Maurice Wynn and Thomas Barker, mentioned above).

This list can be compared with one compiled by the Hamburg Senate noting sixty-eight Merchant Adventurers present when the Company returned to the city in 1612: twenty-one of this group were still present in 1620, fifteen of them listed as married; five of these were elders.[158] Of 125 possible merchants present in 1620 (the total number of bachelors and married men living outside of the Company house), about 17 per cent are known to have been resident in 1612, then, attesting to a relatively high rate of overall turnover in the population. The fifty-six women listed as communicants in 1620 seem to have been made up of thirty-six wives, twelve unmarried daughters, and eight servants: little wonder that most men returned home to marry, then.

Despite the small number of eligible single women present in 1620, ninety-one marriages were recorded in the Hamburg church up to 1685 (including six that predated 1620), though the numbers followed a downward trajectory (see Fig. 1.1). The number of recorded new communicants was also in decline,

---

[156] John Quarles–Secretary Dorchester, 5 Jan. 1629, TNA, SP 16/131, fol. 24; H. Quarles van Ufford, *A Merchant-Adventurer in the Dutch Republic: John Quarles and his Times 1596–1646/7* (Amsterdam, 1983), p. 30. For more on this case, see Chapter 7.
[157] Hamburg Register.   [158] Ehrenberg, *Hamburg und England*, pp. 258–62.

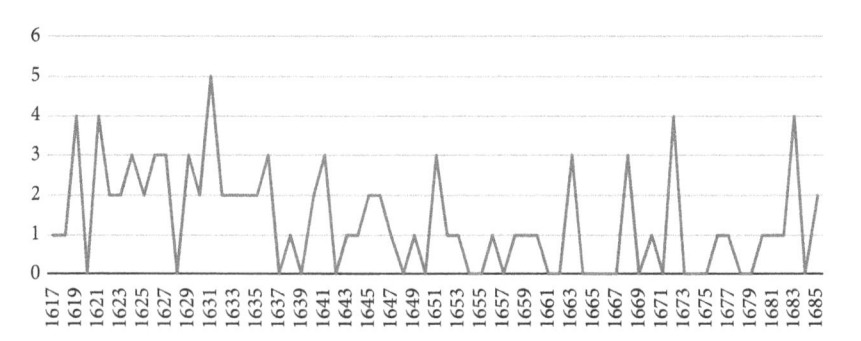

Fig. 1.1 Annual marriages in the Hamburg Company church, 1617–85.
Source: Hamburg Register

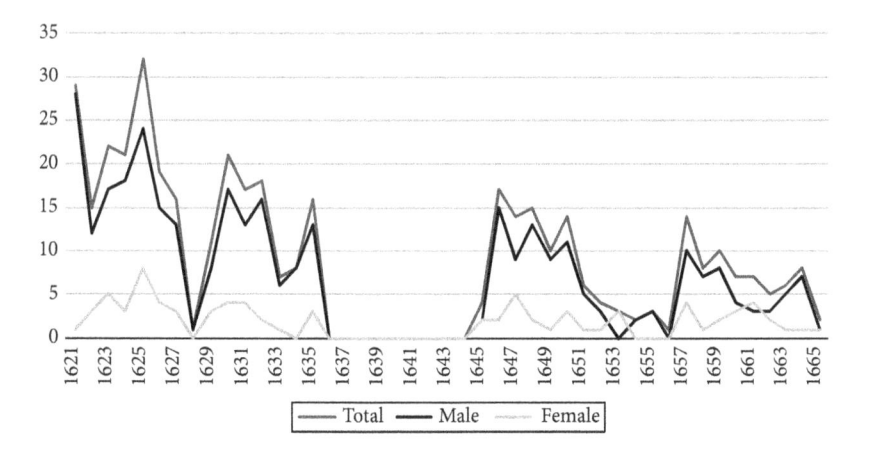

Fig. 1.2 New communicants in Hamburg Company church, 1621–65.
Source: Hamburg Register

although these figures cease in 1665, and there are gaps in the record from 1628 to 1629 and 1635 to 1644 (see Fig. 1.2). Nonetheless, it is notable that the number of newly communicating females was relatively stable (though the number was always low), whilst that of men was clearly falling. If figures were available after 1665, this would likely become more pronounced, as more children born in Hamburg reached adulthood. Baptisms, in fact, seem to have peaked in the 1640s, and only dropped significantly in the 1670s, a low point in the Company's history (see Fig. 1.3). What this seems to attest to is a relative fall in new recruits to the Hamburg merchant community, which probably shifted the balance between bachelors and married men (roughly 2:1 in 1620) in favour of the latter, resulting in a rather more domesticated social environment overall. William Attwood for instance married his partner Walter Pell's step-daughter in London in 1636, ten years after he joined the Hamburg congregation, and had seven children baptized

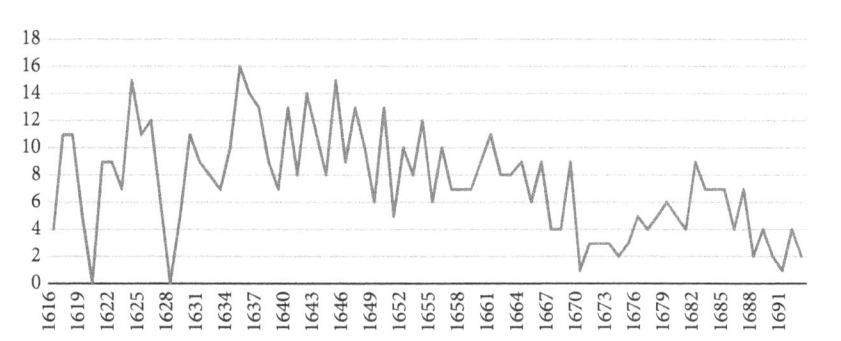

Fig. 1.3 Baptisms in the Hamburg Company church, 1616–93.
Source: Hamburg Register

in Hamburg from 1639 to 1650, before he returned to London permanently in the early 1650s. Attwood continued to correspond with friends in Hamburg like Melchior Wolfenden (a new communicant in the Hamburg church in 1634, and still present in 1682, having had seven children baptized) and George Watson (new communicant in 1632; married in 1641 and still resident in 1669), their letters replete with domestic details ranging from a child's teething to the death of a spouse.[159]

Although even in 1620 there were a significant number of married men amongst the Hamburg merchant community, the above evidence suggests that their proportion within the overall merchant population grew over time even as this population was falling in line with the declining volume of the cloth trade. This would have limited opportunities for new entrants, who previously had been able to launch their careers in the mart towns by combining service, commission agency, and whatever sums they could access from the Company or relatives. As Matthew Ashton complained in the 1680s, 'commission it is noe inheritance because mens mindes are various one time for one man & then after to another being willing to make experience of all men & Partnershipp or a mans owne Stocke that is to bee relyed upon.'[160] Other sources also indicate a growing preference for employing commission agents rather than apprentices or 'servants' on a fixed term and salary, as seems to have been commonplace when John Quarles was trading. We have a relatively detailed portrait of the Hamburg residency for the year 1666, when a number of Company ships heading home were destroyed by the Dutch during the second Anglo-Dutch War in sight of Hamburg. In the course of the crown's subsequent attempts to sue Hamburg for damages, information was collected regarding the cargoes that were lost (largely linen).[161] This

[159] William Strange–Attwood, 2 Nov. 1658, TNA, C109/24; George Watson–Attwood, 17 July 1668, TNA, C109/23/1.
[160] Ashton–Edward Frank, 25 Nov. 1679, Bodl. Lib., Eng. misc. c602, fol. 10r.
[161] TNA, HCA 32/6/1–2.

provides details about some twenty Hamburg Merchant Adventurers. For fifteen of these, it is possible to identify their English principal(s), and amongst these there are only three known examples of apprentices serving their masters: John Ayshford (apprenticed to Lucy Knightley Sr in 1661), Thomas Shepard (Thomas Tyte, 1663), and Samuel Free (Daniel Farrington, 1650). The former was standing in packhouse with a more experienced merchant, Henry Spurway, however, whilst Free had commenced his apprenticeship sixteen years previously, so was hardly a novice.[162] This was typical of this cohort, who can be identified as present in Hamburg for an average of twelve years by 1666, with three trading in partnership with their England-based correspondent, and four awarded damages on their own account.[163] Two individuals, Nathaniel Cambridge and Richard Twyford, handled several accounts, and would continue to reside in the city for decades to come.

The emergence of a settled community of English merchant households in Hamburg also led, naturally enough, to a growing number of children born and raised within its ranks. Reversing the pattern at the start of the period, some sons of Merchant Adventurers raised abroad were sent to England in order to improve their language and to establish themselves amongst the merchant community, as was the case with the aforementioned Richard Twyford, for instance.[164] An added complication for many was the Company's requirement that those with non-English mothers, or born outside of England, could only claim their freedom through patrimony if naturalized subjects of the crown.[165] In 1664, Melchior Wolfenden sent his 16-year-old son John to stay with William Attwood in London, in part so that 'he might not be counted A stranger to our company being our intentions are to bringe him up to our trade as to be an helpe unto me in mine age'.[166] Attwood was happy to house him and arrange his schooling, but advised that the cost and duration of the apprenticeship would be too high to be worthwhile.[167] Attwood himself had paid £300 to apprentice his son with a Turkey merchant.[168] As their traditional commerce withered, successful Merchant Adventurers in London could direct their sons into more flourishing branches of trade, but this was harder for those based in Hamburg. The latter might also struggle to access the apprentice market in England. As the number of his commissions grew, Matthew Ashton found himself in need of an apprentice's assistance,

[162] Another Hamburg Merchant Adventurer, Nathaniel Butler, was apprenticed to Nicholas Lawrence, possibly a relation of his principal Thomas Lawrence.
[163] This is based on data found in the Hamburg Register, along with additional information such as bills of exchange found in merchants' accounts. The partnerships were Humphrey Morrice (Hamburg)–Robert Hunter (England), Peter Watson–John Doggett Jr, and Thomas Shafto–Mathew Carleton.
[164] Twyford–Attwood, 23 June 1666, TNA, C109/23/1.   [165] Laws, pp. 41–2.
[166] Wolfenden–Attwood, 18 Feb. 1665, TNA, C109/24.
[167] Attwood–Wolfenden, 17 Mar. 1665, TNA, C109/23, Attwood's out-letter book 1663–6.
[168] Attwood–William Terkell, 29 Apr. 1664, TNA, C109/23, Attwood's out-letter book 1663–6.

'which I have a greate occasion of findeing the merchants oftens passe by my packhouse unless one bee at doore to speake with them'.[169] But despite soliciting the aid of his correspondents in Leeds, London, and even Narva, he failed to find a suitable recruit.[170]

Although these examples attest to continued ties between Merchant Adventurers in England and overseas, the social world of merchants in Hamburg seems to have been becoming increasingly autonomous from London, therefore, home to a diminishing but intimate community of English families. This is suggested by the reaction of Abigail Boynton of Hamburg to the death of her Merchant Adventurer husband Dru Tindale, in 1665. Three years later Boynton explained to William Attwood how, following her bereavement, she had been 'left a cumfortles poor cretur in a straing cuntry', having failed to secure her rightful inheritance.[171] But rather than return to England, Boynton chose to remarry one of her husband's associates in Hamburg (the Merchant Adventurer Francis Boynton), 'so that i have not demend my dere doue in his grave hee is one he had a gret love and openion of when he lived'. Evidently some English residents had come to feel at home in the mart towns, as was the case with one longstanding Hamburg resident whose death in 1660 was reported to Attwood. Happily lodged with his family in a house 'on the Barge', this 'Ould Mr Suite was very much affected with this place, pretending this Climent did suite well with his Crasy bodye, & was a great lover of rennish wine'.[172]

For others, however, long-term residence in the mart towns was more of a necessity than a choice. Following an agreeable visit to London in 1667, William Attwood's Hamburg factor Thomas Scott (a new communicant in the Hamburg church in 1649) wrote that 'I like London so well that Hamburg doth not please me as it formerly did but I am not Ballasted sufficiently for London & the North is liveless in Trade'.[173] The cost of setting up household could thus preclude against an aspiring merchant's return home, particularly if he had chosen to marry overseas.[174] Impatient to commence a family as well as launch his mercantile career, Matthew Ashton married his landlady's daughter in 1683 in a match frowned on by his brother due to the small size of the dowry. To this, Ashton countered that 'I never could expect one with any greate fortune & your constantly pressing of me to marry, hath occationed me to take one that I could fancy'.[175] In fact the cost of

---

[169] Ashton–Jeremy Whichcote, London, 22 Feb. 1684, Bodl. Lib., Eng. misc. c563, fol. 136r; Ashton–Joseph Kitchingman, Leeds, 6 May 1684, ibid., fol. 160r.

[170] Ashton–Whichcote, 4 July 1684, ibid., fols 169–70; Ashton–Erasmus Darwin, Narva, 12 Dec. 1684, ibid., fol. 207v.

[171] Boynton–Attwood, 27 June 1668, TNA, C109/19.

[172] Jones–Attwood, 31 July 1660, TNA, C109/20.

[173] Scott–Attwood, 19 Oct. 1667, TNA, C109/20.

[174] Scott–Attwood, 11 Dec. 1667, TNA, C109/20.

[175] Ashton–Edward Frank, July 1683, Bodl. Lib., Eng. misc. c602, fol. 28r. See also Grassby, *Kinship* p. 67.

establishing his household seems to have pushed Ashton into several risky ventures which eventually contributed to his insolvency in 1685. He continued to reside in Hamburg, at a safe distance from his creditors, for several years, raising his young family and sheltered by a community of merchants aware of the importance of maintaining peace in its ranks.

Conclusion

In 1615, it was claimed that 'long & thriftie service, with sparing out of their factories & wages, & the use of bequest monyes', had been the means for many young Merchant Adventurers lacking 'the help of large patrimonies' to accumulate their 'best portion & first Capitalls', making the Company 'a perpetual seminary & succession of merchants planted and nourished by the trade it self'.[176] Although this was an overly optimistic depiction of the openness of the Company to new entrants, it was possible for young men like George Lowe to launch a successful mercantile career by exploiting the opportunities open to them through their apprenticeships. To an extent these opportunities were controlled by masters: this was a highly hierarchical commercial, as well as social, regime. However, distance weakened patriarchal control, and the social worlds of the mart towns provided ample occasion for sociability and the formation of new alliances outside of the household, the relationships on which, paradoxically, the attainment of independent status depended. Merchant Adventurers were aware that success depended on the support and patronage of others as much as individual initiative—young merchants were 'raysed up to great busines', as Thomas Wotton put it—but this was never entirely in the control of masters. The youthful environment of the mart towns allowed for ample intergenerational turnover within the merchant community, exemplified by the rapid rise of Lionel Cranfield. Certainly Cranfield's success owed much to his insider status, as the scion of a successful merchant family, something which probably encouraged his master Richard Sheppard to prefer him over his unfortunate fellows Robert Swaddon and Thomas Wotton. Even so, Cranfield's success surely depended too on his ability to fashion alliances amongst peers like Daniel Cooper who could recognize in Cranfield a young merchant on the rise, one who might offer a means to escape their own state of dependency.

Over time, however, this regime shifted, to one which was in some senses less hierarchical, but not necessarily more open to new entrants. Although the mart towns were always home to a combination of factors, partners and servants, there appears to have been an increasing switch from the latter to the former, at least in

---

[176] Members of the King's Merchant Adventurers at Hamburg to the Governor and Company at London, 27 Nov. 1615, KHLC, U269/1/B82/6.

Hamburg (with partnership probably stable throughout). Commission agency, characterized by its informality, relative egalitarianism, and flexibility, represented a weaker form of tie than the master–servant relationships that characterized the earlier part of the period, and this had an attendant effect on relations between the Company's English branches and its mart towns. It may be that the decline in the volume of the cloth trade beginning in the 1620s destabilized the traditional merchant life-cycle, with diminishing opportunities at home forcing more residents of the mart towns to extend their stays overseas, leading to an increase in the number of long-term resident commission agents. In turn, this limited the opportunities for new entrants seeking to launch their careers in the mart towns, contributing to a decline in the overall size of the merchant community, as seen by the falling numbers of new male communicants in the Hamburg church.

Also significant were the reforms of the Company that were forced upon it by the crown in the 1620s, in response to the depression in cloth exports. In 1624 the Company was ordered by the Privy Council to open its ranks to all 'mere merchants' on the payment of a reasonable fine. This invitation may not have been widely taken up, as it was accompanied by an extensive opening up of trade to Germany and the Low Countries in all but undressed cloths, but when in 1634 the Company's monopoly was restored, membership was still kept open on the payment of a £50 fine (£25 for merchants from the outports). As well as representing a considerably lower sum than the £200 required at the start of the period, the principle that admission was the right of all qualified English merchants compromised the Company's ability to define its own membership. In the 1660s these sums would drop even further, to just 20 marks (£13 6s. 8d.). It is possible that these changes brought to an end the previous requirement that those seeking admission travel to the head court overseas to swear their oath of loyalty to the Company, with the London court instead taking responsibility to admit new members.[177] Although the lack of admission records makes it difficult to assess how many merchants took advantage of these opportunities, those who did were less likely to have personal experience of the mart towns, making them more reliant on experienced factors to market their goods. Such developments opened new opportunities for Merchant Adventurers overseas to earn commission, though dealing with merchants who had not followed the standard career path of fellow members might create tensions. A suggestion of this appears in a letter written to William Attwood by the London-based Eastland merchant Humphrey Wightman, who was sending perpetuanas for sale in Hamburg in 1632 (so taking advantage of the 1624 liberalization of trade). When Wightman complained of

---

[177] This is suggested by a petition of Merchant Adventurers from York, Hull, and Newcastle complaining that the new requirements for admission would allow many clothiers and other unqualified persons from the north to be admitted to the Company in London, to their prejudice: TNA, SP 16/307, #74.

the quality of the linen Attwood had sent in return, Attwood had apparently not concealed his irritation, leading Wightman to protest that 'though I was never at Hamburg, I have bine abroad In other places & know a litle what belongs to busynes as well as another'.[178] Clearly Attwood had been stung by criticism from one he perceived as an outsider.

For the earlier part of the period at least, recruitment and training provided a significant element of shared experience for a majority of Merchant Adventurers, which contributed to their sense of belonging to a cohesive merchant community. The experience of arriving in the mart town as a young merchant would have been replicated across the generations, and this was capable of generating a sense of group identity and solidarity. Changes within the wider community of Merchant Adventurers, and relationships within it, were a challenge to the unity of the corporation overall: as ties coalesced between the increasingly intimate residents of Hamburg, their sense of identification with the rest of the Company was accordingly weakened. But whereas the Hamburg community became more closely integrated, by the 1650s the Merchant Adventurers' Dutch residence was in danger of dissipating entirely, as members became absorbed into a wider English merchant community that stretched beyond the boundaries of the Company. The effect of these changes on how the Company functioned as a corporation will be a major theme for the rest of this book.

Solidarities, and the social capital which was generated through group affiliation, were resources which could provide social support for Merchant Adventurers, even if the boundaries of these groups were subject to change. However, membership of the Company was not the only group affiliation which acted on Merchant Adventurers. Although they were united by their membership of the Company and their enjoyment of the privileges that this bought, the reality of their trade meant that fellow Merchant Adventurers were also rivals and competitors. As this chapter has suggested, the Company was bifurcated by networks formed by Merchant Adventurers to manage their businesses and to access opportunities. The next chapter will consider how these two forms of identification—the group and the network—played out in Merchant Adventurers managing the core part of their businesses: the export of cloth.

---

[178] Wightman–Attwood, 8 Dec. 1632, TNA, C109/10.

2

Show Days

The Government of Trade

For those Merchant Adventurers who followed the path of apprenticeship, the reward of their labour was to partake in a share of that trade which the Company's privileges were designed to capture for the exclusive benefit of members. A central argument in favour of these privileges was that only under Company government could commerce thrive in the interests not just of members, but of the commonwealth of England. The training discussed in Chapter 1 provided Merchant Adventurers with the skill necessary to ensure that English cloth would be valued at its true worth. Furthermore, Company regulations limited damaging competition amongst members by distributing the gains of commerce equitably, so upholding the reputation and the price of English cloth. By virtue of the Company's ability to coordinate collective action, it was able to negotiate preferential terms overseas, concentrating trade on the mart towns and creating a seller's market. This was an orderly market, then: membership of the Company of Merchant Adventurers entailed a particular way of doing business.

Leaving consideration of the effectiveness of the Company's attempts to confine commerce to its mart towns to Chapter 4, this chapter examines the routine aspects of managing a business centred on the export of cloth, reflecting on how far this corresponds to the image the Company sought to convey. On the surface, Merchant Adventurers performed a relatively simple role, exporting English cloth to the continent in return for money or wares for import, an archetypal bilateral commerce. Indeed, for critics of the Company this was a trade which required little skill: insulated from risk by their monopoly, members relied on rents earned in a non-competitive market, at the expense of cloth producers and the English economy generally. However, the challenges of managing a business across seas were numerous: controlling agents at a distance, coordinating decision making, exchanging information efficiently, and coping with the many caprices of foreign trade. All of these were familiar to long-distance merchants in general, but the markets in which the Company's members operated brought their own challenges, and success was far from guaranteed. This chapter examines the routine tasks of business for established Merchant Adventurers as they sought to exploit the opportunities open to them, the daily dramas of their business lives.

As with other branches of trade, Merchant Adventurers met these challenges through the construction of networks of individuals cooperating at a distance,

Fellowship and Freedom: The Merchant Adventurers and the Restructuring of English Commerce, 1582–1700.
Thomas Leng, Oxford University Press (2020). © Thomas Leng. DOI: 10.1093/oso/9780198794479.001.0001

and this will be a major theme of this chapter. Business management was an intensely social affair: status as a Merchant Adventurer was earned and measured through the quantity and strength of one's ties with others. Just as successfully joining the ranks of the Fellowship of Merchant Adventurers was a social journey which required more than simply purchasing privilege, so managing business over the course of a successful career was dependent on retaining, and enhancing, one's status within the Company's ranks. Reputation and connection coalesced, contributing to success or failure. The embeddedness of business in social relations meant that commercial decisions were never made purely with simple calculations of profit and loss in mind. Having invested such time and energy in establishing their status within the whole network of Merchant Adventurers, members of the Company had a considerable incentive to maintain their position, to uphold the relationships on which this was based, and to concentrate their trade on predictable, known settings where they could rely on multiple connections and sources of information. Social connection, as well as corporate belonging, could be a powerful source of loyalty in a particular market. It also shaped the distribution of trade within the Company's ranks, competing with corporate regulations intended to do the same, whilst acting as a barrier which newcomers had to overcome. Social connection might also be an obstacle to those seeking exit from the Company's protected marketplace. If status within this particular merchant community depended on conformity to certain received norms, then innovation might be suppressed and diversification disincentivized. Connection could also bring opportunities for Merchant Adventurers to transcend the limitations of their trade, however. The Company was bifurcated by a multitude of overlapping networks which might extend beyond its ranks, though these were not accessed equally. Social, as well as commercial, competition was a feature of the trading world of the Merchant Adventurers, then, and the networks which members constructed to manage their trades were not content-free 'structures', but dynamic chains of relationships which were continually being negotiated. Mastering this social context of commerce was as important as understanding the nature of the products that Merchant Adventurers traded in, or the markets in which they operated.

The first part of this chapter will consider how Merchant Adventurers went about building their networks, focusing on specific examples of merchants fashioning and consolidating ties with their peers over the course of their careers. These stories unfolded over a period when the Company's trade was undergoing significant structural change, meaning that the challenges and opportunities that Merchant Adventurers were presented with were hardly stable. The second section considers how Merchant Adventurers managed the business of exporting cloth in the context of these changes. As well as the cloth trade experiencing changes to its structure, English commerce in general underwent a more profound restructuring that opened up significant new possibilities. The final part of

the chapter will consider whether loyalty to their core markets precluded Merchant Adventurers from participating in these changes, and the role that networks played in accessing them.

The Formation of Networks

Long-distance commerce in the early modern period was dependent on cooperation between individuals at a distance: the principal purpose of business networks was to meet this geographical challenge. Even the Merchant Adventurer trading on his own stock was reliant on an agent to handle his goods. In practice, merchant businesses generally relied on networks larger than this simple bilateral relationship, which were used to pool resources including capital, credit, contacts (social capital), and information. These networks were comprised of a variety of different relationships, bringing together partners, masters and servants, professional factors and principals, and merchants acting reciprocally for each other on an ad hoc basis; we might even include customers and suppliers, particularly those who entered into long-term relationships with a merchant.

In recent years the role of networks has come to dominate studies of premodern trade; as David Hancock put it, 'The personal, multidimensional, nonhierarchical, and voluntary nature of networks made them the organizational mode of choice in a long-distance, preindustrial, precorporate world.'[1] Historians have presented these flexible, informal structures as allowing merchants to cooperate across long distances with a range of agents who were capable of performing a variety of different services rather than conforming to specific roles.[2] In particular, networks have been seen as a response to a major problem of long-distance trade, that of trust.[3] Information about the reliability of individuals was shared between correspondents whose interests were aligned in an egalitarian manner that, as Hancock notes, is implicitly opposed to the more hierarchical model of the firm (with the emerging joint stock companies presenting an alternative model for the government of long-distance trade).[4]

---

[1] David Hancock, 'The trouble with networks: managing the Scots' early-modern Madeira trade', *Business History Review* 79, 3 (2005), p. 489.

[2] See for instance David Hancock, *Citizens of the World: London Merchants and the Integration of the British Atlantic Community, 1735–1785* (Cambridge, 1995); Perri Gauci, *The Politics of Trade: The Overseas Merchant in State and Society, 1660–1720* (Oxford, 2001); Francesca Trivellato, *The Familiarity of Strangers: The Sephardic Diaspora, Livorno, and Cross-Cultural Trade in the Early Modern Period* (New Haven and London, 2009); Sheryllynne Haggerty, *'Merely for Money'? Business Culture in the British Atlantic, 1750–1815* (Liverpool, 2012); Siobhan Talbott, *Conflict, Commerce and Franco-Scottish Relations, 1560–1713* (London, 2014).

[3] Gelderblom, *Cities of Trade*, p. 77.   [4] Hancock, 'Trouble', p. 470.

Chapter 1 demonstrated that the businesses of Merchant Adventurers do not straightforwardly correspond to this common picture of premodern mercantile networks. The importance of the master–servant relationship, at least in the earlier part of the period, meant that the networks of Merchant Adventurers often possessed a hierarchical dimension that can be downplayed in studies of business networks.[5] Over time, it appears that commission agency became a more common form of agency relationship, though considerations of status and rank persisted, and so the egalitarian nature of these relationships should not be overstated. The stages of the merchant life-cycle provided opportunities for merchants to enter into various types of relationships: apprentices and 'journeymen' offered a different sort of service to the well-established merchant, who might be a potential partner or factor. Relationships varied in duration and degree of formality, and often overlapped or shifted in nature over time. Business networks were thus characterized by fluidity, and the deployment of a range of institutional combinations to manage their constituent relationships: kinship, apprenticeship, legally binding contracts, informal alliances, correspondence, the rhetoric of service or friendship, and so on.

Business networks were not static structures with clear boundaries, then: the relations which constituted them were continually under negotiation, and through these interactions individuals were able to change their position within the broader 'whole network' of Merchant Adventurers. Ability to traverse through this network effectively required mastery of what Paul D. McLean has called 'the art of the network'.[6] As sites of social interaction, networks are the forum in which individuals are able to 'project' themselves 'into an identity', to be recognized as such by others, and to accumulate the social capital that comes from connection and from adopting recognized roles and acquiring the prestige attached to them.[7] These roles and relationships are not stable: social rank is always subject to interpretation, and an individual can assume a range of different identities. Social ties can be construed in different ways. Nor do the roles which individuals assume determine conduct: whilst an ability to conform to normalized behaviour might be important in gaining recognition, the possibility of strategic improvisation allows these norms to be challenged, and new roles to be forged.[8] But networks are not simply open for the socially skilful to fashion themselves on a blank canvas: social relationships are relations of power, and social capital can be withheld as well as shared. Access to privileged information and sources of credit depended on maintaining network relationships through continued acts of exchange, the

[5] One study which is more attentive to the importance of rank in merchant networks is Jessica L. Goldberg, *Trade and Institutions in the Medieval Mediterranean: The Geniza Merchants and their Business World* (Cambridge, 2012), though this examines the eleventh century.
[6] Paul D. McLean, *The Art of the Network: Strategic Interaction and Patronage in Renaissance Florence* (Durham and London, 2007), pp. 6–7.
[7] Ibid., pp. 1, 10–12.   [8] Ibid., pp. 17–18.

effect of which could be to restrict opportunities to insiders and limit competition.[9] Merchant Adventurers would certainly have recognized 'the transformative power of connections to powerful others'.[10]

Network building was a means to achieve status within the merchant community, to access the opportunities that came through connection, and to insulate these opportunities against danger through establishing durable relationships of trust. The changes in the structure of the whole network of Merchant Adventurers identified in Chapter 1 influenced how this happened, privileging some sorts of relationships over others. This can be usefully demonstrated by the career of William Attwood, which spanned the shift away from a commercial regime characterized by master–servant relations to one where partnerships and commission agency predominated. Attwood was a new communicant in the church at Hamburg in 1626, a year after he commenced his apprenticeship under Nicholas Backhouse, very much in line with the expected career-path that was then dominant. However, rather than return home to establish himself as a London Merchant Adventurer, Attwood apparently remained in Hamburg for much of the following twenty-five years, almost the entire duration of his career as an active cloth trader. More than his master, Attwood relied on connections made amongst his peers in Hamburg when embarking on his career. Particularly important was Walter Pell, one of eighty-five bachelors listed as communicants of the Company church in 1620, and at that point in the service of the Merchant Taylor Francis Harrington, though he was already an assistant in the Company court. By the time of Attwood's arrival, Pell had married the widow of another of the 1620 residents, William Hampton, whose daughter Attwood went on to marry, in 1636. By then, Pell was back in London and trading in partnership with Attwood, who handled the Hamburg end of their business. Attwood held a one-quarter part this partnership, as well as a share of another one with Pell and Ralph Sarocold, a relative of Pell by his second marriage, which seems to have been largely in the export of tobacco and copperas. Attwood's largest account at this time, at least if the amount he paid out in petty charges for it is any guide, was on behalf of Hugh Windham and George Hawkins, and focused on imports of linen and diapers. George Hawkins was another former Hamburg associate, who would write to Attwood nearly thirty years later from as far away as the Caribbean island of Nevis, asking after their shared friends, and he was perhaps the source of Attwood's other accounts with members of the Hawkins family.[11] As Table 2.1 shows, Attwood's accounts tended to focus on different goods, in a complementary manner.

[9] Pierre Gervais, 'In union there was strength: the legal protection of eighteenth-century merchant partnerships in England and France', in Simon Middleton and James E. Shaw (eds), *Markets, Ethics and Practices, c.1300–1850* (Abingdon and New York, 2018), pp. 167–71.
[10] McLean, *Art of the Network*, p. 1. See also Haggerty, *'Merely for Money'?*, pp. 104, 162–8.
[11] Hawkins–Attwood, 31 May 1662, TNA, C109/19.

Table 2.1 Petty charges for William Attwood's Hamburg accounts, April
1635–December 1636

Hugh Windham & George Hawkins (linen & diaper imports; export of perpetuanas and stockings)	£1,570 16s. 4d.
Walter Pell (¾) & William Attwood (¼) (cloth exports & various imports)	£496 3s. 8d.
Walter Pell, Ralph Saracold & William Attwood (tobacco & copperas exports)	£447 2s. 6d.
Worshipful Isaac Jones (perpetuana & cloth exports; imports)	£250 15s. 3d.
William Hawkins junior (perpetuana exports)	£195 15s.
William Hawkins senior (cloth exports; various imports)	£102 8s.
Ralph Saracold (tobacco & copperas exports)	£94 8s. 8d.
Arthur Bostock (export of dozens)	£10 9s. 7d.
Abraham Ashe (export of galls)	£8 6s. 3d.

Source: Attwood's petty cash book, TNA, C109/20

Only fragmentary glimpses of Attwood's career survive before the 1650s. We
know that in 1632 he was acting as agent for the Eastland merchant Humphrey
Wightman, who had capitalized on a recent opening up of trade to export perpetuanas and import linen.[12] In 1649 he was handling the goods of the Hull merchant Daniel Heringe, and in 1652 was selling pepper for the Merchant
Adventurers Thomas Andrews (a future East India Company governor) and
Richard Clutterbuck, and indigo for the clothier Richard Shute, as well as running
exchange accounts for many Eastland merchants.[13] Doubtless these were just a
fraction of the many commissions he would have taken on over the previous
twenty-five years. By then, however, these were supplementary to Attwood's
major business, which was on his own account. Attwood was still trading in partnership with Pell, now joined by his brother-in-law and Pell's stepson Walter
Hampton, as well as in another partnership worth £6,000 with Hampton and
William Strange, who had been a fellow resident in Hamburg since 1647.[14]
Strange had perhaps been co-opted into the partnership with a view to taking
over its management in Hamburg once Attwood returned to London, which he
eventually did in 1653. The account of Pell–Attwood–Hampton meanwhile was
taken over by a factor, William Edline. In 1654 Attwood reckoned the value of his
investment in the former account as £2,288 4s. 8d., and the latter £5,050, out of a
total estate of £18,700 which now included an estate in Hackney, valued at £2,040:
by then, Attwood was beginning to shift his estate away from commerce into
other assets that might provide an inheritance for his three sons and dowries for

[12] Wightman–Attwood, 31 Nov. & 8 Dec. 1632, TNA, C109/19.
[13] Heringe–Attwood, 28 Aug. 1649, TNA, C109/19; Hamburg journal, TNA, C109/21.
[14] Calculation of accounts dated 31 Oct. 1653, TNA, C109/19.

his daughters.[15] The partnership of Pell–Attwood–Hampton was valued at over £20,000 in January 1658, shortly before it was wound up, probably due to Pell's retirement.[16] Attwood also dissolved his partnership with Hampton and Strange, which by then also included Attwood's London-based son-in-law Edward Halford (cousin to Edward Halford of Hamburg, Attwood's sometime agent). By 1664, when Attwood next drew up the value of his estate, it had grown slightly and included further lands and properties in his native Essex and London.[17]

Attwood's business career was characterized by a high degree of stability in his choice of partners, which was reinforced through marriage, but his intimate knowledge of Hamburg also allowed him to draw in multiple commissions, both from former Hamburg acquaintances and from outsiders like Wightman: clearly Attwood possessed deep personal knowledge of this market. Attwood's exit from it essentially entailed shifting his capital into the traditional alternatives of land and property, though he did invest in the East India Company and engage in some ventures to other markets like the Mediterranean. For the latter he depended on family connections in the forms of his sons-in-law, however (see below). Much of Attwood's surviving correspondence dates from this stage in his career, though he continued to have occasional dealings with Hamburg, importing linen and speculating on the exchange. This gradual withdrawal from the cloth trade seems to have been typical of Merchant Adventurers, which created opportunities for others to move into previously occupied market territory. However, Attwood's status was such that he continued to attract suitors keen to draw him back into business.[18] He was often approached by Hamburg associates looking for a reliable agent in London to sell a parcel or two of goods, but had little patience for these time-consuming commissions, now that he was more preoccupied with other tasks such as managing his property. For instance in 1660 when Cuthbert Jones of Hamburg sought an agent in London to accept his consignments of linen, he turned to Attwood, a previous employer, invoking Attwood's 'former free declaration of yourselfe to be willing to vndertake the trouble of my inconsiderable imployments there'.[19] Jones framed their relationship in terms of both shared interest and service, writing of his hopes that they might pursue 'a mutuall Amicable Correspondency sutable to that relation wee have stud ingaged by on to the other, yowe, as my master & I, your servant (which is the honorablest title I beare this day)'. Despite this, Jones had little he could offer given Attwood's disinclination to trade. Reciprocity was the key element of these relationships, and so

---

[15] As recorded in his ledger, TNA, C109/21.
[16] In total £20,616 6d. (£9,313 6s. 9d. in England, £10,792 13s. 9d. in Hamburg, including £7,868 11s. 1d. in unsold cloth, and £510 in Dordrecht). TNA, C109/19.
[17] 1660s ledger, TNA, C109/20. A copy of his will is in C109/20.
[18] See for instance his former apprentice John Ramm, discussed in Chapter 1. See also Harrington–Attwood, 7 Sept. 1658, TNA, C109/20.
[19] Jones–Attwood, 3 June 1660, TNA, C109/20.

they were difficult to sustain if there was an imbalance between the needs of each party. This meant that relationships tended to remain open over time, sustained by promises to return a favour at a future date.

These suitors all wished to capitalize on Attwood's reputation through association, showing how status continued to structure this merchant community, even as commission agency and partnership pushed out servitude as the most common agency relationship. The formulaic language of letter writing shifted over time, from the characteristic salutation ('Sir my humble dutie remembered with praier for your health & hope of your welfare'), and accompanying valediction ('your humble servant'), routinely deployed by apprentices like George Lowe, to the more egalitarian language of friendship which merchants of an equivalent rank tended to use, an etiquette that regulated informal social relations in the absence of written contracts.[20] Nonetheless, awareness of status persisted. Nathaniel Cambridge of Hamburg, occasional factor for Attwood, preferred the less familiar 'Worthy Sir' to 'Friend', and commonly closed his letters 'your humble servant'. Although by then he had been resident of Hamburg for over twenty years, Cambridge was clearly conscious of Attwood's seniority, reassuring him when they had one difference over accounts that 'I have the respect for your Age & Justice as to beleave you will seeke nothing but what is Just & fayre.'[21]

As the use of servants as agents decreased, partnerships could be an alternative means to stabilize agency relations, more so if they were overlain with kinship ties. John Sanford was another who partnered his father-in-law, Lucy Knightley, who was also his former master. Sanford was in Hamburg in the early 1660s, though he was based in London from 1665. By the end of the decade, Sanford and Knightley were dividing their Hamburg business between two agents, another of Knightley's former apprentices (and Sanford's cousin), John Ayshford, and Henry Spurway, a long-term resident of the city. Spurway however had an erratic business record, and in 1671 Knightley's apprentice Thomas Biggs was sent to stand in packhouse with him, as Ayshford and possibly Sanford had previously done. When Ayshford left Hamburg, his business was entrusted to the factor John Baron, who was shortly joined in packhouse by Lucy Knightley Jr, who could thereby monitor this new recruit into the network as well as learn his trade. Ayshford was later enlisted into the Sanford–Knightley partnership, each contributing £3,000 to this new joint stock.[22] Kinship of course was a means to enhance trust, though such high levels of intimacy between partners could prove claustrophobic.[23] Sanford clearly found his overbearing father-in-law difficult to deal with and at one point considered breaking with him, writing to Thomas Biggs of

[20] Trivellato, *Familiarity of Strangers*, p. 180.
[21] Cambridge–Attwood, 5 Jan. 1675, TNA, C109/19.
[22] Sanford–John Ayshford, 7 March 1672, SRO, DD\SF/7/2/1.
[23] Grassby, *Kinship*, pp. 287, 306.

'som private reasons which you may immagine haveing lived so long in the family but they are not convenient to be Comitted to paper.'[24] This reference to the firm as a family highlights the degree of intimacy invested into these relationships, which could generate confidence and security, although sometimes also anxiety. This was certainly the case with Spurway, whom Sanford and Knightley were reluctant to break with in spite of his dubious conduct (see Chapter 3).

Deploying kinship to consolidate business networks was a common practice, allowing inter-generational cooperation, with older merchants contributing their reputations to less well-established, but perhaps more energetic, counterparts. These businesses were rarely handed from father to son, however: merchant businesses were highly personal in nature, with little fixed capital to bequeath, and that most important of assets—a merchant's reputation—was not easily passed onto an heir.[25] Aspects of a merchant's business which could be perpetuated beyond retirement—his network of clients, customers, and suppliers, for instance— might be appropriated by former apprentices, partners, and associates who were able to move into a merchant's territory as his trade was winding down, enabling a degree of fluidity in the Company's ranks. Networks did not have simple lifespans centred on individual careers, then, and 'The organization chart of a major business resembles a family tree.'[26] John Kendrick, for instance, had been enlisted into a partnership with his former master John Quarles, who was keen to keep him as his Middelburg agent, but after this relationship ended, Kendrick joined with Quarles' other apprentice George Lowe, specializing in coloured cloths as Quarles had done. Two of Kendrick's own apprentices at the time of his death in 1626, Andrew Kendrick and Christopher Packe, were themselves trading in partnership by 1640.[27]

By then Packe was the largest cloth exporter amongst the Company in London, and clearly there were benefits from being part of the network of an already well-established Merchant Adventurer. Partnerships could also be formed amongst relative newcomers seeking to pool their limited resources. John Quarles' other apprentice, William Calley, broke with his master acrimoniously, and in 1600 entered into a seven-year partnership with another Merchant Adventurer, Ralph Stint, in order to 'better encrease and augment their substaunce and creditt', as their articles agreement termed it.[28] The contract stipulated that any 'Ambiguitie, doubt, question or controversie' that the two partners could not settle within forty days was to be presented to the London court of the Merchant Adventurers for adjudication. This may have been a common practice: when John Ramm's

---

[24] Sanford–Biggs, 16 Feb. 1672, SRO, DD\SF\7\2\1.
[25] Richard Grassby, 'English merchant capitalism in the late seventeenth century: the composition of business fortunes', *Past and Present* 46 (1970), p. 107.
[26] Grassby, *Kinship*, p. 271.
[27] *The last will and testament of Mr Iohn Kendricke late citizen and draper of London* (London, 1625).
[28] WSA, 1178/324/1.

partnership with one [Dru?] Tindall ended acrimoniously, the case was bought before the Company's Hamburg court, with Ramm demonstrating Tindall's guilt in breaking it.[29] The court proceeded to award him damages, although some of Tindall's friends successfully argued that if this was made public Tindall would thereby be 'registered for a deceitfull person', and so the court consented to an informal arbitration by Company members, 'being naturally inclined to peace then Contention'. The Company therefore did adjudicate in its members' networks, though this was essentially a voluntary service.

Calley and Stint were both based in London at the outset of their partnership, but as we have seen partnerships were sometimes established as a means to respond to the principal–agent problem, and some of the most prominent Merchant Adventurers in the mart towns probably acted in this capacity, as did William Attwood.[30] In fact, writing in the 1680s Matthew Ashton complained that merchants trading in partnership had an advantage over commission agents like himself, as they could save 'provition both wayes soe that they may undersell any that payes provition for buying & selling'.[31] Ashton's career provides an example of the difficulty that a young Merchant Adventurer could face when seeking to establish his position within the overlapping networks that comprised the Company's trading world, particularly in the second half of the seventeenth century. Although they might be a part of several different mercantile networks, commission agents might be marginal within each of them, the informality of their role making them rather disposable. Turning this position of marginality into one of centrality, the sign of independent merchant status, was no easy task.

At the outset of his career Matthew Ashton was handling the business of Godfrey Lawson and a handful of other Leeds and Hull Merchant Adventurers, but he was continually looking for opportunities to trade on his own account. This, however, was a careful balancing act, as factors had to demonstrate that they were not neglecting their principals' businesses. If, as was the case with Lawson, a principal also happened to be a former master, then agents also had to negotiate the additional expectations of deference that came from such a relationship. Lawson seems to have resented his declining influence over his former servant now that Ashton was doing business for several others. Ashton was forced to respond to a 'scruple' from Lawson, 'that you thinke severall of my princepalls charges upon me & forces me to sell theire goods for the most I can gett', which had the effect of bringing down the price of Lawson's own cloth, and had to reassure him that he did not 'let your goods runn amongst them'.[32] As he went about establishing his reputation, Ashton had to be similarly solicitous towards

[29] Ramm–Attwood, 10 May 1659, TNA, C109/24.
[30] See, for instance, William Jones, who died in Hamburg in 1615: Chapter 6.
[31] Ashton–Robert Trippett, 24 Aug. 1683, Bodl. Lib., Eng. misc. c563, fol. 97r.
[32] Ashton–Lawson, 1 Jan. 1684, Bodl. Lib., Eng. misc. c563, fol. 126r–v. For similar concerns, see Starkie–Warner, 2 June 1643, TNA, SP 46/84, fol. 330.

his other principals: after one disappointing deal, Ashton assured Philip Wilkinson of Hull that 'there neither hath beene nor ever shall bee any neglect on my part to doe for you or any other whome you are pleased to recommend unto me'.[33] Commission agents like Ashton depended on such recommendations, made with the expectation that they would lead to reciprocal favours; Ashton asked his correspondent Joseph Kitchingman to 'speak in my behalfe as I have done for you to Mr Biggs & Co' (probably Lucy Knightley's servant Thomas Biggs, now well established in Hamburg).[34] Correspondents also shared information about prospective collaborators, as when Ashton asked Kitchingman for intelligence about John Preston of Leeds, 'soe would know something of his Condition before I either receive his goods or order his freinds to charge upon me'.[35] Through such means, Ashton was able to gradually extend the number of his ties, and the opportunities that came with them.

Expanding business came at the risk of upsetting existing principals, however. Although he commenced business with a consignment of cloth on his own account, following its dispatch Ashton scrupulously rejected offers to partner others in the trade in northern cloths. As he explained to one merchant, this was because it was 'of late the Custome in this place, that if a merchant sends goods by Commission (unless it bee to a partner) he expects his Correspondent should not bee concerned in the same sorte of goods for his proper Account'.[36] When supplementing his commission trade, Ashton was thus limited to importing such 'interlopeing goods' as sugar, and exporting linen, flax and so on.[37] However, frustrated by his slow progress, he was eventually tempted to enter into a partnership for cloth with Kitchingman and Jeremy Whichcote of London, although he kept this secret from his other principals.[38] Such secret dealing did not help Ashton when some bad deals brought his estate into question, and he could rely on few allies to support him, as Chapter 3 will discuss.

In spite of the decline of master–servant agency relations, personal ties were clearly still central to the commercial networks of Merchant Adventurers, and these were likely to be concentrated on whichever mart town they had most personal experience of. Ever since the emergence of the dual-mart system in the 1580s, there was a degree of divergence between the Dutch and German branches of the Company's trade. According to Astrid Friis's study of the 1606 London port book for cloth exports, over 65 per cent of the total cohort of 219 exporters traded to Germany, the Netherlands or Calais exclusively. This had fallen slightly to 60 per cent in 1640 (with Dunkirk taking the place of Calais), albeit in context of a smaller merchant community numbering 143 (see Table 2.2). As these figures

---

[33] Ashton–Wilkinson, 8 July 1681, Bodl. Lib., Eng. misc. c563, fol. 6r.
[34] Ashton–Kitchingman, 10 June 1684, Bodl. Lib., Eng. misc. c563, fol. 166v.
[35] Ashton–Kitchingman, 23 Jan. 1683, Bodl. Lib., Eng. misc. c563, fol. 62v.
[36] Ashton–William Pickering, 28 Feb. 1682, Bodl. Lib., Eng. misc. c563, fol. 23r.
[37] Ashton–Jeremy Whichcote, 25 Apr. 1682, Bodl. Lib., Eng. misc. c563, fol. 31r.
[38] Ashton–Whichcote, 2 Jan. 1683, Bodl. Lib., Eng. misc. c563, fol. 59r–v.

Table 2.2 London cloth exporters to Germany, Netherlands, and Calais/Flanders, 1606/1640 (figures in brackets denote percentage of total cohort)

	1606 (old draperies only)	1640 (old and new draperies)
Germany	95 (43%)	31 (22%)
Netherlands	40 (18%)	31 (22%)
Calais/Flanders	8 (4%)	23 (16%)
Total one market	*143 (65%)*	*85 (60%)*
Germany, Netherlands	40 (18%)	32 (22%)
Netherlands, Calais/Flanders	10 (5%)	17 (12%)
Germany, Calais/Flanders	14 (6%)	2 (1%)
Total two markets	*66 (29%)*	*51 (35%)*
Germany, Netherlands, Calais/Flanders	12 (5%)	7 (5%)

Sources: 1606: Friis, *Alderman Cockayne's Project*, p. 77; 1640: TNA, E190/43/1, 4

show, the number of cloth exporters to Germany had fallen much more sharply than was the case for the Netherlands. Furthermore, German traders had largely withdrawn from the alternative market of the Spanish Netherlands, which in 1606 had been accessed via Calais.[39] In fact in 1640, 83 per cent of London cloth exporters concentrated 80 per cent or more of their trade (in terms of value according to customs rates) in one of these three markets (46 to Rotterdam, 44 to Hamburg, and 28 to Flanders).

This regional specialization appears to have grown following the Restoration, by which point the Company could only claim effective monopoly rights over cloth exports to Hamburg. In 1677, thirty London merchants exported old draperies to Hamburg, and just two of these were counted amongst the seventy-five old drapery exporters to the Netherlands, although there may have been more cross-over when it came to new draperies.[40] The exporters of old draperies to Hamburg thus appear as an increasingly separate group, although in the 1680s a growing number did begin to export to the Netherlands, as will be discussed in Chapter 8.

---

[39] The corporate affiliation of those merchants trading to Calais/Flanders is not always clear, particularly in 1640. Although trade to this region was reserved for the Merchant Adventurers in the 1634 royal proclamation restoring its privileges, this market seems to have been harder to control than Germany or the United Provinces and had no formal mart town. The relatively large number trading exclusively to Flanders in 1640 might include some former interlopers specializing in narrow and dyed cloths, who had taken advantage of the 1634 proclamation to purchase the Company's freedom. However, a significant number of Merchant Adventurers trading to Rotterdam also partook in this trade.

[40] TNA, E190/67/2. Examining the port books for 1678, Newman identified eighteen old drapery exporters from London to Hamburg, two of whom exported to another market, but for new draperies the equivalent figures were twenty-one and twenty. The total number of exporters from London to Germany, Netherlands, and Flanders was 129 (old draperies) and 164 (new draperies), though there was probably considerable cross-over between the two groups. Newman, 'Anglo-Hamburg trade', pp. 136–7.

William Attwood was typical, therefore, in concentrating the bulk of his trade as a Merchant Adventurer on Hamburg, where he could rely on multiple sources of information, and a range of potential partners to choose between. When in the 1650s he launched a modest venture to Rotterdam, he relied on the professional factors Robert Gay and Thomas Bale. George Warner, too, focused on Hamburg, relying on Pearce Starkie as his agent from at least 1638 to 1643, although it is unclear whether he had previously spent time in the mart town himself. Warner reflected the division in the Company's ranks when in August 1641 he complained that the 'Rotterdamers' in the Company were buying up all the cloth in London, pushing up prices for Hamburg merchants like himself.[41] This prompted Warner to launch his own venture to Rotterdam, and he spread his risk by selecting two agents to handle his white and Spanish cloths respectively, one William Lee, agent of Warner's former partner Edward Wastfield, and Brian Ball, who like Warner had Warwickshire connections. Neither merchant was a complete stranger, therefore, but Warner was still frustrated by their poor sales, and so kept his consignments at a fairly low level. Although Lee professed that he would have happily received more, he explained that his first obligation was to his principal merchant: 'for me to sell 100 or 200 clothes more in a yeare then I doe & not to give my principall resonable incouradgement would greive mee'.[42] Brian Ball, meanwhile, was an even more reluctant agent in Warner's Spanish cloth business, which Ball found to be not worth the trouble given the small amount Warner was willing to venture.[43] When Lee moved to Hamburg, Warner was forced to turn to yet another Rotterdam agent to dispatch his cloth, but with no more success.[44] Established relationships dominated the market, therefore, influencing which custom agents were willing to take on, and presenting an obstacle even to Merchant Adventurers seeking to redirect their trade, let alone non-members. Given the trust that merchants had to place in their agents, it is unsurprising that they were likely to concentrate business on places where they had stronger ties, providing them with greater opportunity to monitor their agent's behaviour through reputational mechanisms based on the provision of information in multiple channels.

As we will see in Part Two, the division between the Company's German and Dutch traders could at times threaten corporate unity. This was far from the only potential source of conflict that the Company's government had to contend with, however. Network building was a competitive process, with agents competing for commissions whilst their principals sought to exert as much leverage as possible over their agents' decisions without souring the relationship; partnerships were

---

[41] Warner–Starkie, 13 Aug. 1641, TNA, SP 46/85/1, fol. 67v.
[42] Lee–Warner, 6 Sept. 1641, TNA, SP 46/84, fol. 96.
[43] Warner–Ball, 21 Feb. 1642, TNA, SP 46/85/1, fol. 80r.
[44] Bolles–Warner, 1 Aug. 1643, TNA, SP 46/84, fol. 340.

fashioned on the basis of evaluations of creditworthiness, ability, and future prospects, as well as personal affection. The distribution of opportunities within the Company's ranks was shaped by such interactions. Equally, these competing networks influenced the distribution of trade: competition between members could undermine the fraternal values, which corporate government was intended to sustain, as well as the Company's claim to be able to maintain the price of English cloth overseas. The next section considers the nature of this market, in terms of the skills and resources needed to master this trade, how it was regulated, and how its structure was changing over time.

Managing the Packhouse

The Fellowship of Merchant Adventurers was synonymous with the export of a particular commodity, broadcloth, or more specifically, the unfinished 'white' cloth which it was illegal to export above a certain price without licence. The Company's 'free licence' to export 30,000 notional shortcloths annually, acquired in 1564, was perhaps its most valuable privilege, supplemented by the exclusive rights it won to other licences leased to courtiers, at a cost (for instance, 2s. 2d. per cloth for the licence possessed by the Earl of Cumberland, agreed in 1602).[45] Allocation of access to the free licence was used by the Company to distribute trade equitably, as part of the measure known as the stint. As John Wheeler put it, this aimed to ensure 'an oeconomicall, and discreete partition, or approportioning amonge the members, and Brethren of the Companie, of the commodities of the same', as in the 'maner of a well ordered common wealth, or familie, wherein all are prouided for'.[46] The stint, however, reflected assumptions about the normal career path of members, with its level rising according to seniority, beginning with a maximum annual level of 400 cloths in the first three years after taking the freedom, and increasing at the rate of fifty a year up to 1,000.[47] This figure included an allotted portion of the free licence, beginning at 120 and rising by fifteen a year to a maximum of 300. Exceeding the stint was punishable by a fine of 40s. per cloth.

These levels, as recorded in the surviving copy of the Company's 'Laws, Customes and Ordinances', were set by an order dated 2 July 1609, but the stint was certainly in place before then. However, there is some uncertainty as to the

---

[45]   Richard Turfitt Spence, 'The Cliffords, Earls of Cumberland, 1579–1646: a study of their fortunes based on their household and estate accounts', unpublished D.Phil. thesis (London, 1959), p. 257. This sum was raised to 2s. 8d. in 1612. Ibid., p. 263.

[46]   Wheeler, *Treatise of Commerce*, pp. 78–9.

[47]   *Laws*, pp. 67–70. It is rather unclear whether these levels referred to 'notional shortcloths' according to the 1606 book of rates, or pieces. The phrase used is 'Clothes or the quantitie thereof in all sortes of Englishe woollen Commodityes'. These figures included wrappers, which went custom free. At some point the limit for aldermen was raised to 2,000 cloths: BL, Add. 28079, fol. 64r.

dates when it was actively being enforced. Around 1598 a critic of the Company alleged that a decade earlier the House of Lords had forbidden the stint, only for it to be revived in the last two years.[48] A later published attack on the Company printed a court order dated 27 April 1605 increasing the levels of the stint, as well as one from October 1606 instituting an annual oath whereby members disclosed the number of cloths they had exported, on pain of a fine of £20, and the loss of the benefit of their free licence.[49] In fact a similar oath was in use in 1597, though George Lowe believed that the punishment for refusing to take it was only the loss of the free licence, which was no trouble to a coloured cloth trader like his master Quarles, so perhaps the fine was subsequently added to target others like him.[50] The 1609 order added a fine of £200 for those who continued to refuse to swear after being warned.[51]

The stint was often seized on by enemies of the Company who presented it as artificially retarding the size of the cloth industry. It could also be accused of unfairly limiting the ambitions of members. One anonymous author suggested that the stint of 400 cloths would only produce £200 profit, not enough for a merchant to live on, and poor returns for the investment of the gentleman who might have provided as much as £2,000–3,000 stock for his son's starting capital.[52] In fact already by the time this was written, a Company order of June 1618 had confined the stint to white cloths, although the author argued this was no consolation, the coloured cloth trade requiring specialist knowledge that was beyond the majority of Adventurers.[53]

For all the criticism levelled against it, there are questions as to the effectiveness of the stint in preventing engrossment by the richest traders. Friis' analysis of the 1606 London port books identified twenty-six Merchant Adventurers exporting over 1,000 cloths.[54] In fact, in 1620 the Company at London ordered that exceeding the stint be punished by the payment of double Company impositions and impressed money, following 'Complaint made by the yong men, that some great traders, doe buy vp such quantities of Clothes weekly, that the yong men cannot get Cloth for their money'.[55] Thus the Company's claim in 1622 that the 'ancient order' of the stint had not been used for twenty years, was possibly not quite so brazen a falsehood as it first appears, and may reflect the difficulty of putting the measure into effect.[56] Although in 1648 Henry Parker still defended the stint as a practice adopted by 'the whole Company by common advice, and

---

[48] HL, Ellesmere 2387.
[49] *A discourse consisting of motives for the enlargement and freedome of trade* (London, 1645), p. 31.
[50] Lowe–Quarles, 3 Nov. 1597, TNA, SP 46/176, fol. 236v.   [51] *Laws*, p. 72.
[52] 'Reasons that the stint of the Merchant Adventurers in White Cloth may be prejudicial for the growth of yonge men, & soe to the Commonwealth', 1621/41?, Whitelocke II, #15.
[53] *Laws*, p. 135.
[54] Friis, *Alderman Cockayne's Project*, p. 78. Note that in these figures, Friis did not convert broadcloths into their notional equivalent, although she apparently did this for narrow cloths.
[55] *Laws*, p. 135. For these charges, see Chapter 1.   [56] TNA, SP 16/535, fol. 82.

consent', he also argued that the size of the trade was now so diminished that many members were far from reaching their allotted stint in any case.[57] This was clearly the case, as the breakdown of undressed broadcloth exports amongst the 118 merchants/merchant partnerships exporting old draperies from London to Germany, the Netherlands, and Flanders in 1640 demonstrates (Table 2.3).

As well as demonstrating that exceeding the stint remained common, these figures show how many merchants were not taking up their full allocation, or were avoiding the commodity altogether (although many of these concentrated on Flanders, which was not a significant market for undressed broadcloth). In 1640 white broadcloth accounted for only 57 per cent of total exports of old draperies from London to these markets (as notional shortcloths), compared to 80 per cent in 1606, with Spanish cloth, a high-quality coloured variant pioneered in the Somerset–Wiltshire border and Devon, now accounting for over a quarter of woollen cloth exports (see Table 2.4).[58] Spanish cloth was beginning to eclipse the main variants of coloured cloth previously exported by Merchant Adventurers, dyed-in-the-wool cloth of Kent and Reading, which was exported in its finished state.[59] Despite the rise of Spanish cloth, overall old drapery exports in 1640 were less than half of the 1606 figure, although Spanish cloths were probably undervalued in the customs rate (along with longcloths and Reading/Kents), so the fall in the total value of exports was not as pronounced as this suggests.

This decline would continue into the Restoration, by which point London was exporting around one fifth of the total volume of old draperies (in notional terms)

Table 2.3 Distribution of undressed broadcloth exports (as notional shortcloths) from London to Germany/Netherlands/Flanders (denizens), 1640

Total number of undressed broadcloths exported per merchant	Number of merchants (% of cohort)	Total number of undressed broadcloths exported by each group (% of total)
1,000+	11 (9%)	16,170 (53%)
800–999	2 (2%)	1,796 (6%)
600–799	5 (4%)	3,514 (12%)
400–599	8 (7%)	4,090 (13%)
200–399	9 (8%)	2,807 (9%)
1–200	30 (25%)	2,051 (7%)
0	53 (45%)	0

Source: TNA, E190/43/4

[57] Henry Parker, *Of a Free Trade* (London, 1648), p. 22.
[58] For Spanish cloth, see Supple, *Commercial Crisis*, pp. 149–52; Ramsay, *Wiltshire Woollen Industry*, pp. 102–4.
[59] This was a legacy of an act of Parliament of 1566 sponsored by the London Clothworkers' Company, which enacted that all dyed-in-the-wool Kent and Suffolk cloths were to be finished before export. The main market for Suffolks was the Baltic. Ramsay, 'London Clothworkers'; Friis, *Alderman Cockayne's Project*, p. 59.

Table 2.4 London cloth exports by denizens (old draperies), 1606/1640, as notional shortcloths

	1606				1640			
	Stade	Middelburg	Calais	Total	Hamburg	Rotterdam	Flanders	Total
Undressed shortcloths	50,190	29,285	3,025	82,500	11,058	12,601	657	24,316
Undressed longcloths	2,791	3,939	483	7,213	3,639	2,392	81	6,112
Dressed shortcloths (inc. Suffolks)	512	61	49	622	20	76	0	96
Dressed longcloths	225	56	5	286	569	68	0	637
Dressed Reading/Kent cloths	4,996	2,388	5,616	13,000	717	2,475	1,358	4,550
Kerseys	4,238	49	240	4,257	117	37	870	1,024
Northern dozens	108	31	66	205	2	121	1,606	1,729
Devon dozens	1,239	263	484	1,986	511	404	208	1,123
Spanish cloths					4,033	6,089	3,630	13,752
Others	870	100	41	1,011	0	6	0	6
Total	65,169	36,172	10,009	111,350	20,666	24,269	8,410	53,345
As % of annual total	59%	32%	9%		39%	45%	16%	

Note: 1606 figures exclude interlopers, as identified by Friis; for difficulties in differentiating between Merchant Adventurers and interlopers trading to Flanders in 1640, see footnote 39, above.

Sources: For Holland and Germany (1606), Supple, Commercial Crisis, pp. 260–2; for Calais (1606), Friis, Alderman Cockayne's Project, pp. 454–5; for 1640, TNA, E190/43/4.

to Germany and the Low Countries that was the case at the start of the century (see Table 2.5). Most pronounced was the fall in shortcloth exports, to around 5–7 per cent of its former size, although these figures do not differentiate between dressed and undressed broadcloth.

To an extent this decline was mitigated by rising new drapery exports, although we lack figures for 1606. In 1640, the four main types of new draperies exported to Hamburg, Rotterdam, and Flanders were valued at almost £60,000, over half of this being perpetuana exports to Hamburg.[60] In total, £2,993 was paid in tonnage and poundage for the main types of new draperies, compared to £17,782 custom for woollen cloth exports, which therefore still accounted for over 80 per cent of the total customs paid for old and new draperies combined, excluding impositions (which were not charged on cloth).[61] New drapery exports from London to Germany seem to have remained relatively stable over the subsequent fifty years, but as the volume of old drapery exports continued to fall, the relative importance of the former was growing.[62] Contemporary estimations of the value of different types of cloth, which correct the undervaluation of Spanish and longcloths when converted to notional shortcloths, show a shift after 1660 towards new draperies, although old draperies continued to be more valuable (Table 2.6; by comparison, the value of old drapery exports in 1606 using these figures was about £788,000). Cloth exports to Hamburg held up better than to the Netherlands, partly because of the Anglo-Dutch Wars, though some of this trade may have shifted from London to the outports, particularly Exeter, which enjoyed a boom in perpetuana/serge exports.[63] Overall London was losing its pre-eminence in the cloth trade: by the 1680s, Hull was rivalling the capital as the major exporter of old draperies to Germany as well as the Netherlands.[64]

Over the period, then, the structure of the Company's cloth exports was transformed, with the long-term collapse in the continental market for undressed shortcloth the major development. That said, even in 1606 the range of types of

[60] TNA, E190/43/1.
[61] Tonnage and poundage was charged at the rate of 5 per cent ad valorem, according to the book of rates; this is close to the figure of 6s. 8d. per notional shortcloth measuring 24 yards, if these are valued at £6. This is a reasonable figure for shortcloths, which were each rated as 1⅙ notional short-cloth (i.e. £7), although longcloths (rated at 1⅓ notional shortcloths per cloth, i.e. £8, whether finished or unfinished) and Spanish cloths (rated at $1\frac{1}{12}$ notional shortcloths, to match the average length of 26 yards) were undervalued in terms of notional shortcloths. Of course the book of rates did not straightforwardly match market rates, and so these figures do not accurately measure the value of exports. For these customs, see Michael J. Braddick, *The Nerves of State: Taxation and the Financing of the English State, 1558–1714* (Manchester and New York, 1996), pp. 49–55.
[62] Although new drapery exports from London to Germany were rated at £63,630 in 1669, other years were closer to the 1640 value (£27,553 in 1663; £38,193 in 1678; £36,641 in 1686). Newman, 'Anglo-Hamburg trade', p. 108.
[63] W. B. Stephens, *Seventeenth-Century Exeter: A Study of Industrial and Commercial Development, 1625–1688* (Exeter, 1958), p. 130.
[64] Ibid., pp. 107–9.

Table 2.5 London cloth exports by denizens (old draperies), 1660s/1678, as notional shortcloths

	1663/9 average				1678			
	Germany	Holland	Flanders	Total	Germany	Holland	Flanders	Total
Shortcloths	4,966	1,899	765	7,630	3,117	848	54	4,019
Longcloths	1,921	727	913	3,687	2,098	1,268	368	3,734
Kerseys	208	218	850	1,275	220	402	231	853
Northern dozens	304	138	1,362	1,804	86	399	107	592
Devon dozens	93	0	11	104	0	0	0	0
Spanish cloths	5,614	2,238	4,632	12,483	4,378	2,246	1,143	7,767
Total	13,230	5,220	8,532	26,982	9,898	5,163	1,903	16,969
As % of annual total	49%	19%	32%		58%	30%	11%	

Note: Although both broadcloth and Spanish cloth were re-rated in terms of notional shortcloths in the 1642 book of rates, I have used the previous rating, with longcloth rated as 1⅓ notional shortcloth per piece, shortcloth as 1⅙, and Spanish cloth as $1\frac{1}{12}$, to allow comparison with the figures in Table 2.4.

Sources: 1663/9: BL, Add. 36785. 1678: Newman, 'Anglo-Hamburg trade', p. 319.

Table 2.6 Value of old and new drapery (main varieties) exports from London by denizens, 1640–78 (£)

	1640		1663/9 average		1678	
	Old	New	Old	New	Old	New
Germany	168,959	40,483	122,735	55,138	93,038	30,595
Netherlands	208,630	8,333	48,436	11,577	50,938	17,789
Flanders	90,401	12,434	91,151	27,731	19,515	8,493
Total (% of annual total)	467,990 (88%)	61,250 (12%)	262,322 (74%)	94,446 (26%)	163,491 (74%)	56,877 (26%)

Note: Values have been calculated based on the rates given in BL, Add. 36785, as follows (per piece): longcloths £12; shortcloths £8; Spanish cloths £12 10s.; Northern dozens single £5; Devon dozens £2 10s.; kerseys £1 10s.; double bays £6; single bays £2 15s.; serges/perpetuanas £2 10s. For 1678 perpetuana and serge exports are given in pounds rather than pieces, so the valuation according to the book of rates has been used instead.

Sources: 1640: TNA, E190/43/1, 4, 1663/9: BL, Add. 36785; 1678: Newman, 'Anglo-Hamburg trade', pp. 319–20

cloth available enabled both specialization and diversification. For instance John Quarles' exports were almost entirely confined to coloured Reading and Kent cloths, whereas Lionel Cranfield, although something of a specialist in northern kerseys (which accounted for almost 60 per cent of his sales in Germany from 1599 to 1603) also dealt in packcloth and fine cloth (around 18 per cent each) and smaller numbers of coloured cloths.[65] Quarles and Cranfield, however, were relatively unusual, given the dominance of undressed cloth exports, and both coloured and narrow cloth exports tended to be concentrated in few hands. In the 1606 port books, according to Friis, three merchant firms exported half of all Reading/Kent cloths from London, namely Henry Robinson, Paul/Richard Bowdler, and William Calley, whilst in 1614 a similar proportion of dyed/dressed cloths were in the hands of George Lowe, Robert Angell, and George Morgan.[66] Lowe and Calley were former apprentices of Quarles, who was also connected to the Bowdler family, whilst Quarles' other servant John Kendrick was by 1620 the chief London exporter of coloured cloths.[67] Similarly, almost all northern kerseys exported from London in 1606 were sent by Thomas Moulson, Lionel Cranfield, and Sir Thomas Lowe.[68]

As late as 1628 (a year which briefly bucked the overall trend of decline in old draperies), most London Merchant Adventurers focused on undressed broadcloth. In that year, 121 merchants/partnerships (denizens only) exported more

[65] For John Quarles' sales, George Lowe's journals, TNA, SP 46/19, fols 106–20; TNA, SP 46/176, fols 94–104. For Lionel Cranfield, Rawstorm's journal, KHLC, U269/1/AB98. Subsequent references to sales data for these two merchants in this section come from these sources.
[66] Friis, *Alderman Cockayne's Project*, p. 130.   [67] Ibid., p. 282.   [68] Ibid., p. 130.

than 100 notional shortcloths from London; 54 of these devoted 80 per cent or more of their exports to undressed broadcloth, 17 to varieties of narrow cloth (mainly Devonshire dozens), and 13 to dressed cloths.[69] Of those who combined different varieties to a significant extent (each amounting to more than 20 per cent of their total), only 7 combined undressed cloth with either narrow or dressed cloth, compared to 30 combining the latter two. The relatively high number focusing on narrow and/or dressed cloth reflects the fact that these varieties had been exempted from the Merchant Adventurers' privileges in 1624, although most of the largest traders in coloured cloth were still Merchant Adventurers, with over half of Reading/Kent cloth exports by four merchants. This group also led the way in the export of Spanish cloths, which amounted to 3,478 notional shortcloths in total. Almost a third of these were exported by Lawrence Halsted and Co., the leading exporter of Reading/Kent cloths and a former partner of John Kendrick. The subsequent rapid growth of Spanish cloth exports as well as new draperies shifted the overall profile of London cloth exports away from white cloth. In 1640, 92 merchants/partnerships (denizens only) exported the equivalent of over 100 notional shortcloths in either old and new draperies from London; 34 devoted 80 per cent or more of their exports to undressed cloths, 16 to dressed cloths, 1 to narrow cloths, and 6 to new draperies, leaving 35 who exported some combination, 38 per cent of the total compared to 31 per cent in 1628 (albeit the latter figure does not include new draperies).[70] This shift was more pronounced amongst the largest traders: just half of 22 merchants exporting the equivalent of over 1,000 notional shortcloths in 1640 focused their trade on undressed cloth, whereas the figure in 1628 was 22 out of 25 exporters.

George Warner was quite typical, then, in spreading his Hamburg exports from 1638 to 1643 between Spanish cloth (55 per cent of total sales) and undressed shortcloth (43 per cent).[71] William Attwood's sales for the partnership of Pell–Attwood–Hampton in 1652 reflected the shift from shortcloth even more strikingly, which in this case amounted to 3 per cent of total sales, compared to 69 per cent for Spanish cloth and 21 per cent for bays (the rest made up by a variety of other sorts).[72] Already in 1640 over half of the cloth exporters from London to Germany, the Netherlands, and Flanders handled some new draperies, though the most buoyant sector, perpetuana exports to Hamburg, was dominated by four specialists who were responsible for about half of the total. The growth of Spanish cloths and new draperies further diminished the centrality of white broadcloths in the Company's trade into the Restoration. Shortcloth was now becoming something of a niche product: in 1677, 90 per cent of exports of this type from

---

[69]   TNA, E190/32/3.   [70]   TNA, E190/43/1, 4.

[71]   Accounts/journals of Pearce Starkie, TNA, SP 46/85/4, 6. Subsequent references to sales data for Warner in this section come from these sources.

[72]   Attwood's Hamburg journal, TNA, C109/21. Subsequent references to sales data for Attwood in this section come from this source.

London to Hamburg were handled by just two Merchant Adventurers, Jeremy Elwes and William Gore, though longcloths were more widely distributed.[73]

Over the period, therefore, the commodity structure of the Company's cloth exports had changed significantly; no longer could the majority of Merchant Adventurers base their career on undressed shortcloth, or packcloth as it was often known, reflecting the fact that it was often sold by the pack of ten.[74] According to statutory regulations, shortcloth measured from 23 to 28 yards in length, distinguishing it from longcloth, which paid a higher rate of custom, though regional variations existed for both sorts. Similar specifications were given for the different narrow kerseys and dozens, largely made in Hampshire, Devon, and Yorkshire.[75] Packcloth came in 'many sorts', as Cranfield explained to a potential foreign customer, with packs ranging in price from £50 to £80 (in sterling, 'first penny').[76] This was even more the case for longcloth: Cranfield accounted the best as Worcesters of 31 yards, costing £8–50, but Gloucester and Wiltshire cloths of 28 yards had the same price range. As for other sorts, 'mingled' (i.e. dyed-in-the-wool) coloured cloths ranged from £7–11 for northern products of 31 yards, to £12–16 for Readings of 34 yards, with the best sorts of Kent cloth reaching £40. Cranfield's speciality, kerseys, were simply described as 'several kinds' and 'prices', although only Devonshire and Hampshire varieties at that point came in colours, with bays priced at 1–5s. a yard.

The range of products and prices available meant that the market in cloth was never entirely predictable, and English-based Merchant Adventurers relied on good 'advice' from their agents about which cloths were in demand, on the basis of which they would 'regulate' their purchases.[77] News that a particular type of cloth was in demand in the mart towns could lead to a rush to buy it up before the departure of the Company fleet, and because the supply of cloth was relatively inelastic (due to the length time it took to be manufactured), prices could rise rapidly. The market was equally susceptible to gluts which could leave factors struggling to dispatch their remainders before the arrival of the next fleet. One response to this unpredictability was to fashion direct relations with suppliers. By the sixteenth century the size of the cloth trade had outgrown Blackwell Hall, which instead was becoming a site for deals to be struck between merchants and clothiers or, increasingly, their factors, sometimes based on samples, with cloth then being delivered direct to a merchant's warehouse. It was a short step to placing advanced orders with suppliers for particular sorts, bypassing Blackwell Hall entirely.[78]

---

[73] This was a very poor year for shortcloth exports, however, with just 1,733 exported to Hamburg (in terms of notional shortcloths). Note that this portbook does not distinguish between dressed and undressed broadcloth exports. TNA, E190/67/2.

[74] Friis, *Alderman Cockayne's Project*, p. 50.   [75] Ibid., p. 47.

[76] HMC Sackville II, p. 146.   [77] Starkie–Warner, 16 June 1642, TNA, SP 46/84, fol. 203.

[78] Eric Kerridge, *Textile Manufactures in Early Modern England* (Manchester, 1985), pp. 216–17.

This appears to have been a particular feature of the coloured cloth trade, which as late as 1642 was considered to be a more volatile commodity than white cloth, necessitating regular intelligence: as George Warner put it, 'he that will follow a Coloured Cloth trade must have constant advice of all alteracons: else its impossible to doe good by it'.[79] The tendency of Reading and Kent cloths to be dominated by small numbers of Merchant Adventurers was probably a reflection of this volatility, which encouraged close personal links with clothiers, so acting to confine the market to those with good connections (Kendrick, at least, came from a family of Reading clothiers). John Quarles directly contracted with the suppliers of his Reading and Kent cloths, though this carried its own risks: his servant Lowe complained that the high prices these cloths were commanding at London was 'bycause yowe havinge all the best makers in bargayne for weekely [delivery] litle alteration could be amongest the Rest'.[80] This was part of Quarles' strategy to corner the market. Unwelcome newcomers could be fought off by taking 'the price of the markett', which would 'weary most men in this place from dealinge in cullord cloth'.[81] This strategy proved to be impossible to keep up indefinitely, however, and Lowe was soon complaining that coloured cloth was 'soe abundant that scarce any packhouse in towne is without cullors'.[82] Even a niche product such as coloured cloth was difficult to monopolize effectively, although Quarles' servant John Kendrick managed to achieve a dominant position in this market in the early 1620s.

Kendrick's success was mirrored by that of his former servant Christopher Packe in 1640, but Packe exported twice as many Spanish cloths as he did Reading and Kents. The rise of this product meant that increasing numbers of Merchant Adventurers were now involved in the vagaries of the coloured cloth trade, with customers prone to 'run after fresh new Collers'.[83] The market in Spanish cloth was more open than that of Reading and Kent cloth, with sixty-four merchants/partnerships exporting the commodity from London to Hamburg, Rotterdam or Flanders in 1640, though it continued to be accounted a difficult commodity to master. George Warner complained that his factor Pearce Starkie sold his 'knowne sorts' for 'noe profit', adding that the rates he sold at would 'not pay 2 pc: for all ventures and 6 monthes Interest'.[84] Little wonder, then, that Starkie preferred the easier trade of packcloth, explaining that 'for Good sorts of w[hite] Cloth...a man may alwayes have his mony againe without any losse for the most parte'.[85]

[79] Warner–Ball, 7 April 1642, TNA, SP 46/85/1, fol. 85v.
[80] Lowe–Quarles, 2 Feb. 1595, TNA, SP 46/176, fol. 411v.
[81] Lowe–Quarles, 28 Oct. 1593, TNA, SP 46/176, fol. 8v.
[82] Lowe–Quarles, 9 July 1596, TNA, SP 46/176, fol. 138v.
[83] Starkie–Warner, 7 Apr. 1643, TNA, SP 46/84, fol. 319. For similar sentiments, see Ashton–Lawson, 25 Oct. 1681, Bodl. Lib., Eng. misc. c563, fol. 16.
[84] Warner–Starkie, 6 Dec. 1639, TNA, SP 46/85/1, fol. 10v.
[85] Starkie–Warner, 16 Oct. 1641, TNA, SP 46/84, fol. 105.

Acquiring exclusive access to a popular clothier's mark was one way to mitigate the force of competition. John Sanford corresponded with some of his more important suppliers, sending patterns and making orders on the promise of further custom if they were satisfactory. Sanford wrote to one clothier that 'I have a designe to further you in the world though I gain little thereby', and hoped to persuade another to send serges with 'lively Cullors and very substantial thick goods and as Cheap as any if not Cheaper' on the promise that 'we shall in a short time have a learger Correspondency to the advantage of each other' (adding that 'we have great and subtill ones to vie with').[86] At the same time, Sanford continued to buy cloth on the open market at Blackwell Hall, and was not above using this as a way to cajole his regular suppliers into lowering their prices.[87]

Packcloth was also commonly known by the clothier's mark, with 'Knowne sorts' being particularly valued.[88] Pearce Starkie favoured those made by Thomas Flowers, particularly his fine blue marks bought for £75, and he instructed George Warner to advise Flowers to 'make more of them and also the course at 53li'.[89] This suggests direct relations with the clothier, but in general the market for shortcloth seems to have been fairly open: the 697 shortcloths sold by Richard Rawstrom from 1599 to 1603 were produced by at least twenty-seven different clothiers. Indeed, the stint on the Company's free licence guaranteed a significant number of Merchant Adventurers trading in this product at a relatively low level, at least before the decline of the trade after the Restoration. Shortcloth was an ideal product for newcomers, with customers often purchasing several packs at a time. Longcloths by contrast tended to be sold in smaller packages, fitting for a product that varied considerably in length and quality: the 515 fine cloths sold by Richard Rawstorm for Cranfield from 1599 to 1603 ranged in price from £9 to £36 vls. These were made by forty-seven clothiers, though 295 were produced by one William King, all of 32 yards length, and were sold for between £12 and £12 10s. vls, suggesting that Cranfield had a special relationship with him. Cranfield's main export to Germany was northern kerseys, a cheap product often sold in bulk: just five merchants were responsible for 85 per cent of Richard Rawstorm's sales for Cranfield from 1599 to 1603. But if this is to suggest that the trade in kerseys was a particularly easy one, a different impression is given by Rawstorm's letters. The major market for northern kerseys was Nuremburg, from whence they were traditionally distributed to consumers in eastern and central Europe, but in the early years of the century this market was apparently at a virtual standstill.[90] This cheap product, however, was easy to come by in England, and in

---

[86] Sanford–John Foster, 26 Dec. 1671; Sanford–Jasper Radcliffe, 21 Jan. 1673, SRO, DD\SF/7/2/1.
[87] Sanford–Foster, 29 June 1672, ibid.
[88] Warner–Starkie, 6 Dec. 1639, TNA, SP 46/85/1, fol. 10v. For cloth marks, see Ramsay, *Wiltshire Woollen Industry*, pp. 50–1.
[89] Starkie–Warner, 22 July 1642, TNA, SP 46/84, fol. 220.
[90] HMC Sackville II, p. 31.

June 1601 Rawstorm complained that they were 'in so many men's hands, and unrequested, I fear the price will be greatly debased'.[91] Another problem was competition from northern ships: Rawstorm complained that the 'Hullners' had 'made such a beggarly price that themselves I am sure are losers and have spoiled our markets'. Eventually those with small parcels of 150–200 kerseys were willing to sell cheaply as a means to help the sale of their other cloths, leaving those with larger stocks with a hefty remainder of unsold cloth.

Cranfield's response was to tighten his control over the supply of kerseys to Stade by entering into partnerships with other leading merchants such as Richard Venn and Thomas Moulson.[92] Rawstorm fully approved of these efforts, and encouraged Cranfield to renew his agreement with Venn whereby they could 'buy and sell here together' which 'would be the more profitable for you all'.[93] Alongside these collusive practices, Cranfield joined those Merchant Adventurers sending kerseys to Nuremburg on their own accounts, so violating the orders of the Company (see Chapter 4). This was successful in the short term—in September 1603 his Nuremburg agent was accounted to have the 'market in his own hands'— but eventually this only served to glut the market and discourage his customers in Stade.[94]

Given that kerseys were often sold in bulk, customer loyalty was particularly important, but Merchant Adventurers in general were aware of the need to maintain good customer relations. This was another aspect of the market which Company rules attempted to regulate in order to limit competition. Accordingly, cloth was to be sold only on designated 'show days', taking place thrice weekly following the arrival of Company ships.[95] Further orders were intended to preserve decorum amongst brethren: 'No persone shall stand watchinge at the Corners or ends of streetes, or at other mens Packhouses or at the house or place where anie Clothe merchant or draper ys lodged, nor seeinge anie suche in the Street shall rune or ffollowe after hym with Intent to Entyce or lead hym to his packhouse, vpon paine of fyve pounds ster.:'[96] It was forbidden to interrupt any bargains in progress. The ideal, then, was for merchants to remain with their goods in the packhouse and wait for customers to come to them, in an open and public market.

The account of Edward Misselden of the state of the market at Stade in 1611, gives a rather different picture, however:

There is scarsely any marchaunt soe slight or meane, but is sought & sued unto by our factors, each snatching & catching at them to prevent his fellowes; and

[91] Ibid., p. 27.
[92] Tawney, *Business*, p. 59; HMC Sackville II, pp. 97, 132; Cranfield's ledger, 1604–12, KHLC, U269/1/AB3.
[93] HMC Sackville II, pp. 140, 143.   [94] Ibid., pp. 140, 177.   [95] *Laws*, pp. 88–9.
[96] Ibid., p. 91.

that in such unseemely & unmarchantlike fashion, that I cannot compare them better, then to the watermen plying a fare at a common stayres, or the sale-men in Burchin Lane, labouring the utterance of a suite of Apparrell. And when they have by this base kinde of solliciting gotten the Marchaunt into the Packhowse; then, rather then to let him goe againe without buying somwhat they will not only goe too neare for price, but give 9.10. yea 12 monthes day of Payment, for that Commodity, which a good while before, cost reddy money here in England. By this meanes basely prostituting soe noble & necessary a commodity upon vile Termes to a Company of slight fellowes; who upon our servile demeanoure to them are become soe nice, that almost nothing will please them, and soe proude, that they think us much beholding to them, for but comming into our Packhowses, without offring one penny for any cloth shewed him.[97]

A subtly different impression is offered by William Lowther's instructions to his brother Christopher about the appropriate conduct for Hamburg show days, however:

…upon which dayes we are to waite dewly either in our packhowse or at our packhowse doore and after you have the language yow must alwayes be inviting your marchts. to come to yow, for they are somewhat prowde and doe exspecte it, and as yow will find, some have good judgement, some little or none, soe yow must goe seeke out there disposition to apply with them, which I found the onely way to draw them to my owne ends.[98]

Actions which for Misselden entailed servility were for Lowther critical to securing custom, but he suggests a much more circumspect strategy than Misselden allowed. It might be tempting to take advantage of an inexperienced merchant to rid oneself of some unvendible goods, but because sales were usually made on credit, this could be dangerous: 'to deale with weake men, is not good in these tymes'.[99] It was vital 'to know whom to sell & when to refuse mony'.[100] Lowther also advised about the need to 'observe the nature and the disposition of all men', revealing the very personal nature of this marketplace.

Company requirements to deploy freemen as agents overseas, and rules against marrying foreign-born women or acquiring land overseas, may suggest a parochial or indeed xenophobic outlook, hardly conducive to the flexible and adaptive conduct often seen as necessary to bridge cultural divides in international

---

[97] Misselden, 'Discourse', fols 10v–11r.
[98] Hainsworth (ed.), *Commercial Papers of Sir Christopher Lowther*, p. 203.
[99] Starkie–Warner, 7 July 1643, TNA, SP 46/84, fol. 336.
[100] Starkie–Warner, 2 Aug. 1642, TNA, SP 46/84, fol. 227.

trade.[101] Edward Misselden's hostile representations of the Company's customers, both the 'Netherlanders, who are naturally cunning & brought up in trade from their childhood', and 'blunt Dutches alsoe who were wont to be accompted the rudest & slightest people of Europe', can be found echoed in private merchant correspondence and the Company's public statements.[102] However, these were stereotypes which had accrued over years of close contact, meaning that it is problematic to frame relations between Merchant Adventurers in terms of 'cross-cultural trade'. By the late sixteenth century the Company had been established on the continent for many generations. Antwerp and London were part of a closely bound commercial system, which was also a channel for the communication of mercantile norms, as customs from the south, such as double-entry bookkeeping, entered into English usage thanks in part to the participation of Merchant Adventurers in the cosmopolitan Antwerp marketplace.[103] Although the fall of Antwerp scattered its merchant population, the Merchant Adventurers included, its members were followed to their new mart towns by many of their customers, who continued to deliver English cloth to much the same markets. Merchant Adventurers belonged to a larger mercantile world characterized by shared expectations about acceptable practices which rendered commerce predictable enough to enable exchange across various religious, national, and legal boundaries.[104] The sort of intimate alliances with locals necessary to penetrate new markets and supplant existing trading networks, which can be seen in the actions of English merchants in this period ranging from the Venetian Empire to Japan, were arguably unnecessary in the case of the Merchant Adventurers, at least in their core markets: 'straggling' beyond the mart towns, something discussed in Chapter 4, might demand different tactics.[105] Instead, Merchant Adventurers tended to concentrate on network building within the Company's ranks, although this did not preclude them from diversifying their social contacts once their reputation as a Merchant Adventurer was secured.

Company regulations confining overseas business to members were intended both to ensure its cohesiveness as an economic community capable of offering opportunities to new entrants, and to keep the cloth trade in English hands: the rationale behind the Company's existence was to that extent exclusionary.

---

[101] For a penetrating overview of the theme of cross-cultural trade, see Francesca Trivellato, 'Introduction: the historical and comparative study of cross-cultural trade', in Francesca Trivellato, Leor Haveli, and Cátia Atunes (eds), *Religion and Trade: Cross-Cultural Exchanges in World History, 1000–1900* (Oxford, 2014), pp. 1–23, and for examples, the essays within this collection.

[102] Misselden, 'Discourse', fol. 10v.

[103] Gelderblom, *Cities of Trade*.   [104] Trivellato, *Familiarity of Strangers*.

[105] Maria Fusaro, *Political Economies of Empire in the Early Modern Mediterranean: The Decline of Venice and the Rise of England, 1450–1700* (Cambridge, 2015), p. 211; Maria Fusaro, 'Cooperating mercantile networks in the early modern Mediterranean', *Economic History Review* 65 (2012), pp. 701–18; Alison Games, *The Web of Empire: English Cosmopolitans in an Age of Expansion 1560–1660* (Oxford, 2008), pp. 81–115.

Merchant Adventurers may have observed their customers with circumspection, even prejudice, but this was reflective of the insecurities of exchange in a credit-based economy rather than sign of a deep cultural divide. These were relationships of mutual dependency, but in which each party was aware that the other had their own interests at heart.

The mart towns bought Merchant Adventurers and their customers together in a predictable setting, allowing the latter to place their trust in the corporate affiliation of the former: this was a significant advantage of being a member of the Company. Because commerce was concentrated temporally and spatially, interactions between English merchants and their customers were dense, and this enabled the rapid circulation of information about goods, as well as the reputation of individual merchants. Brokers were deployed in this market, but do not seem to have occupied a central role, and much interaction between Merchant Adventurers and their customers was direct; the former were expected to master the local language during their training. By lowering the costs of information, the mart towns were thus able to generate a relatively large pool of buyers and sellers, but this was far from an anonymous marketplace.

Information about customers was commonly exchanged between members of the Company verbally and in correspondence. Matthew Ashton enquired after the reputation of certain local merchants on behalf of Godfrey Lawson, finding that the Company in general 'esteemes them to bee good', although one Anthony Schott required careful treatment: 'if they bee not to urgent with him he will pay them all, but at present he hath a greate many debts standing out, therefore his Creditors must have patience till he can get his debts in'.[106] Another customer, Ephraim Joseph, was 'in that repute with our merchants that most of them [deliver] him goods upon his obligation', though one Frederkin was reported 'a very tedious paymaster'.[107] Information could be acquired in other ways, however. A litmus test of a merchant's reputation was how readily he was able to sell bills of exchange on the burse, as well as whether or not his bill of obligation could be sold at discount. Richard Rawstorm justified selling to a merchant unknown to his principal Cranfield on the basis that 'he is so well thought of that Boudwins or any of the Netherlands will take his bill for 100 or two as soon as the best man's on the bourse, and likewise most of our folks will give him credit'.[108] Merchants thus responded to the signals given by their contemporaries when evaluating the creditworthiness of potential customers; credit was a 'public means of social communication', played out in the social arenas of the mart towns, and effectively crossing boundaries between Merchant Adventurers and their customers.[109]

---

[106] Ashton–Lawson, 16 Sept. 1681, Bodl. Lib., Eng. misc. c563, fol. 14r.
[107] Ashton–Lawson, 14 Feb. 1682, Bodl. Lib., Eng. misc. c563, fol. 22r; Ashton–Kitchingman, 17 July 1683, ibid. fol. 90r.
[108] HMC Sackville II, p. 33.   [109] Muldrew, *Economy of Obligation*, p. 2.

When in 1600 a new merchant, Hans Cornelius, arrived in Emden seeking to purchase large numbers of northern kerseys for Danzig, Cranfield initially warned Rawstorm off him, but in September Rawstorm explained that 'Now the man begins to be known, both amongst the townsmen and Netherlanders, his bills begin to pass.'[110] Cornelius rapidly became one of Rawstorm's chief customers.[111]

Information from surviving account books and journals suggests that Merchant Adventurers were able to sustain trade with a large number of customers in the mart towns: William Attwood sold cloth to no fewer than 144 merchants in 1651 alone, nearly all on credit. But all merchants relied on a smaller selection of merchants for a substantial proportion of their sales, and retaining these 'chief customers' was essential. Factors like George Lowe and Richard Rawstorm active at the start of the period largely dealt with customers who had followed the Company from Antwerp to its German mart towns, further binding their interests together as strangers reliant on the goodwill of their hosts. Names of Dutchmen such as Hans Bernberg, Francis and Jeremias Bowdwins, Johann Verpoorten, and Hans and Adam Boots commonly recur in their letters to their principals Quarles and Cranfield, who had a deep personal investment in this market: the role of their agents was to manage these personal relationships on their behalf, and cloth was probably marketed in their own names. Lowe was willing to go to some lengths to ensure that his chief customers were furnished with cloth in time for the major fairs at Nuremburg, Frankfurt, and Leipzig, and often sent his master patterns that they had requested to be made up in advance.[112] Occasionally Quarles arranged deals himself, communicating via his customers' London agents. In July 1594 he arranged a shipment of cloth to Emden to be consigned to a kinsman of Diricke Vermewrs, who would have first sight of them in time for the Frankfurt mart. This deal was an attempt to win Vermewrs' custom from his previous supplier, Thomas Bennett, and Lowe was instructed to 'promise him further frendship therin'.[113] Lowe was under the impression that he was to set a price on the goods on their arrival, but when it turned out that Quarles had agreed on this in advance, Lowe had to face the consequences. Some of his regular customers had got wind of the price paid by Vermewrs, and were 'very angry...that he beinge noe customer of yours should be furnished by yowe agaynst the marte, they notwithstandinge their ernest desire to be neglected, wherin they have iust cause to complayne'.[114] Lowe warned Quarles about 'theffect

[110] HMC Sackville II, p. 45.   [111] Ibid., pp. 44, 49.
[112] See for instance Lowe–Quarles, 13 Dec. 1593, TNA, SP 46/176, fol. 410v; 23 April 1594, TNA, SP 46/176, fol. 38v.
[113] Lowe–Quarles, 19 July 1594, TNA, SP 46/176, fol. 42r.
[114] Lowe–Quarles, 14 Aug. 1594, TNA, SP 46/176, fol. 48v.

of a bad president', but he was also clearly stung at having been marginalized by the deal.[115]

This example shows the dilemmas faced by a merchant seeking to expand his business whilst keeping hold of existing customers. In fact, as the decade went on, Lowe increasingly complained that 'men will not be carried away with fayre wordes or ould acquaintance to bad barganes but as Reason is soe they will buy where they fynde best cloth & best cheape'.[116] Lowe's labours to uphold his prices were straining customer relations, leading him to warn that 'I have scarce recovered the good willes of many of them since I forced them to pay 20li a cloth...but many of them beare yt yet in theyr mouthes & myndes & dayly cast yt in my teeth'.[117] Longstanding customers were 'by some others soe feasted to drawe them from me that I could scarce come to deale with any of them'.[118] Lowe complained of Vermewrs' efforts 'to bringe Mr Butler into a trade of cullord cloth for Emden where he is as a factor for such matters'.[119] In this competitive environment retaining custom was an uphill struggle: 'by good wordes I keepe them to my self, & soe have their advise at all tymes eyther to perswade or diswade yowe in makinge your provision of cloth, accordinge as they finde the likelyhoode of the tyme/ and if yowe consider the state of your trade yowe shall finde that yt standeth cheefly bothe here & at middlebr upon some few principall men, whome yt is easier to keepe in custome then to Recover beinge lost'.[120] This reliance on certain 'principall men' was even more the case in Quarles' trade to Middelburg, where his factor John Kendrick considered that his chief customer, Michael Verhagen, purchased between one third and a half of Quarles' cloth at one shipping, '& therby set price upon your whole remainder'.[121]

Although customers were willing to shift their attentions elsewhere, they could form durable alliances. When a parcel of kerseys which he had a claim on at Nuremburg was attached by an Italian merchant, Lowe relied on the help of a customer, Francis Bowdwins, to help him recover the goods.[122] Following the Imperial Mandate, Lowe planned to leave business in Bowdwins' hands, a course which Lionel Cranfield took by relying on the services of Gottfried Gortzen at Hamburg: in extraordinary circumstances, Merchant Adventurers were not averse to deploying foreign merchants as their agents.[123] New customers in the mart towns were seen as long-term investments; Richard Rawstorm sold an assortment of kerseys to Hans Cornelius 'more to keep his acquaintance in hope

[115] Lowe–Quarles, 25 July 1594, TNA, SP 46/176, fol. 44r.
[116] Lowe–Quarles, 20 Nov. 1595, TNA, SP 46/176, fol. 86v.
[117] Ibid.   [118] Lowe–Quarles, 6 Dec. 1595, TNA, SP 46/176, fol. 92r.
[119] Lowe–Quarles, 27 Dec. 1597, TNA, SP 46/176, fol. 262v.
[120] Lowe–Quarles, 17 Apr. 1594, TNA, SP 46/176, fol. 37r.
[121] Kendrick–Quarles, 5 Nov. 1597, TNA, SP 46/176, fol. 238r.
[122] Lowe–Quarles, 1 March 1597, TNA, SP 46/176, fol. 177v.
[123] Lowe–Quarles, 29 Nov. 1597, TNA, SP 46/176, fol. 254v.

of further dealings than otherwise'.[124] He agreed to supply John Tolner and company with a parcel of 400–500 northern kerseys 'because I would not have them seek another', being optimistic that 'they are likely to vent a great store and are greatly addicted to deal with me before any other, and being once entered into credit and trade with them may do much good thereby'.[125]

In contrast to these letters, those of Pearce Starkie to George Warner in the 1630s and 1640s, and of Matthew Ashton forty years later, give much less information about specific customers beyond general assurances that they had sold to 'good men'. This was a symptom of how several decades of settled residence in Hamburg had transformed the nature of the Company's German mart town, as well as relations between the membership there and in England. As Hamburg became home to a community of long-term resident Merchant Adventurers and cloth buyers, it seems that principals in England were more willing to entrust customer relations to their agents. When offering to purchase bills of sale on William Attwood's behalf in 1659, Edward Halford of Hamburg promised that 'I have reason to be able to guesse at mens abillities, by the longe experience I have had of their performance'.[126] By then English factors would have been particularly familiar with those chief merchant dynasties which had grown up alongside the Company in Germany, many of whom were by now pillars of the Hamburg community. When he reported news of the failure of several merchants including Paul Berenberg—a descendant of the Dutchman Hans Bernberg who was a customer of Lowe and Rawstorm at the turn of the century—Thomas Scott commented that 'these are sad things when these greate & Cheife of the Towne goe & yet here is such excess in pride...that you would say Hamburg is turnd upside downe', such that 'our Chief Cloth buyers not a bil of them will sell'.[127]

Long-term residents had the advantage of possessing intimate knowledge of customers whom they may have dealt with for many years, making it harder for newcomers to establish themselves without prior connections. Even so, in the mart towns, as in England, Merchant Adventurers were engaged in a competitive market, even if access to it was controlled. Indeed, the concentration of trade on the mart towns only intensified competition between brethren, and may have done as much to depress prices as to maintain them: as Matthew Ashton explained to one principal, 'here beeing soe many Packhouses in this place that unless I will give the same prices with my neighbours I must keepe your goods upon hands'.[128] Similarly, John Sanford advised a correspondent that their rivals 'will undersell us doe what wee Can unles wee sell to loss for they will admit of no Compettytors but will Rather lose one ey if it may Pick out two of annother Mens'.[129]

---

[124] HMC Sackville II, p. 29.   [125] Ibid., p. 19.
[126] Halford–Attwood, 27 Sept. 1659, TNA, C109/24.
[127] Scott–Attwood, 7 Dec. 1669, TNA, C109/20.
[128] Ashton–Lawson, 25 Oct. 1681, Bodl. Lib., Eng. misc. c563, fol. 16r–v.
[129] Sanford–John Barron, 20 Jan. 1673, SRO, DD\SF/7/2/1.

Prices for cloths can only be glimpsed intermittently, and it is even rarer to have information about their purchase price. Using the early-seventeenth-century account book of the Stade factor John Morley, Baumann calculated that both short and longcloth was sold for around 50 per cent more than its purchase price in London, for him evidence of monopolistic price fixing. With an estimated £7 of additional costs on each pack, the profit on each pack of shortcloth bought at an average of £60 and sold for £88 would thus amount to 31 per cent.[130] However, Morley recorded his sales in Flemish pounds rather than sterling, as Baumann assumed, and when this is taken into account (at an exchange rate of 25 Flemish shillings to the pound), sale price would be about 17 per cent above purchase price, and profit less than 6 per cent once other charges were taken into account.[131] These figures are in fact closer to those which can be pieced together from sales data in other account books.[132] Richard Rawstorm, for instance, sold his packs of shortcloth at prices ranging from £74 to £109 vls (£59 4s.–£87 4s. sterling), and at an average of £9 7s. vls a piece (£7 10s. sterling). Pearce Starkie sold his packcloths for an average £14 13s. 6d. vls (£8 8s. sterling, the par exchange now being 35s. to the pound).

It is rarer to have the prices that cloth was bought at. Rawstorm reported that the longcloths of William King that were sold for £12–12 10s. vls were bought in London for £8, giving a mark-up of 20 per cent minus other costs. Quarles' Reading/Kent cloths were bought for around £13 and sold for £15 8s. sterling on average, giving a figure of about 18 per cent. George Lowe also reported pack-cloth being sold at '29s the li accordinge to the prices of them at London'.[133] At the start of the period, then, it seems that the standard price to aim at was indeed 50 per cent above the cost 'first penny' in England, as Baumann conjectured, but in Flemish money rather than sterling. This suggests much more modest profit margins, although these may be underestimates given that the exchange frequently fell under the official par of 25s.; a drop of just 2s. would increase the mark-up on packcloth according to Baumann's estimate (including £7 costs per pack) from 6 per cent to about 16 per cent. This would more closely match the return of 15 per cent which Richard Sheppard anticipated on his trade to Stade, but this was still modest compared to the 30 per cent that he hoped to make from an adventure to the Barbary coast.[134] Statements from later in the century suggest that returns on the cloth trade were if anything falling. In 1672 John Sanford complained of 'having not this 2 years past made 6 PC of our Capitall besydes our loss at sea and bad

[130] Baumann, *Merchants Adventurers*, pp. 162–3.
[131] Ledger of John Morley for Randall Mannynge, 1601–14, SRO, DD/HY/Box 12 (Hylton of Ammerdown MS).
[132] See also figures for returns on trading capital quoted in Richard Grassby, 'The rate of profit in seventeenth-century England', *English Historical Review* 84, 333 (1969), pp. 721–51, which vary considerably, but which he estimated as falling from 10–15 per cent before 1650 to 6–12 per cent (p. 733).
[133] Lowe–Quarles, 25 July 1594, TNA, SP 46/176, fol. 44v.
[134] Sheppard–Thomas Wotton, 30 Jan. 1602, HMC Sackville II, p. 110.

debts', and later swore 'not to run so headlong into trade againe and trust such fellows at 6 or 8 PC Profit who keep us out of our mony 12 or 18 months: and it may be not pay at all'.[135] Profit was scarce enough to bear losses, and with insurance he and his partners would not have made 3 per cent on their capital. In 1684 Matthew Ashton advised that 'to sell Cloth for 10 or 12 PC profitt is much better profitt then any of our Company hath made of theire Cloth trade this late yeares occationed by the small vent wee have had & the dearness thereof in England'.[136]

The effect of these changes was to decrease the size of the merchant community as well as the volume of cloth exports, and limit opportunities for newcomers. Even in its early-seventeenth-century heyday the Company's trade did not quite live up to its ideal of an 'oeconomicall, and discreete partition' of trade between brethren (as John Wheeler put it). Nonetheless, the stint on the free licence in particular may have had some effect in allowing new entrants to have a protected share of the market, and although it was difficult to retain this or to grow business, a significant minority were able to do so. Friis, for instance, identified 35 per cent of the small-scale London cloth exporters in 1606 (those who exported fewer than 100 cloths) appearing as cloth exporters in later port books; the figure for those trading over 1,000 cloths was 61 per cent.[137] The decline in the volume of exports of shortcloth, a more accessible product to small-scale traders than expensive longcloth or volatile coloured cloth, therefore had a significant influence on the changing structure and size of the merchant community. Already in 1623 Maurice Wynn was complaining that the effect of the current depression was that 'the greate ones devoure the leatle, like pikes in a ponde the small Fry', and that even a stock of £600 was too little to make a profit.[138] A reduction in domestic opportunities for aspiring Merchant Adventurers in the mart towns like himself was one consequence. Of 125 male communicants in the Hamburg church in 1620 (excluding those resident in the Company house), only eleven appear as active London Merchant Adventurers in 1640, indicative of a high rate of attrition, only partially compensated for by the increasing numbers of long-term residents in the mart towns. By 1640 the size of the Merchant Adventurers' community in London at least had shrunk, although the old draperies could still sustain a core of large-scale traders exporting more than 1,000 notional short-cloths annually, representing a stock of at least £6,000, alongside a pool of smaller traders (see Table 2.7).

The shrinking size of old drapery exports from London after the Restoration entailed a smaller community of Merchant Adventurers trading in general on a smaller scale, although the inclusion of figures for the new draperies and imports

---

[135] Sanford–Henry Spurway, 23 Jan. 1672; 6 Dec. 1672, SRO, DD\SF/7/2/1.
[136] Ashton–Whichcote, 11 April 1684, Bodl. Lib., Eng. misc. c563, fol. 151v.
[137] Friis, *Alderman Cockayne's Project*, p. 78.
[138] Maurice Wynn–Sir John Wynn, 18 Oct. 1623, NLW 9059E/1154.

Table 2.7 Distribution of old drapery exports by denizens from London, 1640 (as notional shortcloths)

Cloths exported per merchant	Hamburg		Rotterdam		Flanders		Total	
	No. of merchants (% of total cohort)	Combined total (% of total)	No. of merchants (% of total cohort)	Combined total (% of total)	No. of merchants (% of total cohort)	Combined total (% of total)	No. of merchants (% of total cohort)	Combined total (% of total)
1,001+	8 (16%)	10,944 (53%)	6 (8%)	7,878 (32%)	1 (2%)	1,444 (17%)	19 (16%)	28,854 (54%)
601–1,000	5 (10%)	3,855 (19%)	10 (14%)	7,386 (30%)	1 (2%)	713 (8%)	13 (11%)	10,158 (19%)
201–600	13 (26%)	4,620 (22%)	19 (28%)	6,618 (27%)	12 (28%)	4,205 (50%)	29 (25%)	10,613 (20%)
1–200	23 (40%)	1,248 (6%)	36 (51%)	2,386 (10%)	29 (67%)	2,049 (24%)	57 (48%)	3,720 (7%)
Total no. of merchants	49	20,665 (422 per merchant)	71	24,269 (342 per merchant)	43	8,410 (196 per merchant)	118	53,345 (452 per merchant)

Note: These figures can be compared with the breakdowns given by Friis, *Alderman Cockayne's Project*, pp. 78, 93, 98–9, for 1606, 1614, 1618, and 1622, which show a similar distribution. However, this is problematized by the fact that Friis apparently did not adjust short/longcloths to their equivalent in notional shortcloths (which she did in the case of narrow cloths), meaning that the figures are not directly equivalent, and Friis underestimated the total numbers exported in terms of notional shortcloths.

Source: TNA, E190/43/3

would complicate this picture somewhat. Figures for Hamburg, which by then was the limit of the Company's effective monopoly, in 1677 indicate that old drapery exports were effectively in the hands of just eight merchants, each trading between 201 and 1,000 notional shortcloths (between them 4,930 notional shortcloths, or 87 per cent of total exports).[139] All of these were still active as old drapery exporters to Hamburg a decade later, compared to just one of twenty-two small-scale traders in 1677 who exported fewer than 200 notional shortcloths (this being John Banckes, whose business interests were particularly varied: see Chapter 4).[140] Possibilities to rise within the ranks of London's cloth exporters were becoming increasingly limited, therefore.

The politician William Coventry voiced a common criticism of the Company in 1662 when he wrote of how its 'Charter restraining others trading gives them opportunity to pursue their intrest by clogging the market at home, & keeping it hungry abroad', allowing them 'to buy cheape & sell deare', whereas the nation's interest was 'to sell deare here for the encouraging the manufacture, & upon light gaines abroad to gett vent'.[141] In fact, it would appear that the gains on cloth were lighter than Coventry suspected. However, this was partially compensated for by the proximity of the Company's markets, meaning that turnover could be faster than in longer-distance trades. Ashton accounted that the ability of 'the greatest of our traders' to sell to such 'Little profitt' depended upon their making 'a double return' on their investments.[142] Cloth, however, was not the only commodity Merchant Adventurers dealt in, and their commercial horizons extended beyond the regulated settings of the mart towns. Turnover was important to release capital for further cloth exports, but also for imports. Other goods could also be exported to the mart towns, whilst Merchant Adventurers were involved in trading to other markets, whether or not in cloth. The next section considers the nature, and limits, of their engagements in such enterprises.

Beyond Cloth

The competitive environment of the mart towns ensured that it was difficult to 'Rule the markett' even in specialist varieties like coloured cloth.[143] Throughout the period Merchant Adventurers were drawn to other goods, whether as imports or exports, in the hope that they might be able to briefly corner the market. Lionel

[139]   TNA, E190/67/2.
[140]   TNA, E190/141/2. These figures can be compared with those of 1678, as examined by Newman, which despite being a better year than 1677 show a dramatic fall in smaller exporters. 'Anglo-Hamburg trade', pp. 136–7, 321–2.
[141]   Coventry–Sir George Downing, 17 Jan. 1662, BL, Add. 22919, fol. 186r.
[142]   Ashton–Kitchingman, 30 Oct. 1683, Bodl. Lib., Eng. misc. c563, fol. 112v–113r.
[143]   Lowe–Quarles, 29 June 1596, TNA, SP 46/176, fol. 134v.

Cranfield engaged in various partnerships as he diversified away from cloth with such ends in mind. In 1602 he bought up the goods of a captured Portuguese carrack along with the merchant William Massam, and later joined with him in a venture to export iron ordnance to Hamburg and Amsterdam. From 1607 to 1609 he and his partners managed to effectively engross the market in logwood not just in England, but also in Hamburg and Amsterdam, by having their agents buy up available stocks as soon as they came on their market. These speculative projects were designed in London and were often undertaken under licence, making them dependent on connections with government financiers and contractors such as Cranfield's frequent collaborator Arthur Ingram.[144] Cranfield later turned these connections to good use by acquiring lucrative positions in crown finance, the beginnings of his political career.

Logwood was amongst those exotic goods which were beginning to make their way into European markets in ever greater quantities just as Cranfield was trading. At the start of the period, goods like sugar and pepper were more likely to travel from the continent to England than vice versa, although Daniel Cooper warned Cranfield off East Indian pepper, there being 'more uncertain venturing therein than in any commodity whatsoever'.[145] The unpredictability of the arrival of ships from the far east and the Americas made the prices of such goods volatile, as Cranfield eventually found with his logwood, which soon became a 'drug' that his factors struggled to dispatch. The growing reach of English shipping in the period, reflected in a dramatic expansion of extra-European imports, meant that England increasingly rivalled the Dutch as supplier of spices and sugar to markets including Hamburg, presenting an alternative to cloth, though a risky one. As well as investing in the East India Company, George Warner purchased its imports at Company auctions to sell in Germany and the Netherlands. However, throughout 1641 he was struggling to find a market for several barrels of indigo, the price of which had crashed following the capture of a prize-ship laden with the commodity.[146] Warner sent parcels from Hamburg and Amsterdam to Leghorn, where he was eventually able to arrange their sale at a loss; as his Amsterdam correspondent Henry Whitaker advised him, 'upon a fallinge market none will buye but from hand to mouth'.[147] Similarly, Matthew Ashton found in the 1680s that 'the sugar trade will neither pay Insurance nor provition'.[148]

With English imports of far eastern and American goods competing with those of Portugal and the Netherlands, merchants trading in such commodities needed to have their fingers on the pulse of international commerce, and it might be preferable to sell them on commission rather than risk a personal adventure.

---

[144] Tawney, *Business*, pp. 68–71.   [145] HMC Sackville II, pp. 42–3.
[146] Warner–Starkie, 18 Jan. 1641, TNA, SP 46/85/1, fol. 46r.
[147] Whitaker–Warner, 25 March 1641, TNA, SP 46/84, fol. 73.
[148] Ashton–Whichcote, 26 Sept. 1682, Bodl. Lib., Eng. misc. c563, fol. 45.

William Attwood took this course with pepper and indigo in 1651–2.[149] Thus although Hamburg emerged as an entrepôt for exotic goods in the second half of the seventeenth century, Merchant Adventurers did not dominate this branch of trade in the way they continued to do for textiles. The re-export trade was open to more cosmopolitan networks of merchants with correspondents in all the major European ports, who were able to monitor the different sources of supply and switch between markets more efficiently than a merchant like George Warner was able.[150]

If the range of possible exports available to Merchant Adventurers was growing in the seventeenth century, to an extent imports experienced a contraction. At the start of the period, Company members could supplement their cloth business by importing luxury textiles that had previously been exchanged at Antwerp, but increasingly they faced competition from direct imports from the Mediterranean, something exacerbated by the decline of south German fustian production and the disruption caused by the Thirty Years War.[151] Over the seventeenth century the Company's German trade became more eastwards orientated, with the Leipzig trade fair supplanting Frankfurt and Nuremburg, a shift reflected in the changing composition of Company imports at Hamburg. Silks, satins, velvets and fustians from Italy, which were so important to Merchant Adventurers that the Company permitted members to purchase goods at the Frankfurt mart, were being replaced by linen, whilst Hamburg was becoming increasingly integrated into trade with the Baltic.

As we saw in Chapter 1, the purchase of wares for import by their agents over-seas could be a source of some anxiety for merchants. More so than exports, it was necessary to rapidly and accurately communicate information about prices on both sides of the seas, the purchases of rival merchants, and the prospects of fresh goods arriving in the mart towns, in order to time purchases and sales, meaning success in this aspect of trade was heavily dependent on a well-functioning network.[152] To further complicate matters, few of the imported goods Merchant Adventurers traded in were exclusively available in either of their mart towns, which as a result could be in competition with each other. As was the case with re-exports, the import trade was much more open than that in cloth, meaning that Merchant Adventurers also had to compete with non-English merchants who were unencumbered by the prejudicial custom rates they faced in exporting cloth.

Nonetheless, at the start of the period Merchant Adventurers were well placed to profit from a consumer boom in England. George Lowe claimed that the

[149] Attwod's Hamburg Journal, 1650–2, TNA, C109/21.
[150] Newman, 'Anglo-Hamburg trade', pp. 186–8; Henry Roseveare (ed.), *Markets and Merchants of the Late Seventeenth Century: The Marescoe–David Letters 1668–1680*, Records of Social and Economic History New Series XII (Oxford, 1987).
[151] Newman, 'Anglo-Hamburg trade', pp. 9–10.
[152] See for instance HMC Sackville II, pp. 77–8.

import of 'vendible wares' was 'dayly used by the Richest men of the company'.[153] At the same time he considered imports to be 'soe hazardous as yt is & fallynge out most comonly rather to losse then proffite'.[154] He alleged that 'yonge men which are ample dealers in wares' tended to sell at London 'good cheape for Redy mony, whereby to make Returne by cloth in the next shippes', thus depressing prices.[155] This meant that even 'staple comodytyes' did 'never bringe out a savinge Reconninge beinge bought up by soe many men & soe disbursed there that yt is almost impossible they should make proffitt & to ingrosse any of them is a thinge which cannot be performed for they come hether into all mens handes'.[156] As Rawstorm wrote to Cranfield on the purchase of jean (Genoese) fustians in Stade, 'Our company buy them up as fast as they come to town, everyone seeking to prevent another'.[157] Occasionally, however, something might arrive on the market that was ripe for engrossing. In 1595, Lowe was offered a large consignment of steel hemp in the hands of his landlord Simon de Bocke.[158] Following a trial, Lowe struck a deal for 200 barrels to buy against cloth, and urged that his master keep the deal secret, both for his sake and for de Bocke's, who risked upsetting his own masters by the deal: 'I hope fewe wordes will prevayle in this matter to keepe yourself from disadvantage & mee from blame'.[159] Lowe reported that a rival 'lyeth hand in hand with myne host to buy this which I must have', but thanks to his caution 'neyther doth nor shall knowe that I have bought of till the tyme serve to shippe yt of when yt can be concealed noe longer'.[160] Lowe arranged to have the consignment shipped home 'in peacemeales, therby the quantyty may not be knowen'.[161] By the time the bales were ready to be shipped home, in summer 1596, some more had come into the hands of his rivals, which threatened to depress the price. However, Lowe was hopeful that the quantity in Quarles' hands would mean that he would be able to 'sett the markettes'.[162]

Opportunities to 'Rule the price' of a particular good like this one were probably rare, however, as rival merchants soon got wind of them.[163] Often Merchant Adventurers made ill-judged deals for goods in barter against cloth which they feared was becoming 'unvendible', before ruing their hastiness as these wares failed to sell in London. According to Matthew Ashton, much of the linen sent from Hamburg in the 1680s was acquired through barter. By that point, linen dominated exports from Germany to England, amounting to 89.9 per cent by

[153] Lowe–Quarles, 18 Nov. 1593, TNA, SP 46/176, fol. 12r.
[154] Lowe–Quarles, 7 Mar. 1594, TNA, SP 46/176, fol. 29r.
[155] Lowe–Quarles, 26 Nov. 1593, TNA, SP 46/176, fol. 16r.
[156] Lowe–Quarles, 28 Nov. 1594, TNA, SP 46/176, fol. 69r.   [157] HMC Sackville II, p. 127.
[158] Lowe–Quarles, 16 Oct. 1595, TNA, SP 46/176, fol. 81r.
[159] Lowe–Quarles, 19 Dec. 1595, TNA, SP 46/176, fol. 93r.
[160] Lowe–Quarles, 26 Feb. 1596, TNA, SP 46/176, fol. 123r.
[161] Lowe–Quarles, 9 Mar. 1596, TNA, SP 46/176, fol. 126v.
[162] Lowe–Quarles, 29 July 1596, TNA, SP 46/176, fol. 142v.
[163] Lowe–Quarles, 22 Oct. 1595, TNA, SP 46/176, fol. 168r. See Grassby, 'Rate of profit', p. 735.

value at the close of the seventeenth century, a sign of how Merchant Adventurers were implicated in the growing Atlantic trade, including the slave trade.[164] English merchants, Merchant Adventurers amongst them, had in fact been heavily involved in expanding the linen trade at the turn of the seventeenth century, by establishing direct links with suppliers in Saxony, Silesia, and elsewhere in competition with south German trading houses.[165] This trade entailed violation of the Company's regulations and often involved Merchant Adventurers working in close collaboration with interlopers, as will be discussed in Chapter 4. However, after the Thirty Years War it appears that this trade was increasingly in the hands of Hamburg merchants who purchased linen at the Leipzig and Breslau fairs to supply Merchant Adventurers in the mart town, although a minority of English merchants continued to have direct dealings.[166]

Trading in a cheap, mass-produced commodity like linen presented its own challenges. According to Ashton, 'the Princepall of our merchants that live in this place are men that have greate quantetyes of Westphalia Lynnons & when they will buy a large parcell of goods they will goe to those members of our Company that will take Lynnon against theire Cloth & there makes theire parcell which is the reason that Mr Beale & severall more of our Company vends soe great Parcells of goods' (probably a reference to Richard Beale, who had a direct connection to the colonial market in the form of a brother resident in Barbardos).[167] The effect was to squeeze out the smaller dealers such as himself. Despite this, Ashton was amongst those tempted by the huge volume of linen that was being exported from Hamburg as cloth sales flagged, writing that he planned to 'follow the Lynnen trade rather then runn hazard of beeing Cheated by our Cloth buyers'.[168] In 1684 he invested in several large consignments to be sent to London, despite knowing that 'barter against Lynnons is out frying into the fire, Lynnons soe deare heare & cheape in England'.[169] Ashton's losses in the linen trade, including an estimated loss of £800 on one pack that had cost £2,300, played a significant part in his eventual insolvency in 1685.[170]

As well as linen, Hamburg's growing ties with the Baltic gave Merchant Adventurers access to a new source of goods. In December 1682 Ashton was persuaded to invest £200 in flax to be purchased by Richard Bacon in Narva, and consigned to John Preston of Leeds for sale.[171] Coordinating business across these locations was challenging, however; the purchase of flax at Narva was delayed by

---

[164] Newman, 'Anglo-Hamburg trade', p. 189. For the use of linen to clothe slaves, see Robert S. DuPlessis, *The Material Atlantic: Clothing the New World, 1650–1800* (Cambridge, 2015), p. 131.

[165] Baumann, *Merchants Adventurers*.   [166] Newman, 'Anglo-Hamburg trade', pp. 222–6.

[167] Ashton–William Pickering, 20 Feb. 1683, Bodl. Lib., Eng. misc. c563, fol. 65r; Beale's will was made in Hamburg in 1702, TNA, PROB 11/468/28.

[168] Ashton–Whichcote, 29 Aug. 1684, Bodl. Lib., Eng. misc. c563, fol. 182r–v.

[169] Ashton–Joseph Kitchingman, 16 Sept. 1684, Bodl. Lib., Eng. misc. c563, fol. 186v.

[170] Ashton–Whichcote, 7 July 1685, Bodl. Lib., Eng. misc. c602, fol. 48r–v. See Chapter 3 for more details.

[171] Ashton–Preston, 26 Dec. 1682, Bodl. Lib., Eng. misc. c563, fol. 58r; 20 Feb. 1683, fol. 64v.

breakdowns in communication, which meant that the best prices were missed.[172] Despite this, Ashton hoped to enlarge his stock in the flax trade in 1684, and arranged for Preston to return his earnings in cloth, shipped in Preston's name.[173] Unfortunately, just as Ashton had expanded his investment, he was met by news of 'extraordinary bad' sales from Preston.[174] Although he considered withdrawing his commission, Ashton ultimately gave Bacon a last chance, 'for would not willingly change my Correspondency if can bee as well served by you as other men at your place'.[175] A lack of personal acquaintance in this trade made Ashton reliant on these correspondents, and he was further frustrated by being at a remove from the goods at either purchase or sale, leading him to complain that 'I finde not my goods soe vendible as other mens & where the fault is I am not able to Judge beeing I never see the goods'.[176]

The Baltic was also a potential alternative market for English cloths when their usual markets were failing, an option explored with little success by Lionel Cranfield. Another market which Merchant Adventurers continued to access was the Spanish Netherlands, which technically remained within the Company's monopoly, though it never hosted a formal residence after the Company's withdrawal from Antwerp in the 1580s. Following the outbreak of the Dutch Revolt, maritime trade to Antwerp was virtually frozen thanks to the rebels' blockade of the Scheldt. However, by the 1590s trade between the north and south was permitted on licence, and the market in the south continued to attract Merchant Adventurers, with a small population of resident English merchants based at Antwerp, many of whom were Catholic converts.[177] In 1612 it was alleged that these licences had been monopolized by a handful of Merchant Adventurers with their Dutch partners, who thereby 'have got & kept that trade ever since, & the Body of the Company & the publique have all this time lost a great & rich trade'.[178] This concession was reportedly so valuable that the merchants in question had allegedly conspired against the lowering of custom charges and the opening of trade from north to south.[179]

However, members of the Company had identified an illicit backdoor to the southern Netherlands soon after they were forced to depart Antwerp, in the form of the ports that stretched westwards of the Scheldt as far as Calais, from whence

---

[172] Ashton–Bacon, 6 July 1683, Bodl. Lib., Eng. misc. c563, fol. 87v.

[173] Ashton–Preston, 22 Apr. 1684, Bodl. Lib., Eng. misc. c563, fol. 155r.

[174] Ashton–Bacon, 29 Aug. 1684, Bodl. Lib., Eng. misc. c563, fol. 182r.

[175] Ashton–Bacon, 5 Sept. 1684, Bodl. Lib., Eng. misc. c563, fol. 183v.

[176] Ashton–Bacon, 30 Sept. 1684, Bodl. Lib., Eng. misc. c563, fol. 191r.

[177] Paul Arblaster, *Antwerp and the World: Richard Verstegan and the International Culture of the Catholic Reformation* (Leuven, 2004), pp. 97–9.

[178] Edward Misselden's observations on the imposition on English cloth in the Prince Cardinal's countries, *c.*1612, TNA, SP 14/71, fol. 244.

[179] Mr Skinner's remembrance touching licence imposed upon English cloth in the Spanish Netherlands, *c.*1632, TNA, SP 16/230, fol. 165.

cloth could be transported to Antwerp overland.[180] Following the Imperial Mandate of 1597, the Governor General of the Spanish Netherlands, Archduke Albert, had barred imports of English cloth from the north, and the Company granted a toleration of the Calais trade to compensate for this.[181] Quarles was amongst those Merchant Adventurers who took advantage of this opportunity, consigning goods to a Dutch factor.[182] He later attempted to obtain a passport that would allow him to transport cloth to Antwerp via Calais on his own account, and although it is unclear whether he succeeded in this, his former servant William Calley later did so, delivering cloth to his servant John Chandler and the Dutch factor John Baptista Roelans at Antwerp in large consignments.[183] This near captive market was evidently lucrative; Calley apparently shipped 3,300 coloured cloths from December 1604 to April 1607 valued at £45,000, largely destined for Antwerp, culminating in a deal to supply uniforms to the Spanish army.[184] George Lowe and John Kendrick were later numbered amongst those Merchant Adventurers with a presence in Antwerp.[185] Lionel Cranfield also attempted to capture a share of the trade in 1604, when an Antwerp merchant enquired about being supplied with no fewer than 6,500 cloths, although disagreements over who would bear the heavy charges imposed by the Archduke on English cloth meant that the venture fell short of expectations.[186] Thus, although according to Friis forty members of the Company were actively trading to Calais in 1606 and twenty-six to Dunkirk, alongside several interlopers, it appears likely that the real rewards of this route were being monopolized by a privileged few who had successfully established the local contacts necessary to trade to the south.[187] However, this situation seems to have changed by 1640, when the cloth trade to Dunkirk was distributed amongst a wide number of merchants, although details of how this trade was conducted are lacking.

Alternative markets for cloth were available in the event of those at the mart towns being depressed, but the integrated nature of the European textile market meant that it was unlikely that they would find better sale elsewhere.[188] As George Warner explained to his agents at Leghorn, trade was dead 'in all Parts where I have any Correspondence'.[189] With the market at Hamburg struggling in the 1630s, Warner hoped to open a new trade by sending goods direct from Hamburg

---

[180] 'Reasons exhibited by the marchantes Adventurers touching their trade and their petition therupon', c.1584, BL, Add. 48009, fol. 555.

[181] HMC Sackville I, pp. 33–4.

[182] Kendrick–Quarles, 19 Jan. 1600, TNA, SP 46/21, fol. 211r.

[183] See his ledger, 1600–6, WSA, 1178/325.

[184] Exemplification of chancery decree in suit of William Calley versus John Quarles, WSA, 1178/333.

[185] TNA, E101/29/23.   [186] HMC Sackville II, pp. 145–7, 154–8; Tawney, *Business*, p. 66.

[187] Friis, *Alderman Cockayne's Project*, p. 75.

[188] Charles Wilson, 'Cloth production and international competition in the seventeenth century', *Economic History Review* 13 (1960), pp. 209–21.

[189] Warner–John Fairfax and Thomas Barnsley, 22 Jan. 1641, TNA, SP 46/85/1, fol. 47r.

to Italy, including 'Corse lynnens of all sorts, Iron, Steele, Copper wire of all sorts, Shaven Latten, Tallow, Wax, dried Goat Skinnes and many sort of fresh fish dried and such like wherewith they are supplied in plentifull maner both out of denmarke and Sweden... yett money may bee Gott as well by them as finer Goods'.[190] However, Warner found it difficult to redirect his capital from his traditional trade, explaining to his Leghorn agent that 'though att this present my hand is soe deep in the Hamburg trade that I Cannot esyly pluck them out yett I will dayly lessen that and increase with you'.[191]

Like Cranfield and Ashton's designs in the Baltic, these efforts were an attempt to re-route trade into more profitable channels during a time of depression, and as such the mentality was defensive rather than expansive. As Warner explained, 'iff my trade Can bee found that way though butt small profitt bee therby I shall willingly Imbrace the same hopeing to torne the wheele Round with a Great deale more ease'.[192] In practice, though, entering a new market was laborious, requiring many 'trials' of different commodities, and relied on unfamiliar agents. William Attwood also dabbled in trade to Italy in the 1660s, sending lead to Livorno, but he relied on the assistance of familial contacts, namely his sons-in-law Thomas Stones and Josiah Child. Rather than undergo the labour of commencing in a new trade at his advanced years, it was easier for Attwood to direct his sons into the more lucrative Mediterranean markets, binding three of them to serve as apprentices with Levant Company members.[193]

To some extent, this picture supports Brenner's account of the Merchant Adventurers becoming left behind by the rise of long-distance imports and re-exports and the emergence of colonial trade.[194] However, whereas Brenner's picture suggests a Company complacently enjoying its monopoly and unprepared to venture into genuinely competitive markets, the above account suggests that there were other reasons why Merchant Adventurers might have been ill placed to capitalize on new opportunities. Expertise in the cloth trade was not acquired easily: mastering this complicated product and the markets where it was sold took many years, several of them often spent overseas. Building up and maintaining the relationships that would allow the effective communication of information from trusted agents was just as time consuming, and this could be a barrier against expanding trade into unfamiliar regions: Ashton turned down an offer from some Amsterdam merchants to consign him East Indian goods, writing that it was out of his 'way of trade'.[195] Similarly, although John Sanford sent goods to a range of

---

[190] Warner–Fairfax, 15 Feb. 1640, TNA, SP 46/85/1, fol. 17r.   [191] Ibid.

[192] Warner–Fairfax, 15 Feb. 1640, TNA, SP 46/85/1, fol. 17r.

[193] Grassby, *Kinship*, p. 282; C109/19/B7; Attwood–William Terkell, 29 Apr. 1664, TNA, C109/23 (1663–6 letterbook); Child's account for lead and pepper, 1663, TNA, C109/19. Details of Thomas Stones' estate can be found in TNA, C109/19.

[194] Brenner, *Merchants and Revolution*.

[195] Ashton–Simon and Pieter De Knudt, 26 Aug. 1684, Bodl. Lib., Eng. misc. c563, fol. 180v.

places such as Messina, he confessed to his agent Johnathan Barker that he was 'a stranger in your way of trade', and so entirely reliant on Barker's discretion in selecting returns.[196] Indeed, D.W. Jones has suggested that by the 1690s most of London's merchants exhibited a high degree of specialization, for many of the same reasons that stood in the way of Merchant Adventurers branching out beyond their core markets.[197] In this light, for the majority such ventures were likely to remain fairly modest, and the easier course was often to diversify out of trade entirely. This was typical of merchants in general: trade was viewed as a means to establish wealth, a 'stepping stone to a broader based fortune' preserved through lower-yielding but more secure investments including land, loans, state contracting, and later the stock market.[198] Lionel Cranfield was particularly adroit at exploiting his social and business connections in order to access valuable opportunities in government finance and office holding, surely the most consistently lucrative business venture throughout the period. Attempts to diversify away from regular trade carried distinctive risks, however, as Chapter 3 will discuss.

Another strategy open to Merchant Adventurers was to attempt 'backwards integration' by investing their commercial profits in cloth production, but this does not seem to have been widely practised. Company rules against members engaging in cloth making were one reason not to do so, but arguably in times of depression for the cloth trade, when a Merchant Adventurer might be looking to channel his stock in new directions, investing in cloth production made little sense. In the long term this opened the door for clothiers to begin exporting goods on their own accounts, something which was occurring in the north before the civil war. Ultimately English merchants faced no real barriers, cultural or legal, to them redirecting their fortunes into the domestic economy. With commerce such a risky and laborious business, and their markets overseas so prone to political disturbance, there was little incentive for successful Merchant Adventurers to do otherwise. Only perhaps with the creation of an Atlantic empire do we see significant numbers of English merchants establishing more lasting, multi-generational, and expansive commercial businesses, confident in the durability and stability of its political structures.[199]

Conclusion

Unquestionably there are examples of Merchant Adventurers throughout this period transcending the limits of their customary trade. In the early stage of commercial expansion, several members of the Company participated in the

---

[196] Sanford–Barker, 14 Feb. 1673, SRO, DD\SF/7/2/1.
[197] D. W. Jones, *War and Economy in the Age of William III and Marlborough* (Oxford, 1988), pp. 260–73.
[198] Zahedieh, *Capital and the Colonies*, p. 65.
[199] See for instance ibid.; Hancock, *Citizens of the World*; Haggerty, *'Merely for Money'?*

corporations established to access new markets, often at an executive level, and many continued to have multiple corporate affiliations.[200] Joint stock investment was an easy means to invest in these markets passively, although those trades which required active participation, such as to the Mediterranean, could be harder to penetrate, as the example of George Warner indicates. However, there continued to be a stratum of Merchant Adventurers whose businesses cut across several markets, whilst many merchants involved in new areas of enterprise began their careers in the Company.[201] There are also examples of Merchant Adventurers integrating their core businesses into more expansive trading networks, notably the case of John Banckes in the Restoration, which will be discussed in subsequent chapters. The re-export of far eastern and colonial goods into the Company's mart towns was one way to achieve this, but perhaps ultimately most significant was the sourcing of linen to supply the needs of plantation slavery, something which appears to have had a transformative effect on the Hamburg trade in the Restoration period. Matthew Ashton blamed the depressed state of the market in Hamburg on those large-scale linen traders who bartered their cloth for 'miserable prices which I imagine must bee onely to beate others out of trade, they makeing greate advantage by theire Commission trade that they can afford theire owne goods at a very easy price & keepe the trade with other men'.[202] This suggests that the gains of the linen trade were being engrossed by a minority of Merchant Adventurers, probably those with strong contacts in the Atlantic, making it all the harder for new entrants to establish themselves. Merchant Adventurers were not untouched by the structural changes to England's overseas trade or blind to new opportunities, then, but these opportunities were enjoyed unevenly. This only increased the diversity of experiences amongst the Company's membership, and the potential for division within its ranks.

We are now in a position to summarize the changes to the structure of the Merchant Adventurers' trade that have been identified in Chapters 1 and 2. Up to the 1620s, cloth exports were extensive enough to allow for a substantial number of London-based Merchant Adventurers to maintain either an apprentice or a salaried servant (often a former apprentice) in the mart towns, who was responsible for marketing cloth in their name. Such strong ties ensured that London-based Merchant Adventurers maintained a high degree of control over decision making, and allowed their corner of the market to be protected even in the event

---

[200] Edmond Smith, 'The global interests of London's commercial community, 1599–1625: investment in the East India Company', *Economic History Review*, early view.

[201] For examples from the early part of the period, see the Company governors discussed in Chapter 4, pp. 151–152 Brenner noted a cohort of leading royalist Merchant Adventurers in the 1640s who were involved in the Levant and East India companies. *Merchants and Revolution*, pp. 384–5. Sir Nicholas Crisp was a pioneering trader to Africa who began his career as a Merchant Adventurer: Eveline Cruickshanks, 'CRISP, Sir Nicholas (c.1598–1666), of Hammersmith, Mdx.', in B. D. Hening (ed.), *The History of Parliament: The House of Commons 1660–1690* (1983), online edition [https://www.historyofparliamentonline.org/volume/1660-1690/member/crisp-sir-nicholas-1598-1666].

[202] Ashton–Lawson, 20 Nov. 1683, Bodl. Lib., Eng. misc. c563, fol. 116v–117r.

of a change of servant. Merchant Adventurers could also look to gain an advantage by entering into direct relations with cloth producers. The evidence suggests that this was prominent in the coloured cloth trade, which tended to be dominated by a small number of merchants with close connections to clothiers (something which the greater degree of volatility in demand for coloured cloth necessitated), and to each other; information on the white cloth trade is less available, but these sorts of relationships probably played a part in structuring the market here too. Connections, then, were important, but the market was not entirely closed to newcomers. The Company stint probably helped to keep the lower end of the market in broadcloth relatively open, even if it did little to constrain the larger traders: distribution of the free licence ensured that a wide range of members had access to broadcloth at a competitive price. Because market dominance was rarely perpetuated beyond a Merchant Adventurer's own career, opportunities to expand business were continually opening for the well placed. Small-scale exporters had to be content in deploying agents overseas on commission, providing an additional source of income to some servants in the mart towns, but also enabling the existence of a class of independent factors which is clearly in evidence in Hamburg by 1620. Commissions were also available from dealing in goods other than cloth (imports and exports), although here Merchant Adventurers competed alongside foreign merchants and 'interlopers', who were less likely to deploy Company members as their agents. Also present in the mart towns were a number of Merchant Adventurers trading in partnership with English-based merchants and probably residing overseas for longer periods. In general, however, as in England the mart towns were home to a fluid population of Merchant Adventurers, with a high degree of turnover as many aspiring merchants pursued a normalized career path that saw service overseas as the prelude to a career as a cloth exporter in England.

The subsequent eighty years saw a number of major changes, most notably a decline in the continental market in undressed broadcloth, especially shortcloth, which was only partially compensated for by a growth in demand for coloured variants including both high-quality Spanish cloth and cheaper new draperies. The major consequence of this was a decline in the overall size of the Merchant Adventurer community in London and the mart towns, which shifted the balance in favour of certain outports where the volume of exports was stable (e.g. Hull) or rising (e.g. Exeter, in the case of the Netherlands). Limited opportunities at home resulted in a rise in the proportion of long-term residents in the mart towns, especially Hamburg, with commission agency displacing servitude (partnership was probably more of a constant over the period). Apprentices were now more likely to acquire experience overseas by 'standing in packhouse' with an experienced partner than being solely responsible for business.[203] This, in turn, limited

---

[203] For instance, Humphrey Morrice sent his apprentice Richard Morse to stand in packhouse with his partner in the northern trade, Solomon Slater, in 1682: TNA, E134/3Ja2/East35.

opportunities for newcomers hoping to launch their careers as Merchant Adventurers in the mart towns. The competition for commissions amongst factors probably opened up the market to merchants of the outports, though if Matthew Ashton is any guide then provincial merchants still favoured agents from their own region. Factors could also broaden their commissions away from cloth, thanks to a diversification of English exports which encompassed non-European re-exports, though as before, these were only partially handled by Merchant Adventurers. Even more significant to the Hamburg merchant community was a change in the structure of imports, with linen becoming the pre-eminent imported good, a high proportion of this probably destined for colonial markets. The growing volume of imports of this cheap product meant that finding a reliable market in England could be a challenge, as witnessed by Ashton's travails, and here connection to wider trading networks encompassing the Atlantic was an advantage. Meanwhile, as subsequent chapters will discuss in more length, there was significant disruption to the market for cloth in the Netherlands, linked to the Anglo-Dutch Wars and the failure of the Company to maintain its effective monopoly by the 1650s, leading to the collapse of the mart-trading system there.

Overall the market continued to be structured by a combination of weak and strong ties, then, but the pattern of these relationships had changed. Whereas the cloth export trade was previously dominated by strong ties of servitude, with Merchant Adventurers centring their network building on achieving rank within this community of merchants, an increasing proportion of cloth exports were managed through the weaker tie of commission agency, although partnership—a different sort of relationship to servitude—persisted and may even have become the dominant relationship for the largest-scale merchants. Partnership did not serve to reproduce the Company's commercial system effectively across generations, as was the case with servitude. Participation in networks that extended beyond the ranks of the Merchant Adventurers may have become a prerequisite for success in some of the more burgeoning areas of trade—linen imports and the re-export of non-European goods. Finally, the informational needs of the cloth trade had become more complicated as the product diversified, particularly with the rise of coloured, and in the case of new draperies, cheaper, varieties, for which the exigencies of fashion increased the volatility of demand. The way was open for direct links between English producers and foreign buyers, cutting out the merchant middleman entirely.

The domination of old drapery exports from London to Hamburg by the 1670s by a handful of Merchant Adventurers is perhaps a sign of the challenges that this new commercial context posed to newcomers. Even so, Merchant Adventurers continued to portray this as a competitive marketplace, fraught with rivalries, much as they had done eighty years previously. Unsurprisingly, this environment could lead to underhand tactics. Richard Rawstorm complained how 'some evil members of our Company, that have no cloths to sell, persuade the Hamburgers

that our ships will be here within this 14 days and bring better cheap cloth, which makes them refrain.'[204] John Sanford warned his agent John Ayshford of the arrival of a rival merchant in Hamburg, whom he expected to 'fight very low', though he was confident that Ayshford would 'aford to keep markett with him'.[205] Factors also competed amongst themselves for commission, and could attempt to undermine the reputations of their rivals. On one such occasion, Daniel Cooper warned Lionel Cranfield not to listen to those 'clawbacks who envy my welfare because I will not suffer them to make a fool of me'.[206] On another, Cranfield's Amsterdam agent Samuel Passfield complained 'that there was never man yet but had ill-willers who would not stick to belie him upon the least occasion whereby they might bring him into discredit'.[207] When his master's household was visited by plague, Lowe reported that he had been forced to move from the packhouse he was sharing, as his companions feared that their 'enemyes reportes (if I stayd in packhowse with them with your cloth which came out of an infected howse) might harme them in their sales'.[208] And Ashton complained to one of his principals that any reports he had recently received 'of my cheape selling' merely reflected 'the malice of some men', who were themselves guilty of that practice.[209]

The Company attempted to police such disputes, devoting a section of its 'Laws, Customes and Ordinances' to 'Injuries in woord or deed quarrellinge fightine misdemeanour excesse and playe', which expressly ordered against malicious speech and writing, in 'Ryme letter or libell to the slaunder Infamie or discredite of anie other persone of the said ffellowshippe'.[210] However, merchants were also conscious of the need to conform to standards of decorum in order to preserve their reputation, and this helped prevent simmering feuds from boiling over. The complex tangle of obligations and connections in which all merchants were enmeshed meant that they were aware of their mutual interdependence, so that even the failure of a rival could ultimately have harmful ramifications.[211] But this was a brittle harmony, continually tested in a time of major structural change in their trade, and rivalries within the Fellowship could come to the surface in times of stress. This chapter has identified some of the regular challenges which faced Merchant Adventurers, but other sources of danger abounded in the choppy waters of north-west Europe. How merchants responded to these risks, and what happened when they failed to do so effectively, is the subject of the next chapter.

---

[204] HMC Sackville II, pp. 119–20.   [205] Sanford–Ayshford, 11 July 1671, SRO, DD\SF/7/2/1.
[206] HMC Sackville II, p. 85.
[207] Ibid., pp. 218–19.   [208] Lowe–Quarles, 3 Nov. 1593, TNA, SP 46/176, fol. 9v.
[209] Ashton–Kitchingman, 10 June 1684, Bodl. Lib., Eng. misc. c563, fol. 166v.
[210] *Laws*, p. 169.   [211] Muldrew, *Economy*, p. 189.

3

Running on the Exchange

In July 1660, Cuthbert Jones of Hamburg wrote to William Attwood in London about the fate of one of their shared acquaintances, James Harrington, who had been resident in Hamburg for over thirty years:

> Mr James Harrington was Constrayned to summon his Creditors togeither, mak-
> ing knowne his deplorable Condition that he had not any estaite to Content
> them, if Mr Waynewrite paid him not, having lost a 1000li starl by Geo Gost, and
> I here [200?]li more by another, wheare upon, he was soly disinabled to Content
> them, having nothing remaininge save only a little houshould stuff, and uppon
> the faire hopes Mr Wainew giveth him that he shall not be any sufferer by him his
> Creditors have given him a monthes Liberty to follow his imployments, & to see
> what Performance dito wainewright will make, but I feare the Contrary, There are
> above 6 of our Company in with him by exchange; besides 2 for mony lent him
> for he was often nessesitated for monies, which occasioned him to borrow.[1]

James Harrington's insolvency bears many of the characteristic features of early modern mercantile failures. Like many other cases, Harrington's was but one episode in what threatened to be a chain reaction of bankruptcies. On such occasions, merchants would anxiously check to see whether they were implicated in the estate of the insolvent in question, which could prompt relief, and reflection on the caprices of a merchant's estate:

> Mr Strange saieth, that he is Cleare of him & I heere not anything to the
> Contrary; I reioyse for his deliverance which in my esteeme is noe small one, for
> he was very intimate with him, and did befriend him frequently in lending him
> large somes of mony. Oh how gallantly might he have lived had he not wanderd
> out of his way & left a hansome estaite behind him & now I feare he, & all his are
> totaly reuined his wife layeth it much to heart, as she hath reson, & his sonn
> Thomas is much diected, God in mercy preserve us all from such sad disastures.

We do not have to look far for potential causes of business failure for Merchant Adventurers in our period. The English cloth trade in the seventeenth century was subject to multiple short-term shocks, taking place in context of a growth in

---

[1] Jones–Attwood, 24 July 1660, TNA, C109/20.

Fellowship and Freedom: The Merchant Adventurers and the Restructuring of English Commerce, 1582–1700.
Thomas Leng, Oxford University Press (2020). © Thomas Leng. DOI: 10.1093/oso/9780198794479.001.0001

foreign textile production, and long-term changes in demand. Supple's classic account of the cloth trade demonstrated its proneness to crisis, with few barriers to entry meaning that production could expand rapidly in response to rising demand, before suffering sudden downturns if merchants withdrew their capital when the market slowed.[2] Clothiers, clothworkers, spinners, and weavers might have borne the brunt of such depressions, but Merchant Adventurers themselves had to contend with sudden collapses in sales overseas, coupled with the long-term decline in demand for broadcloth in their core markets. However, as Thomas Max Safley has argued in his analysis of business failures in sixteenth-century Augsburg, specific bankruptcies are rarely directly attributable to such structural changes in the economy; failure instead tended to come to those who 'suffered misfortune, miscalculated risk, or wasted capital.'[3] Without the statistical tools available to assess risk today, the merchant bankers he studied 'relied instead on personal reputation and insider information' when deciding where to invest and whom to trust, but reputations could rapidly collapse when rumours spread throughout close-knit business communities, leading to a sudden loss in confidence in a merchant's estate.[4] Merchants were thus very much a part of what Muldrew described as early modern England's 'economy of obligation', whereby credit acted as 'a sort of knowledge which could be communicated through chains of friends and business associates', acting as 'the basis of deciding who could then be added to structural chains of obligation.'[5] For overseas merchants, these chains were longer and more geographically dispersed than for other sectors of society, meaning that they had to communicate and sustain their credit within cosmopolitan mercantile communities, conforming to transnational standards of 'merchant-like' behaviour that dictated the appropriate decorum for commercial exchanges.[6]

Merchant Adventurers were certainly aware of the capricious nature of overseas trade: as Maurice Wynn put it, 'a man may bee now a ritch man & tomorrow a begger.'[7] Indeed, awareness of such risks was an important influence on businesses management.[8] But this was not particular to their trade, and indeed the contagious nature of business failure could remind Merchant Adventurers that they belonged to a larger, interdependent mercantile world. For instance, when reporting the loss of one ship laden with silver, George Warner observed that 'we shall all be verry sencible off here in London & I be=leeve that most partes where trade is used will Feele this as well as wee': confidence, to an extent, was

---

[2] Supple, *Commercial Crisis*.

[3] Thomas Max Safley, 'Business failure and civil scandal in early modern Europe', *Business History Review* 83 (2009), p. 40.

[4] Ibid., p. 41.   [5] Muldrew, *Economy of Obligation*, p. 152.

[6] Ibid., p. 188; Trivellato, *Familiarity of Strangers*.

[7] Maurice Wynn–Sir John Wynn, 9 Apr. 1623, NLW, 9058E/1083.

[8] Julian Hoppitt, *Risk and Failure in English Business 1700–1800* (Cambridge, 2002); Emily Kadens, 'Pre-modern credit networks and the limits of reputation', *Iowa Law Review* 100 (2015), p. 2450.

generalized within the mercantile community at large.[9] However, this chapter will argue that there were distinctive aspects of the culture of failure amongst members of the Merchant Adventurers, in terms of the causes of insolvency, the way that failures unfolded within this particular business community, and how its members responded to such episodes. As Saffley has noted, like other types of social scandal, bankruptcy 'focuses the community's attention on a certain form of behavior, allows that community to express its outrage, imposes at the very least an informal, social sanction, and, so, marks the behavior as deviant and unacceptable.'[10] By submitting to his creditors quietly and openly, James Harrington gave himself the opportunity of being judged a 'good bankrupt', which might allow him to salvage some of his damaged credit. Others, though, were less compliant. The reaction of the Company of Merchant Adventurers to these 'bad bankrupts', at both a corporate and an individual level, offers an opportunity to assess the codes of conduct that regulated membership of this merchant community.

An important theme of this chapter will be the distinctive geography of business failure within the community of Merchant Adventurers. As was generally the case amongst premodern merchants, business failures were a collective experience, involving the collapse of a credit network, and this made them particularly contagious. As confidence in a merchant's estate came into question, their ability to ride out such crises was largely dependent on the strength of their social ties: once a merchant's closest collaborators began to desert him, others would quickly follow. Because these ties also extended across space, failures within the ranks of the Merchant Adventurers are also revealing about the changing relationships between its different residences. One particularly important institution that allowed merchants to cooperate across space was the exchange, which was used both to transfer money across borders and to borrow or lend money for short periods, drawing on the reputation of a merchant's name. On one level, individual exchanges were nodes within a larger network that bound the merchant world together, but they were also distinctive social sites with their own particular rhythms, knowledge of which Merchant Adventurers had to master.[11] The burse therefore was a central site for the communication of mercantile reputation, where merchants were able to judge the creditworthiness of their peers even in their absence: on the exchange, the names of Merchant Adventurers divided by distance ran together. All merchants needed to maintain a careful balance between public and private, displaying their honesty and sufficiency, whilst defending the secrets of their business, especially in times of difficulty. The exchange could expose the inner state of their business to unwelcome scrutiny; once a merchant's name became too often heard on the exchange, his reputation

[9] Warner–John Fairfax & Co., Leghorn, 1 Oct. 1641, TNA, SP 46/85/1, fol. 74.
[10] Safley, 'Business failure', p. 44.
[11] For the social nature of the exchange, see Haggerty, 'Merely for Money'?, pp. 2–3.

was likely to come into question. More than any other part of business, therefore, the exchange demonstrates how a merchant's credit was dispersed, vested not so much in the physical site of the household as the strength of his relationships with others, and it was here that much of the drama of business failure played out.[12]

Desperate Times

Overseas trade in the premodern era carried inherent risks, as merchants had to contend with slow communications, transportation problems, and limited information about distant markets.[13] For Merchant Adventurers in our period, such challenges were compounded by a long-term decline in demand for broadcloth in their traditional markets. This challenging climate was a common theme in correspondence, from John Kendrick's complaint in 1597 that he was living in 'desperate times, wherin all thinges are uncertaine', to Matthew Ashton's warning in 1681 that 'our trade is at present soe bad that I know not scarce whoe to trust and those men that pay well will either buy goods cheape or else they will not have them'.[14] In the midst of the 1620s depression Maurice Wynn explained to his father 'that man that did but see our trade 20 yeares agon & looke upon the state of yt at this present would much pittie that the Staple of our land in vent in thes partes showlde bee soe much Impaired as reducted from 30 shipes a yeere for this place onelie to 6 & yet for thoes few noe vent nether'.[15] The diminishing volume of cloth exports to Germany and the United Provinces was paralleled by the decreasing size of the active membership of the Company. However, this was not necessarily the result of a growing number of insolvencies: Merchant Adventurers might simply respond to the bleak prospects of their trade by withdrawing from it for more profitable or secure ventures, as was the case with William Attwood in the late 1650s, when he was at the height of his mercantile success. Attwood's Hamburg factor Edward Halford was another contemplating leaving the cloth trade, 'times both at home and heare beinge very dangerous, and marketts very slowe and what is sould, giveinge litle encouragemt to goe on'.[16] Falling levels of recruitment also likely diminished the size of the community, with fewer numbers of apprentices being taken on by Merchant Adventurers, and a greater number of these choosing to pursue other opportunities than the cloth trade.

Unquestionably, adverse commercial conditions could create a climate in which business failure became more likely. In May 1597, George Lowe gave a vivid account of one such moment, when a disastrous combination of 'godes

---

[12] Ibid., pp. 98–9.   [13] Hoppitt, *Risk and Failure*, p. 69.
[14] Kendrick–Quarles, 19 Nov. 1597, TNA, SP 46/176, fol. 246r; Ashton–Lawson, 19 July 1681, Bodl. Lib., Eng. misc. c563, fol. 8r.
[15] Wynn–Sir John Wynn, 5 Dec. 1622, NLW, 9058E/1054.
[16] Halford–Attwood, 16 Aug. 1659, C109/24.

3 pryncipall plagues...vz famine, warre, & pestylence' threatened to hit the market for broadcloth at Stade:

> the tyme is here very daungerous & untowardly for our trade, god amend yt if yt be his holy wyll/ & grant better successe then the likelyhood of the yere doth prognosticate. else yt wyll goe hard with many men, which stand uppon theyr credytes & are not soe sufficyently grownded wherby they can of them selfes overcome theyr busynesse without usynge of credyte for never were eyther the strangers more Jealous of us then nowe they are, nor our company more suspy-cious of another then at this presente, every man fearyne one an other & none almost without suspicyon.[17]

Merchants were particularly vulnerable in such circumstances. With little fixed capital, it was theoretically easy for merchants to quickly withdraw their stock from trade and sit out any depressions, but because much commercial capital cir-culated in the form of credit, in moments of crisis this capital tended to become immobilized as debtors struggled to meet payments, causing chains of credit to grind to a halt. Those with sufficiently liquid capital reserves could ride such crises out, but those who had stretched their credit through 'over-trading', or locked their capital up in longer-term investments, struggled to meet their debts or ride them out through generating extended credit. This in turn could trigger a collapse in confidence about their ability to meet outstanding debts, which could lead to an onrush of anxious creditors calling in payment.[18]

Such credit crunches, however, generally seem to have been precipitated by unpredictable events which caught merchants off-guard, rather than by the decline in demand for broadcloth, which unfolded over a longer period and could thus be planned for, the sudden depression of the early 1620s notwithstanding. The threat of warfare was one factor which could bring markets rapidly to a stand, as when Matthew Ashton reported how his customers at Hamburg had become 'alarmd with the bad news of the Turks beeing come as farr as vienna with 200000 men'.[19] Natural disasters were even less predictable: as well as losing his five London properties in the great fire of 1666, William Attwood reported that the warehouses of all but one of the Company's traders had been consumed, as well as many others of his former customers.[20] Perhaps the greatest source of anxiety for overseas merchants was the threat of losses at sea, whether through accident or design. The Company's practice of shipping in convoy to an extent sheltered Merchant Adventurers from these risks, but still, when winter storms caused the

[17] Lowe–Quarles, 16–17 May 1597, TNA, SP 46/176, fol. 203v.
[18] Hoppitt, *Risk and Failure*, pp. 165–6. See also Grassby, 'Rate of profit'.
[19] Ashton–Robert Trippett, 10 July 1683, Bodl. Lib., Eng. misc. c563, fol. 88v.
[20] Attwood–Richard Twyford, 11 Sept. 1666, C109/23 (1663–6 letterbook).

grounding of two of the Company's Middelburg fleet and the loss of several others, George Lowe lamented the likely effect on merchants in such 'bad tymes which doe skarce yeld any man sufficient recompence for his labours, & adventures'.[21] Even though the Company's ships had been spared the worst fate, the prospect of the disaster causing bankruptcies amongst the merchants of Middelburg and Amsterdam presented a wider threat: 'yt behoveth a man that shall give credyte in those countreys to forsee whome he trusteth, & to be circumspecte therin'.[22]

These circumstances could bring to light those merchants whose estates were vulnerable because of some other reason, but businesses could fail at any time, and go on to precipitate a wider collapse in confidence. Without any reliable means to measure the overall number of Merchant Adventurers whose careers ended in insolvency, it is impossible to make an overall assessment of the causes of business failure. However, certain factors do recur in the surviving evidence which were distinctive to their trade. Several business failures appear to have been linked to attempts by Merchant Adventurers to diversify beyond their core cloth-exporting businesses. John Quarles, for instance, was subject to a statute of bankruptcy in 1608, but his problems dated back at least to 1596 due to the insolvency of his brother-in-law and debtor William Beecher. Beecher had contracted with the Treasurer at War Sir Thomas Sherley to supply uniforms and victuals to the queen's forces in France and the Low Countries, and Quarles' lending was a means to participate indirectly in this business, which was characterized by embezzlement on a massive scale.[23] Although Quarles acquired large landholdings from both Beecher and Sherley, for several years he was denied possession of his estate at Cotesbach whilst his affairs were under an Exchequer investigation. At the same time, Quarles entered into further risky ventures by lending large sums to the interloper Thomas Jackson, who was active in the trade to inland Germany. These ventures stretched his stock, and by the time he regained possession of Cotesbach, Quarles attempted to make up for lost time first by raising his tenant's rents and then enclosing the manor. In 1606 Cotesbach would be at the centre of the so-called Midlands Revolt, its enclosures thrown open by a reported 5,000 rioters.[24] Quarles subsequently faced investigation in Star Chamber, and such costly distractions were surely one cause of his bankruptcy: his servant George Lowe's warnings about becoming 'overmastered' by his trade had proved prescient.[25]

[21] Lowe–Quarles, 29 Dec. 1593/10 Jan. 1594, TNA, SP 46/176, fol. 19v.
[22] Lowe–Quarles, 6 Jan. 1594, TNA, SP 46/176, fol. 23r.
[23] Janet Pennington, 'Sherley , Sir Thomas (c.1542–1612)', ODNB.
[24] L. A. Parker, 'The agrarian revolution at Cotesbach, 1501–1612', Transactions of the Leicestershire Archaeological Assocation 24 (1948), pp. 57–71.
[25] Lowe–Quarles, 18 Dec.1594, TNA, SP 46/19, fol. 126v. For the link between 'overtrading' and failure, see Hoppitt, Risk and Failure, p. 166.

Lowe himself, however, also risked his estate on an equally speculative venture. After he departed Quarles' service, Lowe followed his contemporary Lionel Cranfield by venturing into several concessions in crown finance, before joining the financier Arthur Ingram in his Yorkshire alum farm project. Lowe spent about two years as resident manager of this ill-fated venture, which swallowed a substantial part of his fortune. From 1619 to 1625 he was reduced to living with his former partner John Kendrick in his London household whilst he strove to recover his debts. Quarles was in fact a fellow resident, employed by Kendrick as his bookkeeper on an annual allowance of £50. Kendrick's early death provided Lowe with an inheritance which allowed him to recover his estate somewhat, and in the 1630s he served as an MP and the Company's London deputy governor, a post reserved for members who had quit active trade: resuming a career in commerce was all but impossible for those whose credit had suffered such blemishes. Another of Quarles' former servants, William Calley, also attempted to tap into the market for military contracting, in his case by sealing a contract to supply coloured cloth to outfit the Spanish forces under the marquis of Spinola in the Spanish Netherlands in 1606.[26] However, meddling in the financial affairs of early modern states was risky; Calley was forced to spend a decade in Madrid lobbying to be paid, whilst his impatient creditors in England waited for his return.[27]

Although these are only a handful of cases, there is good reason to see these attempts to branch into new enterprises and thereby to exit the trade of Merchant Adventurer as particularly prone to failure. Such ventures frequently involved taking on new risks and trusting in partners outside of one's immediate social circle; in such circumstances, miscalculation was a greater danger than in routine trade. At the other end of the merchant life-cycle, failure could be associated with those seeking to establish themselves as an independent Merchant Adventurer in the first place. Matthew Ashton became insolvent in 1685, having over-extended himself in his efforts to set himself up as an independent merchant and householder. Another Hamburg commission agent who became insolvent at a point when he was establishing his household was William Attwood's sometime factor, Nathaniel Butler. Butler's failure was seen as just deserts for one who had overstepped his rightful place in the merchant social order: Attwood reported that 'men talke that his household stuff & plate was worth halfe the valew that hee owed how trew it is I know not, but it is good for younge people to begin lowe for it is a creditt to rise but a shame to fall espetially when it commeth in that way of furnishing their house above their estate or by their owne neglect'.[28] To these cases, we could add those examples cited in Chapter 1 of servants who, in their impatience to escape their state of household dependency, engaged in risky ventures.

---

[26] Articles of agreement between Calley and Gabriel Colford of Brussels, 1606, WSA, 1178/326.
[27] See his letterbook from Madrid, 1610–11, WSA, 1178/327.
[28] Attwood–Wolfenden, 20 June 1674, C109/19 (1671–83 letterbook).

Although these examples are too limited to draw any definitive conclusions, they do suggest that business failure for Merchant Adventurers was in some circumstances a product of the particular constraints of their trade, then.

Like many others, Matthew Ashton's insolvency played out largely on the merchant exchange, which he was increasingly drawn to use as his dealings escalated beyond his control. Ashton had invested heavily in linen, but when his London partner Jeremy Whichcott failed to make a timely dispatch of his packs, Ashton was left out of cash and was increasingly forced to charge Whichcott on the exchange in the hope that he would find sale before the bills became due. When these failed to materialize, Whichcott in turn charged the sums back on Ashton, so in short time there were large sums running between them.[29] Thus Ashton was drawn into the downward spiral of running on the exchange, racking up greater and greater losses as he did so. By the time he became insolvent in April 1685 his debts amounted to over £5,000 vls.[30] Ashton attributed his breaking to 'severall billes of Exchange' being 'charged on me for other mens Accounts & moneys happening at that time to bee very scarce, what with a bad trade & other bad newes from London of men absenting'.[31]

Nothing illustrates the centrality of the exchange to the lives and reputations of merchants so much as the fact that failure to show up on the exchange was generally accounted a signal to begin proceedings against suspected insolvents, a custom accepted in merchant circles throughout Europe.[32] All merchants were aware of the importance of discharging bills of exchange at the day of payment, 'elce a mans Credit is presently lost'.[33] The protest of a bill by the designated payor was a particular affront to the honour of the original drawer, a signal that they did not trust in their ability to be recompensed. Mercantile honour was particularly bound up in the exchange, and the relationships on which this traffic depended.[34]

The burse was always inhabited by a mixture of merchants seeking to buy or sell bills to meet their immediate needs, and speculators who profited from the 'spread' between the rate in London and overseas when they rechanged their money home.[35] As cloth exporters, Merchant Adventurers commonly had cause to order their factors to remit money home by buying bills, or to draw on their balances overseas by selling bills in London, but they often had call to raise funds in the mart towns too, meaning that there was always a lively market for the

---

[29] Ashton–Whichcott, 17 Oct. 1684, Bodl. Lib., Eng. misc. c563, fols. 196v–197r.
[30] Ashton–Whichcott, 7 July 1685 Bodl. Lib., Eng. misc. c602, fol. 48.
[31] Ashton–Edward Frank, 8 May 1685, Bodl. Lib., Eng. misc. c602, fol. 30v.
[32] Gelderblom, *Cities of Commerce*, p. 125.
[33] Ashton–John Rookes, 5 June 1683, Bodl. Lib., Eng. misc. c563, fol. 81r.
[34] John Smail, 'Credit, risk, and honor in eighteenth-century commerce', *Journal of British Studies* 44 (2005), pp. 439–65.
[35] For the workings of early modern exchanges, see Raymond de Roover, *Gresham on Foreign Exchange: An Essay on Early English Mercantilism with the Text of Sir Thomas Gresham's Memorandum for the Understanding of the Exchange* (London, 1949), pp. 94–172.

buying and selling of bills amongst Merchant Adventurers. Understanding the intricacies of the exchange was an essential skill. A factor overseas needing to raise money would hope for a high exchange which would allow him to sell bills at a reasonable rate, although in these conditions a shortage of deliverers might make it difficult to find a good bill. It was necessary to plan well ahead of large payments falling due and to consider whether money was likely to be 'scarce' at that point.[36] To an extent the movement of the exchange in the mart towns could be predicted, with the rhythms of commercial life dependent on the arrival of Company shipping and the continental trade fairs. Lowe wrote that 'I doubt by Reason of the longe stay from here of our fleete & the buyinge of corne mony wylbe sckarce & thexchange lowe here in Apryll when my principall occasyons fall out.'[37] On another occasion advised Quarles that 'Thexchange begyneth nowe to Rise & I hope wilbe shortly at 24s wherby the next payment to Verporten wilbe chardged here at a higher Rate, & I could wishe nowe that yowe had chardged me with some mony from there bycause it is there soe lowe as at 23s [4]d which would have brought out great proffytt.'[38] But the exchange could behave in unforeseen ways. In March 1596, Lowe reported that news of the delay of the Company's fleet from London had caused a rush to sell bills on the exchange resulting from many merchants who 'had a longe tyme shifted out theyr wantes in hope of the hasty cominge of the shippes hither nowe seeing mony growe skarce'. This in turn had caused it to plunge by 10s. in eight days; Lowe was amongst those 'driven to shift' by this fall.[39] However, those with the wherewithal could gain from such movements: Lowe advised that if the exchange in London fell to 24s., Quarles should charge him 'with as much mony as yowe can fynde at that rate, for by the tyme that may fall due I make full accompt thexchange wilbe here agayne at 24s'.

The exchange was also a means for factors to boost their earnings by charging commission for exchanging money. It was normal custom for factors to accept bills from their principals to the value of those of their goods they had in possession, but merchants might also agree to do so on the proviso that they were given direction from where to draw money for their reimbursement. Opportunities for factors in Hamburg to take on such commissions expanded in the seventeenth century, as Hamburg was increasingly used as a route to deliver money to the Baltic, where there was a persistent imbalance of trade with England. Both William Attwood and Matthew Ashton profited from this opportunity. However, these multi-polar exchange networks were vulnerable to breakdowns of communication or trust. For example, Ashton had been reimbursing himself for bills

---

[36] Lowe–Quarles, 18 Nov. 1593, TNA, SP 46/176, fol. 12v; Starkie–Warner, 4 Jan. 1642, TNA, SP 46/84, fol. 131.
[37] Lowe–Quarles, 8 Mar. 1597, TNA, SP 46/176, fol. 190r.
[38] Lowe–Quarles, 25 June 1595, TNA, SP 46/19, fol. 135r.
[39] Lowe–Quarles, 9 Mar. 1596, TNA, SP 46/176, fol. 127r.

charged by Richard Daniel of Riga on Jacob Veen of Amsterdam. However, he had cause to rethink the arrangement, having been approached 'by some to whom I have given out my bills upon Mr Veen', who reported that 'they doe not very well approove of him', leading him to ask Daniel to provide an alternative.[40]

On this occasion Daniel was able to satisfy him that Veen was a 'very substantial & honest man'.[41] It was important to have confidence in the designated payor of the bill, as a protested bill would lead to blemish on the drawer's credit, not to mention additional charges. Another of Ashton's arrangements involved accepting bills charged by John Cockin of Stockholm, and drawing on his agent at Hull, John Collings, for recompense. However, when Collings received a smaller than expected consignment of goods from Cockin, he refused to accept his bills, leading Ashton to complain about Collings' 'strange way of Correspondency', and to warn him to 'put noe such slurs on me, for this is the 1st parcell I have done for him & shall bee last unless a more punktuall answer'.[42] The episode led Ashton to withdraw from this business, finding 'much prejudice in my own imployment by haveing money to charge for other mens Account'.[43]

Having a bill protested was considered a particular affront, but it could also lead to questions being raised about the estate of the party who had refused to accept the bill. This was the case for William Attwood's correspondent Richard Twyford of Hamburg, who had been accepting bills for the Danzig merchant Samuel Travell. As Travell's charges began to spiral, Twyford complained that 'his bills come tumbling every post', having 'wound me in against my will or Consent' to accept large sums. In May 1666 Twyford refused to accept a bill drawing on Travell's account, but he feared that this action had led to some bad reports of his own credit in London. Twyford thus asked Attwood to 'vindicate my reputacion which is strucke at by some malitious spirits but I hope I am above their power'.[44] Although Attwood's enquiries uncovered no wrong doing, Twyford was still convinced 'that there was a most wicked intention of mischiefe intended against me by some at London'. Twyford's anxieties about his vulnerable credit led him to suspect a wider conspiracy: he had been informed that one George Marwood 'was a great stickler in it, & its well knowne that he was allwayes one of Fr Ts Creatures & much made use of here when they were at this place, But he is a young man & knowes not what measure may be returned him by others in the like kinde before he dyes, I pray if possible find out these unworthy actors that I may but knowe them'.[45]

---

[40] Ashton–Daniel, 21 Mar. 1684, Bodl. Lib., Eng. misc. c563, fol. 146r.
[41] Ashton–Daniel, 29 Apr. 1684, Bodl. Lib., Eng. misc. c563, fol. 157r.
[42] Ashton–Collings, 30 Sept. 1684, Bodl. Lib., Eng. misc. c563, fol. 190r.
[43] Ashton–Daniel, 16 Dec. 1684, Bodl. Lib., Eng. misc. c563, fol. 208r.
[44] Twyford–Attwood, 15 May 1666, TNA, C109/23.
[45] Twyford–Attwood, 12 June 1666, TNA, C109/23.

Merchants were so keen to uphold the honour of their bills because the exchange was such an effective communicator of their reputations throughout the larger mercantile community. A merchant whose bills were protested too often risked being shut out of exchange networks, and thereby being unable to raise money through selling bills. At moments when credit was scarce, this could be exacerbated, as when Ashton reported that 'the Exchangers timerous beeing lately brought on by a person that absented soe scruples the delivery of theire moneys unless to Persons very well knowen'.[46] But even a merchant with an unblemished record risked discredit if they were seen to be too urgent in selling bills. Merchants had to be careful as to how they used the exchange, therefore, particularly when dealing with the more specialized exchange dealers, who were seen as making easy prey of incautious takers of money. George Lowe reported that the losses of those 'younge men' who were 'soe ample debtors wherby here are comonly 4 takers in thexchange for 1 deliverer' could amount to 20 per cent. By contrast, he commended those who were content to use the proceeds of their sales to fund their returns rather than stretch their credits, and who were 'thereby continually Masters of their trade'.[47] Similarly, and ironically given his fate, Matthew Ashton explained to one of his principals hoping to charge money on him that 'it weakens a man to bee alwayes drawing beeing our Exchange traders are but few soe theire hands soon filled & therefore they see where greate Summes are charged on a man'.[48] Pearce Starkie, too, warned his principal George Warner that 'some of our Company here begin to wonder I should Charge you soe deeply by exchange backe againe', adding 'I write not any thinge out of an ill meaneinge or intent but shall be very willinge to doe you any service I can'.[49]

Factors like Ashton and Starkie always had the option of refusing to accept a bill, though at the risk of losing a commission, but servants had little option but to accept those bills charged on them by their masters. John Kendrick complained to his master Quarles about being 'put to such extremeties that in my time I have not beine put to the like', and feared that 'unrecoverable disgrace will ere longe befall me'.[50] Later he complained that 'I am much perplexed & knowe not almoste which waye to turne by sealf for healpe'.[51] It was thus some relief when Quarles promised not to overcharge him again, which Kendrick hoped would 'stoppe mens mouthes that talke heare'.[52] Another who George Lowe reported was 'driven to bad shyftes' by the flurry of bills charged on him was the servant of the London Merchant Adventurer Robert Burleigh.[53] Because he held Burleigh 'good', Lowe

---

[46] Ashton–Robert Trippett, 17 Oct. 1684, Bodl. Lib., Eng. misc. c563, fol. 196v.
[47] Lowe–Quarles, 18 Dec. 1594, TNA, SP 46/19, fol. 126v.
[48] Ashton–Richard Daniel, 10 Oct. 1684, Bodl. Lib., Eng. misc. c563, fol. 193v.
[49] Starkie–Warner, 9 Mar. 1642, TNA, SP 46/84, fol. 152r.
[50] Kendrick–Quarles, 1 Mar. 1600, TNA, SP 46/21, fol. 215r.
[51] Kendrick–Quarles, 12 Apr. 1600, TNA, SP 46/21, fol. 222r.
[52] Kendrick–Quarles, 19 Apr. 1600, TNA, SP 46/21, fol. 223r.
[53] Lowe–Quarles, 26 Feb. 1596, TNA, SP 46/176, fol. 122v.

asked that Quarles keep the news secret, 'for bad Reports are nowe easily Raysed uppon small occasions as yor self well knowe'. Despite this, soon Burleigh's bills of debt were being offered against cloth, a sure sign of a loss of confidence in his credit, although it took until March 1597 for Burleigh to finally become insolvent.[54] Fortunately by then Lowe had ensured that he was not amongst those of the Company who were 'deepely intressed with hym'.

The length of time between Burleigh first coming into question and his eventual failure is indicative of how reluctant creditors were to push a merchant into insolvency, which could lead to a domino effect of failures which could bring down even the blameless.[55] This caution might be amplified if an indebted merchant had influential allies: George Shipp of Hamburg promised to be 'very tender' with one debtor, 'being most unwilling to presse so forward as to expose him to that may be inconvenient to him, & displeasing to his Friends; whom I have in a very reverent esteem'.[56] Merchants could be highly reticent about causing one of their own network to fail, particularly if they were long-term collaborators. John Sanford and his partners' suspicions about the actions of their Hamburg agent Henry Spurway's 'chargeing & rechargeing' had built up over several years, and Sanford frequently complained that they were 'weary of his Correspondency and shall not be at rest till we are fre of him'.[57] In fact, Spurway's estate had allegedly failed once before, in the early 1650s.[58] Sanford continued to send him business, hoping that somehow his condition would improve, but allies could quickly desert a merchant once their estate came into doubt. Following Burleigh's failure, Lowe advised Quarles to avoid any dealings on the exchange with 'such as were Burleyghes companions…not that I knowe any ground occasyon but that I perceive their credyte here begyneth to wax scant on thexchaunge in generall'.[59] Similarly, Sanford and company were prompted to take action over Spurway following the breaking of another merchant, the aforementioned Nathaniel Butler, by attaching Spurway's goods, though Sanford swore this was done with 'all Imaginable privacy'.[60]

In order to reverse the tide of rumours that were generated by running on the exchange, merchants depended on their ability to rally enough allies to suppress such talk. Attwood asked his factor Thomas Scott to send word of the business of one such merchant to whom he had delivered money by exchange, though Scott was able to give a positive report of his ample trade in such markets as Barbados.[61] Similarly, Matthew Ashton consistently defended the credit of another Hamburg

[54] Lowe–Quarles, 29 Mar. 1597, TNA, SP 46/176, fol. 299v.
[55] Gelderblom, *Cities of Commerce*, p. 105.   [56] Shipp–Attwood, 31 Oct. 1663, C109/19.
[57] Sanford–Spurway, 23 June 1674, SRO, DD\SF/7/2/1; Sanford–Thomas Biggs, 17 Jan. 1673, ibid.
[58] See Chapter 7.
[59] Lowe–Quarles, 16–17 May 1597, TNA, SP 46/176, fol. 204r.
[60] Sanford–Spurway, 29 Jan. 1675, SRO, DD\SF/7/2/1.
[61] Attwood–Thomas Scott, 13 Jan. 1665, C109/23 (1663–6 letterbook); Scott–Attwood, 28 Jan. 1665, C109/19.

factor, Grenville Tregagle. When asked 'Whether there is any defect in GT', Ashton assured one principal that 'he hath as good a trade as ever he had & as dilligent in keepeing show doore & giveing his Correspondents satisfaction to all theire demaunds as he hath formerly beene', and his credit was 'very good & large'.[62] As Ashton was in a position to take up any commissions that Tregagle lost, this reluctance to undermine him is notable. When Richard Mann of Leeds requested that Ashton take custody of the cloth he had in Tregagle's hands, Ashton wrote that he was 'unwilling to disgrace any man by useing extreamityes especially one of Credit at this place as GT is'.[63] This loyalty was partly personal: Ashton and Tregagle eventually married two sisters in Hamburg, on the same day, and after his own insolvency Ashton entrusted much of his remaining business to his brother-in-law (though Ashton would soon have cause to repent this decision, as Tregagle himself failed shortly after).

In such circumstances, it was vital that merchants had reliable agents. John Quarles faced 'envous Reports of some men' in February 1596, which caused him to fear that his servant George Lowe's credit had been 'impayred'. In reply Lowe boasted that the opposite was the case:

rather by this slanderous Reports of some that peradventer wished you harme in my Judgement increased for I perceive that from thence generally men did wryte to theyr factors & servants for good lykynge of yowe, that I have bene offred more since then before in Regard of my abatement of credyte, ... for I doe thinke noe man in this place whatsoever could have more credyte then my self on thexchange if neede Required havinge since that slander bene privately spoken to by many [deliverers] of mony to take of them when I had occasion, which cortesye before they never offred[64]

Quarles faced greater danger at the end of the year, following his collaborator William Beecher's insolvency. Having had early warning of this coming, Lowe travelled to Nuremburg in order to take possession of some of Beecher's goods. However, Lowe explained that 'some after the newes of Bechers Breakynge & intelligence of my absence gave yt out that I was undone & soe Runne away, & withall some wryte from London doubtfully concerning yor self in Regard yowe were iudged to be soe deeply interessed with Mr Becher'.[65] Fortunately Lowe had made timely arrangements to satisfy his outstanding debts in Stade, 'soe my speedy Returne gave them more content & amased my enemyes which tyll then dyd not forbeare theyr secret mutterynge'. However, when the crown launched an

[62] Ashton–Alexander Horne, 1 Aug. 1682, Bodl. Lib., Eng. misc. c563, fol. 40r.
[63] Ashton–Mann, 4 Apr. 1682, Bodl. Lib., Eng. misc. c563, fol. 27v.
[64] Lowe–Quarles, 28 Feb. 1596, TNA, SP 46/176, fol. 124r.
[65] Lowe–Quarles, 1 Feb. 1597, TNA, SP 46/176, fol. 173r.

investigation into Beecher's dealings with Sir Thomas Sherley, this did not go unnoticed by Quarles' enemies. Lowe reported that 'there are many evyll tonges amongst our company & some that wyll rather speake evyll then good of yowe more for mallice then uppon any grownde'.[66] Lowe soon heard rumours that Quarles' counting house in London had been raided and sealed up by Exchequer officials, and although he initially attempted to suppress these reports by complaining to the Company deputy—'yt would not stande for yor credyte or myne that I should heare them & be sylent'—unfortunately they proved to be true.

It was possible to survive these trials. Lowe had met most of his master's outstanding debts, and so Quarles was able to weather this particular storm and continue trading for several years. However, it is likely he had sustained a lasting stain on his reputation, contributing to his eventual failure in 1608. Over time, doubts about a merchant's estate would accumulate, leaving his credit vulnerable to sudden crises, though this process could be slowed by awareness of the socially destructive impact of insolvencies. But a merchant's fortunes could collapse much more rapidly, and spectacularly. Such was the experience of Lionel Cranfield's father-in-law, Richard Sheppard.

The Failure of Richard Sheppard

We do not have a complete picture of what caused Richard Sheppard's business to fail. However, the surviving letters of Thomas Wotton in Amsterdam show this story unfolding from the point of view of his increasingly desperate servant, who struggled to uphold Sheppard's credit in the face of a growing tide of bills being charged on him from London. The reasons why Sheppard began to borrow so heavily on the exchange from summer 1601 onwards are unclear, but Wotton's letters to Sheppard, as well as several references in Cranfield's correspondence, vividly illustrate the downward spiral of declining credit that such behaviour prompted.

In 1600 Sheppard's Middelburg factor was Francis Greenowes, the servant of Paul Bowdler, whilst his Emden account was in the joint hands of his own servant Wotton, and his son John Sheppard. When John returned to London, Sheppard chose to give his business to the factor William Ellim rather than leave it with Wotton, who was sent to Amsterdam instead. There Wotton sold kerseys and bought various wares for Sheppard, as well as his son John and son-in-law Lionel Cranfield. However, from the outset Wotton struggled to raise credit in this unfamiliar town which lacked a formal Company residence, the local merchants being 'curious and my continuance here has been so small a time that they know

---

[66] Lowe–Quarles, 24 May 1597, TNA, SP 46/176, fol. 205v.

me not'.[67] He complained that 'My credit will not serve to take up any money for Stade, and here is no Englishman that I can hear of has any money to deliver for London', and claimed to be 'greatly troubled and abashed at these great sums charged upon me'.[68] Sheppard arranged for one local merchant—Gertson Metzu— to assist his servant by underwriting his bills of exchange, and for a time he was Wotton's 'best refuge'.[69] However, Wotton was soon forced to pursue other courses in order to raise money, borrowing from Thomas Armitage, another English merchant based in Amsterdam. He even warned Sheppard that his inability to raise money on the exchange would force him to use Cranfield's bills of sale to satisfy his master's debts.[70] Wotton's letters register the growing desperation of a servant struggling to keep up with his master's charges. In one letter he swore that he would 'rather live at home basely than to be thus perplexed, never enjoying rest of mind for care how to discharge so many sums, having here no such credit as your factors at Stade and Middelburg have', and claimed to be 'dismayed and perplexed in mind continually to make payment of your bills of exchange'.[71] Again Wotton reminded his master that his 'means' were 'so weak and credit amongst the Dutchmen nothing at all. For men will not deliver their money to young men who are strangers'.[72] Wotton's urgent need to raise money forced him to cut the prices of his cloth, and he complained to Sheppard that 'I shame to write how basely I have been forced upon necessity to sell away the northern kersies'.

It appears that Sheppard was facing an acute liquidity crisis at home which was forcing him to draw heavily on Wotton at Amsterdam. Cranfield meanwhile was becoming concerned about his father-in-law's fortunes, as well as the security of his assets in Wotton's hands. In September Wotton wrote to Sheppard about some 'variance betwixt Mr. Cranfield and you' which 'is noted by divers and misconstrued to the worst on your part, so that as good as to my face it has been rehearsed that by reason of your variances and your deep running on the exchange both for Middelburg and this place men make doubt of your estate'.[73] A few months earlier, Cranfield had written to Daniel Cooper at Middelburg asking for his opinion about Wotton's trade, and particularly the security of his bills of debt in Wotton's possession. Cooper suggested a ploy: 'to try whether he has employed them for Mr Sheppard's use or not you may give him order to send the bills to me in form of giving contentment for wares I have bought for you'.[74] When Cranfield eventually put this plan into execution, Wotton was thrown into a panic, writing to his master that the request to deliver his bills of debt to Cooper 'so greatly disquiets me that if I were not to discharge so many sums for you I would return into England'.[75] Cranfield's suspicions were soon confirmed: Wotton complained to Sheppard that 'if it had been for any other in the world

---

[67] HMC Sackville II, p. 233.   [68] Ibid., pp. 68, 71.   [69] Ibid., pp. 83–4.
[70] Ibid., p. 80.   [71] Ibid., pp. 83–4.   [72] Ibid., p. 94.   [73] Ibid., p. 86.
[74] Ibid., pp. 80–1.   [75] Ibid., pp. 233–4.

than for you, whom in duty I acknowledge to have absolute command over me as being your servant, I should show myself very simple and trustless to use one man's bills for another's account, neither would I have done so'.[76]

This acrimonious business prompted much damaging gossip in merchant circles. In September, Cooper reported that this 'grumbling about Mr Sheppard' had reached Middelburg, leading to a further decline in Wotton's credit at Amsterdam.[77] In the following month Cooper advised Cranfield that 'if you will be your own friend clear your hands of him, his master and your brother John, unless you know better grounds of their proceedings than the world generally expects'.[78] Sheppard in fact began to suspect that Wotton was disclosing his affairs to others including Cranfield, which Wotton hotly denied. Sheppard was soon facing further 'rumours raised against you at Stade'.[79] This talk cut off all of Wotton's remaining sources of credit. Metzu refused to underwrite any more of his bills of exchange—'it is noted and has been spoken to him of many, and he finds that it brings him great discredit'—and the few English merchants in Amsterdam would no longer deliver him money.[80] Even a modest bill of £70 charged on him in December was enough to throw Wotton into 'dismay', writing 'that I would to God I were quietly laid in grave rather than to sustain the shame and disgrace which I can see no means to avoid'.[81]

As well as Wotton, Sheppard was heavily charging his factors Ellim and Greenowes, with the same harmful impact on his reputation.[82] With his credit declining and the option of raising money on the exchange beginning to close, Sheppard turned to his son-in-law for support. Sheppard's letters to Cranfield combined protests of innocence—'For God's sake let me not sink under so small a burden, for I do not owe unto any Dutchman beyond the seas either at Stade or Middelburg for one penny'—with warnings that his failure would hurt Cranfield as well as himself—'some discredit besides will redound to you, all which although you little weigh in respect of your money I would wish you to consider it'.[83] Sheppard also emphasized their familial connections, protesting that 'To support your credit I would pawn all the plate I have'.[84] He was particularly outraged when Cranfield sent his servant Richard Perrott at night to demand payment of £260 balance of their accounts, which was 'not a little to my disgrace'. Sheppard was also angry that Cranfield had disclosed the business to his son John, and became increasingly obsessed about secrecy, writing to Cranfield 'I pray you do not lay my letters abroad where they may be read by others'.[85] In fact some of his letters had gone astray. Cooper reported that Greenowes had opened one of his to John Sheppard, then visiting Middelburg, calling on him to return home, 'for his credit began much to fail and he foresaw great troubles to come upon

---

[76] Ibid., p. 89.   [77] Ibid., p. 88.   [78] Ibid., pp. 91–2.   [79] Ibid., p. 100.
[80] Ibid., p. 235.   [81] Ibid., p. 105.   [82] Ibid., p. 105.   [83] Ibid., p. 113.
[84] Ibid., p. 97.   [85] Ibid., pp. 104–5, 106.

him and therefore desired to have him at home with him to comfort him. This is a bad sign.'[86]

Despite the acrimony between them, Cranfield did attempt to shore up his father-in-law's credit.[87] Cranfield eventually consented to purchase Sheppard's bills for £200 charged on Ellim and £110 on Greenowes, although on condition that Sheppard made over some cloths and kerseys at Middelburg as security—Sheppard complained to Wotton that this revealed his true character as 'a most lewd man, but keep all this to yourself'.[88] However, in January 1602 Ellim refused to accept the bill in question, along with several others, and thereafter Sheppard's estate quickly unravelled; now 'all will be nought', Cooper prophesied.[89] Cranfield's factor Rawstorm entered a protest about the bill before witnesses, and although he made every effort to keep it secret 'both for Mr Sheppard's and your credit', this was the beginning of the end for Sheppard.[90] Fortunately for Cranfield, Cooper (who was visiting Stade) had arranged for his friend William Hawkins to take up the cloths and kerseys at Middelburg that Sheppard had granted him for security, so keeping them out of the hands of Sheppard's creditors when their attachments began to come in.[91] Sheppard also conveyed his London properties to Cranfield, although perhaps this was a deal to keep his estate in the family's hands; certainly Sheppard asked Cranfield to keep this secret, as 'It might cause my creditors to think I make things away.'[92]

Then followed the painful and protracted experience of insolvency: imprisonment in the Counter and Queen's Bench, action in the City of London court, his goods attached by anxious creditors—'for God's sake let me have all done at an instant.'[93] Sheppard was particularly fearful that Cranfield would connive with his creditors to have him subjected to a formal statute of bankruptcy, writing that 'If you suffer that to be performed by underhand cunning I may wish myself unborn.'[94] Eventually, however, he secured his release when Cranfield and his other son-in-law became bound on his behalf, but his credit was so broken that he claimed to be unable to pay a shilling in the pound to his creditors, who continued to dog him with law suits for years to come.[95]

The reasons why Sheppard failed in this dramatic manner can only be speculated at. Sheppard himself attributed his declining credit to the failure of another Merchant Adventurer, Ferdinando Clutterbock, which had brought him undeserved attention. In November 1601 he wrote to Ellim at Stade:

not only those vile caterpillars the Netherlanders but also our own folk have got me upon the stage like most vile and wicked men, who so ever they be, for they may by their slanderous report take away a man's credit, which is so dear unto a

---

[86] Ibid., pp. 106–7.   [87] Ibid., p. 108.   [88] Ibid., p. 112.   [89] Ibid., p. 114.
[90] Ibid., pp. 109–10.   [91] Ibid., pp. 113–15.   [92] Ibid., p. 115.
[93] Ibid., pp. 115, 117.   [94] Ibid., p. 118.   [95] HMC Sackville I, p. 55.

merchant as nothing can be more precious, which when they have infringed they cannot make whole again much less restore him unto. So that if I knew the authors and might come where they are I would spend my life upon them, trusting that God will never let me live the day to be bankrupt.[96]

Perhaps the climate of suspicion that followed the breaking of a prominent merchant did play a part, but Sheppard must have made some serious mistakes in his business management to leave his credit so vulnerable. The part of his business for which we have most evidence—Wotton's trade in Amsterdam—certainly had significant flaws. Wotton continually complained about the market for kerseys in Amsterdam being glutted, and the fact that he was breaking Company rules by trading outside of the mart towns forced him to keep his dealings beyond the eyes of Company members who commonly had business in Amsterdam.[97] This did not help Wotton's efforts to establish his reputation amongst the local merchants.

But a few months of slack sales in Amsterdam were unlikely to have been the root cause of his failure. More serious perhaps was his apparent inability to manage his network of agents effectively, as shown by his deployment of the inexperienced Wotton in Amsterdam. Wotton resented Sheppard's use of a factor in Middelburg instead of himself, complaining that it would be better to have 'committed your business there to some servant of your own rather than turn and toss it into so many hands as I have known you to do'.[98] Sheppard's over-reliance on his son John, who lacked a merchant's training, was another flaw: when they were based at Emden together Wotton complained that he 'never knew one that will run so headstrongly upon all base wares'.[99] William Ellim's refusal to accept Sheppard's bill of exchange, the trigger for his ultimate breaking, is suggestive of an inability to retain the confidence of his agents; Francis Greenowes at Middelburg was also reportedly keen to 'clear his hands of Mr. Sheppard's business if he can'.[100] But the actual business decisions which forced Sheppard into his dire liquidity crisis in summer 1601 are essentially lost to us, although it is likely that, like others, Sheppard had overstretched himself by seeking to expand into new areas. On the cusp of his failure Sheppard wrote to Wotton that he now intended to 'draw myself away from all other trade' and concentrate on cloth, explaining that he was expecting some returns on an adventure to Barbary imminently.[101] With his 'stock being dispersed' in this manner, Sheppard was vulnerable to a sudden decline in his credit.[102] Once it became apparent to his contemporaries that he was not fully in control of his business, Sheppard was quickly stripped of the status of a capable and reputable Merchant Adventurer,

---

[96] HMC Sackville II, pp. 95–6.   [97] Ibid., pp. 67, 75.   [98] Ibid., pp. 62–3.
[99] Ibid., pp. 21–2.   [100] Ibid., p. 98.   [101] Ibid., p. 110.   [102] Ibid., p. 111.

the master of his trade. As Daniel Cooper put it, 'His proceedings are very monstrous childish and without discretion.'[103]

'A walking, talking, dead man': The Consequences of Failure

Given the interdependent nature of their business community, the first priority for Merchant Adventurers following the breaking of one of their fellows was to ensure that they were not caught up in the chain reaction of failures that often ensued. Following Richard Sheppard's breaking, Lionel Cranfield was faced with the innuendo of 'ill willers', although Daniel Cooper was confident that he was 'well armed against them', and agreed that the best strategy was to 'maintain your trade royally to spite your enemies, though you use more of your mother's money, some of your lame brother's and some of your brother Osborne's'. Thanks to such action the 'carpers' at Middelburg had had 'their mouths...stopped'.[104] When another of his associates, Thomas Wright, failed, Cooper reminded Cranfield that 'you may thank God and good friends that you are so clear of him, for by the reports of him here he is the wickedest man alive'.[105] Once again, the importance of having strong social ties is clear. The risks of failure in international trade could thus encourage Merchant Adventurers to deepen their connections with fellow members as a source of security, although paradoxically this could itself increase exposure to the risks that such affiliations carried with them.

The next task was for creditors to recover their debts, which could be a competitive process where, again, good connections were an advantage. Merchants who failed in England were covered by bankruptcy laws which provided a system for managing the claims of creditors, although many insolvents were never subject to formal bankruptcy commissions; temporary insolvencies could allow a merchant to continue in business in order to satisfy creditors, whilst even more permanent cases might be subject to informal composition amongst creditors.[106] Merchant Adventurers who failed overseas, or whose estates were dispersed across different legal boundaries, were out of the reach of English law, however, and legal fragmentation was a persistent problem for merchants seeking to recover their debts.[107] This was partially mitigated by the emergence of standardized practices with regard to commercial disputes, including accepted procedures for arbitration and identifying bankrupts, though the precise legal regimes varied. Merchant Adventurers in the mart towns were also under the jurisdiction of the Company's court, which had its own procedures for policing disputes between

---

[103] Ibid., pp. 101–2. For the connection of economic independence and manhood, see Shepard, 'Manhood, credit, and patriarchy'.
[104] HMC Sackville II, pp. 113–14.   [105] Ibid., p. 150.
[106] Hoppitt, *Risk and Failure*, pp. 29–30.   [107] Gelderblom, *Cities of Commerce*, chapter 5.

debtors and creditors. The Company had strict rules intended to marginalize bankrupts, who were barred from holding Company office along with any other 'Infamous persone', and publicly identified alongside those guilty of 'anie notirious offence or Cryme'.[108] This coupling of bankrupts with criminals was typical of contemporary attitudes, which tended to see bankruptcy as an economic sin that harmed innocent creditors, the implication being that it signalled an intent to defraud. However, in practice it was recognized that there were degrees of culpability, and that the inherent risks of trade could lead the innocent to fail. Accordingly the Company ruled that only those members who failed to demonstrate to the Court of Assistants that their failure 'proceedeth of pure necessitie or of suche accydents or occasions as no merchant or trader can well eschew' were to be 'dismissed of and from the libertyes of this ffellowshippe, Never to Enioye or recover the same again'.[109]

This still left the question of how to deal with the claims of creditors. Any Merchant Adventurer seeking to reclaim a debt from a fellow member in the mart town, bankrupt or otherwise, was to enter an attachment with the Company secretary or clerk with two sureties binding them to abide by the Company's decision. The debtor was required to do the same, but if they refused or absconded, they were to be apprehended until they were able to give security.[110] The goods of suspected bankrupts could also be attached, and their packhouse or chamber sealed up.[111] Once both parties had been examined alongside witnesses, the Court was to give sentence, appointing four members of the Company to apprise the value of the goods in question once a debt was proven. Creditors were then given a fifteen-day limit to come forward, and were paid 'each one in order accordinge to the Enteringe of his Attachement', although only following the satisfaction of debts owed to the Company, for victual or rent, or for the hire of servants.[112] This would appear to be a different system to contemporary bankruptcy laws which were intended to equalize the claims of creditors, and which were becoming increasingly common across Europe, though it is not entirely clear how these rules were actually applied. In cases where the Court failed to make judgement, the plaintiff could be granted licence to pursue the debts in other forums. Rather than providing a service that was unavailable elsewhere, these rules were intended to ensure that disputes were settled within Company ranks; the Company also barred members from suing each other in any foreign court for a civil cause.[113]

For English-based Merchant Adventurers, the successful pursuit of debts in the mart town was dependent on the timely and effective action of their agents. On one occasion John Quarles requested that George Lowe attach the goods of one Thomas Piggott of Stade, on behalf of William Turner. Unfortunately the request

---

[108] *Laws*, p. 7. [109] Ibid., p. 117. [110] Ibid., p. 156. [111] Ibid., p. 158.
[112] Ibid., pp. 160–2. [113] Ibid., p. 155.

arrived too late—Piggott's partner Hugh Griffin had pre-emptively ensured that his goods were made over to him by bills of sale.[114] Quarles had more success in claiming his debts from William Beecher when he failed in December 1596. Because of his close involvement with Beecher, Lowe was able to take possession of his goods at Nuremburg before any attachments came in. This, however, provoked an outcry amongst the remaining creditors, who believed that Beecher had fraudulently conveyed his goods to Quarles, leading to Lowe being summoned before the Company Court of Assistants. When Lowe refused to answer he was imprisoned for three days until another court was called, although on that occasion he was able to clear himself by taking an oath that none of the goods were Beecher's, Lowe arguing that 'his comissyon was to deliver over all thyngs to me for your use & to your use I Recieved them'.[115]

These examples show the importance of having access to inside information, something which certainly advantaged Company members over outsiders. According to Company rules, any strangers or unfree English people with a demand against a Company member could initiate proceedings in the court, as long as they could muster two sureties from the Company's ranks.[116] But an example from 1634 shows the challenge that outsiders faced when trying to recover debts in the mart towns. In that year, the Merchant Adventurers Carew Sanders and Robert Awbury had become bankrupt, leaving behind a long chain of over 250 creditors in England, who were reportedly owed £15,000 between them, but who found that much of Sanders and Awbury's estate was out of their reach overseas. Only because their number included some of the king's household servants were they able to secure the support of the Privy Council, who demanded that Sanders and Awbury's Delft factor, Thomas Clutterbuck, return to England to make satisfaction. Their Hamburg partner, William Gore, was also accused of refusing to give up their assets, whilst other members of the Company were alleged to have made fraudulent claims on their goods.[117]

Merchant Adventurers could thus exploit their information advantages in order to pre-empt the Company's own rules for arbitrating disputes, or turn them in their favour, although they could use this against the claims of other members as well as outsiders. When in 1624 Richard Lambe of London failed, several of his creditors ordered their Hamburg factors to attach his goods in the hands of his factor, Thomas Stubbing, according to Company rules. However, having been given six months' liberty to settle his affairs by the court, Stubbing presented a bill of sale to himself for all goods suspected to be Lambe's, and then refused to answer any questions on examination. Faced with this 'refracturines &

---

[114] Lowe–Quarles, c.1595, TNA, SP 46/176, fol. 84r.
[115] Lowe–Quarles, 25 Jan. 1597, TNA, SP 46/176, fol. 171r.   [116] *Laws*, p. 165.
[117] Privy Council to Company at Delft, 9 Apr. 1634, TNA, PC2, Vol. 43, fol. 302; Certificate, 12 May 1637, TNA, SP 16/356, f. 25; Privy Council to Company, 22 May 1637, TNA, SP 16/357, f. 27.

opposition', the Hamburg court preceded to imprison Stubbing, only for him to 'violently brake away out of the Officers custodie'; on his recapture, he was sent to the town prison. Following this, several of Stubbing's other principals in London then petitioned the crown, complaining that he had been the victim of a miscarriage of justice. In response, the Hamburg court under its deputy governor William Balden protested that the Company's independence was under threat by the action of those members who had appealed to an outside authority rather than follow Company rules:

> you will see that the Complaints of these men (being all brethren of our Companie) proceeded either out of much levitie and indiscretion in themselves, or ells out of a faint distrust of the weaknes of their cause; besides their grosse presumption, on so groundles an occasion, and by such sinister informations, to sollicite his sacred Majestie, before they had once made known their grievaunces, either unto our Fellowshippe at London, or ells from us: from whom they might have bene relieved, or have received at least satisfaction by being informed in the trueth & ground of our proceedings.[118]

The Company struggled to contain disputes between its members in the aftermath episodes of insolvency, when social relations in the community were at their most strained. In any case, the complexity and informality of relationships within merchant networks could lead to confusion about liability in the event of failure, let alone culpability: proving ownership of goods was not always straightforward. In order to establish the truth of these affairs, contemporaries analysed events leading up to a merchant's insolvency, and their subsequent behaviour.[119] Insolvency generated suspicion that merchants were defrauding their creditors, conveying goods in secret to their allies in order to avoid a just settlement. The verdicts on these 'bad bankrupts' were uniformly harsh. In January 1601 the Company imprisoned one William Higgs, whom Daniel Cooper (who had delivered him money by exchange) described as a 'cosening villain' whose 'vile course to cosen other men' would 'much disgrace' his kinsman, 'Old Higgs'.[120] Cooper reserved his harshest words for Thomas Wright, however: 'I think the like damned villain was never heard of, neither will he be heard of, for I think his throat will be cut and be thrown into some jakes. Some like end he will have for a more profaned, swearing, riotous, drunken villainous fool ever lived.'[121]

There was thus considerable moral pressure on insolvents to take what was seen as the least damaging course of action, in order to avoid such ostracism. One

---

[118] Hamburg Company to Conway, 1624, TNA, SP 14/170, fol. 127.
[119] Saffley, 'Business failure', p. 48.
[120] Cooper–Cranfield, 24 Jan. 1601, HMC Sackville II, p. 51.
[121] Cooper–Cranfield, 6 Nov. 1604, ibid., pp. 151–2.

merchant who succumbed to this was George Mitley of Hamburg, whose estate failed in 1676. This was a source of some embarrassment to William Attwood's factor Nathaniel Cambridge, who had delivered money for Attwood's account to Mitley, but he was relieved to report that the 'young Man is very Candid—& throwes himselfe & all he hath freely in to the Creditors hands—you shall fare as well as I'.[122] Unfortunately Mitley's creditors rejected the 20 per cent composition which was all that he was able to propose. Attwood's debt was still outstanding five years later, by which time Cambridge had written it off, Mitley's 'Condition growing worse & not better as I feare'.[123] Voluntary submission to one's creditors could draw a merchant into protracted negotiations from which they might never recover, and so it is unsurprising that many preferred the course of flight.[124] This was the choice made by Nathaniel Butler of Hamburg, who had been recommended to William Attwood by his father-in-law Melchior Wolfenden. Following his failure in 1674, Butler, together with his pregnant wife, sought refuge from his creditors in nearby Altona, then under Danish rule.[125] Attwood's reprimands about this young merchant overspending on his household, mentioned above, severely strained his relations with Wolfenden, which stretched back some forty years. Wolfenden, though, was ultimately keen to avoid losing such an influential friend, reassuring him that 'I hope this unhappy buisenes shall make any breach of frendship betweene us were we can serve you by day or night'.[126] For one thing, he hoped that Attwood would be able to intercede on Butler's behalf with his London creditors, although all that Attwood could do for Butler was advise him to submit to them willingly, and thus 'gett into some way againe whereby to gett a livelyhood in the world...although I feare not as a marchant'.[127] Credit lost in this way was scarcely recoverable.

Social ties could mitigate the effects of bankruptcies, as could an awareness of the contagious nature of failure, which acted as a constraint on creditors pursuing their debts. Overzealous actions were frowned on as anti-social, damaging the peace of the merchant community: Butler complained that his fall was 'occasioned by the violent, unlawfull, sudden prosecution of mee by my partners in England'.[128] It was too late for Butler by then to reverse his fate, but merchants could be reluctant about hounding an insolvent from the mart town, as recovering their debts would become very difficult. This was the case with the Hamburg factor John Snowden, who became insolvent in 1681, his case falling under Company arbitration. Matthew Ashton was charged with recovering the debts

[122] Cambridge–Attwood, 20 Oct. 1676, TNA, C109/19.
[123] Cambridge–Attwood, 24 January 1682, TNA, C109/19.
[124] For examples, see HMC Sackville II, p. 154; William Strange–Attwood, 15 Feb. 1659, TNA, C109/24.
[125] Wolfenden–Attwood, 11 June 1674, TNA, C109/23/1.
[126] Wolfenden–Attwood, 27 Oct. 1674, TNA, C109/19.
[127] Attwood–Butler, 7 Nov. 1674, TNA, C109/19 (1671–83 letterbook).
[128] Butler–Attwood, 23 June 1674, TNA, C109/23/1.

Snowden owed to several of his principals, including Joseph Kitchingman of Leeds, whom Ashton represented in negotiations with other creditors that took place before the Company deputy. These discussions culminated in a proposal for Snowden to pay his debts in instalments, although this was resisted by two other creditors, Henry Lee and [John] Staines.[129] With the settlement in the balance, Ashton advised Kitchingman to 'doe good against evill' and accept the deal, 'that then the complaints of other men will be quieted, whoe thinkes the proposition that Mr Snowden hath made to bee a very faire one considering his condition'. Ashton claimed to be under some pressure to bring the case to a friendly settlement or else 'put Mr Snowden upon some desperate designe'.[130] Members of the Company were keen to preserve peace within their ranks, but they were aware that it was generally in their interests to do so; as Ashton warned Kitchingman, 'here is severall of our Company which hath severall demands upon him from freinds in England which dare not adventure to bee urgent with him for feare they should force him away'.[131]

Eventually Ashton persuaded Kitchingman to accept the settlement, against the wishes of Lee and Staines, who wrote to Kitchingman alleging that Ashton had failed to defend his interests in the case. Ashton warned Kitchingman that to renege on the deal now would be frowned on in Hamburg:

> I must tell you that you will likewise impaire your Credit as much here as in any other place, it beeing the generall opinion that you tooke the wisest course to put your busyness into another person hands, soe if you will dishonour the Agreement I doe not looke upon it to bee merchant like...therefore if you will have Credit at this place act merchantlike & doe not beleive every Idle story wrotte you by Lee & Staines & if you have any respect for me let me know what they have written against me & I will vindicate myselfe & I doe feare but very much to theire disgrace for theire unhansome actions.[132]

In this context, then, 'merchantlike' standards entailed a willingness to compromise and accept some losses in favour of preserving concord, and Ashton continued to recommend 'faire meanes' over 'extremitye'.[133]

If this instance indicates how in the event of insolvencies merchant communities could favour peaceful settlements which allowed the course of business to continue with minimal disruption, it also shows how they could breed resentment and rivalry. There was clearly no love lost between Ashton and his rivals Lee and Staines, who were partners. The situation was complicated by the fact that

---

[129] Ashton–Kitchingman, 24 May 1681, Bodl. Lib., Eng. misc. c563, fol. 1v.
[130] Ashton–Kitchingman, 28 June 1681, Bodl. Lib., Eng. misc. c563, fol. 4r–v.
[131] Ashton–Kitchingman, 5 July 1681, Bodl. Lib., Eng. misc. c563, fols 5v–6r.
[132] Ashton–Kitchingman, 9 Aug. 1681, Bodl. Lib., Eng. misc. c563, fols 11r–12v.
[133] Ashton–Kitchingman, 25 Apr. 1682, Bodl. Lib., Eng. misc. c563, fol. 30v.

Lee was also indebted to Kitchingman. Ashton suggested that Lee's reluctance to allow the Snowden composition was due to his own pressing financial needs, and he advised Kitchingman to 'please endeavour to gett cleare of him as soone as you can for I doe not looke upon his Estate to bee soe large as Mr Staines doth suppose it to bee; for I can assure you that his bills of Exchange at this place are not very Currentt'.[134] Ashton was quite happy to undermine the reputation of a merchant whom he felt had crossed him: the desire for social peace in merchant communities only went so far.

Thanks to their gentle treatment, Snowden's creditors ensured that unlike Nathaniel Butler he did not take flight, but they still faced an uphill struggle when recovering their debts, and Ashton was still pursuing his principals' claims several years later. Perhaps because of this experience, Joseph Kitchingman proved to be rather less willing to show mercy when Ashton himself failed in April 1685. Initially Ashton had fled to Altona, conveying some of his principals' goods to his brother-in-law Grenville Tregagle, who then failed himself. Several months later Ashton secured a protection to visit Hamburg in order to settle with his creditors, including Kitchingman, who had come over in person. Ashton was coaxed to attend a meeting where they were to discuss how to recover the goods in Tregagle's hands, but on the way Ashton began to suspect that Kitchingman intended to 'have me before the Deputy & make me give Security for his debt & let him know where GT Estate was'.[135] Panicked by this, Ashton attempted to escape, only for Kitchingman to call out 'stopp theife', leading to Ashton's arrest. Eventually he was brought before the Company deputy, but even then the deputy was reluctant to begin formal bankruptcy proceedings, and instead left the two parties alone for a time 'to see if wee could make an end before it was publickly knowen'. Unfortunately Ashton's very public arrest had come to the attention of his other creditors, who, fearing that a deal would be struck in Kitchingman's favour, 'ordered the Deputy to continue me unlesse JK would release me'. Faced with the choice between consenting to Ashton's release without having reached a deal, or seeing him imprisoned, Kitchingman reluctantly agreed to the former. This gave Ashton the opportunity to play off his creditors against each other in the protracted negotiations that followed.

Another failed Merchant Adventurer at Hamburg who struggled in vain to restore his condition was Peter Clerke, whose creditors included George Warner. In order to lay a 'good foundatyon' for his recovery, Clerke proposed that Warner furnish him cloth to sell in his own name with profits going to Warner, so allowing Warner to bypass the Company's stint on exports of undressed cloth.[136] As a further incentive, Clerke offered to take on an apprentice on Warner's behalf, with

[134] Ashton–Kitchingman, 24 May 1681, Bodl. Lib., Eng. misc. c563, fol. 1v.
[135] Ashton–Edward Frank, 8 Sept. 1685, Bodl. Lib., Eng. misc. c602, fol. 52.
[136] Clerke–Warner, 27 Nov. 1638, TNA, SP 46/84, fol. 8.

Warner receiving the anticipated £200 premium without exceeding the Company limit on apprentices; this servant would then be able to supervise Clerke's dealings. Clerke promised to pay Warner 6s. 8d. for each cloth thus delivered, an arrangement which had been allowed in the case of another merchant who 'is com forward therby'. Clerke assured Warner that his intention was simply to satisfy his creditors—'for noe fysh longeth soe much after the water; as I doe to gyve every man that which is due to hime'—closing his letter 'yours not my owne till you have that which is yours'.[137] Warner, however, did not bite at this offer, and when he began to suspect that Clerke was simply delaying him with 'good words', he threatened legal action. This, Clerke claimed, had done him irreparable damage: 'for the very reports of this course of yours, hath soe filled all mens Letter[s]; that I am nothing, but a walking, talking, dead man'.[138]

Clerke was still present in Hamburg in the early 1650s, and the lingering presence of broken merchants like him in the mart towns served as a living reminder of the consequences of failure.[139] But they also show that, in practice, expelling bankrupts from the Company's ranks was difficult, given that creditors needed to keep them close in order to retain at least some prospect of making good their losses. This was probably more pronounced in the mart towns than in London, and particularly in the close-knit merchant community of Hamburg. Although he continued to reside in Altona, for instance, Matthew Ashton had three children baptized in the Company church at Hamburg in the decade after his insolvency, before the death of his brother Edward Frank led him to inherit the manor of Campsall. He followed his brother by renaming himself Matthew Frank, so ensuring that his children would not carry the stain of a broken name.

In certain cases, the stigma of bankruptcy could indeed persist into subsequent generations. Even before his failure, Richard Sheppard feared that bankruptcy would 'defame my children married', and 'leave such a perpetual shame unto my sons, whose credit I am'. He was particularly fearful for John, 'being now coming into the world, whose countenance I should be with my credit and reputation, and am so slandered that with my credit I shall not be able to do him any good'.[140] Sheppard's prophecies unfortunately proved to be accurate, giving his father cause to lament that 'There is no hope that ever he will be reclaimed and therefore I rest contented. It is a punishment that God hath laid upon me in my posterity'.[141] Thomas Wotton, too, seems to have suffered an enduring blemish to his credit by Sheppard's failing, demonstrating how intertwined the reputations of masters and servants were. Although his immediate movements after this event are not entirely clear, in 1605 Wotton was on the run from his own creditors, including

---

[137]   Clerke–Warner, 8 Mar. 1639, TNA, SP 46/84, fol. 17.
[138]   Clerke–Warner, 7 June 1639, TNA, SP 46/84, fol. 20.   [139]   See Chapter 7.
[140]   Sheppard–Cranfield, 5 Nov. 1601, HMC Sackville II, pp. 95–6.
[141]   Sheppard–Cranfield, 1610, HMC Sackville I, pp. 228–9.

Cranfield, who wrote to his correspondents as far afield as Venice for news of the whereabouts of that 'ungrateful villain Thomas Wotton', adding that 'never man did so much abuse the love of his friend as he has mine'.[142] But a year later Wotton was begging Cranfield to confer with his creditors on his behalf, swearing that his intention was 'to lead an honest life in the world to the joy of all my friends'.[143] Cranfield in fact seems to have been remarkably patient with his sometime fellow apprentice, offering Wotton employment in his household.

Richard Sheppard also found refuge in Cranfield's household, although it must have been hard to swallow this charity from his former servant. Eventually in 1611 Cranfield employed his father-in-law to manage his estate at Pishobury, Hertfordshire.[144] The ability of such loyalties to survive the catastrophe of mercantile failure is perhaps best illustrated by the fate of John Quarles after his bankruptcy in 1608. Sixteen years later, Quarles was to be found residing with his former servant John Kendrick, employed as his bookkeeper, counting out a fortune which, he must surely have wondered, could have been his.

Conclusion

Kendrick's continued loyalty to his former business associates, who were generously rewarded in his will, attests to the durability of such relationships. Indeed, the fear of failure may have served to increase the density of ties between Merchant Adventurers in general, as members were aware of the importance of strong allies to ride out moments of crises. The decision to abandon a failing associate could thus be painful, as seen in John Sanford's protest to his former mentor in Hamburg, Henry Spurway, that ''tis I that shall be the only sufferer here which I could not have expected from you who I intrusted with my all when I was first comeing into the world' (though admittedly this emotional pressure was also calculated to provoke Spurway into submitting quietly to him and his partners).[145] The importance of a merchant's social relations was never more apparent than in times of crisis: their credit was the product of the confidence that others had in their ability to command the support of others, as much as in their perceived honesty.

As well as straining individual relationships, the failure of Merchant Adventurers also exposed the rivalries that existed within its ranks, and insolvents were commonly suspected of favouring their allies. This was a strain on the Company's efforts to regulate trade in the interests of members. However, failure also sharpened an awareness of the ties that bound this merchant community together as a whole, which meant that bankruptcies threatened to spread

[142] Cranfield–Geoffrey Luther, 12 Nov. 1605, HMC Sackville II, pp. 161–2.
[143] Wotton–Cranfield, 3 Oct. 1606, HMC Sackville I, pp. 126, 132.
[144] HMC Sackville I, pp. 243–4.   [145] Sanford–Spurway, 29 Jan. 1675, SRO, DD\SF/7/2/1.

indiscriminately, following the channels of obligation that extended throughout the Company's ranks. Rivalry between Merchant Adventurers was balanced by a shared commitment to the peace of the community, which, however brittle it was, limited the damage that insolvencies could cause. Merchantlike behaviour did not just entail being a 'good bankrupt'; it also demanded merciful treatment of debtors, though this came more from a recognition that it was in the shared interests of the merchant community as a whole, than from any sense of Christian obligation: 'taking part in a credit network may have meant engaging in acts of generosity in order to maintain one's status in the network'.[146]

Such an aversion to conflict was far from exclusive to early modern merchants, for whom arbitration was usually preferred over costly and disruptive legal action. Even so, episodes of failure could remind Merchant Adventurers of their shared identity as members not just of the Company, but of a merchant community characterized by dense overlapping ties between members. The density of connections amongst members of the Company was itself a source of risk, increasing the likelihood that failures would be contagious. But these ties were more concentrated in the mart towns, particularly in Hamburg as the period progressed, and this changed the nature of those relations that bound this geographically disparate community together. Joseph Kitchingman's experiences of trying to pursue his debts in Hamburg are instructive: the merchants in the mart town appear to have closed ranks against him, forcing him to conform to their own attempts to maintain the peace of the community. This is a sign of how Hamburg in particular was becoming home to an increasingly autonomous community of merchants, as previous chapters have discussed. In light of this, identifying the collective interests of the Company's members became increasingly difficult, as we will see in Part Two. Company government, however, was always shaped in response to the pressure of a membership whose interests might be at variance. The final chapter in Part One will assess the nature of the Company's institutional structures, considering how Merchant Adventurers interacted with them in their routine business lives.

---

[146] Kadens, 'Pre-modern credit networks', p. 2451.

4

Disorderly Brethren?

Merchant Adventurers and the Company

In correspondence between Merchant Adventurers, the Company figures as a subject less often than we might expect, particularly compared to the attention given to the prosaic details of managing trade. This might give the impression that it was a distant presence in their business and social lives. Of course the three previous chapters have shown that corporate affiliation framed the activities of Merchant Adventurers in a much more fundamental sense that this suggests. Rules about admission shaped the career paths of members, whose business lives revolved around the regulated settings of the mart towns, which owed their existence to Company privileges. But even if we accept that Company membership defined the parameters within which Merchant Adventurers conducted their businesses, we might still question whether corporate affiliation meant anything more than partaking in this protected marketplace. Did membership of the Merchant Adventurers simply entail enjoying the fruits of their Company's monopoly, or was it capable of fostering a sense of corporate loyalty or belonging that shaped members' identities? What did it mean to be a Merchant Adventurer?

In its public statements, the Company presented a consistent image of an idealized Merchant Adventurer. Most famously, John Wheeler's 1601 *A Treatise of Commerce* presented members of the Company as honourable, skilful and self-disciplined merchants, renowned for their 'seemlie dealing, cariage, and orders'.[1] As well as emphasizing such qualities, Company discourse frequently highlighted members' status as good public servants, supporting the crown whilst upholding the honour of English cloth overseas. Loyalty to Company, crown, and commonwealth naturally coalesced. These texts were intended to convince often critical outsiders of the value of the Company's 'moral economy', but they also had another potential audience: the Fellowship itself. We rarely have information about the drafting of specific Company letters and petitions, and often it is unclear whether they originated in London or overseas, but as this was a corporation governed, as Wheeler put it, 'by common consente of all the Merchantes, free of the said Fellowshipp', it is likely that such texts would often have come under the scrutiny of members in some form.

---

[1] Wheeler, *Treatise of Commerce*, p. 60.

Fellowship and Freedom: The Merchant Adventurers and the Restructuring of English Commerce, 1582–1700.
Thomas Leng, Oxford University Press (2020). © Thomas Leng. DOI: 10.1093/oso/9780198794479.001.0001

In fact, Wheeler's *Treatise* was aimed at convincing members, as well as outsiders, of the advantages of obeying the Company's government. The fact that the book was published with these different audiences in mind explains why Wheeler included discussion of the tendency of members to transgress Company orders by 'straggling' beyond the mart towns to places like Nuremburg, evidence which undermined the orderly image emphasized elsewhere in the book. As we will see in Chapter 5, the *Treatise* emerged in a period of crisis within the Company that followed its expulsion from the Holy Roman Empire in 1597, but throughout its history the Company had to contend with governing members who were not always as disciplined as it liked to pretend. One of the chief intentions of the following chapter will be to consider the mechanisms which were used to enforce Company rules, and how the membership responded to them. But in a sense this is to erect a false separation between the Company, on the one hand, and its members, on the other. It is therefore necessary to consider how the Company functioned as a self-governing corporation, and how this system shaped the development of its regulatory system, a task which, given the non-survival of the Company's court books and the rather baroque nature of its governing structures, is no simple task.

Fortunately, the constitutional structure of the Company and its procedures for selecting officers are outlined in detail in the opening chapter of its 'Laws, Customes and Ordinances', or at least the surviving manuscript copy which was produced in 1612. This 201 folio text, copied from a version created in 1608 by John Wheeler in his capacity as Company secretary at Middelburg, is perhaps the single most important source for understanding the Company's constitution, but it is no more a straightforward representation of how this functioned in practice than Wheeler's *Treatise*. Individual Merchant Adventurers would not have possessed their own copies of such a bulky text, and the ways in which these elaborate regulations were propagated to an ever-changing membership is unknown. The surviving manuscript copy explains that its contents had been 'Collected And digested into order by John Wheeler', clearly from a pre-existent set of texts.[2] It was thus an accretion of rules and practices that had come into existence over time, raising questions about the extent to which many of them were actually in execution by that point. The 1612 copy was probably produced to coincide with the removal of the chief court of the Company from Middelburg to Hamburg, and at some point it came into the possession of the London residence.[3] Into the copy was entered a handful of orders made by the London court up to 1621, but then nothing further until a controversial agreement between the London and Hamburg courts made in 1688 (and discussed in Chapter 8), as well as a final few orders of the Hamburg court added in London as late as 1770 and copied from a

---

[2] *Laws*, p. 1. The manuscript is held at the British Library: BL, Add. 18,193.
[3] Friis, *Alderman Cockayne's Project*, pp. 87–8.

now lost volume described as 'William Alderseys booke', referring to the Company's Hamburg secretary in the late seventeenth/early eighteenth centuries.[4] A manuscript summary of the 'By-laws of the Hambro Company', made after the Glorious Revolution by a critic of the Company and abstracted from a book sent from Hamburg to the London court in 1675, included content not in Wheeler's manuscript.[5] The status of the latter, particularly after 1621, is therefore unclear. As we will see, there is evidence of uncertainty amongst the membership about Company's regulations, which suggests that in practice they were less stable than the 'Laws, Customes and Ordinances' might suggest.

In order to understand the extent to which members internalized the values expressed in Company discourse, we need to think beyond texts such as this one, and consider the settings in which they might have been encountered. Exposure to corporate values did not happen in a vacuum; membership was an intensely social experience, and it was during its collective gatherings that most members would have come face-to-face with the Company as an organization, a set of rules and practices, and a community of individuals. This aspect of Company membership can only be glimpsed fleetingly, but it is important to address how the Company functioned as a community as well as an organization, and how this shaped the authority that it was able to exercise over members. Alongside the Company's official courts was the informal court of members' opinions, and this arguably had as much say over which practices were considered legitimate as any formal regulations.

The very meaning of 'company' entailed a coming together: as Wheeler put it, the Merchant Adventurers originated when 'men of olde time linked and bounde them selues togither in Companie', a foundational act predating any formal grant of privilege or charter.[6] But the dispersed nature of the Company's membership meant that it was never possible for all members to meet as one, and the social occasions in the mart towns were of a different nature to those in London or the provincial bases. The dispersal of the Company's governing structures made it difficult in practice to govern such a membership. Nor was the Company simply comprised of a mass of members operating as individuals; the networks through which Merchant Adventurers managed their trade were similarly difficult to govern. As the head court of the Company was overseas, prosecuting offences committed there appears to have been easier than in London, but offenders might have been acting on orders given by their principals or masters at home. The dual-mart system complicated things further; at any one time, the Company was effectively being governed by several different disciplinary regimes.

---

[4] *Laws*, pp. 30–1.   [5] BL, Add. 28079, fol. 68r.
[6] Wheeler, *Treatise of Commerce*, p. 22. See Phil Withington, 'Company and sociability in early modern England', *Social History* 32 (2007), pp. 291–307.

The social worlds to which particular Merchant Adventurers belonged thus varied in space as well as time, something which, as we have seen, was often linked to the stage of their career. Whereas the established, London-based Merchant Adventurer was part of a large and cosmopolitan business community, in the mart towns the distinction between insiders and outsiders was sharper, and this surely would have had a corresponding effect on the degree to which members identified with the Company. But even when overseas, the lives of Merchant Adventurers commonly crossed over with non-Company members, both strangers and those English merchants castigated in Company discourse as 'interlopers'. These interactions also varied, however; the mart system functioned in different ways in Germany and the Netherlands, increasingly so over the period. At points in the period certain 'grey areas' opened where the Company's status was uncertain, and in such locales collaboration between Merchant Adventurers and interlopers became likely, but these frequently dynamic zones were rarely stable. In order to understand the meaning of being a Merchant Adventurer, then, we must understand both of these elements of variation in space and change over time.

The Nature of Participation

One statement of corporate values which all Merchant Adventurers would have been exposed to was the oath which freemen were to take on admission, the first of a series of oaths which the Company used to govern its membership. Here, the taker swore obedience to their sovereign as well as the governor and assistants of the Company, promising to keep to all its statutes and ordinances, 'having no singuler regarde to yor selfe in hurte and preiudize of the Commonweal of the sayd fellowship', and to keep its secrets.[7] The oath (at least in its 1582 form) added one specific proviso relating to commercial practice, that members were not to 'color or free any forreins goodes which is not free of this fellowship', so ensuring that the distinction between freemen and unfreemen was made manifest from the commencement of a member's freedom.

The act of taking this, and other oaths, was one way in which members were exposed to corporate values, and (as we will see) there is evidence that they were taken seriously, if not always observed according to the spirit intended.[8] Just as important as the content of the oaths themselves is the setting where they were taken. The freeman's oath was typically to be taken in the Company's General Court in the chief mart town, though members could be admitted at the equivalent court in London if this was 'for the good and servyce of the

---

[7] This text comes from a copy in possession of Lionel Cranfield, KHLC, U269/1/B82/1.
[8] Unfortunately, the text of these oaths is not included in *Laws*, so their content has to be surmised from other references.

ffellowshippe'.[9] For the majority, taking the freedom entailed making a commitment before not just the Company's governing officials, but the assembled members in the mart town, who were thereby repeatedly reminded of the commitments they had made themselves at the outset of their careers.

General Court meetings were but one of many social occasions which brought members in the mart towns into regular proximity with one another. Members worshipped communally, and although most members arranged their lodgings privately rather than in the Company house, provision was made for collective dining at the latter. The Company arranged special deliveries of English beer, at least to its residences in the Low Countries, the members having 'found the English beer more wholesome and better agreeing with their bodies than that which the Netherlands can afford'.[10] Such occasions would have offered informal opportunities for the dissemination of corporate values alongside the routine sociability of Englishmen drawn together in a foreign land. But it was at the meetings of the Company's courts that members encountered the Company's government most directly, and were offered an opportunity for participation. These meetings were the living embodiment of Company government in practice.

As its charter made clear, the Fellowship of Merchant Adventurers was entrusted with the government of members overseas. As soon as they arrived in the mart town, freemen were required to register their presence with the secretary or a sworn clerk, in order to acquire up-to-date information about the rates which the Company set for services such as crainage, as well as whichever tolls they were currently subject to.[11] Once registered as present, the member in question was then bound to attend any meetings of the Fellowship, on pain of a fine.[12] At such meetings, all free brothers were permitted to speak on any matter for a maximum of three times. Interruptions were prohibited, and speeches were to be directed to the governor or deputy rather than other members. Members were to absent themselves when they were the subject of discussion, or the brother, partner, factor or servant of such a person. Apprentices attended but sat separately, and were deprived of a voice or hand in court 'except they bee their maisters factors and Atturneyes'. However, an apprentice could 'deliuer his mynde' if he came forward with 'dew Reuerence'.[13]

The General Court meetings were thus an inclusive forum where all members were able to participate on some level in the Company's decision-making process. Presiding over the membership were the Company's officers, who were personally entrusted with the 'Authorities (so ffarre as the Priuileges and orders will permitte) in all thinges lawfully to Governe and rule the foresaid fellowshippe, according to the Lawes, Statutes Actes and Ordinances of the same'.[14] These were the governor or his deputy and twenty-four assistants, who met as the Court of

---

[9] *Laws*, p. 35.   [10] HMC Salisbury 21, p. 43.   [11] *Laws*, p. 25.
[12] Ibid., pp. 15–16, 21.   [13] Ibid., p. 20.   [14] Ibid., p. 6.

Assistants, which seems to have handled disciplinary cases. Although the 'Lawes, Customes and Ordinances' are vague on the precise relationship between the two courts, these officers were formally entrusted with significant power over the membership. However, they were accountable, being 'Chosen martly or as occasion shall serue from tyme to tyme by the brethren of the said ffellowshippe or by the most parte of them'.[15] They were also bound by their own oaths, with the governor and deputy committing to uphold Company privileges, and the assistants swearing to act indifferently and maintain 'the Comon weale of the ffellowshippe of merchants Adventurers'.[16] The governor or deputy was not to make any law without the consent of the majority of his assistants, and together they were not to enter into any business 'in the name of the ffellowshippe, without the lykinge and agreement of the same, vpon pain to bee deemed and holden insufficient and vnworthy of the place of Government in the said ffellowshippe'.[17]

These rules suggest that the principle of consent was of real importance, and it seems likely that new orders were drafted by the Court of Assistants before being subject to discussion and potentially vote in General Court. However, this is complicated by the fact that the Fellowship was always dispersed, and so it was never possible to summon them to any one meeting. In contrast to most other English trading companies whose government (in the form of either a governor and court or a board of directors) tended to be based in London, the head court of the Company met overseas, largely a consequence of its historical origins in privileges secured from foreign rulers, but also because it was in the mart towns that Company regulations were concentrated. The Merchant Adventurers also had a London court but, as the deputy governor at London Robert Edwards explained in 1641, its major functions were to organize Company shipping and to give 'Accompt to the State', although this latter responsibility gave it particular importance, and the London brethren were commonly consulted on matters concerning the fate of the Company in general.[18] As the Company did not have its own residence in London, it had to find other premises to conduct meetings, and in the fifteenth century, meetings took place in Mercers' Hall, which also held some of the Company's records.[19] The Company continued to pay rent to the Mercers' Company up to 1666 (when the hall was destroyed in the fire), and the chapel of Mercers' Hall hosted a meeting of the court of assistants as late as 1619, but already by then the same court was also meeting in Founders' Hall in Lothbury, another casualty of the great fire.[20] This lack of a settled residence in the possession of the

---

[15] Ibid., p. 5.   [16] Ibid., pp. 8–9.   [17] Ibid., p. 9.

[18] Petition to the Commons Committee for Trade, presented by Deputy Edwards, 5 Jan. 1641, Whitelocke Papers VIII, #28. For an example of the London Company meeting at the calling of the Privy Council, see APC 1619–20, pp. 289–90.

[19] Sutton and Visser-Fuchs (eds), *Book of Privileges*, pp. 42–3.

[20] In 1654 the Company was paying £2 a quarter rent to the Founders' Company: Merchant Adventurers receipt book, 1654, TNA, C109/24.

Company might have had a corresponding effect on the sociability that came with meetings, though we have frustratingly little evidence of this, and we do not know of any regular Company feasts or other occasions of conviviality. Provincial affiliates of the Company also would have had occasion to meet to decide on such matters as shipping, though in some cases such as Hull and Newcastle corporate loyalties were complicated by an overlap with local merchant companies which incorporated all overseas merchants within the town (London, of course, had no equivalent institution). The location of the chief court in the mart town, so often identified with inexperienced youths, was a potential source of tension within the Company's ranks, and in 1633 the Privy Council labelled it 'a thing in it selfe very incongruous.'[21] This was particularly the case because the head court was responsible for electing all the chief officers of the different branches, including those at London, in its annual midsummer elections, and much of our knowledge about electoral procedures comes from the disputes which this system could precipitate.

Although the chief officer of the Company was the governor, in practice by our period governors resided in London rather than the mart town, where they could wait on the crown and Privy Council. Governors were thus chosen for their reputation as public men, demonstrated by some from the earlier part of the period: Richard Saltonstall, Richard Goddard, Henry Rowe, Christopher Hoddesdon, and Thomas Lowe. All were knighted, Saltonstall, Rowe and Lowe were sometime Lord Mayor of London and the latter two also Members of Parliament, whilst Goddard and Hoddesdon were aldermen. Most had considerable interests in other commercial ventures and companies (Hoddesdon had a long involvement in trade to Russia, and Lowe was governor of the Levant Company; Saltonstall was a founding member of the Muscovy Company and was named in the 1592 Levant Company charter; Goddard was involved in the foundation of the East India Company).[22] Probably their ability to speak in defence of the Company in Parliament and at the Council Table was more important than up-to-date knowledge of the state of trade. Thus in practice the labour of enforcing the Company's government fell on the deputy governors, particularly those resident in the mart towns (often a deputy was also appointed for London), though they had the support of the assistants and other officers, notably the treasurer and secretary.

---

[21] TNA, PC 2/43, fol. 95.
[22] For Saltonstall, see A. M. Mimardière, 'SALTONSTALL, Richard (d.1601), of London and South Ockendon, Essex', in P. W. Hasler (ed.), *The History of Parliament: The House of Commons 1558–1603* (1981), online edition [https://www.historyofparliamentonline.org/volume/1558-1603/member/saltonstall-richard-1601]; for Lowe, see Andrew Thrush, 'LOWE, Sir Thomas (c.1546–1623), of Broad Street, London and Putney, Surr', in Andrew Thrush and John P. Ferris (eds), *The History of Parliament: The House of Commons 1604–1629* (2010), online edition [https://www.historyofparliamentonline. org/volume/1604-1629/member/lowe-sir-thomas-1546-1623]. For Goddard, T. K. Rabb, *Enterprise and Empire: Merchant and Gentry Investment in the Expansion of England, 1575–1630* (Cambridge, Mass., 1967), p. 299; for Hoddesdon, J. Hodsdon, 'Hoddesdon, Sir Christopher (1533/4–1611), merchant', *ODNB*.

The convention was that the deputy was not actively involved in trade, and the office came with a £200 salary, as well opportunities to ingratiate oneself with statesmen by assuming the role of foreign correspondent.[23] As they were deeply implicated in the enforcement of discipline, these deputies could be amongst the most controversial figures in the Company.

As for the role of assistant, the Company seems to have faced difficulties in recruiting sufficiently experienced members to serve overseas. The identity of eight of the Hamburg assistants for 1620 is known, and all but one were listed in the Hamburg church book for that year as a bachelor, suggesting that this office ranked lower than that of church elder, all of whom were married.[24] Any member chosen for the part-time roles of treasurer or assistant was subject to a £50 fine if they refused to serve, a penalty John Quarles was prepared to take.[25] When George Warner was selected as treasurer by the Rotterdam court in 1641, despite having (as he complained) 'of my owne occasions nothing to doe there', he excused himself by claiming pressing business in London.[26] Such problems may have eased as more merchants became long-term residents in the mart towns— William Attwood was Hamburg treasurer in the early 1650s, for instance—but is likely that the supply of potential assistants was too small for these selections to be contested in anything but exceptional circumstances.

The choice of deputy was potentially another matter, however. Much of our knowledge of the Company's electoral practices dates from the middle decades of the seventeenth century, when, as Chapter 7 will discuss, political and religious divisions led to three deputies being de-selected in acrimonious circumstances— Edward Misselden as Delft deputy in 1633, Joseph Avery at Hamburg in 1645, and Richard Bradshaw, also at Hamburg, in 1654. The selection of Misselden and Bradshaw's successors also became embroiled in controversy due to attempts by the crown and Protectorate respectively to impose their re-election, in the face of resistance from the Company. These experiences seem to have made the Hamburg Fellowship particularly jealous of their electoral independence. In 1659 William Attwood's factor Edward Halford reported that the London court had recommended as deputy one William Meade, 'but the Election passed with much opposition', with many calling for it to be deferred so that 'some as had noe knowledge of the man, might informe themselves', though Halford speculated that 'some perhaps had other ends in their opposition'.[27] Members were clearly sensitive

---

[23] See, for instance, Thomas Ferrers–William Cecil, Lord Burghley, 18 May 1596, TNA, SP 82/4, fol. 36.

[24] These were Nicholas Backhouse, Thomas Barker, George Franklin, John Greenwell, Isaak Lee, Edward Mead, Walter Pell, and John Powell, all dedicatees of a book of spiritual poetry written by the Hamburg pastor William Loe, *Songs of Sion* (1620).

[25] *Laws*, p. 8; Lowe–Quarles, 3 Dec. 1596, TNA, SP 46/176, fol. 16v.

[26] Warner–Edward Bolle, 16 Apr. 1641, TNA, SP 46/85/1, fol. 54.

[27] Halford–Attwood, 6 Dec. 1659, TNA, C109/24 (Hamburg folder).

about the arrival of an outsider, though in the following April Halford reported that 'the Company receives much satisfaction under [Meade's] Government'.[28]

Meade's successor in 1664, Sir William Swann, was also the crown's resident in Hamburg and thus a political appointee rather than a member, as had been the case with Bradshaw before him, and like Bradshaw he was frequently eyed with suspicion. During the midsummer 1672 election, for instance, one Thomas Shafto had alleged in General Court that Swann had earlier that day warned him to mind his speech, lest he be summoned to explain himself in England. This had caused the court to send a committee of six members to raise the matter with Swann, who had retreated from court along with the other candidate in order to allow open discussion, 'that soe they might be freed from the feare of such dangers in deliueringe their Judgements in Court as they stood obliged by the orders and their Oath'.[29] According to the court's register, Swann reassured these members that he would only report the misbehaviour of a member to the crown if the court itself had failed to punish the recalcitrant member themselves, and he preceded to be re-elected. Swann, however, would later allege that his words had been misrepresented by the secretary, who had 'forged a Register out of some words, that passed in discourse amongst us, and some in his owne coyning'.[30]

Evidently the fellowship valued their freedom of speech in elections and the possibility of a genuine contest, even if the outcome was to endorse the incumbent. We owe our knowledge of this episode to the fact that it was raised during the midsummer elections of 1675, during which the incumbent governor Sir Richard Ford was de-selected, only one of two examples for this period of a governor actually losing office in this way (to be discussed in more detail in Chapter 8). Swann had come to Ford's defence, leading to some old resentments about his outsider status being raised, with Shafto allegedly flinging a copy of the court register detailing the 1672 incident in Swann's face. When Swann continued to obstruct the Hamburg court's efforts to replace Ford in subsequent sessions, Shafto proclaimed that Swann 'did not deserve to sitt in the Chaire', and another critic, Francis Stratford, inferred that Swann was not 'one of the Company'.[31] Stratford also allegedly opined that 'they could do well enough with a Martly Deputy that is one of the Company chosen to sitt in the Chaire from Quarter to Quarter'. This was a reference to the fact that the 'Laws, Customes and Ordinances' mentioned elections happening 'martly' (i.e. for the duration of each of the Company's four seasonal marts), a practice which seems to have been abandoned by the seventeenth century in favour of annual elections, although the precedent had been deployed in recent years to undermine Bradshaw. Swann eventually

[28] Halford–Attwood, 3 Apr. 1660, TNA, C109/24 (Hamburg folder).
[29] Copy of minutes of a General Assembly of the Court at Hamburg, 1 July 1672, Coventry Papers 39, fol. 144.
[30] Swann–[Coventry], 13 Sept. 1675, Coventry Papers 39, fol. 141v.   [31] Ibid.

reached an accommodation with his critics, but following his death in 1678 the position of Hamburg deputy resumed to a member of the Company, the Hamburg court 'being unwilling the Kings Minister should be theire Deputy'.[32]

Swann's successor as Hamburg deputy was Samuel Missenden, previously Hamburg secretary and son of the infamous Edward Misselden: it was he who Swann alleged had forged the account of the quarrel during the 1672 elections.[33] Missenden's role in this dispute demonstrates how the authority of the deputy could be rivalled by other Company officers, with the secretary holding extensive power over the production and interpretation of Company records. This was epitomized by the figure of John Wheeler, secretary at Middelburg from the early 1590s. Wheeler was far more than a faceless bureaucrat; as well as a practising merchant, he was described by the governor Christopher Hoddesdon as possessing 'a sharp sight and quick conceit to prevent any mishap', being 'of good estimation and long acquainted with the manners of the Netherlands', as well as possessing excellent language skills and correspondents from as far afield as Prague and Cologne: an exemplary humanist scholar.[34]

However important the principle of consent was in the government of the Company, then, key officers were able to exercise a significant influence on the course of Company politics, though the plurality of posts spread over the various branches meant that authority was effectively dispersed. Chapter 7 will show in more detail how this could undermine the role of deputy governor, though it should be noted that the terms of several deputies seem to have passed without significant controversy. For instance, the Hamburg deputy in 1620, Richard Gore, was in post from 1611 to 1622, the interregnum of the Cokayne Project excepted, and was fondly remembered; one of his successors, Edward Bennett, governed from 1628 to 1638 with no obvious signs of opposition. Gore had previously been London deputy, and Bennett was Misselden's predecessor at Delft. These experienced administrators helped to ensure a degree of continuity in Company government: other examples would include William Towerson, London deputy in the years before and after the Cokayne Project, and Thomas Skinner, secretary of the London residence from the 1630s to the 1650s. Much of their business would have been devoted to routine matters such as the admission of new members, rather than the potentially controversial business of Company elections. Most important was the elaborate regulatory framework which was intended to channel trade into the mart towns and distribute it amongst members equitably, whilst

---

[32] Bevil Skelton–William Blathwayt, 13 June 1682, BL, Add. 37983, fol. 219v. For more details, see Chapter 8.

[33] The reasons why Samuel chose to the change the spelling of his surname are unclear, but perhaps linked to his father's controversial reputation.

[34] Quoted in P. Wauchope, 'Wheeler, John (d. 1617), secretary of the Company of Merchant Adventurers', *ODNB*. For Wheeler's role as custodian of the Company's history, see Wheeler–Sir John Hobart, 24 Sept. 1611, Bodl. Lib., Tanner 74, fol. 5.

keeping it out of the hands of interlopers. The remainder of this chapter will focus on how this system worked in practice.

The Costs and Benefits of Membership

Being a Merchant Adventurer brought many advantages besides a share of a valuable monopoly. The system of appointing shipping spared members the labour of freighting their own ships. Overseas, the Company secured privileges from local rulers such as exceptions from certain tolls and taxes and other burdens, rented warehouses and space at docks, and arranged services including carriage and cranage. But there were costs to being a member, as well, most obviously financial (in the form of Company impositions), but also the limitations imposed on their commercial independence; as Wheeler put it, 'he looseth a piece of his libertie well, that being restrained of a little, fareth better in that estate, then if he were left to his owne greedy appetite'.[35] The weight of attention paid to enforcing the Company's regulations in its 'Laws, Customes and Ordinances' suggests that conformity to them was far from automatic, though the extent of the misbehaviour of 'disorderly brethren' varied over the period.

Company rules stated that the governor and deputy had the authority to 'correct and punishe' transgressors against its laws 'by fines Imprisonment, or otherwis'.[36] In practice the system centred on the imposition of fines or 'brokes' for particular violations, the amount of which ascended according to seriousness as well as for repeat offences, with disenfranchisement (pronounced in General Court) the ultimate sanction; imprisonment was reserved for members persistently resisting Company discipline. Initial refusal to submit to the Company's orders was punishable by a £100 fine, rising to £200 for a second offence and £300 for a third, with the member placed under arrest until this had been paid.[37] Imprisonment could also be used in cases of irreverent behaviour in court, which was subject to an initial fine of 40s., rising to £4 if such 'disorderly behauiour' continued. If the member in question refused to 'bee ruled reclaymed or take annswer, but replyeth against or provoketh the Governour or his Deputie', the fine rose to £10 and the member was imprisoned until further order was given. Most serious was disloyalty towards the Company: 'anie thinge in woord or deed to the breach preiudice disanullinge or makinge void of the Priuileges, ffreedomes, Charters or grannts to the ffellowshippe' was accounted a violation of the freeman's oath and thus perjury, which was punished by being 'disfranchised and banished from the liberties of the said ffellowshippe for ever'. The seriousness of this offence is shown by the fact that it was discussed alongside cases of

---

[35] Wheeler, *Treatise*, p. 54. For impositions, see Chapter 1.
[36] *Laws*, p. 6.   [37] Ibid., p. 11.

'cooseninge, felonie or other heynous or Capitall Cryme', which also bought disenfranchisement.[38] The emphasis, though, was on ensuring that members recognized the authority of the Company and were willingly bought back into its ranks, with exclusion a last resort.

This meant that it was possible for members to occasionally stray from the letter of the Company's laws and continue to enjoy the freedom, as long as they were willing to ultimately submit to its discipline. This left a degree of latitude which could be exploited by those willing to test the boundaries of acceptable practice. Their ability to do so was assisted by the challenge that the Company faced in effectively governing a dispersed membership. On the continent, outside of the mart towns the Company's authority was limited and there was ambiguity over certain places where members might trade by 'toleration' such as Emden or the Spanish Netherlands, whilst in London members were part of a cosmopolitan business community and monitoring their practices was clearly difficult. In the provincial towns, there was often a lack of will to comply with Company rules even from those who were supposed to be enforcing them. Thus it was in the mart towns that the brunt of Company government was felt, although the two different mart towns often seem in practice to have followed different regimes. Exacerbating the complexity of governing such a dispersed membership were the limited powers of detection that were at the disposal of an organization whose officials were largely recruited from the ranks of the Company itself, with only a small number of salaried positions. The Company's response to these challenges was to rely on the consciences of members through a series of oaths, to be taken at strategic moments and/or places through which all members would theoretically have passed, and designed to bring malfeasance into the open so that it could be acknowledged, punished, and the Company's authority confirmed. The Company also relied on information about offences being presented to its officers, though subsequent investigations by the Court of Assistants commonly involved examination under oath.[39]

Because the Company's 'Orders in Feat of Merchandise' concentrated on regulating business in the mart towns, this was where most investigations would have taken place, but certain regulations transcended any one location, including the stint, discussed in Chapter 2. Probably a more popular service was the organization of shipping in 'appointed' ships which sailed in fleets, traditionally in the spring and the autumn. This was one of the chief planks of the mart-trading system, which was designed to create a seller's market by ensuring all cloth arrived together, keeping customers waiting until demand reached its highest point. News of the departure of Company ships was keenly awaited in the mart towns, though factors commonly complained that the London court had dispatched its

---

[38] Ibid., p. 12.   [39] Ibid., pp. 147–53.

fleet too late to coincide with the fairs at Frankfurt or Nuremburg.[40] The timing of Company fleets had a significant influence on the markets in England and overseas; factors frantically sought to rid themselves of remaining cloth before the arrival of fresh wares, whilst the departure of the cloth fleet from London precipitated a fall in prices at home. A merchant who wished to benefit from this falling market might then be tempted to arrange for these goods to be laden on the appointed ships after the last permitted day, or even to freight their own ships, a course which might also be taken by those wanting to get their goods to market before the arrival of the Company fleet.

Such practices were labelled as 'mis-shipping' and were punishable by fines: 40s. for each cloth mis-shipped in non-appointed ships, and 20s. for each cloth laden on appointed ships over their allocated number, plus 6s. 8d. for each cloth sent to the ships after they had left London.[41] This system was enforced by members described as 'appointers', whose job it was to survey the cloths in their packhouses, and to furnish the shipmasters with this information.[42] Further measures were intended to guard against members entering cloth for another individual in their own name. An oath printed in an eighteenth-century compilation and dating from the early part of our period required members to disclose where any cloths they intended to ship were bought and by whom, and to swear that they were to be shipped to the mart towns.[43] This might be the oath 'that noe cloth shalbe shipped but such as are entred at the poynters', which according to George Lowe was introduced in summer 1594.[44] Three years later, Lowe mentioned another oath 'to fynde out indyrect shippers' introduced by the Company at Stade, requiring members in the mart towns to swear how many packs they had received from appointed and unappointed ships, and how the cockets had been entered. Evidently the 1590s were a time when the Company was seeking to crack down on mis-shipments, though Lowe hoped the oath would soon be withdrawn.[45] The Company's regulations also demanded that a duplicate of the inventory of goods on each ship was to be sent to an officer in the mart town in order to check this against the cockets provided by the shipmaster, who was also to be 'purged by his Corporall oathe' as to whether he had laden more goods than had been appointed.[46] The shipmaster was subject to a £5 fine for any pack of goods to be found to have been mis-shipped.

As well as avoiding this penalty, the key incentive for shipmasters to comply with these rules was the prospect of repeat custom, and any found to be taking on

[40] See, for instance, Richard Rawstorm–Lionel Cranfield, 26 Oct. 1600, HMC Sackville II, pp. 42–3; 29 Mar. 1604, ibid., p. 145.
[41] *Laws*, pp. 57–9.   [42] Ibid., pp. 62–3.
[43] *The Book of Oaths* (London, 1715), p. 19.
[44] Lowe–Quarles, 19 July 1594, TNA, SP 46/176, fol. 43v.
[45] Lowe–Quarles, 4 June 1597, TNA, SP 46/176, fol. 211r; 21 June 1597, TNA, SP 46/176, fol. 214r.
[46] *Laws*, pp. 78–9.

packs after clearing from London was banished from serving the Company for three years.[47] But shipmasters were still independent of the Company, and so one possible weak point in its regulatory system. When Lionel Cranfield mis-shipped some packs on the Company fleet to Middelburg, and feared that he would there-fore 'Come in the Companyes danger', Daniel Cooper reassured him that he had intercepted the ship in question 5 miles out of port in order to dispose of the cockets, and had persuaded the shipmaster to unlade the trusses onto hoys before the appointers had a chance to examine them, 'for avoyding of suspition of Reasevinge soe mannye'.[48] Nor were the Company's own officers entirely reliable; Cooper assured Cranfield that he had 'Thomas the offysser sewre yf hee Coulde hee woulde nott present me'. Failing that, members might simply hope to avoid detection through negligence. On learning that one of his principals had laden a pack in the Hull ships after the last appointed date, Matthew Ashton was optimis-tic that 'if noe notice taken by the Appointers at Hull I hope there will bee noe dispute aboute its beeing unduely waterborne'.[49]

The above cases all involved mis-shipping in the appointed ships, but the use of non-Company ships was a more serious business. Letters from the earlier part of the period make frequent reference to 'interloper' ships arriving in the mart towns, although the designation is rather misleading: these ships carried those goods which could licitly be traded in by non-Merchant Adventurers, including strangers, as well as occasionally taking in imports by Company members, though no doubt they were a conduit for interloping. To Company members, these ships presented an alternative option to the appointed fleet.[50] In March 1600, following unexpectedly good sales at Middelburg, John Kendrick hoped to arrange an indirect shipment to supply one of his customers. He explained to his master John Quarles that the cloths should be consigned to another Dutch merchant, Martin Vander Sande, 'of whome they may be Received without knowledge of anie of our company'.[51] Interloper ships also frequented ports other than the mart towns, and George Lowe at Stade advised Quarles that 'for hamburg I make accompt yowe shall finde interlopers shippes redy to lade, in January in which yowe may alsoe lade some cloth under a strange marke & packed like strangers packes'. These could be consigned to a local contact, from whom Lowe could fetch them 'without any danger, as lynen packes or otherwyse as we shall thinke best', though he cautioned Quarles to be 'sure of the shipper that he will not betray them'.[52] It was obviously a short step to the more serious offence of actually selling cloth outside of the mart towns. In fact, in September 1594 Lowe

[47] Ibid., p. 81.
[48] Cooper–Cranfield, 23 May 1601, KHLC, U269/1/CB49 (HMC Sackville II, p. 72).
[49] Ashton–Richard Mann, 18 Apr. 1682, Bodl. Lib Eng. misc. c563, fol. 29r.
[50] Rawstorm–Cranfield, 7 May 1603, HMC Sackville II, pp. 131–2.
[51] Kendrick–Quarles, 15 Mar. 1600, TNA, SP 46/21, fol. 219r.
[52] Lowe–Quarles, 13 Dec. 1593, TNA, SP 46/176, fol. 17v.

mentioned that a new measure had been introduced requiring shipmasters to enter bond in the customhouse at London promising to deliver cloth only to Stade.[53] But the 'Lawes, Customes and Ordinances' of 1608 still complained of Company ships discharging goods at ports such as Flushing, with 'multitude of Interlopers thereby maynteyned, as also of vnorderly brethern whoe by means hereof cannot bee so well mett withall and restrayned'.[54]

How common such practices were is difficult to say, but it seems that they exerted a cumulative pressure on the Company, leading it to change its shipping policies. Some time after the turn of the century the practice of sending two or three large fleets from London to Stade each year began to break down, with the main appointed fleets being supplemented by several smaller shipments, perhaps as a means to discourage mis-shipping. In 1605 Richard Rawstorm at Stade complained that 'cloth sells here very slowly and basely, and the worse in that shipping comes so disorderly, one in the neck of another, which makes our merchants refrain all they can expecting still better pennyworths to come'.[55] In 1622 the Company claimed to have definitively abandoned twice yearly fleets and adopted regular shipping.[56] George Warner's accounts suggest a mixed regime: from 1639 to 1640 he sent cloth to Hamburg in May, September, and November only, but in other years more often. In the 1680s the London Company was apparently not appointing regular fleets for its trade to Hamburg, though the practice was still followed in Hull, to the irritation of some members who had been penalized for mis-shipping. Matthew Ashton, though, warned that 'the London traders themselves are almost weary of free shippinges findeing soe little vent when fresh goods arrives & such greate number of remainders at the conclusion of the yeare, that they wish againe for sett shippinges & then would bee in hopes to give the Enterloper as great an overthrow, as could bee done by free shippings'.[57]

Ashton's mention of interlopers indicates another factor which the Company had to contend with when setting its shipping policy. Like so many aspects of the mart-trading system, the appointed fleets could only be effective if interlopers were effectively suppressed. Regular or 'free' shipping might therefore be an indication that this was not the case. Chapter 8 will consider how the Company dealt with the problem of interlopers through legal, political, and other means, but here it is worth addressing how it sought to control relations between members and non-members, in order to ensure that its privileges were reserved for the former. Company rules forbade deploying 'unfreemen' as agents in the parts covered by its territories, on pain of a fine of 10 per cent of the value of the goods in question. Similarly, no member was to buy or sell goods on behalf of non-members, or

[53] Lowe–Quarles, 5 Sept. 1594, TNA, SP 46/176, fol. 57r. See APC 1595–6, p. 519.
[54] Laws, p. 82.   [55] Rawstorm–Cranfield, 26 May 1605, HMC Sackville II, p. 165.
[56] 'The Answere of the Marchants Adventurers to the Articles of complaint exhibited against them by divers Clothiers of Gloucestershere', 13 Mar. 1622, TNA, SP 16/535, fol. 82.
[57] Ashton–William Pickering, 28 Aug. 1683, Bodl. Lib Eng. misc. c563, fol. 98r–v.

convey them in their name. Using the exchange for non-members was also forbidden, with some exceptions (for instance, for a voyage transporting goods to some other country than England). Even information about purchases of cloth or the price of foreign wares was to be withheld from unfreemen.[58] However, the Company did permit members to take up the goods of non-members if they came from parts not covered by its privileges, such as France and Spain, whilst of course it could claim no jurisdiction over the dealings of its members in such places.[59]

This last point reflects the key problem facing the Company when enforcing the rules against dealing with unfreemen. Merchant Adventurers came across non-members at many points of their business lives, and the flexible and expansive nature of commercial networks made it likely that they would be drawn into cooperating with them in ways that might transgress the Company's rules. Central to this issue was the ambiguous nature of the Company's monopoly, something which extended back at least as far as the 1497 act of Parliament granting all English subjects the right to access the Company's continental markets for a fine of 10 marks (£6 13s. 6d.), as long as they submitted to Company government, following which the Company had a two-tier membership, the 'old' and 'new hanse'. The Company's 1564 charter said little about the Company's powers to exclude non-members, and so a second Elizabethan charter proved necessary to confirm that unfreemen were indeed prohibited from 'intermeddling' in the Company's trade, subjecting them to fines and imprisonment by the Company. Even here, though, there was ambiguity regarding the Company's powers. The attorney general, Sir John Popham, had inserted certain caveats into the wording of the charter, such as qualifying the fines and imprisonment that the company was to impose as being 'reasonable'.[60] He edited the passage outlining the Company's power to punish members as well as interlopers, changing the original text, which specified that they could be imprisoned without bail until such time as 'by the said Governour or his deputie with the greatest parte of the Assistantes he or they shall be set at liberty', to read 'until such time as he or they shall according to our lawes be set at liberty'. This would seem to confirm a domestic right of appeal by any English person imprisoned overseas. The charter also specified that all punishments wielded by the Company on interlopers were to be 'agreeable unto the Statutes Ordinances and Constitutions of the said Fellowship', which could be read to suggest that non-members were merely to be subject to the same regulations as freemen, implicitly legitimizing their presence overseas. Elsewhere, the charter required both members of the Fellowship and 'all other persons which now be not of the said Fellowship nor hereafter shall be which shall of their owne wrong intermeddle in trade of Merchandize in the said Countryes', to obey the governor or his deputies. In fact it was legal for all denizens to trade in these parts

---

[58] *Laws*, pp. 93–4.   [59] Ibid., pp. 93–5.
[60] See his draft copy in TNA, PRO 30/34/2.

for certain strategic commodities, such as horses, munitions, butter, corn, and books, but in practice, given the legal ambiguities, interloping was tolerated for any goods except cloth. Thus, the Company always shared its markets with unfreemen, both in England and overseas. Friis' analysis of the 1612 London port book for non-cloth exports found thirty-four interlopers sending goods to Amsterdam in the first quarter of the year, with a core of twelve who had long-term involvement in this trade; a further nine sent goods to Flushing, and nine to Middelburg, which can hardly have gone unnoticed by members of the Company.[61]

Certainly the letters of individual Merchant Adventurers do at times reproduce the hostility towards interlopers that informed the Company's public rhetoric. To take just a few examples, Francis Ottley of Middelburg reflected in 1605 that 'If the interlopers may be restrained then we may hope of good doings', whilst John Sanford reported that a bale of cloth plundered at sea after the outbreak of the second Anglo-Dutch War 'did not belong to us but to one of our Enimies an Interloper'.[62] A decade later Matthew Ashton closed one letter by 'Wishing our markets were soe quick as yors & not spoiled by interlopers'.[63] Clearly the demarcation between insiders and outsiders did mean something, but in practice this distinction was prone to break down, particularly in cases when Merchant Adventurers were themselves transgressing the boundaries of licit trade. This reality was acknowledged by John Kendrick in 1611, when he suggested that one key reason for the Company to move its German mart town from Stade to Hamburg was 'for suppressing of the stragling, & interloping Trade, which was dryven as well by those, of the Company, as by others which were not free: both in Hambourg, and in other principall Townes of Germany'.[64] Kendrick was well placed to make this comment, given that his former master, John Quarles, had been at the forefront of such collaborations.

The nature of interactions between Company members and interlopers varied in time and place, however. Despite the Company's efforts to stabilize their markets, Merchant Adventurers operated within a volatile European economy, with new opportunities as well as dangers continually tempting members to depart from the mart-trading system. The development of the mart-trading system and the interactions between interlopers and 'disorderly brethren' were thus bound to a larger process of transformation within the structure of the Company's trade.

---

[61] Friis, *Alderman Cockayne's Project*, pp. 110–11.
[62] Ottley–Cranfield, 9 Feb. 1605, HMC Sackville II, p. 157; Sanford–John Ayshford, 7 Nov. 1672, SRO, DD\SF/7/2/1.
[63] Ashton–Godfrey Lawson, 18 Apr. 1682, Bodl. Lib., Eng. misc. c563, fol. 29r.
[64] Kendrick's reasons for the Company's removal from Stade to Hamburg, 1611, TNA, SP 14/67, fol. 105.

The Mart System in Practice

The Fellowship of Merchant Adventurers' ideal of an ordered trade was centred on channelling cloth exports into the regulated settings of the mart towns. As with other aspects of the Company's disciplinary framework, the mart system was sustained through the usage of oaths to reveal transgressions and fines to penalize them, with disenfranchisement the ultimate sanction. The fine for trading outside of the mart towns was 40s. sterling per cloth or 25 per cent of the value of other goods (bought or sold, or indeed displayed), with a third offence met by disenfranchisement. Using the exchange outside the mart towns brought a fine of 10 per cent of the sum in question.[65] Practices intended to circumvent this order by covertly trading under another name, or arranging deals for customers outside the mart towns, were defined as 'Indirect dealinge', and treated in the same way as the aforesaid offences.[66] The less serious offence of trading in the mart towns on non-show days was also punishable by fine (6s. 8d. per cloth sold with a flat fine of 40s. for showing goods).[67] Members were to swear an oath to accord to this last regulation every three months, on pain of a fine of £20, and an oath to keep to the mart towns was also in place by 1605 at the latest. Refusal to take this oath was also punishable by a £20 fine applied for each continued month of non-compliance, 'and the offender to bee held suspect of the breache of the Orders, and not to enioye anie benefyte of the free licence till he have taken the said oathe'.[68] A member could not depart the mart town without having first 'purged himself by the said twoe oathes', the so-called 'purging oath'.[69]

By the time that these regulations were recorded in Wheeler's manuscript, the Company had experienced a half-century struggle to redefine the geographical bounds of its commerce after leaving Antwerp, in which circumstances many members had been tempted to 'straggle' beyond the mart towns. This was particularly the case in the unfamiliar territory of Germany, and as early as 1564 members had responded to the failure of the Emden mart by travelling to Frankfurt to sell their cloth. In fact by the time Wheeler came to compile his manuscript it was lawful for Merchant Adventurers to purchase goods at Frankfurt, if not sell them there, probably an example of how the pressure of members' behaviour could lead to shifts in the Company's regulatory regime, but creating a loophole in the mart-trading system. Also ambiguous by then was the former mart town of Emden, which members were allowed to trade to by toleration. Emden was also recognized as a possible route to the forbidden towns of Amsterdam and Hamburg.[70] From 1579 to 1611, when its German residences were Emden and/or Stade, Hamburg was a particularly tempting destination for the dispatch of cloth, but the 'Lawes' specifically mentioned Nuremburg (also

---

[65] *Laws*, pp. 53–4.   [66] Ibid., pp. 55, 96–7.   [67] Ibid., pp. 88–9.
[68] Ibid., pp. 90–1.   [69] Ibid., p. 91.   [70] Ibid., pp. 54, 60.

singled out in Wheeler's *Treatise*) as a place where members were strictly forbidden to trade.[71] Baumann's extensive researches in continental archives found considerable evidence of Englishmen present in both of these towns as well as many others throughout Germany and central Europe up to the 1620s, including several Merchant Adventurers.[72] What explains this apparently widespread 'straggling'?

One factor serves as an explanation throughout our period. For all the Company's attempts to confine members to the mart towns, there were legitimate reasons for them to depart these regulated settings, and not just to attend the Frankfurt mart. For one thing, as customers rarely resided in the mart towns, the collection of debts often required travel, and in 1611 John Kendrick put forward as one reason to return to Hamburg the burden of having to keep additional factors there.[73] But a Merchant Adventurer did not need to be physically present outside of the mart towns in order to engage in straggling; the close relationships that they often established with customers could be exploited in order to circumvent the mart towns, though to an extent the Company relied on the fact that it was not in the interests of these foreign merchants to encourage activity that threatened their role as middlemen. Even in the absence of cooperation from customers, however, Merchant Adventurers could deploy English interlopers, who were able to operate outside of the geographical constraints imposed on Company members, and (because of the political fragmented nature of the Holy Roman Empire) were largely beyond the reach of the Company's powers. Merchant Adventurers must have been regularly presented with opportunities to straggle, then, but the Company's oath-based disciplinary system ought to have been enough to ensure compliance with its regulations. Here, the casuistic tactics discussed above in relation to shipping again came into play.

Baumann found evidence for English presence in a wide range of towns and cities in the period 1560 to 1620, but certain places stand out. Naturally the important trade fairs of Frankfurt and Nuremburg attracted activity, as did Hamburg, which as well as being an alternative place of sale could also be used as a gateway to inland markets. Each of these cities was large enough to host a reasonably substantial English population, into which rogue Merchant Adventurers could blend. At Nuremburg English merchants gravitated towards a public inn, the 'Golden Goose', where they were able to store their goods, and seem to have been a fairly settled community during the 1580s and 90s, though the Company claimed in a petition dating from the close of the century that the ringleaders of this trade (including the future Company governor Thomas Lowe) had finally submitted to Company government.[74] As well as markets for cloth, these cities

[71] Ibid., p. 100.   [72] Baumann, *Merchant Adventurers*.   [73] TNA, SP 14/67, fol. 105.
[74] Baumann, *Merchants Adventurers*, p. 177; Petition, Merchant Adventurers to Lord Burghley, BL, Lansdowne 86, fols 203–4. This petition is of uncertain date, but must have predated Burghley's death

(particularly Frankfurt and Nuremburg) were a source of imports, and in fact the search for imports encouraged English merchants to venture ever deeper into central Europe. Thus although the fall of Antwerp has long been understood as unleashing an import-driven expansion of English long-distance seaborne trade, this was mirrored by a similar attempt to penetrate the inland European market. Although these efforts have been barely noticed by historians more attracted to spectacular sea voyages, they were, in their own way, as remarkable, involving the transportation of bulky goods across numerous geographical, legal, and political barriers and undertaken entirely through informal networks. The chief target seems to have been humble linen, sourced at southern and western towns like Osnabruck, Paderborn, and Münster, but increasingly from the east, where the Leipzig trade fair rose in prominence, and where English custom and capital played a significant role in stimulating putting out industry in regions such as Silesia and Saxony.

This was the trade which tempted John Quarles to put his corporate loyalties on the line in the 1590s. But rather than stray too far from the acceptable limits of practice, he did so in collaboration with an interloper, one Thomas Jackson, and his factor George Lowe's attempts to evade prosecution by the Company for these activities are perhaps our best record of how its disciplinary regime worked in practice.[75] For Quarles' engagement with Jackson seems to have been open knowledge at Stade, where the actions of one of Jackson's factors in Germany, Lawrence Overton, were accounted 'iestes to laughe at over tables'.[76] Overton and his fellow agents (including William Balden and Ralph Allen) were managed by Jackson from England. Jackson himself had prior commercial interests in France, and had earlier collaborated with Quarles on a venture selling Irish wheat on the continent; in 1588 he was importing a variety of goods from Middelburg, Flushing, and Emden.[77] He probably became acquainted with Quarles via his former master, the Haberdasher Sir Henry Billingsley, who was Quarles' father-in-law. As Billingsley was a Merchant Adventurer, we must assume that Jackson's decision not to take up membership of the Company himself was strategic; by refusing to submit to its regulations he was able to exploit opportunities beyond the mart towns formally closed to Merchant Adventurers. At the same time he was reliant on contacts from within the Company, at least to support his entrance

in August 1598, and the lack of any reference to the imperial mandate might suggest it dated from before July 1597.

[75] This case is discussed in more detail in Thomas Leng, 'Interlopers and disorderly brethren at the Stade mart: commercial regulations and practices amongst the Merchant Adventurers of England in the late Elizabethan period', *Economic History Review* 69 (2016), pp. 823–43.

[76] Lowe–Quarles, 13 Dec. 1593, TNA, SP 46/176, fol. 17r.

[77] BL, Lansdowne 143, fol. 314r; Pleadings in the case of Thomas Jackson and Ralph Allen versus Walter Merriot, 13 Oct. 1587, TNA, C2/Eliz/A7/24; Deposition of Thomas Jackson, in the case of John Quarles versus Thomas and Sir Henry Billingsley junior, 9 Jan. 1608, TNA, C24/340; E190/8/1.

into this trade. Quarles' contribution seems to have been to provide local contacts and lines of credit to finance Jackson's servants' operations, with Balden reportedly unable 'by his goodes billes nor credyte' to 'furnishe himself with 1000 dollers Lybesicke'.[78] These were used to source supplies of linen from Leipzig and its surrounds, though Jackson was also exporting cloth to Hamburg as early as summer 1594, using one of Quarles' customers (Martin Ensberger) as his factor.[79] Two years later Overton was reportedly directly financing cloth production in Silesia, and in 1597 Balden entered into a contract to supply large amounts of cloth to the Emperor.[80] Although these activities extended far beyond Stade, the mart town was still an important financial channel, and George Lowe was continually forced to discharge bills of exchange charged on him for Jackson's use, from both London and Leipzig. Indeed, Lowe frequently complained to his master about being 'inforced to use your name' on the exchange due to the hatred that his countrymen held for Jackson, which was 'noted by many & breedeth talke in the mouthes of such as wishe yowe little good'.[81]

Although Lowe had to contend with the innuendo of his enemies at Stade, where Quarles and Jackson were widely suspected to be partners, it proved difficult for the Company to prosecute him effectively. In May 1595 Lowe was called before the court of assistants on the charge of transporting goods to Balden and making money over to him via the exchange, which was punishable by a broke (i.e. a fine) of 10 per cent of the sum in question, but because he had arranged to deliver money via a customer, Lowe was able to evade the latter charge. He also used the defence of preserving the legitimate secrecy of his master's business, refusing to 'disclose yor busynesse or secrets to a court unlesse they were offensive agaynst the orders'.[82] Further summonses by the deputy, Thomas Ferrers—an inveterate enemy of interlopers—followed over the subsequent months, but Lowe continued to avoid prosecution, exploiting uncertainties in the Company's regulatory regime by demanding to be shown 'any order in our court bookes agaynst which I offended' in accepting bills of exchange from interlopers.[83] Lowe predicted that Ferrers, having been frustrated by the disciplinary procedures at his disposal, would 'eyther make an acte to prevent the assystance of interlopers uppon this occasion or set yt at lyberty for all men to buy goodes at Lybsicke'.[84] This measure would have potentially destroyed Jackson's business, though at the cost of opening another loophole in the mart-trading system. In fact the Company did not take this course, possibly aware that its customers would resent this

[78] Lowe–Quarles, 18 Dec. 1594, TNA, SP 46/19, fol. 126r.
[79] Lowe–Quarles, 25 July 1594, TNA, SP 46/176, fol. 44r.
[80] Lowe–Quarles, 29 July 1596, TNA, SP 46/176, fol. 143v; Lowe–Quarles, 25 Jan. 1597, TNA, SP 46/176, fol. 172v.
[81] Lowe–Quarles, 18 Dec. 1594, TNA, SP 46/19, fol. 126v.
[82] Lowe–Quarles, 30 May 1595, TNA, SP 46/19, fol. 130r.
[83] Lowe–Quarles, 22 June 1595, TNA, SP 46/19, fol. 134r.
[84] Lowe–Quarles, 30 May 1595, TNA, SP 46/19, fol. 130r.

additional competition from English merchants. Instead, it seems that Ferrers responded to Jackson's activities by leading a drive to enforce Company discipline both internally and externally, encompassing the new oaths about shipping discussed in the previous section as well as several complaints about interloping made to the Privy Council. In August 1594 these yielded an order against ships discharging at Hamburg, something Lowe feared 'will force Mr Jackson to seeke a new course & cutt of many interlopers'.[85] But in London Jackson himself seems to have been largely beyond the Company's reach, and indeed he had influential allies: Billingsley was by then an alderman and would later become Lord Mayor of London.

Far removed from deputy Ferrers and the chief court of the Company in Stade, Quarles seems to have been relatively immune to any ill-will that his collaboration with Jackson attracted, and if Lowe felt the pressure of his Fellows' disapproval more sharply in the mart town, even here the Company's authority over its members clearly had its limits. Lowe considered that Ferrers was willing to 'seeke all meanes in his might possible to Redresse & bringe Mr Jackson from his trade or strayne the company purse & his owne authoryty as farr as may possibly be done', calling on his political contacts at home (including his kinsman the Earl of Essex) to buttress his powers.[86] The fact that he needed such support is indicative of the limited authority of his office. Ferrers had previously served as the Company's deputy at Middelburg, which had been home to its chief court at the start of the decade, and perhaps Lowe was not alone in resenting the rigour that he seems to have introduced to the German mart town. In fact Lowe suggested that Quarles support some efforts from within the Company in September 1595 to have the Company's chief court moved back to Middelburg, and with it deputy Ferrers, perhaps restoring to Stade a more liberal regime which would turn a blind eye to instances of 'straggling'.[87]

Eventually this move did take place, but the occasion was the imperial mandate of 1597 banishing the Company from the Empire as a monopoly. As Chapter 5 will discuss, the Company did retain a foothold in the Empire, but this was essentially at the price of abandoning its coercive powers over members and interlopers alike. The letters of Lionel Cranfield show that in this lax environment direct trade to Nuremburg returned on a large scale, with no evidence of any efforts to restrict it on the part of the Company.[88] Similarly, Jackson and his servants were able to extend their operations free from any English opposition, now joined by a growing number of Merchant Adventurers. This was the high point of English

---

[85] Lowe–Quarles, 28 Aug. 1594, TNA, SP 46/176, fol. 53v.

[86] Lowe–Quarles, 1595, TNA, SP 46/19, fol. 149r.

[87] Lowe–Quarles, 12 Sept. 1595, TNA, SP 46/19, fol. 153v; see also 'Reasons set down by the committees in London, touching the removing of the companies authority from Stade to Middleburg. London, Feb. 4, 1595', BL, Cotton Galba D/XIII, fol. 159.

[88] See, for instance, HMC Sackville II, pp. 160–1, 164, 167–8.

involvement in the expansion of linen production in places like Silesia and Saxony, led by individuals like William Balden who became a citizen of Freiburg by 1607, though Jackson and Quarles were forced into an ignominious withdrawal from the trade by their insolvencies.[89] For the first decade of the seventeenth century, therefore, interlopers and Company members in Germany were almost indistinguishable, and even once the Company was officially readmitted into the Empire there seems to have been considerable latitude in the disciplinary regime in place, such that in 1611 one member, Edward Misselden, considered that Company government at Stade had collapsed entirely. Amongst the charges which he laid against the factors at Stade was the sale of goods beyond the mart town, an 'ungoverned' course which threatened to undermine the very foundations of the Company's existence, so that 'the goodly threede that they have formerly spunne; may in tyme be reduced againe into their primitive estate of contemptible pedlery'.[90] Misselden's manuscript treatise, actually written in favour of moving the mart town to the obscure Danish town of Krempe, was first presented to Sir Robert Cecil, and by revealing the deleterious state of the Company's affairs to an outsider Misselden evidently attracted the ire of many of his fellows. At the same time, those who had enjoyed the latitude at Stade for the previous decade probably feared the restoration of government that Misselden's treatise called for.

The Company's situation in Germany in the late sixteenth and early seventeenth centuries thus indicates how much its regulatory regime could vary over time; regulations were enforced with different degrees of rigour, and needed to be responsive to the actual behaviour of members in order to be truly effective. Equally the nature of Company government varied between the mart towns. Once restored to its place as chief seat of Company government in 1598, Middelburg became the focal point for its regulatory energies, supported by the literary efforts of the secretary, John Wheeler, whose *Treatise of Commerce* was printed in both Middelburg and London, in 1601. Whereas in the correspondence of Lionel Cranfield with his German factors the Company was a largely spectral presence, when it came to the Low Countries regulations clearly did mean something; Daniel Cooper had to use all his ingenuity to evade Company officers when fetching up packs of cloth that Cranfield had mis-shipped (see the previous section). However, even Edward Misselden had to concede that in Middelburg, 'where notwthstanding that the Gouernement is according to our owne desire, yet the Interloping ceaseth not; the factors demeane themselves basely towards their marchaunts buyers, & keepe packhowses at Amsterdam'.[91] The commercial and political geography of the Netherlands brought its own challenges; even allowing for the rise of Amsterdam, Antwerp was not succeeded

---

[89] Baumann, *Merchants Adventurers*, pp. 329–31.
[90] Misselden, 'Discourse', fol. 12r.   [91] Ibid., fol. 41r.

by any single distributive centre, meaning that the region lacked a natural staple which the Company could hope to monopolize.[92] Given the politically decentralized nature of the United Provinces, there were always towns willing to welcome English interlopers, notably Amsterdam, whose rulers were unwilling to grant exclusive privileges to corporations such as the Merchant Adventurers, despite the Company's occasional overtures.[93] The Netherlands, of course, was home to a much larger population of English expatriates, not least the military regiments based at Flushing, on the doorstep of Middelburg and a particularly obdurate loophole for interloping. In these circumstances, denying members access to the opportunities enjoyed by interlopers would have been very difficult, and already by 1608 Merchant Adventurers had been granted permission to buy goods for import anywhere in the United Provinces, if not to sell them. As a large proportion of the Company's customers were based at Amsterdam rather than Middelburg, then, there were many reasons for members to depart from the Zealand port.

Confining members' activities to the mart town was as challenging in the Low Countries as in Germany, if not more so. However, Thomas Wotton, acting as agent for Richard Sheppard and Lionel Cranfield in Amsterdam from 1601 to 1602, cut a rather lonely figure there.[94] Unlike in Antwerp, which had risen to prominence by welcoming foreign merchants with generous privileges, Amsterdam's overseas trade was dominated by local merchants or at least recent exiles from the southern Netherlands; the more successful English merchants there were probably long-term residents rather than short-term visitors like Wotton. In the 1590s one English interloper, Peter Allen, was supplying goods for import to the Merchant Adventurer Richard Daniel at Middelburg, and he was still based there in 1618, buying and selling goods for William Cokayne.[95] Allen's partner John Heather had a similarly long career, claiming in 1618 to have been involved in the trade for fifteen years, and his master for a further five or six decades.[96]

In 1612 the Company's chief court had again moved from the Netherlands to Germany, to coincide with the relocation of the mart town to Hamburg, where it would remain. In fact the move to Hamburg removed one source of temptation for members to straggle beyond the mart town, the port by now being the undisputed gateway to the inner German market and thus a natural staple. It is also

---

[92] Gelderblom, *Cities of Trade*.   [93] For more, see Chapter 8.
[94] See Chapters 1 and 3.
[95] Richard Daniel account book, 1598–9, Cornwall Record Office, AD567; Thomas Richardson–William Cokayne, 7 Feb. 1618, NRO, C2654. Peter Allen was still in Amsterdam in 1625, then aged 58, when he was a deponent in a Star Chamber suit of an English-based interloper, Roger Dicconson, against one of Allen's principals, Nicholas Leate. STAC 8/116/2. The Merchant Adventurers at some point brought a suit against Allen and Richard Heather, son of William, in the Court of Exchequer, though unfortunately only a list of interrogatories survives. E134/Jas1/Misc18. For further evidence of connections within this community, see the wills of John Heather Sr, 1618, TNA, PROB 11/131/74, and Peter Allen, 1648, TNA, PROB 11/203/446.
[96] Friis, *Alderman Cockayne's Project*, p. 110.

perhaps significant that one of the first acts passed by the Company after moving to Hamburg, made shortly after the arrest of an interloper's goods, was to agree that henceforth unfree English merchants were permitted to trade in non-English goods in return for paying impositions, and consigning goods to Company members: surely a pragmatic response to the proliferation of English merchants engaged in the linen trade, and the extent of cooperation between interlopers and 'disorderly brethren'.[97] One sign that these boundaries were breaking down, at least in Hamburg, was the fact that by 1625 the former interloper William Balden was acting as deputy governor.[98] In fact, in 1622 the Company claimed to have no rules against selling cloth to Englishmen overseas, if true another sign of growing toleration of English interlopers, as long as their activities did not directly compete with those of members.[99] Four years earlier the Company had passed a rule allowing members to sell all textiles except for broadcloth in any part of the Low Countries and Germany.[100] The liberalization that had set into the Company's government in Germany after the imperial mandate appeared to be spreading, potentially opening the way for further penetration of the continental market by members.

When we come to look at the papers of George Warner, William Attwood, John Sanford, and Matthew Ashton later in the century, evidence for activity beyond Hamburg is minimal, however. Occasional evidence survives elsewhere for the 'straggling trade'. In 1638 the Merchant Adventurer Henry Boothby employed an agent to sell new draperies such as says and stuffs alongside goods like knives and gloves in Nuremburg, Prague, and Leipzig, in contravention of a royal order of 1630 that ended the 1618 freedom to sell textiles beyond the mart towns.[101] In the 1660s one London Merchant Adventurer, John Holman, was alleged to have a servant, Matthias Pfizzer, resident at Leipzig where he was responsible for buying linen, though it is unclear whether he also was selling cloth there.[102] However, these are scattered references compared to the opening decades of the century. Since that time, the impact of the Thirty Years War had probably discouraged direct English involvement in the central European market. By the closing decades of the seventeenth century the linen trade was largely in control of Hamburg firms who supplied the increasingly settled community of English merchants at Hamburg, though some of the latter did occasionally venture beyond the mart town to make their purchases in person.[103] Some modest opportunities to circumvent the mart town did occasionally present themselves. In the

---

[97] *Laws*, p. 32.   [98] See Chapter 3.
[99] 'The Answere of the Marchants Adventurers to the Articles of complaint exhibited against them by divers Clothiers of Gloucestershere', 13 Mar. 1622, TNA, SP 16/535, fol. 82.
[100] *Laws*, p.134.
[101] Lancashire Archives, DDCA 1/45. One of Boothby's agents was the future parliamentarian captain and MP Anthony Buller.
[102] Newman, 'Anglo-Hamburg trade', p. 225; Book of Depositions for the burned ships case, TNA, HCA 32/6/1.
[103] Newman, 'Anglo-Hamburg trade', pp. 222–6.

early 1660s William Attwood was interested in purchasing and shipping linen from a supplier in Bremen, and his Hamburg agent Edward Halford advised that 'though our Companies orders admit not that wee should shipp any goods at any port save the mart towne, though wee may buy out of the mart towne.) yet I say the transgressors of that order need not impeach themselves and therfore it can be privately done I see noe great dainger of being found out'.[104] Should Attwood come to Hamburg, the current version of the mart oath simply bound members to swear to pay impositions for goods bought outside of the mart towns, but not 'to discover whether such goods be shipt from the mart town or not', which actions were thus only revealed by presentments being made to the Company officers. Even then, Halford considered that 'if any man liveing in England should be presented, for such a businesse, then every man must be: for if a presentment be it must be onely on suspition, and if one be suspected without proofe all men ought to be in the like suspected'.[105]

At this point the Company was generally not as concerned with regulating imports as it was exports, and so this tolerance is unsurprising, but it had certainly not abandoned the principle of mart trading. In fact, as opportunities for members to straggle into the German mainland receded, the examples when this did happen may have prompted a stronger reaction than had been the case at the start of the century. This was certainly the case with one instance of straggling beyond Hamburg, in 1672. The occasion was the threat of war between England and Hamburg, which threw the Adventurers in the German mart town into consternation, following a warning from the crown that members should take action to secure their goods. The London Merchant Adventurer John Banckes took this command as a pretext to have his agents at Hamburg, his two brothers, send a consignment of eighty bales of stuffs to be sold at Leipzig, via Luneburg. However, when the threat of war passed, many members of the Company turned on the Banckes brothers, threatening them with the full force of the Company's impositions for goods sold outside of the mart towns, and the prospect of imprisonment until they had paid up. When Lord Arlington upheld Banckes' claim that he was merely following royal orders, the Company at Hamburg made a vocal protest, presenting this as an issue with profound consequences. Banckes' claim to be driven by necessity to send his goods from Hamburg was hardly plausible; if this was the case, then the goods could have been safely stored at Luneburg rather than sent all the way to Leipzig. Clearly it was 'a designe & reall intent to make use of that opportunitie for the sale of them at the Lypsicke Mart'.[106] As well as hurting his brethren by spoiling the market at Hamburg, Banckes' actions had upset their customers, who now refused to send any stuffs to Leipzig in the knowledge that the market there was stocked. Should such behaviour become widespread,

[104] Halford–Attwood, 1 May 1660, TNA, C109/24 (Hamburg folder).
[105] Halford–Attwood, 22 May 1660, ibid.
[106] Merchant Adventurers at Hamburg–Lord Arlington, 18 Oct. 1672, Coventry Papers 39, fol. 26r.

the magistrates of Hamburg were sure to withdraw the Company's privileges, which they granted only for 'the reciprocall advantage they have proposed to themselves, by haveinge our Trade confined unto their Cittie'. But this was not the only threat that the affair posed to the Company: Banckes' disobedience struck at the very roots of its authority, which ultimately depended on the behaviour of the membership and their adherence to the 'sacred Oath' of admission, requiring conformity to its rules. Banckes' actions were thus 'a transgression of so high a nature, & soe intollerably mischeavious in the consequnce, if permitted', that they threatened the very status of the Company, 'For the restreyninge of Our Trade to Our Mart Towne is the fundamental Statute of Our Fellowship, upon which all the rest of our Lawes & Ordinances & consequently Our Government have their dependence.' Were they to see these actions go unpunished, other Merchant Adventurers could not be restrained 'from takinge the lyke liberty', and 'if we once fall into that loose way of tradinge out of Our Mart Towne, we may bidde adieu to our Governement, & Priviledges'.

In spite of these arguments, Banckes retained the support of his English patrons, and a royal letter forced the Hamburg court to cancel its proceedings, 'with all humilitie and obedience', as the deputy Sir William Swann put it.[107] But a month later Banckes was still complaining about the 'dayly affronts & abuses' thrown at his brothers 'by the Company, & Strangers, who threaten their utter ruine, besides at least £2000 sterling dammage already susteined thereby'.[108] As late as 1676 Banckes was still petitioning the crown about the 'arbitrary pro-ceedings' at Hamburg against both himself and deputy Swann, who had until then been a consistent supporter.[109] Ultimately the Company's arguments con-vinced the Privy Council, which in January 1677 finally issued an order requiring Banckes, and other members of the Company, to 'submit to the Companys Jurisdiction with all due Obedience, and acquiesce in the Acts & Determinations of their Court, after they shall have been orderly concluded according to the ten-our & direction of his Majestie's Royall Charter'.[110] But by then the case had become embroiled in a larger struggle over the government of the Company and the nature of its regulatory regime, which pitted members in London and Hamburg against each other, to be discussed in detail in Chapter 8.

Conclusion

This chapter has revealed that the regulatory regime that the Company of Merchant Adventurers imposed on its membership was much less static than is

---

[107] Swann–Arlington, 26 Oct. 1672, TNA, SP 82/11, fol. 216.
[108] 'The State of John Banckes Case', TNA, SP 29/318, fol. 88.
[109] Banckes–Sir Joseph Williamson, 6 Jan. 1676, TNA, SP 29/378, fol. 39.
[110] Privy Council order, 10 Jan. 1677, TNA, SP 29/390, fol. 91.

suggested by the elaborate rules compiled by John Wheeler in 1608. Ever since the move from Antwerp, the Company had been attempting to define the boundaries of its trade, and with it the standards of conduct expected of its members. Although the evidence is often limited, it is possible to suggest a narrative of how the Company sought to make its mart-trading system work in the multipolar commercial environment that emerged after Antwerp. The first generation of Merchant Adventurers operating in Germany seem to have been fairly expansive in their trade, willing to venture beyond the mart town both to sell cloth and to purchase imports. After all, having been liberated from dependence on the Antwerp entrepôt and its Dutch middlemen, why should they willingly recreate this situation in the German mart town? With the Company's chief court located in Middelburg, there was probably little to stop many German traders from venturing to places like Nuremburg and Frankfurt. The relocation of this court to Stade in the early 1590s seems to have precipitated an attempt to crack down on such activities, to restore the principle of mart trading, and to restrict the activities of interlopers who had evidently exploited this liberal environment in order to creep into the trade. George Lowe's accounts of how he sought to evade Company discipline is evidence of an internal struggle within the Company. The imperial mandate gave free rein to those who argued in favour of a liberal regime in Germany, meaning that the focus of regulatory efforts switched back to Middelburg, which from 1598 reverted to its role as site of the chief court. By the time that Wheeler came to compile his 'Laws, Customes and Ordinances', the Company was effectively following two distinct regimes on the continent. Having advocated the principle of confining trade to the mart town in his earlier *Treatise of Commerce*, the 1608 manuscript was an effort to define how this could be achieved, by codifying an accretion of practices which could thus be applied wherever the Company chose to relocate.

In fact, only a few years later the chief court left Middelburg again, this time for Hamburg, and there are signs that this was followed by a watering down of certain Company regulations, notably those concerning cooperation with interlopers. Had these efforts been allowed to take root, a very different Company regime might have emerged over time. But it seems that the outbreak of the Thirty Years War acted as a brake on the activities of Merchant Adventurers and interlopers in central Europe, and by the time that stability was restored the merchant community at Hamburg was largely content to be supplied by German firms (although, as Chapter 8 will discuss, by the 1670s many London members were challenging this arrangement). The return to Hamburg also meant that the Company was now safely ensconced in the major gateway port to the central European market, lessening the potential for interlopers in other ports to rival it. The opposite was the case in the Netherlands, where the Company failed to effectively channel cloth exports into a succession of mart towns, much less imports, which were available in abundance at Amsterdam. Ironically, then, whereas at the

start of the seventeenth century supporters of a rigid enforcement of mart trading looked to Middelburg as a model to be applied in 'ungoverned' Germany, as the century went on the positions were reversed: the Company's regulated trade was sustained at Hamburg long after it was effectively abandoned in the Netherlands.

In part this is a story of adaptation to changing commercial patterns, as reflected in how Company members responded to new opportunities and dangers. In order to be effective, Company regulations needed to be responsive to standards of acceptable behaviour within the Fellowship. The response to deputy Ferrers' disciplinary drive in 1590s Stade is evidence of this; for all that Quarles' dealings with interlopers were resented amongst the Fellowship, too many others were also implicated for this drive to be effective. The general attitude of the Company's members is well summed up by Daniel Cooper, on the occasion of Cranfield's Amsterdam trade being noted by the Middelburg court: 'I think there will be all good means used that may be to make the Company all good brethren. If not, a man finding profit has no reason but to take advantage every way as well as others.'[111] Only those members perceived to be gaining an unfair advantage, like John Banckes in the 1670s, were likely to face the full force of Company discipline, although even here the possibility of appealing to outside authorities could mitigate this.

Banckes' case also illustrates how the Company's shifting regulatory regime was not just a response to the changing practices of its membership. Throughout our period, the nature of Company regulations divided the Fellowship and pitted certain members against those in charge of upholding discipline. Whilst there was a general preference for reconciliation—making recalcitrant members 'good brethren', as Cooper put it—this contention could erupt into open conflict In short, the changing nature of Company regulation was also the outcome of political struggles extending beyond its ranks. Much of this contest centred on the degree of authority that the Company could claim over its members, and the extent of their 'liberties': freedom of trade was not just a principle evoked by the Company's external critics. When John Kendrick described a newly introduced oath as 'soe exceedinge strict & that noe evaision can be made, it if be soe that the companie in Generall are to take it', the implication seems to have been that this was a transgression of the normal levels of authority that the Company could claim, and thus of questionable legitimacy.[112] Over time, this issue became bound up with the increasingly fraught relationship between the Company's different residences, which, as Part One has shown, were being drawn apart by changes in the structure of the trade and the career patterns of members.

Furthermore, because the Company depended on active cooperation with rulers in England and overseas in order to make its authority effective, these

[111] Cooper–Cranfield, 4 July 1601, HMC Sackville II, pp. 80–1.
[112] Kendrick–Quarles, 29 Oct. 1597, TNA, SP 46/176, fol. 235v.

internal contests were deeply intertwined with an external struggle to sustain its position in the face of criticisms. The Company's protracted attempts to ensure that John Banckes was reproved for straggling beyond the mart town reveals the difficulty it faced in prosecuting members who could count on influential patrons. That the Company eventually obtained the support of the crown against Banckes is indicative of how reliant it was on active royal support in order to make its privileges operable, but the affair undoubtedly brought the divided state of the Company into unwelcome light. How the Company sought to contain these internal divisions, whilst upholding its status in an increasingly hostile commercial and political environment, will be the central theme of Part Two of this book.

PART TWO

5

'The odious name of a monopolist'

From the Imperial Mandate of 1597 to the 1604 Free Trade Bill

For the young Stade-based Merchant Adventurer George Lowe, the year 1597 was a frustrating one.[1] Since January he had been requesting permission from his master John Quarles to depart the mart town in order to get his hands on the portion left him by his late father, which might at last allow him to commence his career as an independent merchant (Lowe's apprenticeship indenture being due to expire that May).[2] However, Quarles prevaricated, insisting that he remain in order to supervise the sale of cloths delivered in the spring fleet. There was much else to keep his servant busy. The operations of the interloper Thomas Jackson were expanding, as his servants arrived at Prague in order to negotiate for a contract to supply cloth direct to the Emperor, and Lowe was once again impressed with the task of discharging their bills of exchange, this time in the midst of a severe credit crunch.[3] This had partly been triggered by the failure, in the previous year, of Quarles' brother-in-law William Beecher, alongside several other English merchants, by which 'the straungers are...soe pinched...That they are almost at theyr wyttes endes & feare wee wyll all Runne away & our natyon is growne into exceedynge disgrace & contempte amongest these people'.[4] Lowe's presence was required at Stade as much to shore up his master's sinking credit, as to recover those of Beecher's goods which had been seized in Nuremburg.[5] By the time that the Company's fleet finally arrived, in late May, Lowe was pessimistic about the prospects of good sales, but this did not stop him from requesting a further shipment, to be sent to Hamburg via interloper ships and in Jackson's name, in order to avoid detection.[6] All of this 'extraordinary' business had raised the suspicions of the Company court, which (under the zealous deputy governor Thomas Ferrers) had recently introduced an oath to 'fynde out indyrect shippers',

---

[1] For an introduction to Lowe's career, see above, pp. C1.P25-C1.P28.
[2] Lowe–Quarles, 1 Feb. 1597, TNA, SP 46/176, fol. 174r.
[3] Lowe–Quarles, 19 Apr. 1597, TNA, SP 46/176, fol. 197r; 28 Apr. 1597, ibid., fol. 199r; 16 May 1597, ibid., fol. 203r; 24 May 1597, ibid., fol. 205r.
[4] Lowe–Quarles, 9 Aug. 1597, TNA, SP 46/176, fol. 225v.
[5] Lowe–Quarles, 1 Mar. 1597, TNA, SP 46/176, fol. 177r–v.
[6] Lowe–Quarles, 24 May 1597, TNA, SP 46/176, fol. 205r; Lowe–Quarles, 4 June 1597, TNA, SP 46/176, fol. 211r.

Fellowship and Freedom: The Merchant Adventurers and the Restructuring of English Commerce, 1582–1700.
Thomas Leng, Oxford University Press (2020). © Thomas Leng. DOI: 10.1093/oso/9780198794479.001.0001

though having evaded their grasp up to now, Lowe claimed to be unperturbed: 'how much they envye me I doe not knowe nor much care'.[7] Only in the autumn did Lowe finally manage to extricate himself from this tangle of affairs, and return to England.

By the time that he was back in the German mart town in November, the English community in Stade were in a state of turmoil. In Lowe's absence, the Emperor Rudolph II had issued an edict complaining that 'certain companies of merchants have risen up in England, amongst whom are the Merchants Adventurers', who of late had begun 'to settle themselves in heaps in Germany'. Not only had the Company been guilty of encouraging the English crown to inflict 'grievous oppressions' on the towns of the Hanseatic League, 'with great and intolerable alterations against their ancient and dear-obtained privileges', but the subjects of the Empire had suffered from this 'society, staple, college, confederacy', which had inflated the price of English cloth. In sum, the Company of Merchant Adventurers had proved itself to be an 'unrighteous and very shameful monopoly', and the Emperor gave three months' notice for all its members to depart from his lands, on pain of the confiscation of their goods.[8] Lowe reported that the mandate had been published in Stade on 28 October, and 'the comon people are soe incensed agaynst us' that he anticipated travel would soon become difficult.[9]

So began a controversy that would pit members of the Merchant Adventurers against each other as much as their external enemies, and bring the Company's very existence into doubt. This chapter argues that the imperial mandate controversy represented the first major breach in the dual-mart system of trading that had emerged after the Company left Antwerp, and it had lasting consequences. Often, however, this contest has been framed as the final stage of the long struggle between the Company and the Hanseatic League, with little direct relevance to the Company's subsequent history.[10] The Hanseatic League had been agitating for the expulsion of the Company since the early 1580s, in response to its deteriorating position in England.[11] But after the mandate, the Company was able to retain a foothold in the empire before formally being readmitted in 1607, allowing its members to enjoy the fruits of their victory. Astrid Friis presented the early 1600s as something of a golden age for the Company, its successful regulation of the cloth trade suggested by the minimal presence of interlopers in the 1606 port

[7] Lowe–Quarles, 1 Feb. 1597, TNA, SP 46/176, fol. 174r; 6 Apr. 1597, ibid., fol. 196r; 4 June 1597, ibid., fol. 211r.

[8] 'Cecil Papers: January 1597, 11–20', in *Calendar of the Cecil Papers in Hatfield House: Volume 7, 1597*, ed. R. A. Roberts (London, 1899), pp. 16–31. *British History Online*, http://www.british-history.ac.uk/cal-cecil-papers/vol7/pp16-31 [accessed 11 December 2018].

[9] Lowe–Quarles, 3 Nov. 1597, TNA, SP 46/176, fol. 236r–v.

[10] See especially Friis, *Alderman Cockayne's Project*, p. 71.

[11] Lloyd, *England and the German Hanse*, pp. 325–45.

book for London.[12] Although Supple paid more attention to the commercial instability of the last years of Elizabeth's reign, he still saw the years leading up to the Cokayne Project as 'the calm before the storm', with London's cloth exports peaking in 1614.[13] In both accounts, the Company's problems really began thereafter, particularly during the 1620s depression.

To be sure, the Company did face other challenges in the first decade of the seventeenth century, notably in 1604, when it was once again labelled a monopoly, this time in the famous free trade bill that passed the House of Commons in 1604 (though it never made it through the Lords). Typically, Friis presented this as merely the product of the jealousy of ignorant MPs under the sway of provincial interests, rather than the sign of any serious problems in the Company's commercial system.[14] Supple reached a similar conclusion: 'It is much more likely that the agitation for the bills for free trade, which coincided with the Spanish peace, expressed the pressure of provincial, and perhaps London, mercantile capital at the prospect of trade expansion than any long-term discontent with company organization provoked by the economic dislocation of the 1590s.'[15] Although they differed in their interpretations of the social basis of the free trade campaign, Rabb and Ashton essentially framed the 1604 free trade controversy as a contest over how best to organize the anticipated expansion of English trade following the Spanish peace, as well as who would be its chief beneficiaries.[16] The implication of these accounts is that whilst the imperial mandate controversy closed the door on one stage in England's commercial history, the free trade bill was associated with the opening of another: the expansion of English commerce away from northwest Europe. However, the connections between the two events were noted by Ephraim Lipson, who considered that the victory which the Company secured over the Hanseatics in the imperial mandate controversy ultimately 'carried with it the seeds of its destruction: its organization had been severely shaken by the contest: and for some years after the edict of expulsion from Germany its authority was largely in abeyance'.[17] For Lipson the 1604 free trade bill was a sign that this had not gone unnoticed by the political nation: 'the whole outlook of Englishmen had been radically changed by the years of disorganization and freedom'. But as well as providing opportunities for interlopers, the imperial mandate controversy encouraged many members of the Merchant Adventurers to question corporate government, at least in its present form, before audiences including the Privy Council. Arguably these internal contests were as damaging to the

---

[12] Friis, *Alderman Cockayne's Project*, pp. 113–14.   [13] Supple, *Commercial Crisis*, pp. 31–2.
[14] Friis, *Alderman Cockayne's Project*, pp. 149–56.
[15] Supple, *Commercial Crisis and Change*, p. 30.
[16] T. K. Rabb, 'Sir Edwin Sandys and the parliament of 1604', *American Historical Review* 69 (1964), pp. 646–70; Robert Ashton, 'The parliamentary agitation for free trade in the opening years of the reign of James I', *Past and Present* 38 (1967), pp. 40–55; T. K. Rabb, 'Free trade and the gentry in the parliament of 1604', *Past and Present* 40 (1968), pp. 165–73.
[17] Lipson, *Economic History of England. II*, p. 214.

reputation of the Company as any interloping activity, and as much of a foretaste of challenges to come.

'Devyded into Three partes'

The summary of George Lowe's activities in 1597 that opened this chapter illustrates several features of the Company's situation in Stade on the eve of the imperial mandate.[18] As argued in Chapter 4, the German mart town had been the site of a contest within the Company's ranks that probably originated with the arrival of its chief court earlier in the decade, and the selection of a deputy, Thomas Ferrers, who was a zealous opponent of both interlopers and members inclined to 'straggle' to the mainland. It may be that this contest had some bearing on the issuing of the mandate—it is striking that Thomas Jackson's servants were negotiating with the imperial court during this period, and perhaps they were willing to voice complaints about the oppressive actions of the Company at Stade—though the Hanseatic protests were most important.

Whatever the precise cause, in England the mandate was seen as an affront to royal honour, leading to the dispatch of several outraged letters to recipients across the Empire.[19] It also encouraged the Company to act to secure the status of its privileges at Middelburg, which were yet to be ratified by the States General. Early in 1598 commissioners from Middelburg, who were keen to secure the whole trade of the Company, were hosted by the Company in London, where they were warmly welcomed by the governor, Richard Goddard. Then in May Goddard travelled to The Hague accompanied by the experienced diplomat Dr Giles Fletcher, and three other members of the Company, Alderman Thomas Bennet, Thomas Smith/Smyth (probably the future East India Company governor), and William Romney, in order to secure recognition from the States General.[20] But there is evidence that this mission was not welcomed by all members of the Company, a foretaste of the contest to come. The reasons for this may be suggested by the queen's letter in support of Goddard's mission, which advised the States General to consider the advantages they might receive if 'the whole trade of her said Marchantes bee planted there'.[21] Clearly the mission had ramifications not just for the Company's Middelburg residence, but for the overall organization of its trade.

---

[18] The quotation in the heading of this section is from the Petition of the Stade and Emden traders to the Privy Council, c.Apr. 1600. KHLC, U269/1/B83/1.

[19] 'A Memoriall of Certain thinges to be done Concerning the Emperors mandate against the Merchant Adventurers', c.Aug. 1597, TNA, SP 82/4, fol. 72.

[20] C. te Lintum, *De merchant adventurers in der Nederlanden* (Den Haag, 1905), p. 47; Extract of an Act made at The Hague, 14 July 1598, TNA, SP 12/268, fol. 11.

[21] TNA, SP 84/56, #120.

This was certainly the conclusion drawn by an anonymous discourse, which feared that the mission would result in the 'transferring the trade which hath ben at Stoade, into the United Provinces'.[22] The author conceded that the privileged status of the Company rested on its ability to bring order to its trade by establishing it 'in some place propise for the same'. However, this had always been the result of 'great deliberations amongst themselves not onelie of them of longest experience, But alsoe of others, of largest experience of matters in presente use'. The author (clearly a London Merchant Adventurer) went on to argue that this traditional deliberation had not taken place following the late 'interupcion of trade'. Although wary of directly criticizing a crown-sponsored mission, he suggested that 'the Cause is soe waightie as that it ought not to be guyded, ordered and determined by 3 or 4 or anie fewe, buy by the soundest reasons, and perfectest Arguments of the brethren at London (either in generall or by a Committee) being the parties chiefelie or altogeather tradinge bearing chardge, and in all respectes of best quallitie to geve direction'. Above all, it was necessary 'not to depende any thinge or verie litle on that parte of the worshippfull Companie which is at Middleboroughe of whose integritie and indeliberate deallinge in the Companies busynes, thoughe much more might be saide'.

The suggestion of this paper, then, was that the Goddard mission had been undertaken largely on the initiative of the governor, perhaps with encouragement from those Middelburg traders who stood to advantage most from a redirection of trade into the Netherlands, but with little consultation from the wider membership. The mission should therefore be delayed in order to allow those 'discreete persons bothe of Ancient experience, and of present practize' in London to be consulted about appropriate locations for a second mart town in the Netherlands. Much of the paper, however, critiqued the policy of concentrating trade on the Netherlands at all. For the Company to abandon Germany would be to give up markets hard won from strangers, so placing the trade 'into the handes of the undermyninge netherlander whoe to our coste & the burthen of this comen wealthe will mainteyne a middle trade betwixt us & the nowe merchantes'. The conclusion was clear: in 'this variable tyme' when 'everie daye bringeth with it a newe alteration', it did not do to 'cleave onelie to Ancient presidentes', notably the belief that the Company 'did never better then being altogeather in one place in Antwerpe'.

The accuracy of this account of the Company's internal politics after the mandate is difficult to ascertain in the absence of its court records. The queen's letter presented the mission as the Company's own initiative, and it had certainly received many suitors from the Netherlands. But the reaction of George Lowe suggests that many members of the Company in Stade were reluctant to give up

---

[22] BL, Cotton Galba D/XIII, fols 182–3.

their market for the Netherlands. Lowe considered 'groninge Campen haslinghen dort & others' to be 'unfytt for our Resydence bycayse they are to neare mydleburghe', though of these the former was best because of its proximity to German markets.[23] Lowe's letters reveal that initially the Company in Stade had been highly disturbed by the mandate, holding back some ships from the autumn fleet in the event of having to make a hasty departure. Lowe anticipated that the exchange would soon fall as merchants sought cash rather than wares for their sales, and expected that many would struggle to call in their debts before departure.[24] This uneasy mood worsened when four Merchant Adventurers were arrested on their way from Hamburg, in retaliation for one of their fellow members who had taken goods to Spain, presumably without paying.[25] Soon Lowe reported that his countrymen were 'soe desirous to cleare themselves of the country that they cast away theyr cloth at most base prices', whilst their customers did 'hold of, tyll the last cast, thynkynge to have our company at a liste'.[26] However, as the anticipated date of departure grew closer, sales proved to be surprisingly buoyant, and Lowe reported that his countrymen's 'harts are much eased'.[27] They were further heartened by reports that three of the imperial electors had refused to publish the mandate, raising the prospect of the Company remaining in Stade.[28] These hopes were disappointed, and soon the Company's members were ordered to keep to their houses by the Lords of Stade. But following assurance that the Emperor did not intend that 'eyther our persons or our goodes should be trobled', but rather hoped 'to beete downe & abolishe that monopoly[sing] trade which had bene soe longe complayned of to be mayntayned by us', the Lords granted the English merchants free movement again.[29] Lowe was also relieved to hear that Thomas Jackson's servants at Leipzig and elsewhere continued 'in peace & securyty not Respecting the mandate'.[30] He had already instructed his master to provide more cloth for the spring, expecting that he would come away with commissions to supply his customers by whatever means possible.[31] Clearly Lowe believed that trade with Germany would continue, whether or not under the auspices of the Company.

This was precisely the attitude which the Company's government had to contend with over the following months. Planning for Goddard's mission to the States General would have coincided with the return to London of numerous factors and servants from Stade, many of whom would surely have been as eager as

---

[23] Lowe–Quarles, 3 Nov. 1597, TNA, SP 46/176, fol. 236r.   [24] Ibid.
[25] Lowe–Quarles, 8 Nov. 1597, TNA, SP 46/176, fol. 240r. They included Richard Rawstorm, Lionel Cranfield's future factor.
[26] Lowe–Quarles, 22 Nov. 1597, TNA, SP 46/176, fol. 248v; 7 Dec. 1597, TNA, SP 46/176, fol. 258r.
[27] Lowe–Quarles, 27 Dec. 1597, TNA, SP 46/176, fol. 262r.
[28] Lowe–Quarles, 3 Jan. 1598, TNA, SP 46/176, fol. 265r.
[29] Lowe–Quarles, 1 Feb. 1598, TNA, SP 46/176, fol. 271v.
[30] Lowe–Quarles, 7 Feb. 1598, TNA, SP 46/176, fol. 273.
[31] Lowe–Quarles, 25 Jan. 1598, TNA, SP 46/176, fol. 269v.

Lowe to retain their custom there. However, the policy of confining trade to Middelburg had strong support in the upper echelons of the Company. The reasons for this may be gauged by a report of a committee of the Company dating from early 1596 and published at a general court at London, which argued in favour of returning the chief court to Middelburg.[32] Stade had been found unsuitable for this due to its distance from London, meaning that 'intelligence & notice of matters Concerninge & importinge the affaiers & estate of our Fellowshippe can not so speedely & Convenyently pass between us'. Furthermore, experienced London merchants would be more willing to travel to Middelburg in order to serve as assistants, particularly now that the town had been 'enlarged' and the streets 'made more wholsom & sweete'. In any case, the move to Stade had only ever been intended as a temporary expedient whilst the Company at Middelburg was faced by the threats of war and forced loans, and was only to continue so long as the 'Company at London & Midlebrow should thinck yt convenyent'. Once restored to Middelburg, the Company's authority might be enhanced by the court hosting an annual meeting of all assistants from London as well as Middelburg, which would then establish orders to 'stand inviolable withowt change or alteration' for the following year, unless questioned by the court in either London or Middelburg. This was an endorsement of the supremacy of Middelburg, and ultimately London, over the upstart Stade branch, where 'the multitud of greevous domages & discomodities' caused by weak government were readily observable.

With Goddard at the helm, this pro-Middelburg sentiment continued to guide the Company's response to the mandate throughout 1598. Indeed, with its chief court having by default returned to Middelburg as a result of the mandate, and with it the right to elect Company officers, there was little opportunity for opponents of this policy to challenge Goddard's government. Thus in the summer, the Company petitioned the Privy Council requesting that trade to the Empire be prohibited, alongside all Hanseatic commerce with England. This was framed as a diplomatic as much as a commercial matter, the mandate having been procured by a 'Spanish faction' in the Empire in order to hurt the kingdom as much as the Company.[33] The Privy Council followed in August by instructing the London custom house and Admiralty to put this policy into effect, ordering that exporters of woollen cloths into the Company's territories post bond to send them only to Middelburg.[34] But it was not long before the Privy Council began making exceptions, beginning with several Italian merchants who were permitted to ship a specified number of coloured cloths, kerseys, bays, and says to Holland or Emden, on the basis that they were destined for Italy and Turkey.[35] Then in October permission was granted to none other than the interloper Thomas Jackson to

---

[32] 'Reasons set down by the committees in London, touching the removing of the companies authority from Stade to Middleburg. London, Feb. 4, 1595', BL, Cotton Galba D/XIII, fol. 159.
[33] HL, Ellesmere 2380.   [34] APC 1598, p. 25.   [35] Ibid., pp. 165–6.

transport 300–400 fully dyed and dressed cloths to wherever he saw fit.[36] This was a remarkable change of fortune for Jackson, who had been facing a suit in Star Chamber by the Company for continuing in his trade. Jackson was defended in a petition from the Company's old foe, the Clothworkers of London, who used this as an opportunity to restate their grievance about the export of unfinished broadcloth.[37] Another similar petition in the name of London's clothworkers and dyers, probably dating from this time as well, mentioned 'divers other well affected Marchauntes' who had been willing to export finished cloth, only to be prevented by the recent restraint procured by the Merchant Adventurers, 'by whose merciles practizes a greate number of the poorer sorte' would 'endure extreeme myserie'.[38]

At the same time, evidence was being collected of the accumulation of unsold cloths in Blackwell Hall.[39] In response, the Privy Council summoned representatives of the cloth industry and the Company to discuss the case, as well as the shipmasters of Trinity House and some unidentified merchants opposed to the restraint of trade, perhaps numbering Jackson.[40] Faced with these complaints, the Privy Council reversed its position. In November it wrote to customs officials revoking the restraint of trade to Middelburg, but confirming that this action was intended 'neyther to abridge the Merchantes Adventurers of any privyledges graunted them by letters patentes or charter from her Majestie or from any her progenytours, but to leave each parte to that lybertye to trade as they have used heretofore and lawfully that they may or might use before our foresayd letters of retraynte'.[41] This caveat was of little consolation to the Company. It had previously claimed that failure to halt trade into the Empire would 'be a meanes soone to disperse the said marchantes Adventureres & their ancient Fellowshippe'. Now it was unclear whether the Company's privileges even extended to the Empire, a region where it no longer had any official presence.

Fortunately for the Company, it did possess one influential ally in the form of the customs official Richard Camarden, who apparently continued to enforce the restraint of trade to Middelburg well into the new year. This resulted in a new torrent of complaints by clothworkers about the 'sinister and hard dealings of the Marchaunts Adventurers' and their failure to support the domestic cloth finishing industry.[42] This time the Privy Council referred the matter to a committee comprising Stephen Soames, the Lord Mayor of London and an enemy of the Company, Dr Julius Caesar of the Admiralty Court, and Robert Beale, the Council's clerk, who attempted to placate the clothworkers by encouraging the Company to purchase more dyed and dressed cloth, though to no avail.[43] Eventually the Privy

---

[36] Ibid., p. 248.   [37] HL, Ellesmere 2393.   [38] HL, Ellesmere 2390.
[39] HL, Ellesmere 2399, 2400.
[40] For the position of Trinity House, see its petition. HL, Ellesmere 2376.
[41] APC 1598, pp. 325–6.
[42] BL, Lansdowne 152, fols 151–2.
[43] APC 1598–9, pp. 619–20; TNA, SP 12/270, fols 301–2. For Soames, see Chapter 6.

Council hit upon what it doubtless hoped would be an acceptable compromise; in June 1599 trade to the Elbe and Weser was once again forbidden, but it was permitted to Emden as an act of toleration. The anxious report of this measure sent by Lionel Cranfield to his Hamburg factor Gottfried Gortzen gives some indication of the scale of trade to the region over the six months of free trade. Cranfield explained that six ships were lading for Hamburg in London, on which he had laden about 300 cloths and over 200 kerseys, only for the order to arrive compelling them to go to Emden instead. This was enforced by bonds being taken of the shipmasters and owners as well as some of the chief laders, and 'the best of our Company'. Clearly the Privy Council hoped that this would be a definitive settlement, and Cranfield considered that it was enforced with 'such strict order that the like has not been known', such that it had 'put men clear out of their bias'.[44]

Albeit the initial opposition to the August 1598 restraint of trade had been spearheaded by clothworkers and interlopers, it is clear that the contest over the subsequent twelve months had also encompassed discontented Merchant Adventurers. A set of questions 'to be demanded of Mr Romney and others which come with the Governor of the Company of Marchants Adventurers', and apparently provided for the Lord Keeper Thomas Egerton, named the leaders of the two rival parties within the Company.[45] The list of the supporters of the Middelburg restraint was headed by Governor Goddard, described here as 'noe trader', with two of the other seven similarly described as 'a small trader' (Thomas Smith) and 'noe trader' (Baldwyn Dircham). The others were Goddard's deputy William Romney, Richard Hull, described as 'the Cheif devisor of all the hatefull oths urged by the Governor', Alderman Sir Henry Rowe, and the coloured cloth merchant Richard Bowdler. Against them were twelve merchants who supposedly represented 'themselves and divers others whoe carrie the greatest burthen of trade and desire to trade elsewhere', headed by two aldermen, Thomas Bennet and Thomas Lowe. Friis' analysis of the 1606 London port book for cloth exports (the closest surviving to this date) to an extent substantiates the paper's claim that the latter group represented the chief traders of the Company. Five of the twelve in this group exported more than 1,000 cloths in 1606, including the Company's largest exporter, William Freeman (the others were William Burneford, John Quarles' half-brother William Quarles, George Huxley, and Robert Brooke), whilst Thomas Lowe was the third largest exporter of northern kerseys (behind Lionel Cranfield).[46] In contrast only two of the seven pro-Middelburg merchants traded at this scale in 1606.

As well as claiming intimate knowledge of the identity of the rival parties in the Company, this paper summarized certain grievances regarding Goddard's

---

[44] HMC Sackville II, p. 6.   [45] HL, Ellesmere 2378.
[46] The others named in this list were Ferdinando Clutterbuck, who had failed by 1606 (see Chapter 3), Thomas Bennet, Robert Clarke, Richard Venn, and Thomas Wood.

government. The use of 'hatefull oaths' figured prominently, and Egerton added his own note on the paper about 'The oath, To reveale any thing concerning any of the Company. whether they have bought the Clothes they saith, & have others in their owne handes', along with two controversial aspects of the Company's regulations, 'Stynt of quantyty. of tyme.' Much of the paper focused on denying that Middelburg was able to support the entirety of the Company's trade, having only vented about one third of its exports in recent years. The various tolls and charges imposed on English cloth by the States General, alongside the cost of then transporting it to Germany, would render the product uncompetitive, providing an opportunity for Dutch merchants 'to get all the wholl tradinge of Germany bothe for clothe and wares into their owne handes'. Another set of questions to be 'demaunded of the Governor and others of the Company', also in Egerton's possession, probed the argument for withdrawing from the Empire more comprehensively.[47] The paper enquired whether it would be possible to have the mandate revoked, or alternatively 'Whether the marchantes of England Coming as marchantes without Company may be well entertayned for trade within all partes of Germany'; its reference to the 'oathes and other hatefull ordenances' by which the Company sustained its government made clear this author's preferred solution. In fact, the paper went as far as to claim that 'the most & gracious traders of the Company of Marchantes fynding the great inconveniences of the trade at Middleborow' did 'rather desier the Company to be dissolved then to Contynew as they doe', preferring 'to be set at liberty then to contynew in that bondage which is nowe laid on them by the evill governement of the Company'.

The author claimed that several Merchant Adventurers were prepared to double or triple their exports if granted this liberty, and thus requested they be permitted a share of the Company's free licence to export unfinished broadcloths. Whether this was the position of the twelve merchants named in the other paper is unclear, though five of them at least were persistent critics of the Company, and may have been responsible for bringing their grievances into wider view. These merchants, headed by Thomas Wood and William Freeman, alongside Robert Brooke, William Burneford, and two others not mentioned on the earlier list of Stade traders (Ralph Freeman and Edward Ottwood [Attwood?]), had apparently been summoned by the Privy Council to debate their grievances against the Company in August 1599, after the opening of trade to Emden. Although the loss of the Privy Council registers for this period makes the precise subject of this

---

[47] HL, Ellesmere 2374. The dating of this and the other paper is unclear, but a reference to the Company being 'in speech with the Hamburgers' about 'enterteyning of trade withe them' suggests early 1599, when the Company had sent one John Alsop on a private mission for informal talks on this subject with Hamburg and other towns (TNA, SP 82/4, fol. 99). This would link the paper to the period following the Privy Council's reopening of trade to Germany, which the Company was no doubt lobbying against, but it could date from almost any period from 1598 to 1599.

dispute unclear, it is indicative of how the Emden toleration had failed to heal the divisions that had emerged within the Company.

This expedient had been a blow to the pro-Middelburg party within the Company, but with the Company's authority now firmly ensconced in Middelburg, this group at least had an opportunity to assert their pre-eminence over the Emden merchants. This they first sought to achieve through the medium of the Company's impositions, charged on each exported cloth. As an order of the Middelburg court explained in January 1600, although the German traders had been found to 'have lytle regarde to observe the lawfull ordenances established for the goverment, rule, and maintenance of the saide Company', they were still dependent on the Company to admit their sons and apprentices to the freedom. Thus the court restated the order that all those seeking admission to the freedom at Middelburg should bring certificate that their master had paid all impositions for cloth shipped to Emden or elsewhere for the previous two years, or pay these arrears, so sending the message that the German traders were still under its government.[48] Then in the following month the court passed a more aggressive act, in the form of the deceptively entitled 'Act for the reconciliation of our brethren as have bene disorderlye traders unto the unitye of the felowshippe'.[49] The act stated that ever since the 'breakeing up of the Companie from Stade', many members had continued shipping cloth to Germany in non-Company shipping, making them liable to the fine of 40s. for each cloth that was 'mis-shipped'. However, the act stated, in the hope of restoring them to obedience it had been agreed that those members concerned could pay a lesser fine of 2s. per cloth if they were willing within the next two months to admit on oath to the number of cloths mis-shipped from 28 January 1598 to 25 December 1599.

Although ostensibly a generous offer, this did not prevent the Wood–Freeman group from petitioning the Privy Council in April in protest against these charges, as well as a further £60 fine they were facing for refusing to attend the court at Middelburg. They were also being deprived of their share of the free licence of white cloth exports until they agreed to take the oath in question. Chiefly, they objected to being penalized for mis-shipping during a 'Tyme of Troble', for at least some of which trade had been expressly permitted by the crown.[50] The complainants considered that the act had been passed in revenge for them having earlier been the chief petitioners for the 'Free Tolleracion for Emden', with the Middelburg traders allying with those who were 'No Traders at all' against the Stade/Emden traders, despite the latter managing two thirds of the whole trade. Furthermore their petition complained that 'to accuse our selves by Oathe In

[48] 'Extracts from the Records of the Merchant Adventurers of Newcastle-upon-Tyne. Vol. I', pp. 109–10.
[49] BL, Lansdowne 152, fol. 170–1.
[50] Petition of the Stade and Emden traders to the Privy Council, c.Apr. 1600. KHLC, U269/1/B83/3.

matters penall' was 'unlawfull'. These were serious criticisms indeed, and the Company responded by disenfranchising the petitioners.[51]

So the matter once again came before a by now thoroughly wearied Privy Council.[52] Although on the surface this was a minor issue, the stakes were high. The Company claimed that the 'straggling' of the German traders in spite of the original royal restraint of trade to Middelburg had discouraged German merchants from travelling there, so causing the project to fail, whilst by petitioning the Privy Council its critics had aimed to 'frustrate all the Charters of privilege' granted to the Company.[53] For their part, the petitioners repeated their charge that the Company's actions were illegal, partly on grounds that they had been denied opportunity to 'complaine to any higher power', and demanded a wholesale reform to ensure that 'the governors & other officers of the said Company bee such as bee traders both for Midelbro & Germanie'.[54] The fact that the Privy Council summoned two of those listed as supporters of the German trade, Aldermen Bennet and Lowe, alongside the vigorously pro-Middelburg Governor Goddard, suggests that its aim was to restore peace to within the Company's ranks.[55] It is notable that the Wood–Freeman group had themselves requested 'Pacification with our company' rather than its dissolution.[56] Eventually the commissioners entrusted with brokering a deal reported that all sides were 'at union touching their trade & adventure for tyme to come', with the complainants agreeing to pay a fine of £250 each and 'to submitt & conforme themselves to th'orders of the Company', though they added the telling caveat 'so as they be not repugnant to the lawes of the Realme'.[57] This might be the reason why the Company subsequently petitioned to complain that in this agreement 'some thinges have bene omytted and some others misunderstood'.[58] Only in October were the rival parties persuaded to come to terms, whereby both parties agreed to 'continue and bee sociable the one to the other'. Although the fine of £250 was confirmed and the complainants agreed to be 'alwaies obsequious and obedient' to Company government, the deal had apparently been 'altered in favour of those disorderly traders' by the Lord Chief Justice.[59]

The Company had thus survived the controversy with its charters intact and its recalcitrant members restored to the fold, but this was a pyrrhic victory at best. Emden still lay largely beyond the control of the court at Middelburg. Its weakened condition was shown in the following year, when the Company faced a

---

[51] 'The matters of greevance betweene the company of the Marchant Adventurers and some members of the same', 12 June 1600. BL, Lansdowne 152, fol. 162r.

[52] APC 1600, p. 277.   [53] HMC Sackville I, pp. 32–3.

[54] 'Matters of greevance', BL, Lansdowne 152, fol. 162v.   [55] APC 1600, pp. 361–3.

[56] Petition to the Privy Council, 8 June 1600, BL, Lansdowne 152, fols 153–4.

[57] Certificate of 14 June 1600, ibid., fol. 158r.

[58] Privy Council order, 22 June 1600, ibid., fol. 157r.

[59] Copy of the agreement, 17 Oct. 1600, Bodl. Lib., North A1, fol. 210. A slightly different copy is in BL, Lansdowne 150, fol. 18.

further challenge in the form of a petition to the Privy Council from some unidentified English merchants trading to Germany. This requested 'free libertye of traffique' to Stade as well as Emden, for 'all Straungers, as also hir Maiesties subiectes', though it claimed to have no objections to the Company's charters.[60] By then the immediate shock of the imperial mandate had faded, and the rulers of Stade were keen to find some way to welcome back English merchants. Accordingly on 29 March 1601 the crown lifted the restraint of trade to Stade for all merchants, Merchant Adventurers or otherwise.[61] All that was left to the Company's deputy Richard Gore was to appeal that the continuation of trade to Hamburg by a 'disobedient crew' (perhaps including the Wood–Freeman group) be halted.[62]

When at the end of that year it appeared that the terms of the mandate might be enforced on the English merchants in Stade, on the basis that the members of the Company had 'taken in againe their former lodginge and packhowses, and used their trade as in former time', the Company at London again considered the possibility of withdrawing from the Empire, potentially to Groningen.[63] This was also seen as an opportunity for the 'false bretheren' of the Company guilty of straggling into Germany to be 'brought in question by the Governour of the said Companye for breaking theire orders'.[64] But the move to Groningen did not happen, and the English merchants at Stade were able to continue in their 'accustomed manner', effectively beyond the reach of Company discipline.[65] The Company's representative at the imperial court John Alsop had communicated news of the danger they were facing to a group of the chief traders at Stade, who seem to have been acting as unofficial leaders of the Merchant Adventurers there.[66] They were headed by William Pennifather, a chief linen trader to Münster and heavily involved in the inland trade, as was another of the group, William Jones.[67] With these 'straggling' traders effectively in charge of the Stade residence, the prospects of the Company withdrawing from the Empire were remote; as Lionel Cranfield's Stade factor Richard Rawstorm reported in December, should they be expelled from Stade, 'the Hamburgers will willingly entertain us and suffer us to trade in their town at our pleasure'.[68] In subsequent negotiations

---

[60] 'The matters which the Marchaunts of England trading to Germanye are suitors for in respect of the better utterance of the commodities of the lande', TNA, SP 12/272, fol. 274r.

[61] BL, Lansdowne 150, fol. 19.

[62] Petition dated 14 June 1601, BL, Lansdowne 150, fol. 24v. For Ralph Freeman's trade to Hamburg c.1600, see TNA, C78/161/4.

[63] John Alsop's report on his proceedings at the imperial court and Stade, 28 Nov. 1601, TNA, SP 82/4, fols 135–8; Senate of Groningen to Privy Council, 17 October 1602, HMC Salisbury, 12, p. 111.

[64] Governor Christopher Hoddesdon–Secretary Cecil, 19 Mar. 1602, TNA, SP 12/283a, fol. 109.

[65] Ibid.   [66] For the response of Richard Rawstorm, see HMC Sackville II, p. 99.

[67] Baumann, *Merchants Adventurers*, pp. 347–8, 357–8. The other two were Thomas Flower and Mr Moore. Pennifather was based in Stade in December 1600, several months before members of the Company were permitted to return there. HMC Sackville II, pp. 46–7.

[68] HMC Sackville II, p. 103.

regarding the status of the English merchants at Stade, the latter were keen to emphasize how they were willing to conform to the terms of the mandate 'towchinge the accursed monopolie', addressing themselves as 'The generall English Merchants heere at Stoad' and studiously avoiding any taint of corporate affiliation.[69] By 1603, the London court was again complaining of the continuation of trade to Hamburg, and appealed to the king 'to worke for them, that they may be able to bear againe the face of a Company In Germany ere it be longe wherby good orders amongst them they may redresse such disorders which through a promis-cous liberty in tradinge of late tymes are Crept in'.[70]

Chapter 4 discussed the liberal environment in which the Company's trade to Germany was conducted in the first decade of the seventeenth century, with 'strag-gling' to places like Nuremburg seemingly winked at. One Merchant Adventurer heavily involved in this trade was Alderman Thomas Lowe, who seems to have played an important though rather shadowy role in bringing the disputes of the previous years to an end, and in fact he had a long history of engagement in the inland trade.[71] It is surely significant, therefore, that he was acting as the Company's governor by 1612, by which time the Company's chief court had moved to Hamburg.[72] The defeat of the pro-Middelburg party was complete.

In this context, rather than being the definitive statement of the Company's political economy, John Wheeler's famous *Treatise of Commerce* appears as a des-perate attempt to sustain an ideal of corporate trade that was in danger of being abandoned by a substantial number of Merchant Adventurers. Published at Middelburg with a dedication dated 6 June 1601, this classic account of the advantages of trading to a single place rather than 'straggling' after customers closed with an exhortation to all 'true hearted Marchantes Adventurers', to 'faint not in your orderlie, and hetherton wel continued course'.[73] Wheeler also warned his brethren not to be tempted by 'daungerous persons, louers of themselues, and enemies to your good, and the welfare of your Societie'. Perhaps he had in mind those petitioners who had called for free trade into Germany three months earl-ier, fearful that many Merchant Adventurers might be more willing to take up such an opportunity than to remain loyal to the Company's orders. As secretary to the Company at Middelburg, over the previous three years Wheeler would have been heavily involved in crafting its response to the mandate, and the

---

[69] Petition of the Stade merchants to the imperial commissioners, 10 Feb. 1603, BL, Cotton Galba D/XIII, fol. 202.

[70] BL Lansdowne 150, fol. 21r; 'An answere of the Merchantes Adventurers...on behalfe of them and their trade unto the Messauge delivered to the Kinges most Excellent Majestie by Reinerus Langius Secretary to the City of Stoade', TNA, SP 82/5, fol. 86.

[71] Baumann, *Merchants Adventurers*, pp. 351–2.

[72] The controversial Goddard had been succeeded by the venerable merchant Christopher Hoddesdon, perhaps in 1600, and then Sir Henry Rowe.

[73] Wheeler, *Treatise of Commerce*, pp. 112–13.

arguments put forward in the *Treatise* were perhaps developed in this context.[74] But if in 1601 his position appeared to be losing ground within the Company, three years later it would have call to draw on his arguments in defence of an ordered trade, in face of a potentially even more serious challenge.

From the Imperial Mandate to the Free Trade Bill of 1604

Over the years during which the imperial mandate controversy had unfolded, the divided state of the Merchant Adventurers had been exposed to a number of influential politicians. The effect of this on the Company's reputation may be gauged by the responses of two who became drawn into arbitrating these disputes. The first, the clerk of the Privy Council Robert Beale, possessed extensive diplomatic experience which had brought him into contact with the Company several times, and this probably influenced his response to the question of whether to open up trade into Germany. Rooting his paper on the subject in classical aphorisms, Beale highlighted the dangers of innovation in what was, because of the importance of the cloth trade, 'a greate matter of State'.[75] His response was impressively well informed on the Company's history, and endorsed the position that overseas trade could only be safely conducted under special privileges. This had recently been proven by the seizure of Thomas Jackson's cloth at Leipzig under the terms of the mandate, which had only been discharged 'uppon a Collusorie oathe made in the behalf of his factor'.[76] Corporate government was particularly necessary in the current polarized international situation, and for English merchants to continue to trade into territories which had openly labelled the Company a monopoly would be to 'ioyne handes with the Enemyes of us all'.[77] Probably the paper was written shortly before the restraint of trade into the Empire was lifted in November 1598, and Beale argued that, despite any assurances that this would not hurt the Company's privileges, the effect would be to the contrary. Any Merchant Adventurer taking advantage of this liberty would be 'exposed to the enemyes danger of the Mandate, unles bothe in worde and deede his Corporacon be broken', whilst those remaining at Middelburg would find their markets spoiled.[78] If this was to be allowed, 'Must not the Companie decaye and come to nothing?'[79]

The pro-Middelburg party within the Company would have heartily endorsed these arguments. However, even as supportive a figure as Beale raised some

---

[74] See, for instance, a manuscript of 'Reasons why Restraint of transporting Cloth and other woollen Commodities to other places foreign, save the Mart Town, is very behoofull for the Common wealth', which presented the issue in very similar terms to Wheeler's *Treatise*, and may have been written by him. HL, Ellesmere 2389.

[75] BL, Add. 48126, fol. 32r.   [76] Ibid., fol. 36r.   [77] Ibid., fol. 34v.   [78] Ibid., fol. 36v.
[79] Ibid., fol. 37r.

cautions which they might not have been so comfortable with. Beale admitted that if the trade was being newly established, and if the present time was one of 'peace, good amitye, open vent for our comodities without emportment or interrupcion', then 'such an alteracon might be the boldlier attempted'.[80] Even more concerning, Beale conceded that it was possible that the Company had 'made orders & rules more, then they ought to have authority to doe', though he called for it to be reproved if this was the case, and not overthrown.

Another experienced politician, the lawyer Sir John Popham, chief justice of the Queen's Bench, took his criticisms of the Company much further, having been called by the Privy Council to adjudicate in its disputes with the clothworkers in November 1598. As we saw in Chapter 4, Popham had acted to limit the Company's powers over non-members when overseeing its new charter a decade earlier, and the mandate only confirmed his reservations about its privileges. On a note itemizing the falling price of cloth overseas from 1594 to the end of October 1598, Popham scribbled a suggestion that the proclamation of 1587 for free export of cloths be reissued.[81] Popham also opposed barring the Hanseatic League from trading to England in retaliation for the mandate, suggesting that this would hurt English merchants outside of the Empire, such as those of the Eastland Company. The efforts of the Merchant Adventurers to channel trade into Middelburg merely demonstrated that they did 'seke to drawe the whole Traffyque that way both outward and Inwardes to them selves onely'.[82] When in early 1600 he heard news that the Company was planning to send an agent to Emden in order to bring some government to the merchants there, Popham strongly objected, writing that 'yt wuld shortly overthroughe that trade'.[83] His hostility to the Company had not waned five years later when the incorporation of trade into France and Spain was under consideration. Popham wrote to the Earl of Salisbury that his experience was that 'what pretences soever the Marchantes make to drawe themselves into companyes, they ever have in yt their privat ends, and all those take their ground from the Marchantes adventurers'. Thus he considered it a principle that 'yt is not Convenient that Marchantes have such power passed over unto them, as that thereby they may govern the estate of thinges both at home and abroad as they list, and they not to be Curbed therein by the State'.[84]

As well as hearing the cases of the Company and its rivals in person, individuals such as Popham and Beale would have been exposed to some of the numerous manuscripts on the subject that have survived in the papers of politicians such as Caesar and Egerton. The majority are anonymous, and many were doubtless produced by those with a direct stake in the contest, particularly those which

---

[80] Ibid., fol. 32v.   [81] HL, Ellesmere 2333.
[82] HL, Ellesmere 2377.   [83] Popham–Salisbury, 22 Feb. 1600, CP 68/45.
[84] Popham–Salisbury, 11 Sept. 1605, CP 112/63. See also Robert Ashton, *The City and the Court 1603–1643* (Cambridge, 1979), pp. 94–5.

focused on restating the cases for and against restraining trade to Middelburg, or restricting exports to fully dyed and dressed cloths.[85] Some at least addressed the issue from a broader commercial perspective, however, suggesting that the mandate controversy was responsible for generating a wider discourse on the advantages and disadvantages of Company government. The majority of these were critical of the Company in some way. Whereas most of the debate between Merchant Adventurers and clothworkers focused on exports, one paper written in answer to the Company's petition of July 1598 emphasized the effect that withdrawing from Germany would have on imports.[86] Stade had previously been a source of goods from across Germany, including many territories 'whoe are noe parties in the Acion of the mandate' and which continued to welcome English merchants, as well as from Italy and other distant parts; all these places would suffer from the measure far more than the intended victims, the Hanseatic towns. To limit imports to the Netherlands would raise their cost dramatically, to the harm not just of the nobility and gentry who purchased imported silks and velvets, but also 'the meane sorte of people' who depended on cheaper fustians and linen. The Merchant Adventurers themselves, of course, would only profit from such a restraint. When it came to exports of cloth, the author favoured encouraging their full dyeing and dressing, and hinted that some merchants were prepared to undertake a project to encourage this, a precursor to the Cokayne Project. Above all, though, the paper stressed that it was expedient to take whichever measures were necessary to dispatch the stocks of unsold cloth that were accumulating, 'it being now, no tyme to aggravate matters of discord & discontent as the said Marchauntes Adventurers by thextremenes of their courses would urge and bring to passe'. The danger otherwise would be that the Emperor would extend his mandate to the banishment of English cloth in its entirety. Unfortunately, the treatise complained, the Company's current policy of tying its members to their mart towns frustrated any efforts to find new markets, particularly for dyed and dressed cloth, and it concluded with a condemnation of the Company's repressive orders, through which 'they have undone and much wronged many of her Majesties Subjectes aswell of their owne fellowshipp as others'. Particular hostility was reserved for the 'suttle oathes' enforced on 'every trifling matter', which had 'brought as it were such an Atheisme amongst a great sorte of them, whoe to save their purses...will rather forswere them selves then confesse the truth'. Indeed, these oaths could be accounted 'but a snare to draw men into their daungers to pray upon them at their pleasures'.

---

[85] See, for instance, 'Reasons for restraint of English Commodities to be transported into the Rivers of Elve and Embs', May 1599, BL, Lansdowne 152, fols 140–1; 'Reasons why Middelboroughe or any parte of the united Provinces are not fitte for the ventinge of the whole wollen Commodities of this Lande', HL, Ellesmere 2395.

[86] 'Exceptions by way of Answere to the Supplication of the Marchants Adventurers, showing how prejudiciall their requests are to the Commonwealth', HL, Ellesmere 2381.

Not all commentators were as openly hostile to the Company as this one, but most were critical in some way. One author computed the annual losses caused by restricting trade to Middelburg at £100,000, a heavy price to uphold at most 300–400 traders, but still recognized the profitable 'service' that the Company had hitherto performed. However, in these changed circumstances 'the generall good & profite of the whole commen wealth is to be regarded & preferred before the private respect of a few particular personns'.[87] Another paper began by admitting 'that the marchaunt adventurers hath beene good members of the common wealthe and therefore not to be dissolved', but argued that the laws passed in recent years by 'their governours and other officers whoe be not traders' had prejudiced the younger sort of the Company, as well as clothiers.[88] Those laws singled out were the restriction of shipping to biannual fleets, the recent restraint of trade to Middelburg, and the enhanced cost of imports due to the great tolls and charges that they were subject to there. But the author objected to the 'Rigorous manner of gouernment' in general, epitomized by the clearing oath being imposed whenever ordinances were breached. In present circumstances, it would be best to dissolve this government and allow open trade, which would provide the opportunity for the Company to assess possible new mart towns, though not in one or two places as had been the case in the past. Rather, 'the dispersing of themselves into sundry places will cawse the magistrates of every place in hope of theire Rezidence with them, favourably to protect them'.

For another commentator, this last point was sufficient to question the existence of trading companies altogether. For all the 'pollished reasons' such companies proposed for their existence, they were essentially preoccupied with controlling the level of imports and exports in order to 'enriche themselves', to the detriment of consumers and producers.[89] Such practices were not limited to the Company Merchant Adventurers, but equally applied to 'those of Tripoly, Eastland, or Muscovy'. Should imports not be restrained in this manner, the paradoxical effect would be that merchants would be encouraged to bring home their returns in money rather than wares, finding that the latter were in such abundance that they offered little gain. The author's focus, however, was on exports, and he concluded that 'It is not one twoe or three places will serve to vent the Comodeties that England maie spare but the more may be gotten, or sought out, the better the vent will be.' Rather than being restrained by geographically defined corporate privileges, merchants should be encouraged to 'seeke out' new markets. The paper ended with the assurance that 'Companies maie in some sorte and within some Compasse be permitted', but their precise status was left unclear.

---

[87] 'Certaine Reasons to prove that a tolleration of shipping for the River of Elve during this mandate of Themperor is very profitable both for her Majestie & the Realme', TNA, SP 12/265 fols 114–15.

[88] Untitled paper on the privileges of the Merchant Adventurers, HL, Ellesmere 2386.

[89] 'For the matter touchinge the marchaunt adventurers', HL, Ellesmere 2379.

Not all of these arguments were novel. Clothworkers and clothiers had for many years been arguing not only that the Merchant Adventurers were negligent in failing to support the domestic dyeing and finishing industry, but also that the Company's practices deliberately limited the scale of exports in order to inflate members' profits. Only 'a Large and Liberall vente' overseas could counteract these monopolistic tendencies.[90] The argument that the full potential level of cloth exports could only be reached by actively seeking out customers rather than waiting for them to attend the mart town had been implicit in the initial move from Antwerp, though the imperial mandate gave added weight to it. The more novel critique of Company rule arguably came from within its own ranks, in the form of those complaints about rigid and restrictive government so prominently voiced by the Wood–Freemen group. By stressing the usage of oaths in administering this system, critics of the Company were able to frame this as a matter of conscience as much as commerce. And by presenting the Company as claiming powers which exceeded its charters, this became an affront to sovereign authority and so a matter of state. It seems too that the Company's legal status was facing scrutiny, in terms of both the precise nature of the powers that its charters established, and the parliamentary acts that could be seen as a limit on them, particularly that of 1497 opening access.[91]

In fact the act of 1497 figured prominently in the next major challenge that the Company faced, the free trade bill of 1604. Much of the debate on the latter has focused on the reasons why the gentry-dominated House of Commons was willing to support this measure, with provincial resentment against the dominant London companies being the usual explanation.[92] Although the Merchant Adventurers were prominent amongst the companies under attack, from this perspective the bill was as much intended to prevent the establishment of new corporations, with Parliament successfully blocking the re-establishment of the Spanish Company in 1606, principally due to the hostility of West Country interests.[93] However, although these provincial interests dominated once the Commons came to debate the issue, the focus on the response of the MPs has been to the neglect of the origins of the bill, and the discussions held before the parliamentary committee headed by Sir Edwin Sandys prior to the parliamentary

---

[90]   Notes on the decay of trade, HL, Ellesmere 2334.
[91]   See, for instance, 'Certaine notes out of the Statutes shewing e the libertie that hath bene graunted to all subiectes for transporting of all woollen commodities', May 1599, TNA, SP 12/20, fol. 303; an extract from the Company's charters, May 1599, BL, Lansdowne 152, fols 144–5; 'Concerninge the Companie of Marchants Adventurers of London', HL, Ellesmere 2387.
[92]   Rabb's attempt to see this in terms of the gentry's growing desire to invest in overseas trade via joint stock companies as opposed to regulated ones such as the Merchant Adventurers was dismissed by Ashton on the grounds that several joint stocks were subjected to parliamentary attack: see works cited in footnote 16, above.
[93]   Pauline Croft, 'Free trade and the House of Commons 1605–6', *Economic History Review* 28 (1975), pp. 17–27.

debate. Attention to this initial stage of the contest suggests that the Merchant Adventurers were more central to it than has sometimes been suggested, and that the Company faced as much hostility from London as provincial merchants.

The bill for 'all Merchants to have free Liberty of Trade into all Countries, as is used by all other Nations', received its first hearing in the Commons on 18 April, to be joined on the following day by one 'for the Enlargement of Trade for his Majestie's Subjects into foreign Countries', though subsequently the concerns of this latter bill were absorbed into the former.[94] According to the Venetian ambassador this was supported by 'a petition complaining of monopolies signed by many merchants', although this has not been located.[95] Whoever had been responsible for presenting these two bills, it is clear that at this point the Merchant Adventurers were very much their chief target. The surviving copy of the bill for free trade began by citing the parliamentary act of 1497, before discussing how the Company had subsequently procured privileges to overturn this act 'by Letters unduly procured to the Customers and Ports and other undue means'.[96] Only having identified the 'Evill Precedent' of the Merchant Adventurers were other companies—for Russia, Eastland, Spain, the East Indies, and Turkey—mentioned as subsequently having received charters 'against the Common wealth of this Realm'. Rather than request open admission to these companies on the lines of the 1497 act, the bill intended to establish free trade for all of the king's subjects who were not 'Cloathiers Retailers Inholders Farmers Mariners nor using any handycraft'. Even so, the only places specified in the bill were 'Holland Flanders Zeland Brabant', in other words the traditional territories claimed by the Merchant Adventurers but not, significantly, its newer German markets.[97]

These last points suggest that the bill represented the wishes of interlopers seeking to break the Company's privileges, particularly in the Low Countries. Potentially they were provincial merchants, but when the Sandys committee met to hold hearings about the two bills, Londoners were dominant, with three out of four London merchants said to support the bill. Although interlopers from London and elsewhere had been a thorn in the Company's side for many decades, the former had recently acquired a new grievance which may have prompted them to take their complaints to the new parliament. In August 1601 the Earl of Cumberland had been granted a ten-year licence to export an unlimited number of undressed cloths, and he had soon begun selling shares of this licence to

---

[94] CJ, I, pp. 176–8.

[95] 'Venice: June 1604', in *Calendar of State Papers Relating To English Affairs in the Archives of Venice, Volume 10, 1603–1607*, ed. Horatio F. Brown (London, 1900), pp. 154–64. *British History Online*, http://www.british-history.ac.uk/cal-state-papers/venice/vol10/pp154-164 [accessed 11 December 2018].

[96] 'An Act for Free Trade for all Merchants into all Countries beyond the Seas', BL, Lansdowne 487, pp. 353–4.

[97] Ibid., p. 355.

interlopers, although he protested that he had been forced to do so as a result of a boycott by Merchant Adventurers, which was a 'malytyus platt' intended to see the licence revoked.[98] In fact, Cumberland also found willing customers for his licence amongst some 'false bretheren' of the Company who had 'long practised to trade to places where the said Marchantes Adventurers be not priviledged'. According to the experienced Merchant Adventurer Christopher Hoddesdon, this threatened 'the overthrowe of the most famous Company of Marchantes in all Christendome'.[99] Very likely Hoddesdon was referring to the Wood–Freeman group. Soon the Company opened negotiations to purchase exclusive rights to Cumberland's licence, warning that otherwise 'the utter dissolcon of our Companye must necessarilye ensue'.[100] Despite the protests of interlopers and the warning of Sir John Popham that this would allow the company to 'beat downe the prices of our Cloathes', the Company eventually struck a deal to pay Cumberland 2s. 2d. for each cloth exported under his licence.[101] Possibly those interlopers deprived of the opportunity to partake in the trade in white cloths were the chief advocates of the 1604 bill.

The Company responded to this threat with its own lobbying initiative, producing several copies of a manuscript which comprehensively denied 'the odious name of monopoliste'.[102] This began with the Company's long history of royal preferment, notwithstanding the 1497 act, which had been violated by those 'irregular, and ungoverned marchantes' who took advantage of the concession by refusing to obey Company orders, as the 1497 act had in fact required of them.[103] The paper proceeded to outline the virtues of a 'governed trade', in much the same terms as John Wheeler's *Treatise of Commerce*, with an emphasis on concentrating trade to 'one or more certayne Townes, where the said marchantes made their residence', as opposed to the disorderly practices of an 'unskilfull multitude'.[104] The paper argued that those privileges which the Company had acquired overseas were conditional on inhabiting such mart towns, and emphasized the good reputation its members had built up overseas by following its orders.[105] The bill itself argued the contrary: such companies had been a 'discredit of the Merchants of

---

[98] Friis, *Alderman Cockayne's Project*, pp. 72–3; Cumberland–Ellesmere, 5 Mar. 1602, HL, Ellesmere 2409.

[99] Hoddesdon–Cecil, 19 Mar. 1602, TNA, SP 12/283, fol. 109v. Spence, 'Cliffords, Earls of Cumberland', p. 256.

[100] 'The humble peticion of the Companye of Marchants Adventurers of England, for a license to transporte undressed Clothe, &c. Against the E. of Cumberland', HL, Ellesmere 2368.

[101] Hoddesdon–Cecil, 6 Mar. 1602, TNA, SP 12/283a, fols 95–6; notes on the case between the Merchant Adventurers and interlopers, BL, Cotton Vespasian C/XIV2, fol. 123. Popham's opinion seems to be represented in a document which, though unsigned, included a note added by him as well as alterations by Ellesmere. 'Remembrances touchinge the Marchants Adventurers', HL, Ellesmere 2382.

[102] 'A Discourse made by the marchant Adventurers upon occasion of a Bill preferred to the highe court of Parliament, requiring free liberties of trade into all Kingdomes & Countries', BL, Harleian 36, fol. 28v.

[103] Ibid., fol. 32r.   [104] Ibid., fol. 32v.   [105] Ibid., fol. 34r.

this Realm in foreign Nations, who are Enemies to such Monopolies and sole Trading, the Canker and Decay of well governed Commonwealths'.[106] Similarly, a petition in the bill's favour cited the 'bitter imputation in forreign Countries of breeding Monopolies', a clear reference to the imperial mandate.[107] Furthermore, another paper argued, the aftermath of the mandate contradicted the Company's argument that the 'skill and Government' of its members were necessary prerequisites for the successful vent of English cloth. This was disproven by the 'late experience at Stoade, where they have had no Government the 4 or 5 yeares past', but 'the Cloath hath had as good vent as before, and our Nation better welcome to the people, who many times before opposed their misgovernment in restraining the trade which of late years the better part of the trading merchants procured from some of your Honours'.[108]

This last reference comes from a manuscript copy of Sandys' report, but belongs to a section which was omitted from the version entered in the Commons Journal when it was presented by Sandys on 31 May, although some of its points appear in a slightly changed form elsewhere in that document. The omitted passage was a series of answers to objections raised by the Company, written in the first person plural and addressed to 'your Honours', suggesting that it was originally part of a document presented to the committee on behalf of certain merchants (the paper mentioned that 'most of the merchants which desire liberty of trade' were also shipowners, so answering the objection that they would favour using foreign shipping).[109] This is indicative of how Sandys' report was a composite document, summarizing several reasons for the bill that had been presented to the committee, rather than simply the opinion of the committee itself. It can thus be said to represent the views of a range of interested parties as well as Sandys and the other members of the committee, who were perhaps responsible for framing the issue in terms of the 'Natural Right' of freeborn subjects, a term missing from the bill itself.[110] Many of its points were probably drawn directly from evidence submitted by the various groups attending the committee. For instance, the argument that a 'more equal Distribution of the Wealth of the Land' was 'a great Stability and Strength to the Realm even as the equal Distributing of the Nourishment in a Man's Body' had previously been made in a paper arguing in favour of distributing trade throughout the 'great Body of this Common-wealth', on the basis that 'The strength of the King consisteth in the riches of many subjects and not of a few'.[111]

---

[106] 'An Act for Free Trade for all Merchants into all Countries beyond the Seas', BL, Lansdowne 487, p. 355.
[107] 'The Copy of the Petition to the Kings Majesty', ibid., p. 335.
[108] 'Instructions touching the Bill for free Trade in the Parliament', ibid., p. 298.
[109] Ibid.   [110] 'The Copy of the Petition to the Kings Majesty', ibid., p 335.
[111] Untitled response to the Merchant Adventurers' answer against the bill for freedom of trade, ibid., p. 321.

This latter paper was probably submitted on behalf of clothiers or clothworkers who were hoping to be admitted to the Company, as the author asserted that the Company's present members would 'find Merchants of other Trades as provident as they are in their practice'.[112] In fact, the possibility of extending the liberty of trade granted in the bill to clothiers was debated in the Commons, though ultimately rejected. The principal beneficiaries of the opening up of trade would therefore be London merchants: as the Sandys report stated, 'the main Trade of all the white Cloth, and much of other Kind, is shipped from the Port of London, and will be still, it being the fittest Port of the Kingdome for Germanie and the Low Countries'. However, once the matter came under debate in Parliament, anti-London sentiment came to the fore. Sandys had drafted the report so as to present it as a matter for the whole commonwealth rather than any particular trade, and perhaps he consciously omitted some of the material focused on the Merchant Adventurers. With provincial sentiment aroused, the attempts of London MPs including the Company deputy Richard Gore to confound the bill were thus convincingly defeated.

Establishing a direct connection between the debates following the imperial mandate and the free trade bill of 1604 is not straightforward, but the emphasis in the latter on the unpopularity of merchant companies overseas is telling. Whether any of the MPs who supported the bill had been privy to the earlier debates is unknown, although two early supporters—the lawyers Francis Moore and Robert Hitcham—had been patronized by Sir John Popham and Sir Thomas Egerton (now Earl of Ellesmere) respectively. The disruption of a substantial branch of England's cloth trade was not a trivial matter, and so it is not far-fetched to imagine that some of those reports of the Company's restrictive practices would have spread beyond court. Even if this was not the case, then the present situation at Stade, where trade was supposedly flourishing in the absence of corporate regulation, was an embarrassment to the Company and played into the hands of the free traders.

One aspect of the imperial mandate dispute apparently lacking from the 1604 free trade debates seems to have been the complaints of certain Merchant Adventurers against their own Company's restrictions. The matter now at stake was the protected share of the cloth trade which all members enjoyed, meaning that such 'disorderly brethren' were unlikely to add their own complaints to those of interlopers, clothiers, and the Company's many other critics. Having successfully rolled back the authority of the Company over their businesses in the Empire following the mandate, perhaps these members were now learning the limits of the liberty that they had achieved.

---

[112] Ibid., p. 322.

Conclusion

If the years 1598–1604 had shaken the Company of Merchant Adventurers, it might appear that thereafter its trade resumed into 'a quite normal character', as Friis put it.[113] The divisions within the Company were seemingly forgotten, the dual-mart system of trade was restored, and, thanks to a more sympathetic House of Lords and the support of the Sir Robert Cecil, Earl of Salisbury, the attacks of the Commons had been withstood. But the pacification within the Company's ranks did not entail a return to the status quo. Although the possibility of an open split between the Dutch and German traders was avoided, this came at the price of sacrificing much of the Company's regulatory powers over the latter, allowing them to 'straggle' into the mainland freely. Even following the formal withdrawal of the mandate in 1607, the Company seems to have upheld a liberal regime in Stade.[114] However, the 1604 free trade bill had at least taught the Company a lesson about the risks of advertising its internal divisions to outsiders. This reluctance about exposing the Company's problems to external eyes was not unfounded; the Company's subsequent engagements with a succession of parliaments indicates that the 'odious name of Monopoliste' was hard to dispel.

Many of the accusations against the Company's practices following the imperial mandate would be resurrected in these campaigns, including criticisms of the restrictions that it placed on members as well as outsiders. The aftermath of this controversy was felt in other ways, too. A prominent theme of the attacks of London's clothworkers had been the Company's failure to dye and dress its cloths, an old grievance that was exacerbated by the Company's purchase of the Cumberland licence to export white cloths. The trade to Stade and Emden having been opened to all English subjects and strangers in March 1601, the Cumberland licence did at least give the Company an opportunity to retain its control over this most important branch of its trade. However, this also raised the question of how the Company's privileges were to be defined: territorially, or in terms of a particular commodity, unfinished broadcloth? For the Company was not the only party with an interest in claiming a share of the latter trade; members of the Eastland Company trading to the Baltic contested the Company's exclusive right to the Cumberland licence as it was negotiated throughout 1602. Twelve years later, this combination of Baltic merchants, interlopers, and discontented clothworkers acting under the auspices of Alderman William Cokayne, would prove to be too much for the Merchant Adventurers to withstand.

If the origins of the Cokayne Project can be located in the disturbances following the imperial mandate, here too we can see signs of the attitude that in 1614 would encourage the crown to turn its back on its long alliance with the Merchant

---

[113] Friis, *Alderman Cockayne's Project*, p. 74.   [114] See Chapter 4.

Adventurers. The Company had proven to be an indispensable arm of royal diplomacy in the 1560s, diverting the course of the English cloth trade in order to thwart Habsburg attempts to exploit the commercial predominance of Antwerp. But having departed from Antwerp, exerting this level of control over a dispersed cloth trade, let alone the activities of its members, became much more difficult, as was painfully exposed following the imperial mandate. For a Company used to arguing that it was the only means to prise open foreign markets for English cloth, to be banished from these very markets was a considerable embarrassment. Although the crown may have held back from sacrificing the Company to its parliamentary critics in 1604, its value had begun to be questioned, long before James I thought fit to dissolve the Company in favour of Alderman Cokayne's audacious gamble.

6

'A new & extraordinary service to be done to the state and Comonwealth of England'

The Merchant Adventurers and the Cokayne Project

In 1614, the Company of Merchant Adventurers suffered perhaps the most dramatic setback in its history, as its charter was suspended in favour of what would become a new corporation formed to achieve a specific goal: to replace the undyed and undressed 'white' broadcloth currently exported by the Merchant Adventurers with the finished product, so adding value to the trade and providing labour to thousands of clothworkers. This represented an effort to close a legal loophole often complained of by clothworkers, the export of unfinished cloth over a certain value having been forbidden by law since 1536, only to be permitted by special licences awarded both to the Merchant Adventurers and to various courtiers, most recently the Earl of Cumberland.[1] As these licences tended to be exclusively granted to the Merchant Adventurers in return for a fee, the licensing system was in many ways the most effective means by which the Company was able to enforce its monopoly over the cloth trade, so long as it was dominated by the export of unfinished cloths. The Cokayne Project therefore entailed a fundamental re-ordering of the cloth trade which, even after its eventual failure, had serious implications for the restored Company.

Historical discussions of the Cokayne Project have focused on four main issues: the motives of the projectors, the reasons why they were able to win the support of the crown, the causes of the project's ultimate failure, and its long-term effect on the cloth trade. Of these, the former has generated most discussion. English clothworkers seeking to expand their role at the expense of their equivalents in the Netherlands and Germany, who currently completed the dressing and dying of most exported broadcloth, were the most obvious beneficiaries of the project. However, since the publication of Astrid Friis' account, focus has tended to be on the merchant who gave the project his name, Alderman William Cokayne, as someone possessing the requisite influence at court needed to turn

---

[1] See Ramsay, 'Industrial discontent'.

Fellowship and Freedom: The Merchant Adventurers and the Restructuring of English Commerce, 1582–1700.
Thomas Leng, Oxford University Press (2020). © Thomas Leng. DOI: 10.1093/oso/9780198794479.001.0001

the long-standing grievances of clothworkers into action. Friis' explanation for the projectors' motivations was tied to the fortunes of Cokayne's trading company, the Eastland Company, whose members were suffering from the competition of Dutch merchants exporting West Country broadcloth which had been dyed and dressed in the Low Countries, at the expense of the dyed Suffolk cloths which were their staple export.[2] For Friis the project was an attempt to starve Dutch rivals of their supply of white broadcloth and so to revive the Eastland trade. Supple offered a more cynical and probably realistic explanation: that the projectors were hoping to establish for themselves a share of the lucrative trade of the Merchant Adventurers, particularly in white cloths, and that the grievances of the clothworkers provided a convenient pretext for doing so.[3] Perhaps the best supporting evidence for Supple's interpretation (along with the suspicions of many contemporaries) was the fact that the Eastland Company had unsuccessfully lobbied to gain a share of the Cumberland licence to export white cloths in 1601–2.

Friis' response to the second question, on the decision of the crown to support the project, has faced less criticism.[4] Deploying Sir Julius Caesar's notes recording the meetings between Cokayne, the Privy Council, and the king, Friis reconstructed in detail how James I was won over by Cokayne's promise to boost English industry at the expense of foreigners. This led the king to ignore the initial reservations of several Privy Councillors, and, once the project was under way, growing evidence for the project's failure, until a steadily rising volume of complaints by clothiers about the 'stop of trade' finally changed his mind. The projectors' excuse for their failure focused on the effects of Dutch retaliation, in the form of a plaacart of the States General forbidding the purchase of imported finished cloth, which brought the market at Middelburg to a stand in 1616. This, they alleged, was part of a wider strategy to encourage the expansion of Dutch cloth making as opposing to simply finishing, a theme later picked up by the Merchant Adventurers in their own complaints about falling sales, meaning the Cokayne Project soon acquired infamy as a turning point in England's commercial fortunes. Supple, however, observed that it was not just the export of finished cloth that faltered; sales of white cloths (unaffected by the Dutch plaacart) also suffered a sharp decline in 1616. Supple therefore argued that it was the insufficient capital reserves of the projectors which sucked the life out of a cloth trade dependent on the Merchant Adventurers' accumulated reserves of credit to provide liquidity in the trade.[5]

---

[2] See the figures in Friis, *Alderman Cockayne's Project*, p. 228.
[3] Supple, *Commercial Crisis*, pp. 36–7.
[4] See, for instance, Joel D. Benson, *Changes and Expansion in the English Cloth Trade in the Seventeenth Century: Alderman Cockayne's Project* (Lewiston, Queenston, and Lampeter, 2002).
[5] Supple, *Commercial Crisis*, pp. 46–9.

Most discussion, then, has considered the motives and actions of the projectors themselves, although this has tended to focus on Cokayne at the expense of his collaborators. The Company of Merchant Adventurers itself, meanwhile, has largely been presented as a rather powerless spectator, its members standing by (for Friis, a sign of their admirable corporate self-discipline), until the project failed. Thanks to this stance, the Company was in a strong position to negotiate a return to its former position unencumbered by any obligations to complete the project which the king had initially sought to foist upon it, albeit at the price of paying off the profligate king with a large loan.[6] To be sure, Friis did note the involvement of a proportion of the Company's membership in the project, initially forced to participate in order to repatriate the profits of their sales overseas, although the wealthiest members were able to sit the project out (signified by an upturn in investment into the East India Company, as noted by Supple).[7] But in general, accounts of the Cokayne Project have presented it in terms of a succession of Whitehall meetings in which Cokayne and his opponents vied for royal support.

However, the corporation which was established to carry the project forward—eventually known as the King's Merchant Adventurers—encompassed a range of interests, including many members of the old Company based both in London and, importantly, overseas, meaning that it could never simply be a vehicle for Cokayne's ambitions. The new corporation also claimed the privileges of the Company which it had displaced alongside many key features of its trading system, and so it also absorbed something of the corporate culture of the Merchant Adventurers, although this sat uneasily within the modified corporate structures that Cokayne had constructed. However much the restored Company might have presented the debacle as a hiatus in its own corporate history, it was thus deeply implicated in the Cokayne Project, which left a legacy more troubling than simply burdening the Company with a new set of financial liabilities.

The Merchant Adventurers on the Eve of the Project

Even if we discount Friis' explanation for the Cokayne Project as a remedy for the ills of the Eastland trade, it does appear that in the years leading up to the project, the commercial hinterlands of the Eastland Company and the Merchant Adventurers were beginning to overlap in ways that were potentially troubling for both companies, defined as they were by regional privileges. Around this time Lionel Cranfield was one Merchant Adventurer who was tempted to join those Dutch merchants who were sending English cloth (though in his case, narrow kerseys) from Germany to the Baltic. Cranfield had been prompted in part by

---

[6] Friis, *Alderman Cockayne's Project*, p. 269.   [7] Supple, *Commercial Crisis*, p. 37.

information which his Stade factor Richard Rawstorm had received from Eastland Company factors at Danzig, though their corporate affiliation meant that they refused to handle the goods of a non-member, and Cranfield eventually sent his servant Richard Perrott to do his business.[8] Cranfield only arranged to take his freedom of the Eastland Company once he planned to send his kerseys to Elbing, the Company's official staple, and appears to have taken the attitude that the Company's jurisdiction did not to extend to the wider region. In fact there had been some tension between the Merchant Adventurers and the Eastland Company regarding their respective territorial limits ever since the latter's foundation in 1579. Initially there was also some resistance from within the Merchant Adventurers about allowing its members to join the new company, although eventually it was agreed that they could join for a modest £10 entrance fine.[9] There was subsequently a degree of overlap in the membership of the two companies, including at the level of their government by such figures as Christopher Hoddesdon, easing some of the potential conflict between the two, but Merchant Adventurers like Cranfield could potentially present unwelcome competition, particularly if they took the option of having their broadcloth finished in the Netherlands or Germany before exporting it to the Baltic, or chose to trade outside of the mart town.[10] This should remind us that Merchant Adventurers were not simply on the receiving end of unwelcome competition from outsiders: the Russia Company was also complaining of incursions into its territories by Merchant Adventurers trading via Hamburg.[11]

On the part of the Eastland merchants, William Cokayne was far from a newcomer to the Merchant Adventurers' territories in 1614. His father had been active as a member of the latter company and traded to Hamburg in the 1570s, although it is possible that Cokayne junior did not himself take up membership.[12] As his agent, the younger Cokayne turned to an interloper, William Craddock, who had been active in Stade and Hamburg since at least the early 1590s. Cokayne's acquisition of a contract to supply the English forces in Ireland in 1598 added a veneer of legitimacy to Craddock's operations, Germany being an important source of munitions, but the Company still resented his presence.[13] In 1598 the Company imprisoned him for receiving kerseys at Stade and Hamburg in contravention of the restraint on trade following the imperial mandate. According to his petition to Sir Thomas Egerton, keeper of the Great Seal, Craddock had been seized by the Company during a visit to Middelburg and confined in the town gaol 'amongst fellons & notorious crymynall offendors', subject

[8] HMC Sackville II, pp. 189, 238–9.
[9] Henryk Zins, *England and the Baltic in the Elizabethan Era* (Manchester, 1972), pp. 119–20.
[10] Friis, *Alderman Cockayne's Project*, pp. 232–3.   [11] PC 2/27, fol. 145.
[12] Declaration of a trading debt, 29 Apr. 1572, NRO, C2489.
[13] Friis, *Alderman Cockayne's Project*, p. 235.

to a fine of £180 which he refused to pay.[14] Although we do not know how the petition was received, Craddock's emphasis on the Company's dubious legal powers, being 'bothe accusers Judges & executioners in theire owne Cause', certainly resounded with the concerns about excessive corporate power being raised by observers like Sir John Popham at the time, as well as some of the Company's own members.

Craddock's imprisonment did not prevent him from returning to Hamburg, where he continued to operate throughout the imperial mandate controversy, apparently setting up household there in 1600.[15] A Privy Council investigation into illicit deliveries to Hamburg made in early 1601, following complaints by the Company, revealed that Craddock was the recipient of a consignment of Devonshire kerseys delivered by one Thomas Wetherall, who normally traded to the Mediterranean and would later join the King's Merchant Adventurers.[16] By 1601, the Company's authority in Germany was seriously compromised, and Craddock engaged in the inland trade which thrived in this period, becoming a leading supplier of linen to Stade as well as selling cloth in Leipzig. Cokayne too partook in this trade, arranging purchases of linen at Leipzig and its surrounds in 1601–2 with one Wilhelm Lackin as his agent, and he might also have had dealings with the linen merchant and interloper into Germany, Peter Muffett, who was a fellow member of the Eastland Company.[17] Craddock also had other collaborators besides Cokayne: he was factor for the London-based interloper Thomas Jackson, with whom he had dealings since before the mandate.[18] In spite of his earlier run-ins with the court of the Merchant Adventurers at Middelburg, by 1614 Craddock would have been well acquainted with its membership in Germany, and the liberal regime that persisted there. Cokayne was already highly involved in the Merchant Adventurers' German trade, then, but the Company's monopoly of the licensed export of white cloths meant that this most valuable aspect of its trade was barred to him and his fellow Eastland merchants. There was thus a clear logic behind breaking down some of the barriers between the two trades.

In 1612, the Company of Merchant Adventurers relocated from Stade to Hamburg, which also replaced Middelburg as the seat of the Company's chief court, raising the prospect that the time of 'promiscuous liberty' in Germany was

---

[14] 'The humble peticion of William Craddock, an Englishe Marchante', to Sir Thomas Egerton, 1598. HL, Ellesmere 2352.

[15] Baumann, *Merchants Adventurers*, p. 341.

[16] 'The examinations of the Mrs of the ships which went to Stade May last', 27 July 1601, BL, Lansdowne 150, fol. 16r.

[17] NRO, C2806–7, C2685. Cokayne was one of the commissioners for Muffett's bankruptcy, in 1609: C3215. For Muffett, see Friis, *Alderman Cockayne's Project*, pp. 76n, 104n, 233n. Muffett was back in Hamburg in 1624: see his letter of intelligence to Sir George Calvert, 30 May 1624, TNA, SP 82/6, fol. 9.

[18] Baumann, *Merchants Adventurers*, p. 341; Lowe–Quarles, 29 Mar. 1597, TNA, SP 46/176, fol. 299v.

coming to an end.[19] It is notable that the former London deputy, Richard Gore, became Hamburg deputy in 1611.[20] As well as leading resistance to the 1604 free trade bill in parliament, Gore had been a vocal complainant to the Privy Council regarding those disobedient brethren who persisted in trading to Hamburg after the imperial mandate.[21] But if his arrival was intended to precipitate a crackdown on the unorthodox practices of the Hamburg Merchant Adventurers, this does not seem to have materialized. On the contrary, one of the first orders of the restored court at Hamburg, following the arrest of the goods of an interloper, was to permit unfreemen to trade in non-English goods, on payment of a toll and submission to Company government, as long as they consigned goods to its members.[22] This endorsement of the activity of interloping linen traders like William Craddock tacitly acknowledged the close ties they had fashioned with members of the Company who relied on them to supply goods from the German interior. Far from upsetting the balance between Merchant Adventurers and interlopers that had emerged in the German residence, Gore was apparently popular amongst these merchants, and resumed his role as deputy following the Cokayne Project. Meanwhile with a governor—Sir Thomas Lowe—who had been a leading supporter of remaining in Germany after the mandate, and had himself indulged in the 'straggling' trade to Nuremburg, there was little chance that the Company would seek to overturn the liberal regime in Germany.

An indication of the increasingly settled character of the Company's residence at Hamburg on the eve of the Cokayne Project is given by the will of one of its principal members, William Jones.[23] Jones had been based in Stade and Hamburg for twenty years, trading in a longstanding partnership with Richard Beale of London, during which time he had amassed a fortune. Without a surviving wife or children, Jones left a huge bequest of £9,000 to his livery company, the Haberdashers', to be used in various endeavours in his home county of Monmouth, plus £1,000 to support 'poor preachers' throughout the country, attesting to his continued ties to England.[24] But his will also demonstrates the social ties that Jones had amassed in Germany, including bequests to the poor of Stade and Hamburg, the family of his local host, and several legacies to his acquaintances amongst the Hamburg Merchant Adventurers. These included his apprentice Nicholas Basse, who received £500, another current servant, Thomas Spurway (£100), and a former one, Gabriel Miles (£50). Smaller awards were

---

[19] 'An answere of the Merchantes Adventurers...on behalfe of them and their trade unto the Messauge delivered to the Kinges most Excellent Majestie by Reinerus Langius Secretary to the City of Stoade', TNA, SP 82/5, fol. 86.

[20] See Gore's letter to secretary Cecil reporting his arrival in Hamburg, 24 Sept. 1611, TNA, SP 82/5 f.141.

[21] Petition dated 14 June 1601, BL, Lansdowne 150, fol. 24v.   [22] *Laws*, p. 32.

[23] TNA, PROB 11/126/240.

[24] Jones' bequest amounted to no less than 27 per cent of the Haberdashers' total charitable bequests by 1680. Ian Archer, *The History of the Haberdashers' Company* (Chichester, 1991), p. 72.

made to the children of several Merchant Adventurers who were based in Stade in the 1590s (including Humphrey Baskerville, John Bladwell, William Ellim, Richard Stevens, Arthur Leakes, and John Bland), to several of the Company's officers and servants at Hamburg, and to a group of more recent arrivals in Germany (Thomas Baylie, Samuel Aldersey, Robert Edwards, William Windover, John Beale, Anthony Biddulph, and Thomas Sheppard). Also generously recognized were his four executors: Jones' London partner Richard Beale; William Pennefather, alongside whom Jones had acted as unofficial leader of the Stade merchant community following the imperial mandate; Samuel Watts, another long-term Stade resident and sometime agent of the current governor of the Company, Sir Thomas Lowe; and William Balden, the former agent of the interloper Thomas Jackson, who had been in Stade as early as 1595. The presence of such a figure as Balden amongst Jones' close allies is not surprising given that Jones himself had been heavily involved in the linen trade into Germany, along with Pennefather. Watts meanwhile had previously sold kerseys for Lionel Cranfield in Nuremburg, and John Bladwell (previously Hamburg factor of Ralph Freeman, who had fallen foul of the Company following the imperial mandate for his German trade) and John Bland had both been involved in the trade to inner Germany.[25] Jones also bequeathed a £600 legacy for young members of the Merchant Adventurers, although he provided alternative arrangements in the event of the Company's dissolution: by then, the looming Cokayne Project was beginning to cast its shadow.

The origins of the project itself are well known and so can be summarized here. We saw in Chapter 5 that the aftermath of the imperial mandate had been capitalized on by London clothworkers to raise their old objection against the export of undyed/undressed cloths, apparently in alliance with certain merchants, including Thomas Jackson, who justified continuing to trade to Germany on the basis that they were exporting fully finished cloth. The export of white cloths had again come under scrutiny in 1601–2 when exclusive access to the Cumberland licence to export these cloths was secured by the Merchant Adventurers in the face of objections by the Eastland Company. Denied a share in this trade, prominent members such as Cokayne then supported further attempts by the clothworkers to have the law against exporting white cloths fully enforced in 1606, putting forward a parliamentary bill to this effect, with Cokayne offering to take up the export of finished cloths himself.[26] The long delay in bringing the project to fruition may have been due to the objections of Sir Robert Cecil, who died in 1612.[27] In any case, the project gradually morphed from an initiative of the clothworkers to one dominated by merchants led by Cokayne, with his closest collaborator apparently being Sir Stephen Soames, whose mercantile career was as itinerant as

[25] Baumann, *Merchants Adventurers*, pp. 347–8, 354–5, 362–3.
[26] See Friis, *Alderman Cockayne's Project*, pp. 237–9.   [27] Ibid., p. 239.

Cokayne's, having moved from the Eastland to the Levant trade. Soames also had a longstanding grievance against the Merchant Adventurers, having allegedly faced the Company's wrath for interfering in its trade in 1588, although its privileges were suspended at the time.[28] Resentment at the over-mighty behaviour of the Merchant Adventurers and the barriers it placed to non-members seeking to fashion connections with their own markets might well have been amongst the motives of the leading participants.

That the project in some sense sought to remove these obstacles to merchant initiative is suggested by the manner in which it was framed in its early stages, notably when it was debated before the Privy Council in December 1613. Sir Edward Coke used this occasion to speak in favour of opening up the cloth trade to all Englishmen as their birthright, connecting this to the famous verdict against monopolies in the case of Darcy versus Allin regarding the sale of playing cards.[29] The Merchant Adventurers' failure to support the cloth-finishing industry was another sign of the baleful effects of monopolies, which countered any legal objections to the withdrawal of the Company's charter and opened the way for more public spirited merchants to take their place. The Merchant Adventurers were thus ordered to match Cokayne's offer to export 50,000 fully finished cloths yearly, or else 'leave the markett free unto such as will undertake the sayd course'.[30]

'No newe service to the state'

The Cokayne Project began therefore as a kind of sequel to the 1604 free trade bill, an attack on the monopolistic restriction of foreign trade as well as the failure to support domestic industry. This is clear from the wording of the royal proclamation of July 1614 which prohibited the export of any undyed/undressed broadcloth in favour of fully finished cloth after 2 November: 'Wee hereby intending to make a Free Trade for all Our loving Subiects that shall undertake the Venting of the aforesaid Cloathes within the Territories where the Merchant Adventurers have formerly Traded'.[31] However, the project was always expected to proceed in an organized manner, with its protagonists accountable for seeing Cokayne's promise come to fruition. All those interested were to subscribe their names in one of several publicly accessible books (kept by the Lord Mayor, Cokayne, Soames, and in a house by the Exchange) before 20 September, noting how much they were prepared to invest in the adventure: a means to participate in the

---

[28] 'Instructions touching the Bill for free Trade in the Parliamt Ao 3o Jac Rs', BL, Lansdowne 487, pp. 298–304.
[29] Friis, *Alderman Cockayne's Project*, pp. 243–6.   [30] APC 1613, 303–4.
[31] *A Proclamation against the Exportation of Clothes, vndyed and vndressed contrary to Law*, 23 July 1614.

project that evoked the recently founded joint stock companies.[32] Many who had previously been excluded by the Merchant Adventurers' monopoly evidently took this opportunity, including interlopers, clothworkers, retailers, and other new-comers to foreign trade. This, then, was an experiment in corporate organization that was intended to balance the advantage of company government with free trade, being open to all merchants willing to support this royally sponsored initia-tive. From the outset the subscribers were referred to as a company, and at some point began meeting in a general court, but without a formal charter the project lacked any institutional means to ensure these promises were kept. The early months of 1615 were thus characterized by minimal progress towards the goal of promoting finishing at home. One objection of the Merchant Adventurers to the original project had been that the domestic industry lacked the capacity to rap-idly begin dying and dressing the number of cloths that Cokayne had promised to export, but this argument only aided the projectors, who won the concession that they could continue to export white cloths under the old Company's 'free licence' of 30,000 undressed cloths, until the cloth-finishing industry had been developed.[33] There was therefore no real incentive for the subscribers to fulfil their initial promises, and by May the clothworkers were complaining that, despite having taken on extra workers, they were receiving no more business than usual.[34] Nor was it just the export of finished cloth that failed to live up to expectations: overall unfinished cloth exports in the first quarter of 1615 were down by 46 per cent on the equivalent period of the previous year, doubtless caused by the withdrawal of so many wealthy Merchant Adventurers from the trade.[35]

It was in this context that the project faced its first real scrutiny, though the king was far from prepared to turn his back on it. Instead, the crown's response was to agree to the projectors' request for letters patent of incorporation, which obliged them to transport a more modest number of finished cloths: 6,000 in the twelve months running from 24 June 1615, 12,000 for the next year, and 18,000 for a third.[36] All thoughts of free trade were now forgotten: the new Company requested, and received, powers to exclude interlopers, with the governor or dep-uty awarded 'full and absolute power and authority to administer an oath' to any members.[37] As the vehicle for a royally endorsed project, the new Company was—for a time—shielded from the sort of anti-corporate sentiment that had initially served the projectors well.

---

[32] Friis, *Alderman Cockayne's Project*, pp. 253–4.
[33] Ibid., pp. 271, 461–3. Cokayne and some of his allies were exporting undressed cloths to Stade and Germany as early as August 1614. Ibid., p. 266.
[34] John Chamberlain–Sir Dudley Carleton, 25 May 1615, TNA, SP 14/80, fol. 287.
[35] Friis, *Alderman Cockayne's Project*, p. 273.
[36] Ibid., pp. 276–7; APC 1615–16, pp. 190, 217–21; TNA, SP 14/80, fol. 174.
[37] Friis, *Alderman Cockayne's Project*, pp. 279–80.

Although the authority of its governor (naturally Cokayne himself) was aug-
mented, in most respects the new Company was closely modelled on the old, and
it was awarded rights not only to the latter's free licence, but also the Cumberland
licence. There was also significant overlap in terms of membership. Sixty-five of
the 221 names mentioned in the charter of the King's Merchant Adventurers
(excepting honorary members) can be identified as former Merchant Adventurers,
although the largest traders were poorly represented in these ranks.[38] Of twenty-
four Merchant Adventurers who exported more than 1,000 cloths in 1614, only
six eventually joined the Company, and only one of those had been trading on a
similar scale in 1606.[39] This was John Gore (brother of Richard and a future Lord
Mayor of London), who was also an Eastland merchant, and was one of twenty-
four assistants named in the new Company charter. Nine of these were Eastland
Company members (out of a total of thirty-one named in the charter).[40] Six more
of the assistants belonged to a group of thirty-three merchants who largely
traded to southern Europe and the Mediterranean, though two of these—Francis
Blissard and Adrian Evans—had previously intruded on the Merchant Adventurers'
privileges. This was also true of another assistant, Thomas Dalby, who would be a
leading member of the new Company (one of twelve interlopers named in the
charter who usually traded to Amsterdam).[41] A further eight assistants were previous Merchant Adventurers—a significant proportion, though not necessarily a
sign of their positive endorsement of the project. Of these, Robert Angell, Robert
Palmer, and John Kendrick all specialized in exporting coloured Reading/Kent
cloths and so the aims of the project would have entailed no disruption to their
regular trade, but Kendrick at least was sceptical of its chances of success.[42] All
three, plus two other assistants (Theophilus Bruerton/Brereton and Hugh Perry)
would later add their names to a petition to the Privy Council signed by forty-six
former Merchant Adventurers complaining that they had been forced to participate or else face ruin, being 'much inferiour to the abilities of the rest of the old
Marchants which stand yet out'.[43]

These petitioners sought to differentiate themselves from the rest of the
Company as 'the old Marchands now ioyned to the New'. Nonetheless their participation in the project put them in a difficult position; although they complained
that they had found 'nothing but discouragementes for venting of died and drest
cloathes in any of the places where formerly our Trade hath bin exercised', the
petitioners were clearly aware that they were potential scapegoats for its failure.

---

[38] Ibid., pp. 281–2 (who puts the figure at sixty-three, to which I have added John Wheeler, and
William Palmer who was free of the Company despite switching his attention to France and the Baltic:
ibid., p. 283).

[39] Ibid., pp. 95–7.   [40] Ibid., p. 282.   [41] Ibid., pp. 283–4.

[42] Kendrick–William Trumbull, 17 Mar. 1614, HMC Downshire IV, pp. 339–40.

[43] 'The most humble petition and declaration of divers of the old Marchands now ioyned to the
New', TNA, SP 14/80, fol. 127.

They were therefore at pains to assert their 'wel-wishing to the happy successe of this great worke', pleading that they be held 'blamelesse and excusable', however it might end. Such circumspection was wise given the king's resentment towards the Merchant Adventurers for having displayed such 'wilfulnesse and inconform-itie' with his wishes.[44] The former members of the Company even had to apply for special permission to 'assemble themselves as in former tymes' in order to con-sider the Privy Council's request that they partake in the project.[45]

These discussions proved unfruitful, and the old Company's representatives continued to argue that the project's aims were unachievable given that there was insufficient demand for finished cloths in their markets, although they did offer the minor concession that they would make a trial of finishing 1,000 cloths to demonstrate this.[46] This would support Friis' conclusion that the old Company successfully maintained its boycott of the project until its collapse, at least at cor-porate level, but clearly many individual members had been drawn to participate, however reluctantly. It is also the case that at least forty-eight ex-Merchant Adventurers named in the new Company charter did not sign the aforementioned petition, suggesting at least some division within its ranks. The absence of four-teen of these names, however, can be explained by the fact that they were based in Hamburg, and they were far from willing accomplices in the scheme. If the advent of the Cokayne Project had presented London Merchant Adventurers with a dilemma about whether or not to withdraw from their trade, the choice was starker still for those members based in its mart towns. Servants expecting to pro-gress through the Company's ranks were at the whim of the decisions of their masters at home, but even more experienced commission agents had much less scope to redirect their businesses than members in London.

A letter from the Hamburg apprentice Richard Ferrar to his father from June 1615 illustrates how the merchant community experienced these unsettling changes.[47] One effect was a withdrawal of commissions for imports from many experienced Merchant Adventurers, but some at Hamburg initially hoped that this could be exploited by 'those that have experience in trad'. However, the influx of 'many newe & not understanding marchantes' arriving in the mart town who were willing to 'buy & barter for such Commodeties that others heretofore would

[44] *A Proclamation prohibiting the Merchant Adventurers Charter from henceforth to be put in prac-tise or execution, either within the Kingdom, or beyond the Seas*, 2 Dec. 1614.

[45] Privy Council to Sir Thomas Lowe and William Towerson, 21 May 1615, TNA, SP 14/80, fol. 164.

[46] This argument had been made in the early stages of the genesis of the project, and continued to be restated at every opportunity: 'The reasons of the Marchantes Adventurers in Aunswere to a peti-tion delivered to his excellent Majestie by the Clothworkers and dyers of London', c.1613, BL, Lansdowne 152, fols 282–92. For the offer to dye/dress 1,000 out of whites, see the petition of the old Company to the Privy Council, TNA, SP 14/80, fol. 172.

[47] Ferrar–Nicholas Ferrar, 17 June 1615, *The Ferrar Papers: in Magdalene College, Cambridge, 1590-1790*, microfilm edition (1992).

never doe' had disappointed these hopes. Cloth sales were for the time being holding up, but in general 'the Trade as it is nowe is most disorderly, & not like to bee otherwise till god send our old Company to there former estate'.

For the Hamburg Merchant Adventurers, the foundation of the new Company bought another change: the head court of the Company, traditionally based overseas, was now relocated to London (as was the case with the Eastland Company, a less democratic body than the Merchant Adventurers), giving Cokayne as governor considerable power to reorganize the trade in accordance with his designs. This shift in the locus of corporate authority prompted the Hamburg members of the Company to launch a protest that almost brought the project to an early end. This took the form of a letter to Cokayne and the rest of the fellowship at London, dated 13 November 1615 and signed by thirty-five merchants.[48] It was written in response to instructions from the London court detailing the reorganization of the trade required to fulfil the aims of the contract. All members were expected to swear an oath to agree to these terms, but in a general court on 11 November the Hamburg brethren scrupled at doing so, explaining their reasons in the subsequent letter. Their first objection, however, was to the person of the deputy chosen by the London court: Cokayne's factor, William Craddock. Whilst respecting his 'vnderstanding and skyll in this trade', they argued that Craddock lacked the respect and reputation both amongst the English merchants, and the rulers of Hamburg, that his predecessor Richard Gore—a 'worthie Cheife'—had possessed.[49] However much he had been accepted within their ranks, therefore, the Hamburg Merchant Adventurers were clearly not reconciled to having this former interloper govern over them. Craddock's presence was only likely to lead to 'dissention and faction' at a time when 'wee haue most need of vnitye & vnanemitye'. If no fitting alternative could be found, the protesters suggested that the position of deputy governor be replaced by the usage of 'dyuerse Comittees'.

As well as their antipathy to Craddock himself, this suggestion reflected the Hamburg merchants' desire to continue to have a say in the regulation of their trade, rather than being subject to orders from London. Although conceding the principle of 'the necessarie subordinacion of the dyuerse vnder courts in there one head', the writers protested that local conditions often dictated that they take the initiative; to be bound by the decisions of London would lose them precious time. Clearly these complaints represented the standpoint of agents burdened with the task of trying to sell the newly finished cloths 'to men vnwilling and enemyes to our Course'; as the letter ruefully added, 'this is the difficultye, this the

---

[48] Members of the King's Merchants Adventurers at Hamburg to Governor Cokayne and the Fellowship at London, 13 Nov. 1615, Lambeth Palace 3472, fols 163–7. Neither this crucial document nor its sequel, discussed below, was available to Friis.

[49] Ibid., fol. 163r.

labor'.[50] Further complaints elaborated on their appeal that their 'experience of this place' be respected.[51]

The Hamburg members of the new Company were thus keen to maintain as much continuity in their business practices as possible, and indeed they noted approvingly that the orders sent from London for the most part were 'framed after the modell of the orders of Late here in vse', again demonstrating the extent to which the new Company built on the foundations of the old.[52] But in certain respects, these orders entailed dramatic changes which presented a particular threat to the Hamburg factors. These were tied to the obligation to export 6,000 cloths dyed and dressed out of whites in the course of the first year of the project. In order to compel subscribers to play their part, the London court had ordered that one out of every pack of ten cloths sold be finished, and that other types of cloth and other goods to the like value be subject to the same condition. For agents impressed with the responsibility of finding customers, this was a particular grievance. First, the Hamburg merchants feared that, given that the States General had already forbade the import of finished English cloths into the Netherlands, a disproportionate share of this burden would fall on them. They were equally concerned that coupling finished cloths with other sorts, and particularly goods such as lead and tin, would put off customers.[53] Another new order requiring all sales to be certified to the deputy was also strongly objected to as a violation of a merchant's customary privacy and a practice 'most intolerable, & in Commerce in merchandizing an vnexampled shriutude'.[54] This was exacerbated by the fact that Craddock was still active in trade and could not fail to benefit from being presented with this valuable information: another reason to object to his choice as deputy.

But the Hamburg merchants found most objectionable a practice which would become increasingly controversial as the project went on. The new Company had brought together merchants trading to a variety of regions, and many of these members had taken to sending their allocated portion of dyed/dressed cloths to these other markets, allowing them to focus exclusively on white cloths in the mart towns. As well as being an 'vnmerchantlike Confusion and mingling of accomptes', the letter complained, this practice was 'of a cleare Contrarie note and nature' to the aim of the project and amounted to 'no newe service to the state'. The Hamburg factors faced the double burden of seeking to find a market for the finished cloth sent by their principals whilst finding the market in white cloths flooded by newcomers: 'there can be nothing more repugnant to that equall Oeconomicall dispensacion & disposicion which ought to be amongst such as are as it were brethren of one and the same family'.[55]

---

[50] Ibid., fol. 166v.   [51] Ibid., fol. 164r.   [52] Ibid., fols 163v–164r.
[53] Ibid., fols 164r–v.   [54] Ibid., fols 165v–166r.   [55] Ibid., fol. 166v.

The threat that such practices represented to the Hamburg factors was restated in a second letter, which amongst other things complained that a number of members of the new Company at London, including Thomas Dalby, had been using as their Hamburg factor a local merchant, John Schroedring, who disregarded their regulations for show days and so forth, and threatened to expose the Company's secrets to strangers. None of Schroedring's principals had been a member of the old Company, suggesting that the Hamburg factors were not picking up new commissions that might have compensated for the other problems they were facing.[56] Also of particular concern to these merchants was a new proviso introduced since their last letter, that all members of the Company be compelled to dye and dress at least twenty cloths out of whites annually, rising by ten for each of the subsequent two years. This measure, the letter complained, would disproportionately affect those young merchants setting out with modest capital, who might therefore have to dye and dress as many as four in ten of their cloths. Those members who wholly depended on commission trade would suffer all the more from this 'unequall' measure. Although the authors conceded that they had agreed to subscribe £500 a year towards the new Company's contract, they protested that the younger merchants had been compelled to do so, 'els he had bene excluded his freedome & tourned to live by new unknowne courses, uncouth & strange to his education'. The Cokayne Project had thus inadvertently undermined the traditional means by which Merchant Adventurers had been able to rise within the Company's ranks, through 'long & thriftie service', 'an institutione, or practise which hath proved to profittable to the Comonwealth'. Far better, then, to stick to the requirement that members finish one in ten of their total exports, which would allow the Company to 'admitt yong men that have bene brought up in trade of merchandize underwriting for such somes only as they are able to Compas'. The letter went on to offer further clarification regarding its objections to members transporting their share of dyed/dressed cloth 'unto other forraigne partes out of our precinct', claiming to have evidence for the buying and selling of members' allocated proportions (particularly by Eastland traders). Again, the authors pointed out, the new Company's charter had been awarded 'for a new & extraordinary service to be done to the state and Comonwealth of England by our trade into *germanie* and *the lowe countries*', and not to these other regions.

These two letters clearly represent the grievances of Hamburg agents who had little choice but to participate in the project, and it would seem that the forty-three merchants who signed one or both of the two letters represented a significant

[56] William Craddock and other members of the King's Merchants Adventurers at Hamburg to Governor Cokayne and the Fellowship at London, 27 Nov. 1615, KHLC, U269/1/B82/6. Two of those mentioned, Dalby and William Payne, had previously interloped into the Company's privileged areas, whilst Clement Underhill, William Fynch, and Thomas Trotter all traded largely to southern Europe; the background of Richard Deane, Robert Garrat, and James Medlycot is unclear, but they may have been non-merchants.

proportion of the total English merchant community there, including several long-established residents. Fifteen of these names appear in a list of sixty-seven English merchants based in Hamburg in 1612, and some of these had been present for much longer, amongst them many who had appeared in William Jones' will, including his former apprentice Nicholas Basse.[57] Most of these were signatories of the second letter, whose twenty-six authors identified themselves as merchants of a certain 'quallitie', distinct from mere servants (which was perhaps the condition of many of the seventeen merchants who only signed the first letter, few of whom had been resident in 1612). These, then, were probably relatively established merchants trading on their own accounts as well as on commission.[58] The most vocal critics of Craddock were named as Samuel Aldersey, Richard Lambe, and Richard Grenowes. Aldersey was by then in his mid-thirties and had been in Stade since at least 1603, sometimes acting as factor for Sir Thomas Lowe (having started his apprenticeship under John Quarles junior), although Grenowes was still an apprentice, having begun his indenture under the Draper Nicholas Walmesey in 1604 (he would not take the freedom of his livery company until 1618).[59] Craddock himself added his name to the second letter, but clearly under duress: he wrote a private letter to Cokayne attacking many of his brethren for their conduct.[60]

All three of these letters eventually came to the attention of the Privy Council, and Lionel Cranfield was called on to investigate the allegations contained therein. Cranfield by this point had left behind his trade as a Merchant Adventurer, having in 1613 become chief surveyor of customs, but his commercial experience was recent enough that he must have had many contacts within the ranks of both the old and new Companies. Indeed, one leading member of the latter—the former interloper Thomas Dalby—had been one of his partners in a venture to engross the supplies of logwood in the main northern European ports, including Amsterdam. But this did not make Cranfield any more sympathetic to the new Company, and he drew on the two letters from Hamburg to fashion a critique to be presented to the Privy Council. His abstract of the two letters passed over the criticisms of Craddock (whilst noting that their rejection of him was doubtless 'uppon good ground'), instead focusing on how the practices of the new Company, and especially the transport of dyed and dressed cloths beyond the mart towns, were a betrayal of the essence of the project.[61] Cranfield suggested an amnesty for any member of the new Company, excepting Cokayne and Craddock, who

---

[57] Those of the 1612 cohort who signed both letters were Samuel Aldersey, William Balden, Anthony Biddulph, John Bladwell, William Christmas, George Crofte, Robert Edwards, Richard Grenowes, and Richard Lambe. Edward Breton, Thomas Daungerfield, and William Elwick signed the first only, and Steven Bailye, Nicholas Basse, and William Craddock the second.

[58] One of this group, John Travell, had been apprenticed to an Eastland merchant, however, and would go on to trade there himself.

[59] For Aldersey, see Baumann, *Merchants Adventurers*, p. 328.

[60] APC 1615–16, 367–8. Unfortunately a copy of this letter does not appear to survive.

[61] Cranfield's summary of the letter of 3 Nov. 1615, KHLC, U269/1/B82/3. See also U269/1/B82/6.

exposed its fraudulent practices such as the partial dying of cloth. He also seized upon the protests of the Hamburg merchants about the 'unconscionable order of tying the porest to as great a proportion as the Richest', and the use of an oath 'Framed preemptory & unconsconably to pryvate ends', evidence that Cokayne's pretence to serve the public good was 'In shewe & by protestacion but in truth Mallice & Gayne'.[62] Cranfield also recommended compiling detailed information regarding how much the projectors had achieved towards the project's original ends, including the volume and destination of all types of exports, and the state of the market in the mart towns.[63]

Such revelations were probably instrumental in turning such a figure as Sir Edward Coke against the project, along with many Privy Councillors, but moving the king was another matter.[64] Having found their charter coming under renewed legal scrutiny by the likes of Coke on grounds of monopoly, Cokayne and the new Company now presented the project as rooted in the royal prerogative and so not subject to such legal niceties.[65] This, it seems, had the desired effect; not only was the new Company absolved of the charge of being 'Proiectors & deluders of the State', but its powers were enhanced in order to deal with 'the dayly disturbances in their trade by Interlopers, and...the backwardnes of the ill disposed brethren of that companie'.[66] The Privy Council thus wrote to custom houses to ensure that no cloth destined for Germany and the Low Countries be entered without a sig-nature from Cokayne or one of his deputies, whilst the obligation of its members to finish a minimum of twenty cloths was confirmed.[67] The new Company won a significant new source of power by having a place reserved for its servants in the customhouses to supervise entries.[68] The refractory brethren at Hamburg were ordered to conform themselves to the Company orders, or be disenfranchised.[69] Finally, members of the new Company were granted liberty to export dyed and dressed cloths to any parts where they were privileged to do so, as long as they had been on sale in the mart towns for three months.

'To be free of all Trade for all places'

This last directive must have been particularly hard for the Hamburg protesters to take. By blurring the geographical boundaries of its customary trade, this

---

[62] Cranfield's notes on the King's Merchant Adventurers, KHLC, U269/1/B82/4.

[63] See KHLC, U269/1/B82/4, 9, 11–12.

[64] Friis, *Alderman Cockayne's Project*, pp. 464–7; Thomas Locke–William Trumbull, 24 Jan. 1616, HMC Downshire V, 413.

[65] Petition of the New Company of Merchant Adventurers to the Privy Council, 4 Feb. 1616, TNA, SP 14/86, fol. 75.

[66] Ibid.; Privy Council order, 8 Feb. 1616, TNA, SP 14/86, fol. 98.

[67] Ibid.; Friis, *Alderman Cockayne's Project*, pp. 298, 467.

[68] Earl of Suffolk to London customers, 27 Mar. 1616, TNA, SP 14/86, fol. 190.

[69] APC 1615–16, pp. 456–60.

measure was as much a threat to the Company's integrity as the attempt to replace the export of white cloths with the finished product. In the early stages of the project, the Company had warned that the implication of abandoning the export of white cloths would be to force English merchants to give up trading in a single residence, in favour of carrying the finished goods direct to their final markets, 'which wilbe the wrack of that auncient government which hath soe longe kept our Clothe in reputacion'.[70] The ethos of the Company's trading system was predicated on cloth being dyed and dressed in or around its mart towns, this being the chief incentive for its host cities to grant the Company privileged status. The Cokayne Project therefore threatened the ultimate dissolution of the Company's trading system, to the detriment of those factors in the mart towns hoping to establish themselves as independent merchants. Increasingly, the Company of King's Merchant Adventurers was becoming defined less by a region than by a commodity, finished cloth.

This is surely why the aspect of the project that so many former Merchant Adventurers found most disturbing was the participation of members of so many different companies representing divergent interests. This was the theme of one paper which presented the new Company as the 'Antithesis' of the old.[71] As well as accusing the new Company of breeding 'a dangerous Innovacion', the author emphasized the negative effects of its hybrid membership:

> Because their Society is Compounded of merchants and Tradesmen of Severall Corporacions & Companies of the Citty of London and elsewhere, (who ayming at Severall ends in their vndertaking) Can not Setle an orderly government in the Course of Trafficque, but breede a Confusion in the end because they have already digressed from their Principle, which was to dresse and dye all the white Clothes within the Realme.

The author went on to detail some of the contradictory ends pursued by these different parties: Eastland and Muscovy Company merchants wishing to access a new trade without allowing reciprocal access to their own for fellow members, 'as a Common Society doth Require and diuers of them do insiste upon'; interlopers trading to Amsterdam who were used to selling cloths at a loss in order to purchase goods for import; London shopkeepers seeking to 'enter in the mistery of the Trafficque of merchantes to provide themselves of the Commoddities for their owne Trade and Retaile'. This body was the antithesis of not just the Company of Merchant Adventurers, but the principle of corporate trading in its essence. And

---

[70] 'The reasons of the Marchantes Adventurers in Aunswere to a petition delivered to his excellent Majestie by the Clothworkers and dyers of London', c.1613, BL, Lansdowne 152, fols 282–92.
[71] 'An Antithesis Betweene The state of the Auncient Company of Merchants Adventurers and the new Company of Merchants pretending The dressing and dying of white Clothes in England', TNA, SP 14/80, fol. 199r.

yet the author implicitly acknowledged that even the Merchant Adventurers had contained within its ranks several different interests, some of which had thrown their weight behind Cokayne's Project. Merchant Adventurers who also traded to Barbary, for instance, could continue to send their finished cloth to the latter whilst reserving their white cloths for Germany and the Low Countries. The author also hinted that some members of the old Company had been persuaded to participate in the hope that they might thereby access newer markets such as Turkey and Barbary, having interpreted the project as implying a 'Generall free Graunt' to do so. Merchants of the outports were said to have particularly hoped 'to be free of all Trade for all places'. Many participants, Merchant Adventurers and otherwise, were attracted by the project's initial promise 'to have a Generall freedome of Trafficque of Cloth for all places'.[72] If this account is accurate, then it suggests that in part at least, the threat to the corporate identity of the Merchant Adventurers came from within its own ranks.

The involvement of a certain number of Merchant Adventurers was certainly instrumental in helping the project weather the storm precipitated by Cranfield's investigations in early 1616. According to figures collected by Cranfield from the port books for exports to Middelburg and Hamburg from 25 March to 15 May 1616, fifty-eight merchants identified by Friis as former Merchant Adventurers exported 63 per cent of the total (counted in terms of notional shortcloths).[73] Their proportion of exported finished cloths was only slightly lower (56 per cent). Only a handful of the largest exporters were not former Merchant Adventurers, a list headed by Cokayne and Thomas Dalby, and, if included in this list, the Merchant Adventurer/Eastland trader John Gore. The majority of this group were exporting on a small scale, however. The project at this point was doing little to achieve its original goal of opening up the cloth trade, then, but Cokayne could at least point towards a promising rise in the export of dressed cloths as compared to 1614, and in fact by midsummer 1616 he was able to show that the contracted end of exporting 6,000 finished cloths in the first year had been met.[74] Together with a promotional campaign that included a lavish reception for the king (featuring a Ben Johnson masque replete with caricatures of Hamburg merchants dressed in 'greate bellyed Dobletts, alle druncke'), Cokayne was able to stave off criticism, and win his knighthood.[75] However, the auspices for the cloth trade as a whole were poor, with a fall of over 16,000 notional shortcloths exported from London from 1614 to 1615, whilst Cranfield's investigations had uncovered the poor state of the market in the mart towns.[76]

---

[72] Ibid., fol. 199v.

[73] 'A Just note of all Entries of clothes both white and drest of all sorts that haue been shipped to Midleborougouh and Hambourough from the 25th of Marche 1616 to the 15th of Maie following', KHLC, U269/1/B82/14.

[74] Friis, *Alderman Cockayne's Project*, p. 303.

[75] G. Gerard–Sir Dudley Carleton, 14 June 1616, TNA, SP 14/97, fol. 117.

[76] Supple, *Commercial Crisis*, p. 42.

Things in Middelburg reached crisis point in summer 1616, when the effects of the plaacart of the States General forbidding the purchase of dyed/dressed cloth became fully felt. Despite this measure the new Company in Middelburg had pressed ahead with coupling the sale of finished and unfinished cloth, as was the case with Hamburg, though possibly this was not introduced until July 1616, by which point one observer noted the Middleburg branch had been bought to 'a settled order by a court government'.[77] We know less about the response of the Middelburg factory to the project compared to Hamburg, though interestingly, one prominent convert was none other than John Wheeler, former Middelburg secretary and the old Company's most eloquent defender. Wheeler was named as an assistant in the new Company charter, and at some point became deputy governor at Middelburg, though he attracted criticism by promoting the removal of the factory to Dordrecht (where, it was alleged, his wife had friends and 'he woulde be a great man, for he is nowe all for the newe Companye as longe as he can perseave them lykly to stande in estimation').[78] This projected move was partly a response to the plaacart, which led some (including Lionel Cranfield) to call for a withdrawal of the Company from the United Provinces to the Spanish Netherlands, though this was another source of division within the new Company.[79] As it happened, a boycott of English cloth by Amsterdam cloth buyers in July 1616 quickly brought the markets at Middelburg to a stand, leading to a flurry of complaints from clothiers.[80] The new Company's response was to issue a further set of demands, including for diplomatic action against the States General, greater punishments for subscribers who had not met their obligations, increased inspection of the quality of cloth making, and for the market in cloth at home to be kept free (this a response to the Privy Council's efforts to compel the Company to buy up unsold cloth).[81] As it came under greater pressure, the new Company repeatedly restated its request that members be free to trade finished cloth outside of the mart towns.[82] Even as the king began to lose patience with the projectors, he still hoped to keep the ends of his pet project alive by encouraging a merger of the old and new Companies, based on the principle that 'the marchants

[77] Daniel Skinner–William Trumbull, 2 July 1616, HMC Downshire V, pp. 541–2.

[78] Sir John Throckmorton–Viscount Lisle, 16 May 1615, HMC De Lisle & Dudley, V, p. 289. The move away from Zealand was particularly opposed by the English garrison at Flushing: ibid., p. 308.

[79] Lionel Cranfield, 'Means to mack the Hollanders know them selves', KHLC, U269/1/B82/7; 'Reasons for a better proceeding and a more speedy ending of the question for the residence at Middleburgh', TNA, SP 14/84, fol. 96 (signed in fact by John Wheeler).

[80] APC 1615–16, p. 673; APC 1616–17, pp. 2–4, 7–9; Petition of Gloucestershire clothiers and reply 2 Aug. 1616, TNA, SP 14/88, fols 70–1.

[81] APC 1616–17, pp. 16–20; Petition of the King's Merchant Adventurers, 11 Sept. 1616, BL, Lansdowne 152 fol. 273; Answer of the King's Merchant Adventurers to the Privy Council, Sept. 1616, TNA, SP 15/40, fol. 223. See Friis, Alderman Cockayne's Project, pp. 311–16, 339–40.

[82] Minutes of the General Court, 8 Oct. 1616, BL, Lansdowne 152, fol. 247; APC 1616–17, pp. 53–4.

must bee made of one faction'.[83] The disunity of purpose highlighted by many former Merchant Adventurers was now clear for all to see.

Aware that the prospect of fulfilling the terms of the second year of their contract was remote, the new Company threw its weight behind this attempted merger, pleading for 'The hatefull words of old and newe company to bee taken away, and it to bee called the Kings company of the Marchants Adventurers'.[84] The response of a General Court of the old Company specially summoned to receive this request, however, reveals the unruly mood that was prevailing within its ranks. Cranfield reported that when made aware of the king's displeasure about their initial 'dilatorye answer', the 'graver and better sorte weare much abashed But the yonger and greater number would not bee beaten from their owld resolutions in a longer time and would have lefte it upon distastfull tearmes...had it not been handled with some arte and often pressing'.[85] The offer to join Cokayne received not a single vote, and when pressed by Cranfield to make some 'Submission to his Majesties pleasure' the majority 'weare Jealious how farr that might extend'. Instead, the General Court made three offers, the first of which was in the event of the Company's charter not being restored, in which case they offered to 'Relinquish the trade of white Cloth wholly' in favour of dying and dressing 1,000 cloths for each of the next two years, an offer which the Privy Council accounted 'mere base and meane'.[86] The two other offers, both of which were conditional on a full restitution of the Company, were accounted 'cautelous and crafty': first, to dye and dress one tenth of their total exports in the first year, rising in proportion over the next two, but if found unprofitable to be replaced by a penalty of 13s. 4d. for each cloth that was exported unfinished; and second, to finish 3,000 in the first year, rising by a thousand each year 'yf they fynd profittable vent'. Cranfield was fully aware that these offers fell far short of what the king was expecting, and indeed what some members of the old Company had promised privately. But however unhappy the king was with the old Company, the capitulation of projectors meant that in January 1617 he was forced to accept a restoration of the former, initially on the basis of the second of its offers.[87]

Eventually, thanks largely to a large loan, the king was persuaded to issue a proclamation in the Company's favour, promising 'to quicken and give a new life unto them'.[88] In practice this meant a new charter, by which the Company absorbed the authority to act against interlopers which Cokayne had procured, including a seat in the customs houses for its officers, as well as for the first time

[83] Sir Julius Ceasar's notes, in Friis, *Alderman Cockayne's Project*, pp. 479–80.
[84] Ibid., p. 479.
[85] Cranfield–Buckingham, 9 Nov. 1616, KHLC, U269/1/B82/8.
[86] Ibid.; Friis, *Alderman Cockayne's Project*, pp. 480–1.
[87] APC 1616–17, pp. 108–10; for a detailed account of these negotiations, see Friis, *Alderman Cockayne's Project*, pp. 347–58.
[88] *A Proclamation for restoring the ancient Merchants Adventurers to their former Trade and Priviledges*, 12 Aug. 1617.

having the new draperies explicitly included within its monopoly.[89] The Company proceeded to launch a crackdown on former King's Merchant Adventurers who persisted in their trade, including many with decades-long experience of interloping to places like Amsterdam. It had already fought off an attempt by some to be admitted into the restored Company, arguing 'that it was directly against their auntient custome and freedome, which did never admitt any adoptives'.[90] But however much the Company sought to purify its trade from the dross introduced by the Cokayne Project, restoring the old order was not so straightforward as excluding a handful of interlopers.

One member to face the wrath of his fellows for collaborating with the new Company was John Wheeler, who complained that his twenty-seven years of loyal service to the Company had now been forgotten.[91] Involvement had probably been too widespread for any such score settling to have been repeated on a large scale, however—evidence has been found for over a hundred Merchant Adventurers joining the new Company—and in any case the Company was preoccupied with such matters as negotiating its loan with the king, seeking to have the placaart of the States General rescinded, and moving to a new mart town.[92] The ambiguous status of the restored Company overseas is revealed by a legal case involving Cokayne himself, regarding the contested title of a large consignment of cloths at Middelburg. Cokayne's agent, Thomas Richardson, had taken possession of these cloths to answer a debt owed by John Carpenter, Cokayne's previous factor, who had subsequently died. These cloths had then been forcibly taken from Richardson's packhouse by a Dutch merchant, Peter van Peinen, who claimed title by right of purchase, apparently with the collusion of Carpenter's secret and 'fraudulent' partner John Holliday.[93] Although Richardson hinted that the Company had initially failed to support Cokayne's case, ostensibly on the grounds that Richardson had attached the goods before the Company had made its own award, he suggested that many members had begun to feel 'ashamed and do stryve to salve upp matters what theye cane manye of theme confessinge your worship in this matter hathe endured a greate dealle of wronge'.[94] The new deputy, Edward Bennett, had therefore taken up the case with the rulers of Middelburg, having been prompted by 'some of the companies complaynting that theare was never the licke disgrace offerde to any brother of the company'. Even so, one of the Middelburg court of assistants who had spoken in Cokayne's favour reported 'that he hath gottone much hatred & distaste amongeste some of his old frends for goeinge so fare in your worships bysynes as he hath done, in so much as he is

[89] Friis, *Alderman Cockayne's Project*, pp. 366–8.   [90] APC 1616–17, pp. 110–14.
[91] Wheeler–Sir Ralph Winwood, *c.*1617, HMC Buccleuch, I, p. 176.
[92] John Chandler–William Trumbull, 12 Dec. 1617, HMC Downshire VI, p. 341.
[93] William Trumbull–Sir Thomas Lake, 18 July 1618, HMC Downshire VI, pp. 448–50.
[94] Thomas Richardson–William Cokayne, 27 Dec. 1617, NRO, C2656. Numerous letters survive detailing Richardson's torturous and apparently ultimately fruitless attempts to resolve this case.

threatned to fare the worse for yte'.[95] But however much delight there might have been at Cokayne's difficulties, the case threatened the Company's right to deal with cases of insolvency in its own court, and Richardson reckoned that 'the companye wold not sture in yt soe muche as they doe But that theare ys some thinge overeseene that maye shake theire pryvylidge'.[96] The Company was aware that the articles of agreement which it had originally made with Middelburg might be considered to have been voided in its absence, and so it was in its interests to emphasize its institutional continuity. On a more modest level, it had to take legal action to ensure that the bequest to the Company made by William Jones in 1614 had not been forfeited on the grounds of its dissolution.[97]

However much it might have liked to draw a veil over its two years' hiatus, the Company had to recognize the effects of the Cokayne Project on its status, as seen in certain measures it took to reorganize its commercial regulations. In 1618 the court at London granted brethren freedom to transport kerseys, bays, perpetuanas and other new draperies to any part of Germany and the Low Countries.[98] This was partly a response to complaints from Devonshire clothworkers about the crackdown on those interlopers who customarily bought their goods: the Company was clearly facing increased pressure to demonstrate that it was actively seeking to find vent for its cloths, potentially at the expense of the mart-trading system.[99] Shortly afterwards the London court enacted that the stint only be applied to white cloths.[100] Any measure which could be interpreted as limiting the sale of finished goods was likely to attract increased criticism given that the king had only grudgingly abandoned the goals of the Cokayne Project, and the Company had to make further token efforts to be seen to support the clothworkers.[101] The Company's vulnerability to criticism was clearly demonstrated in the next decade, when a sharp depression in its core markets brought the value of corporate organization once more into question. The goals of the Cokayne Project may have been abandoned, but the willingness to question the value of the government of the Fellowship of Merchant Adventurers certainly had not.

Conclusion

In many ways the response of the Merchant Adventurers to the Cokayne Project demonstrates the continued loyalty of its members to the Company and its commercial system, as Friis suggested. This was not only the case with those members who responded by withdrawing from trade. By resisting full incorporation into

---

[95] Richardson–Cokayne, 14 Feb. 1618, NRO, C2653.
[96] Richardson–Cokayne, 7 Mar. 1618, NRO, C2649.
[97] Pleadings in case of *Merchant Adventurers v. Richard Beale et al.*, 10 Nov. 1617, C2/JasI/M22/22.
[98] *Laws*, p. 134.   [99] Friis, *Alderman Cockayne's Project*, pp. 371–2.   [100] *Laws*, p. 135.
[101] APC 1618–19. p. 198; Friis, *Alderman Cockayne's Project*, pp. 364–5.

the new Company, maintaining their separate identity as the 'old merchants', those Merchant Adventurers who did participate in the project provided a degree of continuity in the organization of trade which facilitated the Company's even-tual return. By asserting that 'Brethern of the same fellowshipp and equall par-takers in the same Common Cause haue always had freedome to advise one another without measuring this liberty by the difference of wealth or dignetye', the Hamburg protesters kept alive the Company's discursive traditions, resisting the subordination of the mart towns to the London court.[102] In fact, it would appear that the Hamburg brethren were more united in this respect than their equivalents in London, some of whom at least had been willing participants in the enterprise. The withdrawal of so many senior Merchant Adventurers from the trade opened opportunities for others: the leading exporters in 1618 include many names that had risen into the premier rank of the Company over the last three years. In other ways the project revealed divergences between the commer-cial positions of London Merchant Adventurers and members overseas, which would only widen as the century went on. The possibilities to participate in alter-native ventures were greater for the latter than the former, making it easier for London Merchant Adventurers to sit the Cokayne Project out, but equally some at least appear to have welcomed the opportunities which it promised to open up for them to diversify their own businesses. The initial prospect of 'a Generall freedome of Trafficque of Cloth for all places' which would weaken political bar-riers between different markets was attractive for Merchant Adventurers seeking to broaden their businesses, such as Alderman John Gore, as well as to those excluded from the Company's trade. Indeed, the Gore family (in spite of Richard Gore's loyal service as London and Hamburg deputy of the Merchant Adventurers) was notable for the breadth of its operations, having long played a leading role in the trade to Barbary.[103] It was a trait that ran in the family: in 1623 John Gore's son William was disenfranchised from the Eastland Company, but continued to trade there via Hamburg.[104] In the long run, such behaviour had the potential to weaken the corporate loyalties of Merchant Adventurers, particularly those based in England, leaving the overseas branches increasingly isolated.

The ominous ramifications of these structural changes for trading companies in general was noticed by one author, who used the occasion of the collapse of the Cokayne Project to attempt to resurrect its initial promise of free trade.[105] Apparently writing at the end of 1616 when the king was desperately seeking to keep the aims of the project alive, the author warned that 'this new proiect for

---

[102] Members of the King's Merchants Adventurers at Hamburg to Governor Cokayne and the Fellowship at London, 13 Nov. 1615, Lambeth Palace, 3472, fol. 166v.

[103] Willan, *Studies in Elizabethan Foreign Trade*, pp. 127–130, 202–5.

[104] Petition of the Eastland Company to the Privy Council, 2 July 1623, TNA, SP 14/48, fol. 122.

[105] Henry Haibey/Haibley, 'A breife dicourse Concerning free trade', c.late 1617, Bodl. Lib., North A2, fols 71–2.

dying and dressing' was not to be achieved by 'the trifling dalliance between the old & new Marchants', or 'the trial of A tenth cloth to bee manufactured'; these were 'but to worke their owne ends, still lingering after their old manner of Trading'. The failure of the project had only confirmed the inherent inconveniences of trading companies, by whose 'pretext of order deceitfully intended is the extremitie of confusion'. As well as burdening trade with unnecessary charges and drawing the hostility of other nations due to 'their use of conventicles & monopolishe assemblyes' (with the imperial mandate cited as a notable example), companies were guilty of instilling a preference for 'A quiett & secure manner of trading' centered on 'privilidged Cercuits' and 'confined residing places'. The Merchant Adventurers in particular were like the fabled 'dog in A manger having a competency to content them', and thus unprepared to allow 'the industrious to seeke their most advantage till all bee lost'. However, only the dissolution of all trading companies would allow 'the industrious & understanding man' to capitalize on emerging commercial opportunities. The future was represented by the Dutch, whose emerging role as Europe's middleman could be seen in their domination of the 'Inland Trades of Germany', notwithstanding recent examples of English merchants trading in Nuremburg and Silesia. This success was rooted in commercial freedom: 'by libertie are they grown industrious, & by industry gained experience, soe by degrees become the Monarques of Merchants'. Above all, the Dutch had shown how commerce was not just a series of discrete trade routes to be managed separately, but 'A glorious Chaine, which being vnited, scope is offered for much more then all the Kings subiects can possibly compass'. Rather than seeing Germany merely as a market for English cloth, this was a place to vend spices and indigo from the East Indies, sugar and almonds from Brazil and Barbary, and currants from the Straits, all supplied by English merchants liberated from 'incorporated societyes, who thinking they have trade sufficient, suppose it folly to seeke new trades, which their forefathers knew not'. The export of fully finished cloth direct to its final markets would be one component of this 'Libertie & coniunction of Trade', which also encompassed making England a staple of the grain trade and a revived fishery, culminating in what amounted to an anticipation of the navigation system, whereby 'noe ships can trade in this seas, but onely ours'.

The author of this discourse, Henry Haibey/Haibley, is obscure, and in the immediate term more conservative instincts won out, as the Merchant Adventurers were restored in the hope of reversing the damage of the Cokayne Project.[106] However, the damage done to its commercial model can be seen by the response to the cloth depression of the early 1620s, when the Company once again

---

[106] Further copies of this discourse survive in the British Library and Cambridge University Library: see the entry in the online database 'Manuscript Pamphleteering in Early Stuart England', https://mpese.ac.uk/t/HaibleyBriefDiscourseFreeTrade.html.

had to face a barrage of attacks in the House of Commons. The 1621 parliament had hotly debated the Company's privileges, calling as witnesses some of those inter-lopers prosecuted after the Cokayne Project, many of whom could claim a long history exporting new draperies to places like Amsterdam.[107] This ultimately led the Privy Council to allow free trade in the new draperies for merchants from the outports as long as they traded to the mart towns, a measure which the Merchant Adventurers (perhaps with Cranfield's encouragement) reluctantly consented to, though the Company was insistent that this liberty not be extended to London interlopers.[108] In spite of this, in the following year the free trade in new draperies was for a limited period extended to London by order of the Privy Council, in the face of repeated complaints of depression.[109] Two years later, the Commons resumed its attacks, ultimately leading the Company to accept a more significant set of reforms: free trade to all parts of Germany and the Netherlands for kerseys, dozens, and new draperies, with this measure extended to dyed and dressed broadcloth for merchants of the outports, and admission to the Company extended to all merchants on payment of a 'reasonable' fine.[110] Having already conceded that the mart-trading system was inappropriate for its own members seeking to vend these varieties, the Company could hardly seek to exclude others from looking for new markets: Haibey's vision seemed to be coming into being. One observer considered that the Company had thus been dealt a 'last deadly strike', being left with nothing but the præmption of their white clothes'.[111] It is striking how closely the attitude of Parliament was paralleled by the Privy Council, in stark contrast to the situation in 1604, reflecting how the Cokayne Project had brought into question the purposes of corporate organization of the cloth trade.[112] The Company's traditional argument that its government upheld the reputation and therefore the price of broadcloth was being supplanted by a new emphasis on volume and, implicitly, consumer demand, and in this sense corporate regulations which inflated prices could be seen as counterproductive.[113] Sir Thomas Lowe's statement in the 1621 parliament that opening up access to the cloth trade would 'cause a great Fall of the Prices of the Cloth' was countered by a provincial member, who asserted 'That the Merchant Adventurers seek not to vent and utter many Cloths, but to vent and sell them at a dear Rate, whereby they may have the better Return of what they have expended, without any Regard to the Number of Cloths'.[114] More merchants, trading at a more modest level, might be the best way to increase the amount sold: already in 1618 the Privy Council had

---

[107] *Proceedings and Debates of the House of Commons, in 1620 and 1621*, I (Oxford, 1766), pp. 188–90.
[108] Friis, *Alderman Cockayne's Project*, pp. 400–11; APC 1619–20, pp. 392–3.
[109] Friis, *Alderman Cockayne's Project*, p. 414.
[110] Ibid., pp. 428–30; Supple, *Commercial Crisis*, pp. 70–1; BL, Hargraves 321, fols 54–9.
[111] Sir Francis Nethersole–Carleton, 24 May 1624, TNA, SP 14/165, fol. 64v.
[112] Supple, *Commercial Crisis*, p. 71.   [113] Ibid., p. 72.
[114] *Proceedings and Debates of the House of Commons*, p. 204.

asked the Company to admit one of the interlopers it was prosecuting, John Heather, on the grounds that he had been trading for fifteen years.[115]

A persistent criticism that the Company faced during these debates concerned the impositions it charged on its members' cloth exports, which had recently been increased.[116] The Company's defence that this was necessary to defray the debts it had incurred in paying off the crown after the Cokayne Project won little sympathy in the context of falling sales overseas. The requirement that it throw open the doors to all merchants on reasonable terms was thus for the Company potentially tempting, allowing this burden to be shared, but at the price of diluting the privileged share of trade its members enjoyed.[117] Retaining the loyalty of its members in the face of these pressures would be a growing challenge, but the reforms of 1621–4 did not prove to be irreversible. In 1634, the Company's monopoly was restored by royal proclamation. The reasons for this can be located in the Merchant Adventurers' ambiguous relationship with the monarchy in the years of personal rule, something that would be reflected too in the complex response of its members to the civil war that followed, events which divided the Company internally as never before. The implications of these divisions for the Company will be the subject of the next chapter.

---

[115] APC 1617–18, pp. 105–6.   [116] For these rates, see Chapter 1.
[117] Merchant Adventurers to the Privy Council, 9 Apr. 1622, TNA, SP 14/129, fol. 16.

7

'A new spirit of dissention and disturbance'

Religious and Political Divisions, *c.*1630–60

The spring of 1629 found the London merchant community in an unusually febrile mood. The recently dissolved parliament had spent much time condemning unparliamentary impositions on foreign trade: mercantile grievance and constitutional principle were, for once, running in parallel.[1] The result was a widespread boycott of the paying of tonnage and poundage, and in the case of the Merchant Adventurers, the looming cancellation of the Company's customary spring fleets. One hostile observer privy to the 'general discourse of merchants' raised the possibility of 'setting of Trade free by dissolving of such Companies as shall desist from Trade' in order to restore obedience, adding that the Merchant Adventurers were 'fittest to bee dealt with first, in regard the proceeding of that Trade doth most import the good of the State'.[2] As custodians of the nation's staple export, the Merchant Adventurers were particularly vulnerable to political pressure, more so than luxury importers such as the Levant Company, whose members were the other ringleaders of the boycott. The anonymous author thus suggested that if the London court of the Merchant Adventurers voted against appointing its regular spring fleet, the crown should permit individual members to ship their cloth, an action which would bring out the self-interest of those suddenly reluctant to 'loose the benefite of their Trade'.

As it happened, no such threat was necessary. When the London court met in May, it voted by a majority of two to dispatch its fleet, apparently persuaded by senior merchants such as Sir John Gore, brother-in-law to the secretary of state Sir John Coke.[3] Even before then, one member had reported that for many of his brethren, the boycott was an underhand means to drive down the price of cloth at home, whilst increasing demand for their remaining stocks in the mart towns: 'there are privat ends, under a publique show, amongst those marchants one to beguile an other'.[4] By its very nature, a regulated company would struggle to maintain collective action: 'this discouerie of under-hand dealing and traide amongst themselves, would quickly make them resolve of shipping'. In any case,

---

[1] Ashton, *City and the Court*, pp. 129–32.
[2] Report on the stoppage of trade, to Lord President Conway, *c.*Apr. 1629, TNA, SP 16/530, fol. 80.
[3] Coke–Secretary Dorchester, 16 May 1629, TNA, SP 16/142, fol. 133.
[4] Notes on the Merchant Adventurers sent to Secretary Dorchester, 6 Apr. 1629, TNA, SP 16/150, fol. 31.

Fellowship and Freedom: The Merchant Adventurers and the Restructuring of English Commerce, 1582–1700.
Thomas Leng, Oxford University Press (2020). © Thomas Leng. DOI: 10.1093/oso/9780198794479.001.0001

this informant suggested, the boycott was driven more by fear of reprisals from Parliament for agreeing to submit to these duties, than any constitutional concerns about their legitimacy.

Having seen their privileges diluted in 1624, members may have felt they had little to lose in joining the opposition to Charles I's government. In 1634 these privileges were largely restored, however, and we might account for the Merchant Adventurers' dalliance with opposition politics as the consequence of this short-term breakdown of relations between crown and Company. In his study of mercantile political allegiance during the civil war, Robert Brenner placed members of the Merchant Adventurers largely in the royalist camp, although not so markedly as those of the other trading companies which had by then supplanted them at the pinnacle of London's merchant elite. This Brenner put down to the limited influence that the Company's elite members were able to exercise over their brethren in comparison with the more tightly integrated 'Levant–East India group', but even so he identified twenty-three Merchant Adventurers actively involved in the conservative London petitioning campaigns that preceded the outbreak of war, against just three supporting the pro-parliamentary equivalents. That said, Brenner did find several members who eventually drifted towards parliamentarianism.[5] Such pragmatism was reflected at the level of the Company, which, once war was under way, eventually accommodated with a Parliament desperate for financial support, in return for which Parliament passed an ordinance maintaining the Company's monopoly, in 1643. The Company eventually became Parliament's biggest lender in the civil war.[6]

Brenner's London-centric account, however, is complicated when we take into account the Company's membership overseas, amongst whom the divisions of the era had their greatest effect. During Charles I's personal rule, the Delft membership became embroiled in a bitter contest with its deputy, Edward Misselden, who sought to bring its congregation into conformity with the Church of England, going against half a century of Presbyterian-style religious discipline, and the incumbent minister, John Forbes. The head court at Hamburg was subject to similar contentions in 1645, when many members revolted against the deputy governor, Joseph Avery, in favour of subscribing to the Solemn League of Covenant, with their minister, Jeremiah Elborough, providing a figurehead of opposition. There was much continuity between these contests: Elborough had been ordained by Forbes in his capacity as head of the English synod in the Netherlands.[7] But if these instances suggest a stronger commitment to parliamentarianism and the reformed religion in the mart towns than was the case amongst

[5] Brenner, *Merchants and Revolution*, pp. 381–9.

[6] Ben Coates, *The Impact of the English Civil War on the Economy of London, 1642–50* (Abingdon and New York, 2004), pp. 72–4.

[7] Chris De Jung, 'John Forbes (c.1568–1634), Scottish minister and exile in the Netherlands', *Nederlands archief voor kerkgeschiedenis/Dutch Review of Church History* 69, 1 (1989), p. 37.

the generally more wealthy and senior London merchants, the events of the 1650s paint a still more complex picture. In that decade Hamburg saw a bitter struggle within the Company, this time directed against another deputy governor, Richard Bradshaw. Bradshaw also held office as the Protector's official resident, and thus came to symbolize the intrusion of the state into the Company's traditional self-government.

The relationship between the Company and the English state was not the only one at stake in the political contests of the middle decades of the century. Equally important were the relationships that bound together a geographically dispersed merchant community, on a personal and corporate level. As ties of deference between factors and servants overseas and their principals at home were weakened by the growing number of independent merchants resident overseas, the mart towns were increasingly willing to follow their own political courses. The potential for division had been exacerbated in 1624 when the trade in new draperies and the cheaper old draperies was opened up to non-members.[8] Although this brought the prospect of new commissions for the Company's factors, much of this new traffic in the Netherlands went to towns such as Amsterdam, where Company members had been free to export all varieties except white cloth since 1618. Because the new draperies had only recently been specifically encompassed within the Company's monopoly privileges, this may not have had a significant effect on the mart towns, which continued to act as the staples for undressed cloth exports. However, the 1628 port book for cloth exports from London indicates that many Merchant Adventurers were taking the opportunity to send other sorts of cloth to places like Amsterdam, alongside an influx of non-members who capitalized on the 1624 opening of trade. Old drapery exports from London to the mart town at Delft in that year amounted to 44,001 notional shortcloths, compared to 22,745 going to other towns in the Netherlands, which took the majority of narrow cloths and coloured variants, including the rising commodity of Spanish cloth (2,199 compared to 760 going to Delft).[9] Whether these exports were being delivered to members of the Company or interlopers is unclear, but the Company's factors at Delft had cause to be alarmed at the growing volume of trade outside of the mart town. In fact, in 1630 the Company in London complained to the Privy Council about 'the late disorderly stragling trade and scattering of the coloured Clothes, kersies and other wollen Comodities in the severall townes of the United Provinces', which led the crown to order that the trade of members and non-members alike be restored to the mart towns.[10] However, four years later the Company complained that the intrusion of interlopers had caused 'divers of the said Adventurers to disband from the Company and leave the place

---

[8] See Chapter 6.
[9] TNA, E190/32/3. Notional shortcloth exports to Hamburg in that year were 30,435.
[10] APC 1630–1, pp. 64, 90.

of their Residence in the Mart Towne; and to carry their Cullered Clothes also and other draperies to Amsterdam and other places'.[11] The 1624 reforms thus threatened the dissolution of the mart-trading system in the Netherlands, and the absorption of its membership into the wider mercantile community.

The cohesiveness of the community at Delft was already under strain, then, by the time that Edward Misselden launched his assault on the Presbyterian-style system which was a foundation of corporate social order overseas. The ensuing contest, as well as those that followed in Hamburg, centred on the relationship between the Fellowship and its governing officers, notably its deputy governors. In a period of continued debate about the origins and nature of political authority, Merchant Adventurers were asking similar questions about their own Company. Was the power wielded by the Company's officers rooted in the royal charter that established it as a corporation, or did it derive from the consent of the membership which elected them? How was the collective will of the Fellowship to be made manifest given the dispersal of its membership? Given the increasing commercial divergence between its branches, could these members be considered as belonging to a single community of merchants at all? Thus, although the contests discussed below were fought around national issues—the appropriate form of the true church; allegiance in the civil war; the legitimacy of the post-regicidal regimes—they became entwined with questions that were central to the Company of Merchant Adventurers as a political, as well as social and commercial, community.

'To raigne as king in this Company': Edward Misselden and the Merchant Adventurers at Delft

Of the three contests to be considered in this chapter, that between Edward Misselden and John Forbes is best known, being an important episode in Charles I's effort to impose religious conformity on the English churches in the Netherlands, a mission that was eagerly taken up by the Delft deputy governor.[12] The Company church at Delft was an early target of this drive, not least because of Forbes' high-profile position as president of the synod of English churches in the Netherlands, established in 1621.[13] From 1631 to 1633 Forbes was assisted by a cleric who would become an even more controversial figure, the future congregationalist Thomas Hooker, who was based in Delft prior to his emigration to Massachusetts. Forbes was also connected to Hugh Peter, who in 1633 reorganized

---

[11] Petition, Merchant Adventurers to Privy Council, Nov. 1634, TNA, SP 16/277, fol. 226.
[12] Keith L. Sprunger, *Dutch Puritanism: A History of English and Scottish Churches of the Netherlands in the Sixteenth and Seventeenth Centuries* (Leiden, 1982), pp. 233-51; De Jung, 'John Forbes', pp. 17-53.
[13] De Jung, 'John Forbes', pp. 30-43.

his Rotterdam church on congregationalist lines and who occasionally preached in the Company church. These associations, together with the fact that the Delft church adopted its own set of articles asserting the scriptural basis of its discipline and government shortly after the Rotterdam covenant, might suggest that it too was headed towards some form of congregationalism.[14] However, the opposition to Misselden of many Delft Merchant Adventurers was driven by a desire not so much to launch a further reformation of the church, as to uphold a system of church government and discipline which was closely woven into the social fabric of their community. Clearly, too, Forbes was a figure who commanded a high degree of loyalty as spiritual counsellor to generations of Merchant Adventurers. His association with the Company stretched back to 1608, making him a reassuring point of continuity, spanning the disruption of the Cokayne Project and the move from Middelburg to Delft.[15] To Forbes' partisans, Misselden was the innovator, guilty of seeking to overthrow a system of church government that had served the Company well for half a century.

This system had emerged in the 1570s and 1580s, when the Company was re-establishing itself in the Netherlands, and its defenders highlighted its respectability by emphasizing that it was rooted in religious rights acquired by the royal diplomat William Davison in 1579, and later endorsed by the Earl of Leicester. The need to conform 'both in doctrine and discipline with those Churches of the Reformed religion' could thus be presented as a prerequisite for the Company's continued enjoyment of its local privileges.[16] The presence of a series of Presbyterian-leaning ministers helped to enshrine a system of church government encompassing regular consistory meetings, elected elders and deacons, and scrutiny of those admitted to take communion.[17] On at least two occasions in the early years of the church, the deputy governor and minister clashed over its organization, and in 1592 deputy Thomas Ferrers resisted an attempt by Francis Johnson to introduce a written covenant, which apparently led to a period of schism in the congregation that may have still been ongoing well into the next century.[18] But other occasions of conflict between the minister and congregation seem if anything to suggest that the latter were embracing the opportunities for participation which a Presbyterian system offered, rather than rejecting it.[19] Given the presence in the mart towns of a majority of potentially unruly young bachelors, Presbyterian-style moral discipline had its attractions, at least to those senior merchants who would have held office as elders (the seven elders of the

---

[14] Sprunger, *Dutch Puritanism*, pp. 237–9; 'The substance of a late submission drawn from the English Church at Delfe by Mr Forbes & his Elders', TNA, SP 16/252, fol. 56 (#29).

[15] De Jung, 'John Forbes', p. 50.

[16] John Quarles–Dorchester, 27 Dec. 1631, TNA, SP 84/144, fol. 137v.

[17] Polly Ha, *English Presbyterianism 1590–1640* (Stanford, 2011), pp. 122–6.

[18] Sprunger, *Dutch Puritanism*, pp. 25–7. For the Merchant Adventurer Edward Bennett's involvement with Johnson's congregation as late as 1612, see later in this chapter.

[19] Ha, *English Presbyterianism*, p. 123.

Hamburg church in 1620 were all married householders). Even for younger merchants, membership of the congregation could act as a sign of moral probity and creditworthiness, and it was not just the sins of the young which were subject to correction by the consistory, although in 1633 one Merchant Adventurer regretted that 'our predecessors have bene more exact and diligent then the present times'.[20] Even if it had fallen from these pristine standards, the Company church survived into the 1630s as a forum for collective associational life, defining the moral as well as religious boundaries of this merchant community.

This was a boundary which, by 1632, many members of the Delft congregation considered their deputy governor Edward Misselden to have crossed. On his part, Misselden had by then reached the conclusion that the Company's church was 'so contrary to His Majesties government & our Mother-Church, as is neither conformable to the Church of England nor the Reformed Churches of these Countries'.[21] However, Misselden had been in office for over seven years before he was prepared to state this sentiment openly, and it is likely that concerns about his own status were instrumental in encouraging him to do so. Misselden arrived in Delft in 1623 with a reputation for ambitiousness stretching back to 1611, when his presentation of a manuscript treatise decrying the lack of discipline in Stade to Sir Robert Cecil aroused the indignation of many of his fellows. Some allegedly considered that by 'discouering the secrets of the same to forreigne knowledge', Misselden was in breach of his oath of allegiance to the Company.[22] Another of Misselden's complaints—that his fellows did 'iest at my manners, in my presenting of it'—is indicative of a sensitivity and pretentiousness (shown by his liberal usage of Latin quotations) that did not desert him. Some also suspected him of using his office to pursue private ends, and he was accused of seeking to engineer a move from Delft to Amsterdam for his own advantage.[23] Nor did Misselden's character endear him to the English resident in the United Provinces, Sir Dudley Carleton, who was initially sympathetic to John Forbes' activities in the English synod, believing this to be a means to prevent separatist tendencies amongst the English churches.[24] Misselden's complaint about having to govern 'a Company of yong men, who must sometimes smart under the exercise of government' is indicative of how he struggled to win respect amongst the fellowship, something made all the harder to take by the respect that Forbes commanded.[25]

Misselden was also frustrated by Carleton's willingness to rely on other merchants for advice. This had been demonstrated in 1631, when a dispute between the

[20] John Quarles–William Boswell, 2 Mar. 1633, BL, Add. 6394, fol. 96. For evidence of its activities, see the extracts of the register of the Antwerp church, 1579–82, BL, Add 6394, fols 106–7.
[21] Extract of Misselden's letter to the Merchant Adventurers in London, Mar. 1633, BL, Add. 6394, fol. 117.
[22] Misselden, 'Discourse', fol. 39r.
[23] Notes on Misselden, c.Jan. 1630, TNA, SP 84/141, fol. 9.   [24] De Jong, 'John Forbes', p. 32.
[25] Misselden–Carleton, 7 May 1625, TNA, SP 84/127, fol. 44.

Company and its Dutch customers led to a lengthy stoppage of trade at Delft. The issue was the tare, a charge on cloths found to be faulty imposed on the seller, and a practice which the Company frequently complained was abused by Dutch merchants. When the Hamburg court prohibited cloths from being tared outside the mart towns, the Dutch cloth-buyers responded by boycotting English cloth, their actions supported by a placaart of the States General and the seizure of some members' cloths.[26] Misselden was entrusted by the Company at London with the task of negotiating an end to this dispute, with the assistance of Carleton's replacement as royal ambassador, his nephew, also called Dudley Carleton. Finding Misselden's rigid approach to be unfruitful, the younger Carleton brokered his own settlement.[27] As his intermediary in discussions with the Dutch cloth-buyers, he turned to one John Quarles (nephew of the merchant of the same name discussed in Part One). Quarles was a rather controversial figure, having contravened the Company's regulations by marrying a Dutch woman, although not before securing her letters of endenization. The fact that the crown consistently supported his petitions to be allowed to continue to hold the Company's freedom is a sign of how useful Carleton and his uncle, now Viscount Dorchester, found his services: indeed, Quarles' intimate acquaintance with Dutch merchants was a particular asset in ending the tare dispute.[28] In spite of this, the Delft court under Misselden's direction continued to withhold Quarles' freedom, arguing that 'by these duch marriages & allyances with strangers His Majesty looseth such his subjects, The cloth-trade & secrets of our Country are discovered to strangers, & our Companies trade & priviledges hazarded'.[29]

Although Quarles could rely on his eminent allies for protection, later in the decade the Privy Council did begin to harden its stance on overseas marriages. In 1636, it turned down the request of one Jacob Bonnell, an English-born merchant of Dutch parentage, to join the Company, using this as an opportunity to confirm the regulations against all members marrying overseas.[30] The Company had opposed Bonnell's admission, but when it petitioned that the marriage clause be waived in the case of the newly selected deputy governor at Rotterdam, Humphrey Burre, the Council was equally unyielding.[31] This shift in the crown's attitude towards foreign marriages is indicative of a growing concern about the religious and political loyalties of the extensive English population in the Netherlands,

---

[26] Misselden–Viscount Dorchester, 21 July 1630, TNA, SP 84/141, fol. 303; APC 1630–1, pp. 62–4.
[27] Carleton–Dorchester, 7 Feb. 1631, TNA, SP 84/143, fols 37–40; 13 Feb. 1631, ibid., fols 51–2; 22 Mar. 1631, ibid., fols 90–1; 30 May 1631, ibid., fols 172–8; Dorchester–Carleton, 22 Apr. 1631, ibid., fol. 132.
[28] Petition of John Quarles to the Privy Council, c.1629, TNA, SP 16/530, fol. 182; Quarles–Dorchester, 5 Jan. 1629, TNA, SP 16/131, fol. 24; APC 1628–9, pp. 312–13; APC 1629–30, pp. 67–8; Quarles–Dorchester, 12 July 1630, TNA, SP 84/141, fol. 284; APC 1630–1, p. 114.
[29] Misselden–Boswell, Jan. 1633, BL, Add. 6394, fol. 72.   [30] PC 2/45, fol. 226.
[31] Petition of the Merchant Adventurers to the Privy Council concerning Humphrey Burre, Sept. 1639, TNA, SP 16/429, fol. 147; Privy Council order, 8 Sept. 1639, TNA, SP 16/428, fol. 107.

which also provided Misselden with the opportunity to make his move against his rivals Quarles and Forbes.

Misselden first raised equivocations about the nature of the Delft church in November 1631, when his reputation was at a low ebb following the tare dispute. His initial complaint was that non-members of the Company had been partici-pating in elections for elders and deacons, so blurring the boundary between freemen and outsiders, a practice which Forbes agreed should cease.[32] However, Misselden also prepared a paper questioning the role of elders, based on his own investigations into the scriptural basis of such an office. Although he forbore from presenting this in the General Court, he did address it Forbes and the elders in private, to their considerable alarm. According to a note of the minutes of the following General Court meeting (produced by Misselden in defence of his con-duct), the deputy used the occasion to publicly deny any intention 'to alter the course, they now are in', and the court proceeded to vote to continue their church government as before.[33] However, John Quarles provided a different account, suggesting that Misselden had initially succeeded in having an act passed that would have given him a 'civil power' over the church, relying on the support of the younger merchants ('for our Court heer is exceeding weake').[34] Only the intervention of Forbes led to this act being revoked.

Whatever the precise details of this meeting, from that point on the breach between Misselden and the church elders was public, signified by the refusal of the latter to admit their deputy governor to take communion. By October 1632 it was alleged that Misselden could command no obedience as deputy governor, and the following month his London counterpart, George Lowe, led a mission to bring the rival parties to reconciliation, to little effect.[35] However, Misselden's position had been strengthened by the death of Dorchester, and the appointment of a secretary of state, Sir Francis Windebank, who was much more willing to lis-ten to his complaints.[36] The replacement of Carleton as ambassador to the States General by William Boswell, with instructions to bring the English churches into conformity, also helped Misselden.[37] After a series of interventions by Boswell and interviews with the king, the elderly Forbes finally agreed to retire in the win-ter of 1633-4. Already the Company at London had consented to the crown's order that it select a more conformable minister for the Delft residence.[38] For a while Forbes' supporters in Delft attempted to find him a new role in their church,

[32] Minutes of the Company court at Delft, collected by Edward Misselden, BL, Add. 6394, fol. 48v.
[33] Ibid.   [34] Quarles–Dorchester, 27 Dec. 1631, TNA, SP 84/144, fols 137–8.
[35] John Wolstenholm–Boswell, 26 Oct. 1632, BL, Add. 6394, fol. 50; Lowe–Boswell, 29 Nov. 1632, ibid., fol. 54.
[36] Windebank's notes on Misselden's information about the English churches, 29 Oct. 1632, TNA, SP 16/224, fol. 137.
[37] Instructions to William Boswell, c.July 1632, TNA, SP 84/144, fols 220–1.
[38] Charles I to the Merchant Adventurers, 29 May 1633, TNA, SP 16/239, fol. 83; Sprunger, pp. 246–7.

but Forbes' death in August 1634 eventually led to the Company church being brought into line with the Church of England, the office of elder being replaced by a vestry presided over by a conformist cleric, George Beaumont.[39] The crown had achieved its religious goals, then, but persuading the Company to overturn the election of midsummer 1633, whereby the Hamburg court replaced Misselden as deputy governor at Delft with one Robert Edwards, was another matter.[40]

Misselden's de-selection at Hamburg demonstrates how his unpopularity had spread beyond the elders at Delft. Misselden presented his defeat as engineered by a Puritan faction: the Hamburg deputy, Edward Bennett, was father-in-law of one of Misselden's chief adversaries at Delft, Samuel Avery, and had allegedly been recovered from Francis Johnson's separatist congregation at Amsterdam by Forbes.[41] However, Misselden's actions could not fail to offend opinion within the Company more widely. As early as October 1632, Misselden was proposing the removal of the chief seat of Company government to London, with overseas deputies to be chosen there by the senior members under the watchful eye of the crown.[42] He was even willing to suggest that the Company's charter be recalled, or subject to a Star Chamber investigation: arguably a violation of his Company oath.[43] Misselden's proposals about church government were equally prone to upset his brethren. Alongside his investigations into the scriptural warranty for the office of elder, Misselden had scoured the Company's records for information regarding the traditional relationship between its secular and religious offices, eventually uncovering references to the position of chaplain, whose role was to assist the governor or deputy in the administration of discipline.[44] As one critic indignantly pointed out, Misselden was proposing to return to practices predating the establishment of the Company's church and belonging to a time of popery, thus implying that there was 'no difference betwix a privat chaplen in a familie and a publick minister of a congregation'.[45] As deputy governor, Misselden clearly considered that the imposition of discipline within the Company's ranks was his responsibility, and so his exclusion from the church eldership was incompatible with his role. But to his critics, this amounted to claiming 'to himself, and that ex officio, as deputie, the whole and sole power to ecclesiasticall government in this church as well as civil in the companie'. This 'strainge' discipline would amount to

---

[39] Sprunger, *Dutch Puritanism*, pp. 246, 250–1.   [40] PC 2/43, fols 95, 134, 143.

[41] Misselden, Memorial, 16 July 1633, TNA, SP 84/147, fols 45–6. Sprunger, *Dutch Puritanism*, p. 258. In 1612 it was alleged that '*As the King of Spaine is vnto the Pope: so is Master* Benet *vnto Master* Iohnson': Christopher Lawne, *The Prophane Schisme of the Brownists* (1612), p. 12.

[42] Windebank's notes on Misselden's information about the English churches, 29 Oct. 1632, TNA, SP 16/224, fol. 137; Misselden–Boswell, 7 Dec. 1632, BL, Add. 6394, fol. 56.

[43] Misselden–Arundel, 16 Feb. 1633, TNA, SP 84/146, fol. 71; Memorial, 16 July 1633, TNA, SP 84/147, fols 45–6.

[44] Orders concerning the Chaplen compiled by Edward Misselden, BL, Add. 6394, fol. 48.

[45] 'Nature & ground of the differences between Mr Missenden Deputy & the merchants of the Company of Adventurers in Delpf concerning Eccleasiastiq affairs', 10 Feb. 1633, BL, Add. 6394, fol. 82r.

Misselden assuming 'the same supremacie in the Company which is his Majesties Royall prerogative in his dominions, and so in effect to raigne as king in this Company'.[46]

Such sentiments were clearly anathema to the more zealous Protestants in the Netherlands: the Delft treasurer, Andrew Kendrick, allegedly refused to take communion with Misselden on the grounds that he was an enemy to God and man.[47] But the fact that the Company's membership repeatedly refused to accept the king's instructions to re-elect Misselden as deputy governor suggests that his unpopularity extended beyond the ranks of the godly. The Privy Council had initially responded to Misselden's defeat in midsummer 1633 by insisting on his restoration as Delft deputy, but by October it was content that the Company merely select someone other than Edwards.[48] At that point, Misselden was out of favour at court, having been rebuked by the king in person for having 'assumed to himselfe that power, which hee charged the minister and companie to have usurped': the reservations of the Delft congregation were not without foundation, it seems.[49] The Hamburg court eventually decided to replace Edwards with Misselden's leading critic Samuel Avery, a man considered by some at court to be 'of factious & rash disposition'.[50] However, throughout 1634 the crown's focus was on settling the Company's church, and so Avery was allowed to continue in his post. The more contentious aspects of Misselden's proposed reform of the Company, including the reduction of its government to London, also seem to have been quietly dropped.[51] Only in 1635 did the crown again push for Misselden's re-election, the former deputy having continued his campaign to besmirch his enemies as 'a violent faction of malicious men'.[52] This time, however, Misselden was rejected as deputy not only in the mart towns, but also by the London court, attesting to a widespread sense that he was 'unfitt for that place'.[53] Another royal attempt to have Misselden re-elected in 1638 was also spurned, although this time the king was satisfied by the Company's offer to employ Misselden in an alternative capacity, and now called instead for 'a reconciliation of all differences amongst themselves'.[54]

Misselden's new position was to lead a mission to recover £3,000 owed to the crown by the city of Rotterdam, as part of the deal whereby the Company moved

[46] Ibid., fols 82v–83r.   [47] Misselden–Boswell, 1633, BL, Add. 6394, fol. 67.

[48] PC 2/43, fol. 143.

[49] Sir John Coke–Boswell, 26 Oct. 1633, TNA, SP 84/147, fol. 156.

[50] Report to Windebank on Avery's election, 25 Feb. 1634, TNA, SP 84/148, fol. 105.

[51] The Privy Council had included this demand in its initial response to Misselden's de-selection: PC 2/43, fol. 95.

[52] Misselden–Windebank, 26 June 1635, TNA, SP 16/291, fol. 138.

[53] Petition, Merchant Adventurers to Charles I, 18 July 1635, TNA, SP 16/307, fol. 131 (#78).

[54] Charles I's response to petition of the Merchant Adventurers, 4 July 1638, TNA, SP 84/154, fol. 73. The king's inclination to interfere in Company elections had not disappeared, however: in April 1639 the Privy Council ordered that the Rotterdam deputy, Richard Bladwell, should be removed, and his successor, Humphrey Burre, was also rejected (see earlier in this chapter).

from Delft in 1635. This move, which was decided on in 1634, might have helped the new minister, George Beaumont, to implement the changes which he had been instructed by Archbishop Laud to make.[55] Boswell ensured that the terms agreed by Rotterdam included a clause against 'any preaching by anyone in their congregation which might be against the doctrines or discipline of the Church of England'.[56] Boswell also tried and failed to enforce the closure of the existing English reformed church in Rotterdam. However, by providing an alternative place of worship for Merchant Adventurers with a tender conscience, the survival of Hugh Peter's church may have actually helped Beaumont to implement his reforms, even if this weakened its importance in the collective life of its members.[57] In fact, Misselden complained that in 1635 deputy Avery had allowed Peter's church to act as the official English representative at a public day of prayer, in preference to the Company church.[58] Such an attitude may have encouraged the London court to eventually insist on Avery's removal, but in any case Misselden's suggestion that by then 'the principall of that faction are come away, & nowe the knot being broken, the rest will easely be wonne', indicates that a generational turnover was under way in the Rotterdam residence, which might weaken its attachment to the Company's religious traditions.[59] The death of Forbes represented another break with the past, though he evidently still had supporters in the Netherlands.[60]

The end of church government by elders may not have been universally regretted at Delft, however. For all the respect Forbes commanded, it seems that in December 1631 Misselden was able to secure a majority in court in favour of remodelling the church structure, even if this was overturned by Forbes' intervention. Misselden's subsequent failure to build a party is a sign of how widely he had offended Company opinion. In contrast, Forbes' supporters were able to coordinate their actions effectively, drawing not only on a high degree of internal cohesion, but also on strong links to Hamburg and London. But in many senses this was a defensive mobilization. The declaration of seventeen of these ringleaders against Misselden's aspersions of them as 'Schismaticks and Refractory men, and Contemmners of the Royall Authority' emphasized their desire to continue to 'lyve as our Precedecessors have done': not necessarily the position of radicals set on a further reformation.[61] Boswell's discussions with members of the Company persuaded him that they had no 'intention to decline his Majesties Commaunds, though I perceyve a great affection in them unto their present Minister'.[62]

[55] Laud and Juxon to the Merchant Adventurers at Delft, 21 June 1634, TNA, SP 16/270, fol. 4.
[56] Quoted in Sprunger, *Dutch Puritanism*, p. 249.   [57] Ibid., p. 250.
[58] Misselden–Windebank, 26 June 1635, TNA, SP 16/291, fol. 138.
[59] Misselden's notes on the Rotterdam court, 8 Oct. 1635, TNA, SP 84/150, fol. 107.
[60] As suggested by the publication of his *Four Sermons* (1635).
[61] Declaration dated 27 Nov. 1632, TNA, SP 16/225, fol. 146. One of the signers, Edward Morgan, did strike a more combative tone in a letter to Boswell, 5 Mar. 1633, BL, Add. 6394, fol. 103.
[62] Boswell to ?, 8 Mar. 6133, BL, Add. 6394, fol. 109v.

Ultimately, members of the Company were still reliant on strong links with the crown, particularly during the negotiations to move to Rotterdam, which were led by Avery.[63] Even more significantly, the move to Rotterdam was accompanied by a decision by the crown to end the ten-year-long period of relatively open trade, something which might have made even the most scrupulous of the godly reluctant to alienate the crown by resisting its religious policies.[64]

Given the behaviour of the Delft membership, the crown's decision to restore these privileges may seem surprising. Even more alarming than the state of the Merchant Adventurers' church, however, was the existence of thousands of largely unknown English exiles resident in the Netherlands, many of whom had strayed much further from the Church of England. Restoring the Company's monopoly might at least make this English community more governable. The move to Rotterdam was accompanied by an attempt to force English interlopers to relocate to the new mart town, under Beaumont's watchful eye. However, compelling these merchants to obey this command proved impossible, leaving the Company to complain about those interlopers who 'are become as dutch by their dutch marriages, and such as are refractory to the religion and Ceremonies of the English Church'.[65] Perhaps some of Forbes' old supporters amongst the Merchant Adventurers had by then been encouraged to join them.

The one figure capable of uniting a broad swathe of Merchant Adventurers, in London as well as Germany and the Netherlands, was Edward Misselden. Misselden's allegation following his electoral defeat, that the brethren at Delft had threatened in future to show him 'such respect, as belongs to a Banckrupt or insolvent', indicates how he had been cast out of the Company's moral community.[66] Principally, this was because he was seen to have disturbed the peace of the Company, bringing unwelcome attention from the crown. The disputes that erupted within the Fellowship during the next two decades proved to be if anything even less containable.

'Tossed in one tempest': The Rotterdam and Hamburg Residences in the Civil War

In spite of the submission of the Delft church, the relationship between the Company of Merchant Adventurers and the crown remained fraught throughout the 1630s, with Misselden at the centre of most controversies. In February 1640

---

[63] Instructions to Avery and other commissioners for the Rotterdam removal, Sept. 1634, HMC Cowper II, p. 69.

[64] PC 2/44, fol. 37.

[65] Petition, Merchant Adventurers to the Privy Council, 1635, TNA, SP 16/307, #77.

[66] Misselden's statement on the want of obedience of the Merchant Adventurers at Delft and Hamburg, late 1633?, TNA, SP 16/257, fol. 19.

the accusation of perjury was once more raised against him in the London Company court, this time on the grounds that he had refused to present some petitions to the crown.[67] However, by then the recall of Parliament had meant that the Company faced new challenges, and by the following year it was contending with seven hostile petitions and the scrutiny of a parliamentary committee.[68] Its ability to survive these challenges was largely a consequence of Parliament's fiscal needs, but the fact that the Company could draw on members such as Samuel Avery with sound godly credentials was also an advantage. The fruit of this was an ordinance dated 11 October 1643 'for the upholding the Government of the Fellowship of Merchants Adventurers of England', endorsing the Company's monopoly over trade to its territories and its power to exercise discipline over members, though confirming the right of merchants to join for a fee.[69]

Another sign of the Company's willingness to trim its sails to the wind was the dismissal of George Beaumont as minister of the church at Rotterdam, something ordered by the London deputy Robert Edwards in November 1642.[70] Beaumont had implemented a thorough reorganization of his church, including the adoption of that litmus test of Laudian conformity, the railed altar.[71] The Company's London court found it as hard to bring the Dutch membership into line in the 1640s as it had a decade previously, however. In 1644 it selected as Beaumont's replacement the Scottish irenicist John Dury, who had prior associations with the Company at Hamburg and had known John Forbes personally. On arrival in Rotterdam, Dury found that Beaumont's changes had been enthusiastically embraced by at least some of his congregation, notably the incumbent deputy governor, William Cranmer. Although he succeeded in removing the communion table and implementing a new form of service, Dury met with resistance over the election of elders and deacons, and thus found himself unable to perform communion.[72] Beaumont, who was still present in Rotterdam, thus appears to have been remarkably successful in severing his congregation's attachment to the Presbyterian-style discipline which had previously prevailed at Delft and Middelburg.[73] The suggestion by Dury's wife, Dorothy, that many of the congregation considered her husband to be no more than a chaplain is reminiscent of Misselden's attempts to redefine the relationship between deputy and minister.[74] Dury's attempts to restore the 'former laudable Customes used in the Congregation'

[67] The accusation was levelled by one Peter Jones: Misselden–Windebank, 25 Feb. 1640, TNA, SP 16/446, fol. 48.
[68] For details, see Chapter 8.
[69] An Ordinance of the Lords and Commons in Parliament Assembled, for the upholding the Government of the Fellowship of Merchants Adventurers of England (London, 11 Oct. 1643).
[70] Sprunger, Dutch Puritanism, pp. 251–2.   [71] Ibid., p. 250.
[72] Dury–Hartlib, 5 Aug. 1644, HP 3/2/49–50.
[73] Dury–Samuel Avery, 19 Sept. 1644, HP 3/2/63A.
[74] Dorothy Dury–Hartlib, 20 Jan. 1645, HP 21/5/21A.

for admitting members to communion and upholding discipline were now objected to as an assault on the Company's privileges.[75] Cranmer was reported to stand 'much vpon his free charter, and independence', and according to Dury the deputy had argued that 'it is inconsistent with the Orders of the Companie that we should have any church orders or I have any Assistents'.[76]

As well as turning away from its religious traditions, under Beaumont the Company church also increasingly withdrew from previous associations with the wider reformed community in the Netherlands, English as well as Dutch.[77] Like Misselden before him, Dury was cast as an outsider, an intrusive presence in what appears a rather insular community, and the fact that he came with the support of the Company's London court was of no advantage. Dury complained to Samuel Avery in London that congregational elections were opposed on the grounds that 'you there haue Chosen to vs here elders & Deacons'.[78] Cranmer also spurned the orders of the Hamburg church, which continued to adhere to Presbyterian-style government, as being unfit as a precedent for their congregation.[79] The allegations Dury claimed were being levelled against him—that he was 'going about to exalt my self, & tyrannize ouer them, & abridge the Company of their priuiledges'—were reminiscent of those once faced by Misselden.[80] For Dury, this amounted to arguing that 'men should be allowed to sinne by priuiledge', and by 1645 he had resigned his post.

The contrast between the religious loyalties of the Merchant Adventurers at Delft in 1632–3 and those at Rotterdam just over a decade later could not be more striking, and support the suggestion that Beaumont's reforms had indeed encouraged some members to drift away from the Company, or at least its church. This may have been accentuated by the arrival of royalist sympathizers at Rotterdam, and the corresponding return to England of godly members previously in voluntary exile. In 1644 Parliament named several members at Rotterdam as 'Incendiaries and Enemies', including a future Company governor, Richard Ford.[81] Parliament proceeded to write to the Company at London demanding the replacement of Cranmer as Rotterdam deputy, but he was still in post in 1648, a sign of the waning influence of the London court over its Dutch membership.[82] Given this, it is thus somewhat surprising that all members, except for one

[75] John Dury, 'A Memoriall shewing reasons wherefore Assistents for his Comunion are requird & judged necissary by the Minister', HP 3/2/61B.
[76] Dorothy Dury–Hartlib, 20 Jan. 1645, HP 21/5/21A; Dury–Samuel Avery, 19 Sept. 1644, HP 3/2/60A.
[77] Sprunger, *Dutch Puritanism*, p. 250.   [78] Dury–Samuel Avery, 28 Oct. 1644, HP 3/2/70A.
[79] Dury–Samuel Avery, 19 Sept. 1644, HP 3/2/63A.
[80] Dury–Hartlib, 14 Apr. 1645, HP 3/2/109B.
[81] Declaration of the Houses of Parliament, 6 July 1644, TNA, SP 16/502, fol. 91; Dury–Hartlib, 5 Aug. 1644, HP 3/2/49B.
[82] Committee of Both Kingdoms to the Merchant Adventurers at London, 20 June 1645, TNA, SP 21/21, fol. 27; Te Lintum, *De merchant adventurers in der Nederlanden*, p. 264.

notable royalist, apparently ignored Cranmer's wishes by submitting to the House of Commons' order that they subscribe to the Solemn League and Covenant, in summer 1645. This was a sign, perhaps, that Parliament's investigations into their political loyalties in the previous year had been effective.[83]

Although we have no details about how the order to take the covenant was received in Rotterdam, in Hamburg at least it proved to be highly contentious. Hamburg was strategically important following the outbreak of war as a source of arms.[84] Acquiring military supplies was partially dependent on maintaining good diplomatic relations with Christian IV of Denmark, who claimed overlordship over the Elbe as Duke of Holstein.[85] In 1643 Parliament dispatched a mission to Denmark led by Theodore Haak and the Merchant Adventurer Robert Lowther, which was instructed to enlist the support of Joseph Avery, then deputy governor at Hamburg and 'a person of greate partes and long experience'.[86] This assessment was certainly true: prior to becoming deputy in 1638, Avery had served as Company secretary in Hamburg since at least 1620, and in that capacity had fulfilled a semi-official diplomatic role for the crown.[87] Avery was a keen advocate of the cause of the exiled queen of Bohemia, a position he shared with his brother Samuel, now a leading parliamentarian in London. However, in the 1640s the brothers found themselves on opposite sides of the domestic political divide, and Joseph Avery became no less controversial a figure than Edward Misselden before him.

Even before the outbreak of war in England, rumours had been communicated to Samuel Avery that his brother had been negotiating with Denmark to send troops in support of Charles I, leading Joseph to protest his innocence against such 'scoffing Ishmaells & cursing Shimee's & railing Rabshæka's'.[88] Probably thanks to his brother, Joseph retained the confidence of Parliament by the time it dispatched its Danish mission a year later, but soon Theodore Haak was reporting that the Merchant Adventurers at Hamburg were at odds with their deputy. One issue that Haak had been instructed to address was the capture of some English ships by the Danish king in retaliation for Parliament's seizure of a Danish ship delivering arms to royalist territory.[89] However, Haak reported rumours that Avery had 'playd foule' in the matter, forcing members of the Company to pay over the odds to have their goods released.[90] The sense that Avery's royalist

---

[83] Te Lintum, *De merchant adventurers*, p. 175.

[84] Kathrin Zickermann, *Across the German Sea: Early Modern Scottish Connections with the Wider Elbe-Weser Region* (Leiden & Boston, 2013), pp. 146–7.

[85] For Christian's attempts to enforce this, see ibid., pp. 28–44.

[86] Parliament's instructions to Theodore Haak and Robert Lowther, BL, Add. 72436, Sept. 1643, fol. 1v.

[87] Zickermann, *Across the German Sea*, pp. 134–44.

[88] Joseph–Samuel Avery, 16 June 1642, HP 45/3/9A.

[89] Coates, *Impact of the Civil War*, pp. 119–21.

[90] Theodore Haak to ?, 17 Nov. 1643, BL, Add. 72436, fol. 21. Avery also offered his support to a royalist privateer in 1644, leading to further criticisms from members. Avery–Sir Richard Browne, 21 Feb. 1645, BL, Add. 78178, fol. 24v.

sympathies were a threat to the Company had been accentuated by Charles I's issuing of a proclamation in April 1644 which implicitly opened up the cloth trade to all his loyal subjects, part of the king's commercial war against parliamentarian London.[91] Avery revealed his allegiances openly when he published this proclamation, together with a letter from the king, in a Company court, pressing them to agree not to molest any person bringing goods to Hamburg, 'wether he bee a Free man or not'.[92] When some members produced a copy of the parliamentary ordinance of October 1643 confirming the Company's monopoly, Avery dismissed it as 'noe Acte', something which one member (probably Robert Lowther) considered to be contrary to his oath as deputy. Furthermore, Avery went on to impose an oath ('Contrary to his power') against members shipping arms or ammunition to London.

Avery's enemies were presented with an opportunity to challenge their deputy when the London governor, John Kendrick, sent over the Commons' order to take the covenant, in May 1645.[93] Unsurprisingly, when this order was discussed in General Court on 4 June, Avery raised several objections, only for a majority to vote that the covenant be taken by members in court on the 12th.[94] Avery subsequently secured a postponement on the grounds that members of the Hamburg Senate were concerned that it would compromise the city's neutrality in the English conflict (an argument also adopted by Cranmer in Rotterdam, suggesting collaboration between the two deputies).[95] His delaying tactics exhausted, on 17 June Avery announced that he intended to refuse to call a court on the allotted date, leading eighteen members to write an open letter to Elborough, requesting that he administer it to them as a congregation instead. However, when this day arrived, Avery and some of his supporters interrupted proceedings with another letter forbidding Elborough to proceed. This was sufficient to discourage the assembled members from doing so, but forty of them plus Elborough put their names to a resolution declaring their intention to take the covenant when able (for names, see the appendix to this chapter).[96] They also agreed to write to Governor Kendrick explaining their failure to do so, although the copy that was produced the next day only carried twenty-five signatures. Some members, including Francis Townley and Slingsby Bethel, also addressed articles of

---

[91] *A Proclamation for the Vent of Cloth, and Woollen Manufactures of this Kingdome*, 9 Apr. 1644 (Oxford, 1644).
[92] Report, possibly part of a letter by Robert Lowther–Theodore Weckherlin, 8 May 1644, BL, Add. 72436, fol. 144r.
[93] Note that this was a different John Kendrick to the former servant of John Quarles.
[94] The following order of events can be pieced together from a compilation of relevant documents by Avery's opponents. HL, Stowe VIII, Temple Special Subject, Miscellaneous documents, box 10, hereafter HL, Stowe VIII, TSS misc. 10, as well as Jeremiah Elborough's account in a letter to Sir Robert Harley, 20 June 1645, BL, Add. 70005, fols 77–8.
[95] Dorothy Dury–Hartlib, 21 June 1645, HP 3/2/133A.
[96] Copy of the resolution, HL, Stowe VIII, TSS misc. 10, fol. 2r.

complaint about Avery to Parliament.[97] In response the London court advised that he be replaced as Hamburg deputy pending investigation, something which had happened by 31 July.[98] In the meantime, the London court had replied to the letter sent to Kendrick, although nineteen of Avery's opponents still felt the need to draft another letter on 11 August vindicating their stance.

The fact that the surviving evidence of this dispute was produced by Avery's opponents means that it is difficult to identify Avery's supporters within the membership, although the surviving account always presents them as a minority. Avery's own position, however, is clearer. According to his opponents, Avery had initially presented his objections to the parliamentary order as simply prudent, given the dangers that members would face by openly signifying their allegiances (though his enemies emphasized the partisan manner in which he had made this case):

> though wee weere as he said, all tossed in one tempest, yet wee weere not all imbarked in the like bottome of dainger, as they in England, where those under the kinges Commaund, are not free from the miseryes, which acompany warre, and where these under the Parliaments groane, and sigh, under heavie taxes, and oppressions.[99]

As well as making members subject to parliamentary taxation, subscribing to the covenant might encourage the king to 'take our Charters from us', which would endanger the Company's privileges in Hamburg: 'strife, and Contention' would be the result. One unnamed member responded that the order had not been 'sent unto the Company for them to discusse the fittingnesse or unfittingnesse of it'. Avery's decision to put the matter to hands, then, was presented as undertaken 'by his owne single authority', although in fact he lost the vote. The closeness of this vote is unclear, but Avery had already undermined his stance of moderation and neutrality by publishing the king's intimidating declaration the previous year. This probably helped his opponents frame the deputy as aspiring to maintain an 'unlimited authority' reminiscent of Misselden, shown by his continued refusal to put certain matters to vote, his insistence that no act could pass the court without his approval, and above all his outright refusal to summon a court on the date allotted to take the covenant. One member was provoked to ask Avery 'if he Called the Company togeather to no other end, then to Confirme what he would have done', a transgression of the deliberative function of the Company's court. Denied the opportunity to come together in that forum, Avery's critics were able

---

[97] Elborough–Harley, 20 June 1645, BL, Add. 70005, fols 77–8.
[98] Elborough–Harley, 21 June 1645, BL, Add. 70005, fol. 79r; 'A treue, and perfect relacon of Mr Averie (late Deputie unto the Marchant Adventurers of England resideing in Hambrough) his opposing the company takeing the nationall covenant', 31 July 1645, HL, Stowe VIII, TSS misc. 10, fol. 4v.
[99] Ibid.

to turn to the congregation as an alternative means of association, and Elborough as an alternative figure of authority within their community.[100] Avery's behaviour at the ensuing service, which he was said to have attended 'in a grate raige', railing at the minister 'in a passionate, and violent manner', belied his moderate stance. For all his years' service as secretary and deputy, Avery was now cast as the intrusive outsider undermining the Company's harmony. When the deputy denied the allegation (raised by one John Doggett, senior) that 'he aimed at ingrossing the whole power of the Company unto himselfe', the congregation was reported to have unanimously 'Cryed out, it was treu, it was treue'.

The forty Merchant Adventurers who signed the resolution promising to take the Covenant at a future date probably represented a majority of the freemen. However, the fact that they did not proceed immediately to take the Covenant is indicative of how Avery had sown doubt in some minds, forcing the godly party to accept a compromise that would allow them to 'all goe togeather, and be therby tyed the firmlier in love, and amitie, each to other'.[101] The resulting resolution confirmed their intention to take the Covenant, but only 'uppon the recovery and resumption of the Courtes power', perhaps indicating anxiety about acting outside of the Company's constitutional structures. Eleven of the forty members refused to endorse the resolution to write to Governor Kendrick, probably on the grounds that this letter included a promise to take the Covenant on receipt of any further order from Parliament even without the permission of the Company court (and in the event this letter only received twenty-five signatures). It would appear, then, that a core of around twenty consistent enemies of Avery were reliant on the support of a slightly smaller number of members who were more hesitant about openly transgressing corporate norms.

Thus, although the events of 1645 suggest that the majority of the Company at Hamburg were inclining towards Parliament, they did so with varying degrees of enthusiasm. The fact that the Hamburg church had undergone no George Beaumont-style reformation in the 1630s, in spite of some unwelcome attention from Archbishop Laud, was clearly a significant factor. Elborough continued to administer discipline over the flock alongside the elders much as he had done since arriving as minister in 1629, although he did complain about having to use the Prayer Book, and hoped that Parliament would replace it with the Presbyterian Directory of Public Worship.[102] The Covenant implied no disturbing reorganization of their congregation, therefore, and indeed its defenders presented it as fully compatible with the existing discipline of their church: 'so pious a league, and Covenant, which will, wee doubt not, tend to the beating downe of sin, and increasing of godlinesse in every one of us, as likewise, to the begetting of peace,

---

[100] Letter to Governor John Kendrick, 20 June 1645, HL, Stowe VIII, TSS misc. 10, fol. 3r.
[101] 'A treue, and perfect relacon of Mr Averie', ibid., fol. 6r.
[102] Sprunger, *Dutch Puritanism*, pp. 256-9; Elborough-Harley, 21 June 1645, BL, Add. 70005, fol. 79r.

and union amongst us'.[103] The lack of alternative English churches in this Lutheran city, and the much smaller size of its British population in comparison with the Netherlands, ensured that the Company church continued to be central to the collective life of the community in a way that was decreasingly the case for the Company at Rotterdam by the 1640s.

Despite Avery allegedly accusing those members who had gathered to take the Covenant in the Company church 'of faction, and houlding Conventicles', it would appear that his objections to the Covenant were essentially political rather than religious.[104] It is true that Avery harboured resentment against Elborough as early as June 1642, when he complained that the minister had 'put himselfe at a strange distance from me, in a farre higher strayne then becomes the modestie & meeknes of his coate & calling'.[105] However, this was probably a consequence of the opposition that Avery was already attracting for his royalist sympathies, rather than a sign that the deputy was seeking to challenge the organization of the church. Once the crown had effectively turned against the Company in April 1644, parliament began to appear as the best defender of its privileges, allowing the godly party in Hamburg to win a majority against the incumbent deputy.[106] Robert Lowther's conclusion, that Avery was supporting a strategy by 'Our Kings Marchants...to destroye the Marchant Adventurers trade both in Holland & Germanie & soe there Credits & our deputye muche by his power Crush our Estates', may have been widely shared.[107]

In 1642 Avery alluded to a faction of 'foolish proud & malitious men' who resented him for having refused to 'comport with their vicious & corrupt humour', with Elborough's son-in-law Francis Townley marked as the ringleader.[108] Townley was one of the eighteen Merchant Adventurers who originally requested that Elborough administer the covenant against Avery's wishes, a group which included perhaps seven long-term residents whose presence in Hamburg can be traced back for more than a decade, some as far back as the early 1620s, at least five of whom were married.[109] By virtue of his marriage to Hester, widow of Nicholas Basse, Elborough was father-in-law to another of these ringleaders, David Hechstetter, as well as Henry Taylor, who did not sign the initial letter to Elborough but went on to join the covenanters. Hechstetter's sometime partner,

[103] Letter to Elborough, 17 June 1645, HL, Stowe VIII, TSS misc. 10, fol. 1r.

[104] 'A treue, and perfect relacon of Mr Averie', ibid., fol. 5v.

[105] Avery–Samuel Hartlib, 16 June 1642, HP 45/3/14A.

[106] For instance, around May 1644 the Company petitioned the committee of both kingdoms to negotiate with the king of Denmark on its behalf, making no mention of deputy Avery. BL, Add. 72436, fol. 146.

[107] Robert Lowther–Theodore Weckherlin, 8 May 1644, BL, Add. 72436, fol. 145r.

[108] Joseph–Samuel Avery, 16 June 1642, HP 45/2/10B.

[109] See the appendix to this chapter. The William Gore who first communicated in the Hamburg church in 1620 may not have been identical with the individual present in 1645, given the number of members of the Gore family who were free of the Company. The married men were John Doggett Sr, Robert Palmer, Henry Crispe, David Hechstetter, and Francis Townley.

Slingsby Bethel, was another of this group, and would go on to find notoriety as Whig sheriff of London in the Exclusion Crisis.

Those members who signed the resolution to take the covenant, but held back from signing the letter to Kendrick, also included several senior merchants, amongst them Isaac Lee, who was apparently Avery's successor as deputy governor. The fact that Lee was chosen rather than one of the more consistent opponents of Avery suggests that the latter were not fully confident of their ability to rely on a majority. However, one of this party, David Hechstetter, had become treasurer by 1648, and its influence is suggested by the fact that the Hamburg court chose to employ the parliamentarian propagandist Henry Parker as its secretary in 1647, in which capacity he authored a published defence of the Company.[110] These senior merchants had been able to mobilize opposition against their deputy governor as effectively as their counterparts at Delft had done in the previous decade. But just as the latter struggled to maintain their authority over a subsequent generation of Merchant Adventurers, so in the 1650s the grip of the godly party over the Hamburg court began to weaken, and they now found themselves accused of endangering the Company's freedoms.

'Contrary to the good orders of our Fellowship': Hamburg in the 1650s

Support for Parliament amongst the Merchant Adventurers in the civil war had been boosted by the crown's willingness to interfere with Company privileges. However, the regicide introduced new dangers which undermined Parliament's claims to be the best defender of the Company's status. As well as the hostility of the outraged citizens of Hamburg, supporters of the Commonwealth in the city had to contend with the violent tactics of royalists seeking to extort money for their cause, or simply take revenge on known parliamentarians. Surrounded by enemies, the Commonwealth regime was particularly aware of the need to ensure political conformity amongst English people overseas. In March 1649 the Council of State wrote to the Merchant Adventurers, along with other trading companies, to require that anyone employed overseas 'whether as Ambassadors, Agents, Presidents, Consulls, Deputyes, Secretaryes or by what other name soever any of these generall and publique Ministers shall be called, be men of unsuspected & unquestionable fidelity & good affection to this Common wealth'.[111] Increasingly, the officers of the Company were cast as public men whose responsibility was to serve as the eyes and ears of the regime overseas. However, this only added to

---

[110] Parker, *Of a Free Trade.*
[111] Council of State to Merchant Adventurers and other merchant companies, 12 Mar. 1649, TNA, SP 25/62, fol. 81.

their value for royalists seeking to hurt the Commonwealth from a distance. These attacks were often met by the Senate of Hamburg with ambivalence, if not outright approval. The Company's Hamburg residence in the 1650s thus became a litmus case of the ability of the Commonwealth to protect English interests, privileges and lives overseas.

Jeremiah Elborough was an early target of royalist ire, surviving an alleged assassination attempt shortly after the regicide by a supporter of Charles II's agent Sir John Cochrane. Cochrane's attempts to milk the wealth of the merchant community in Hamburg culminated in the abduction of deputy Isaak Lee, alongside two other members (Henry Crispe and Robert Palmer), and their dramatic rescue by certain young Merchant Adventurers.[112] In the face of such threats, the Commonwealth's offer of protection was welcomed, although Lee was reluctant to take on the role of Parliament's representative, preferring the dispatch of one with 'the Caracter of a publique Minister'.[113] On its part, the Company in London was actively adjusting to the new political reality. Samuel Avery, by now the London governor, presented the recent decline in the Company's fortunes as a sign of the crown's failure to protect its privileges at home and abroad.[114] Avery ended with a request that its charter be confirmed, which would counter the claims of those like Cochram that, as a chartered Company, the Merchant Adventurers owed allegiance to the crown, 'the fountayne' of its privileges.[115]

Having failed to convince the Company to elect a new deputy willing to take on the role of its representative, the Commonwealth eventually agreed to appoint its own resident, selecting one Richard Bradshaw, a sometime merchant of Spain and relative of the president of the Council of State. Bradshaw soon found that questions about the status of the Company following the regicide were being raised not only by royalists, but also by Hamburg's Senate. He struggled to gain recognition as agent of the English state, or obtain satisfactory justice against the perpetrators of the attacks on Elborough and Lee, not to mention those royalist exiles who threatened him to his face.[116] Fortunately for Bradshaw, he received a warmer welcome from the Company court, which elected him deputy governor in place of the now departed Lee.[117] However, Bradshaw found that when it came to negotiating with the Senate, his dual role only confused matters, with the

---

[112] Jason Peacey, 'Order and disorder in Europe: parliamentary agents and royalist thugs 1649–1650', *Historical Journal* 40, 4 (1997), pp. 960–3; Council of State to Merchant Adventurers at Hamburg, 9 Aug. 1649, TNA, SP 25/94, fol. 367.

[113] Deputy Isaac Lee–John Bradshaw, 27 July 1649, TNA, SP 82/7, fol. 127; David Hechstetter–Council of State, 19 Apr. 1649, TNA, SP 18/1, fol. 121.

[114] Petition of Governor Samuel Avery and Merchant Adventurers to the Council of State, 1 Nov. 1649, TNA, SP 46/95, fol. 185.

[115] Sir John Cochran–Deputy Lee, c.June 1649, TNA, SP 82/7, fol. 126.

[116] Peacey, 'Order and disorder', pp. 964–5.

[117] Treasurer William Attwood–Council of State, 28 May 1650, TNA, SP 82/7, fol. 190. Jeremiah Elborough had suggested that Parliament appoint a resident who would act as Company deputy during the Covenant dispute: Elborough–Harley, 21 June 1645, BL, Add. 70005, fol. 79r.

Senate insisting on offering him the full dignity of resident only in matters of state, whilst treating him merely as Company deputy on other issues.[118] When this began to have ramifications for the Company's ability to administer discipline upon its own 'refractory Members', Bradshaw considered that the 'very being of the Court & the priviledges of the Company' were now at stake.[119]

Although Bradshaw's election demonstrated that the court was still largely under the sway of the parliamentarians, there are signs that following the regicide political dissent was growing amongst the Company's ranks. One figure who was willing to openly attack the Commonwealth was the bankrupted merchant Peter Clerke, whom Bradshaw caused to imprisoned in the Company gaol.[120] However, following an appeal, the Senate adjudged that Clerke was being imprisoned on matters of state and thus fell outside the Company's civil jurisdiction, which Bradshaw considered a 'totall subversion of the very being of their court'.[121] Bradshaw considered this 'broken merchant' to merely be a front for a party of royalist 'Malignants' within the Company, who made their allegiances clear by refusing to take the oath of allegiance to the new regime, the Engagement.[122] When Bradshaw proceeded to exclude these non-subscribers from attendance at court, one John Metcalfe, described as 'a most imbittered Cavallier', openly declared his allegiance for Charles II. He was then imprisoned on Bradshaw's orders, only to escape with the complicity of the Company officer and find refuge with the Senate, adding to Bradshaw's growing list of grievances.[123]

Bradshaw reported that the rest of the excluded members had departed court merely with grumbles, but shortly afterwards, twenty of them (including Metcalfe) sent a letter of complaint to the Company at London. However, rather than protest at the legitimacy of the Engagement itself, the authors emphasized that they had 'never acted any thinge against the present Government in England'.[124] In support of their readmission, they appealed to the commercial interests of their 'Partners Principalls and Masters' who had been denied a say in the decisions of the Hamburg court thanks to the exclusion of their agents from court. Bradshaw, however, was under no illusions about the political stance of this 'disaffected' party, and he and his supporters strove to prevent their return. One anonymous denunciation presented to the Council of State demanded that the

---

[118] Richard Bradshaw, 'The State & Condicion of the Resident from the Parlement of the Comonwealth', TNA, SP 82/8, fol. 75r. For further details, see Newman, 'Anglo-Hamburg trade', pp. 270–3.

[119] Bradshaw, 'The State & Condicion of the Resident from the Parlement of the Comonwealth', TNA, SP 82/8, fol. 78v.

[120] For Clarke, see Chapter 3.

[121] Bradshaw, 'The State & Condicion of the Resident from the Parlement of the Comonwealth', TNA, SP 82/8, fol. 79v; Translation of the Senate of Hamburg's address to the Company Court, 17 Sept. 1650, TNA, SP 82/8, fol. 52.

[122] Bradshaw–Secretary Frost, 17 Sept. 1650, Bradshaw Letters, p. 431.

[123] Bradshaw–Secretary Frost, 25 June 1650, ibid., p. 428.

[124] Hamburg non-engagers to the Company at London, 16 July 1650, TNA, SP 82/8, fol. 19.

London membership be required to refuse any dealings with the recalcitrant members until they submitted.[125] This would ensure that 'the sole management of all affaires there' would remain in 'the hands of those, that will improve their power, for the Intrest of this Comonwealth'.

This paper emphasized that many of the 'professed Malignants' amongst the non-engagers were 'men of desperate and lost fortunes', and several of their followers 'yonge apprentices', so the Company could only benefit by government being restricted to the 'honest party'. However partisan this representation was, it does appear that several of the non-engagers were recent arrivals at Hamburg, with seven noted in the Hamburg church book as having joined since the 1645 dispute, and only four known to be heads of households by 1650.[126] In fact five years earlier a number of apprentices had supposedly made a 'feint' in court to be allowed to vote on whether to take the Covenant.[127] By 1650 some of these may have been in the position to participate fully, threatening the power of the parliamentarians, whose numbers may have also been eroded by the return of some members (such as Slingsby Bethel) to London. The issue which these non-engagers used as grounds to push for their readmission was an imposition which had been decided on by the court at London to deal with the Company's growing debts, and this too is suggestive of generational tensions within its ranks at Hamburg. The London court had proposed a new impost on cloth exports, but the Hamburg court had suggested instead a 2 per cent levy on the real estate of each member, on the grounds (as Bradshaw put it) that too many of the 'old senators with great estates in the Company' could withdraw from trade to avoid paying their share.[128] This was a position clearly supported by the senior members of the Hamburg court, who relied on the cloth trade in order to earn commission. The non-engagers, however, protested against the 2 per cent levy as well, arguing that it was unfair to burden those whose parents were not members of the Company with its debts, and thereby shrink their 'first capital', a position which younger members had good reason to support.[129]

It may have been the case that some of the newer arrivals in the mart town had left England in part because of their opposition to political developments, something far from limited to civil war royalists. Indeed, three Merchant Adventurers who had been in favour of taking the Covenant in 1645 were amongst the twenty non-engagers (James Wolfenden, William Lee, and John Gilbert). It is also notable that Jeremiah Elborough was apparently slow to take the Engagement, which

---

[125] 'The humble proposalls of certain Marchant adventurers in referrence to the settling their residence at Hamborgh in full pease and quiet', 28 July 1650 (date of presentation), TNA, SP 82/8, fol. 27.
[126] See the appendix to this chapter. The married men were John Gilbert, George Watson, Thomas Aldersy, and John Metcalfe.
[127] HL, Stowe VIII, TSS misc. 10, fol. 4v.
[128] Bradshaw–John Bradshaw, 3 Sept. 1650, *Bradshaw Letters*, p. 430.
[129] Hamburg non-engagers to the Company at London, 16 July 1650, TNA, SP 82/8, fol. 19.

was being actively opposed by many of his fellow Presbyterians at home. Bradshaw noted this as 'something of scandal to others', adding that 'here be some could wish those formalitys were laid aside, and the power of godliness more pressed'.[130] The arrival in 1655 of John Gunter as assistant to Elborough, on the recommendation of Thomas Goodwin, for a while satisfied these urges.[131] The prospect of the schism between Presbyterians and Independents that had by then emerged amongst English parliamentarians extending to Hamburg was one threat to the integrity of the Company church. Another was the willingness of others to separate from it on grounds of their royalism, or adherence to the pre-civil war Church of England. Bradshaw alleged some of the 'archest malignants' of the Company, namely Clement Clarke, George Waites, Thomas and William Lee, and George Wakefield, had left the congregation and taken on Sir John Cochran's former chaplain as their own.[132] All of these five were amongst the non-engagers marked by Bradshaw as 'considerable' (along with John Gilbert, John Dusy, John Metcalfe, and George Sharpulls).

The attempt of the non-engagers to secure their readmission to court appears to have fallen on deaf ears, and in 1651 one of them, Thomas Bellingham, was forced to post £1,000 bond not to criticize the Commonwealth (George Sharpuls was one of his sureties).[133] Bradshaw later remembered this as a period when the 'well afected party, beinge then the greater number remaininge ruled the Court & affaires of the Fellowship to the great content of the Company in general, & in much peace & amity amongst themselves'.[134] The Commonwealth's victory over the Scots at the Battle of Dunbar enhanced its reputation overseas, meaning that Bradshaw at last made some progress with the Senate of Hamburg, and by the end of 1651 the resident was able to visit England.[135] But following his return in the following year, the harmony of the Company was once again under threat.

As Bradshaw later explained, his opponents had used his absence as an opportunity to convince the Company at London to support their readmission to court, on the grounds of 'obtayninge & continuing peace in the Company'.[136] Under pressure from the London court, Bradshaw consented to approach the Council of State for its permission to allow this, possibly in order to rid himself of some unidentified 'base scandalls even upon the Exchange' which he alleged had been spread by his enemies. However, once readmitted to court Bradshaw complained that these members soon showed their true colours, committing various insults against the Commonwealth and scoffing at Bradshaw's efforts to discipline them.

---

[130] Bradshaw–Council of State, 29 Oct. 1650, *Bradshaw Letters*, p. 433.
[131] Sprunger, *Dutch Puritanism*, p. 260.
[132] Bradshaw–Secretary Frost, 24 Sept. 1650, *Bradshaw Letters*, pp. 431–2.
[133] Submission of Thomas Bellingham, George Sharpuls, and George Mitley to the Commonwealth, 1651, TNA, SP 46/128, fol. 200.
[134] Bradshaw's narrative of his insults, 1 Aug. 1654, Whitelocke Papers XVI, no. 30.
[135] Peacey, 'Order and disorder', p. 965.
[136] Bradshaw's narrative of his insults, 11. Aug. 1654, Whitelocke Papers XVI, no. 30.

Notwithstanding his earlier submission of obedience, Bellingham allegedly tore down the arms of the Commonwealth that hung in the Company house, provoked by another merchant's refusal to drink a health to the king.[137] By the end of 1652 Bradshaw was once again complaining to the Council of State of the 'insolent behaviour of some younge men', but apart from a letter from Cromwell he received little support from the state, which only increased the confidence of his critics.[138] In August 1653 he complained of being 'in a worse condition, then trayleing a pike for the commonwealth'.[139] The breakdown in communications from London which Bradshaw complained of was no doubt linked to the outbreak of the Anglo-Dutch war in July 1652, which led to a year-long stop in the Company's shipping to Hamburg.[140] Cut off from their supporters in the London court and the government, Bradshaw's allies at Hamburg now found themselves losing their grip on power.

Although Bradshaw suggested that the bulk of his opponents were drawn from the malignants, the two he identified as ringleaders—Henry Spurway and [Thomas?] Farrington—had not been amongst the twenty known non-engagers, and indeed the former had been numbered amongst the covenanters in 1645.[141] Spurway's insolvency and subsequent flight from Hamburg robbed this faction of their leader, but he was soon replaced by another who had previously been accounted amongst the firmest parliamentarians, namely Elborough's son-in-law Francis Townley. It was Townley who was selected by the Hamburg court as deputy governor in preference to Bradshaw in the elections of midsummer 1654. The remainder of Bradshaw's time as English resident in Hamburg (he departed in 1657 for a posting to Russia) was overshadowed by his contest with Townley, which polarized the merchant community.

For Bradshaw and his supporters, Townley's change of sides was a sign of his ambitious character, which led him to have designs on Bradshaw's post of deputy. Having failed to persuade the 'well affected party' that Bradshaw was acting beyond the bounds of his office by persecuting Spurway, Townley was presented with the ideal opportunity to make himself head of a now leaderless party following Spurway's departure.[142] Townley insinuated himself into the role of this party's head by acting as their defender in court, whilst out of court he solicited the 'youngest sort' with 'wine and good Fellowship'.[143] In one instance, Townley

---

[137] HMC Portland I, pp. 672–3.

[138] Bradshaw–John Bradshaw, President of Council of State, 10 Sept. 1653, Folger Shakespeare Library X.d.483 (110), available online at https://luna.folger.edu/luna/servlet/detail/FOLGERCM1~6~6~677356~146653:Letter-from--Lord--Richard-Bradshaw [accessed 26 July 2019].

[139] Bradshaw–Thurloe, 30 Aug. 1653, *Thurloe State Papers* I, p. 445.

[140] Petition of Slingsby Bethel and other Merchant Adventurers trading to Hamburg to Council of State, 24 Mar. 1653, TNA, SP 18/34, fol. 147.

[141] Bradshaw's narrative of his insults, 11. Aug. 1654, Whitelocke Papers XVI, no. 30.

[142] 'A Narrative of the behaviour of Mr Francis Townley', Bodl. Lib., Rawlinson A31, fol. 310r.

[143] Members of the Hamburg Merchant Adventurers to Company at London, 27 June 1654, Whitelocke Papers XVI, #11.

defended a group who were being reprimanded in court following 'a notorious Riot acted by some of them at Wansbecke upon the peasants of that place', arguing that the examination of witnesses on oath was 'against the priviledge of the subjects of England'.[144] His affronts to the deputy eventually resulted in the imposition of a 40s. fine, which he refused to pay (evidence, to his enemies, that Townley 'designed to overthrow the orders of the Company').[145] When one George Waites was imprisoned and then banished from Hamburg for conspiring to send arms to the Scots, Townley opposed the seizure of his papers on the grounds that 'if it were soe it would be noe living for merchants in Hamburg', and stirred up opposition amongst the city burghers.[146] Most provocatively, Townley allegedly advised the court against too ready compliance with the will of the English state by warning that 'they did not know but Queen Mary might come to raigne againe'.

When a letter from the Protector arrived in March 1654 reprimanding the court for permitting such 'miscariages', Townley argued that its members should vigorously defend their conduct, and he refused to be part of a committee selected to draft a more emollient reply. He also suggested that Bradshaw's complaints to the Council of State were a violation of the Company's privileges, and a dereliction of his duty as deputy: a sure sign of the dangers of confusing the office of deputy and resident. The stage was set for Townley to make his move at the midsummer elections of 1654.

At the election itself, however, Townley held back from directly challenging the incumbent deputy. Instead, the vote for deputy was preceded by one to resurrect the traditional role of martly (as opposed to annual) deputy to hold the post for a three-month period, which passed by four hands. Although Bradshaw was duly elected, he refused to accept the office on these conditions, leading proceedings to come to a halt. However, after the departure of several members, Townley signalled for his party to stay, whereupon he was elected as deputy by the remaining sixteen merchants, who also filled the outstanding governmental posts, in spite of many being young men. For Bradshaw's supporters, these proceedings were no election but 'a mere factious designe and contrived combination contrary to the good orders of our Fellowship', and as well as refusing to attend court under this new regime, fifteen of them proceeded to protest to the Company at London and the Protector.[147]

---

[144] 'A Narrative of the behaviour of Mr Francis Townley', Bodl. Lib. Rawl. A31, fol. 310r.

[145] Ibid.

[146] Ibid., fol. 311r. Waites had been Hamburg agent of William Lowther since 1641, though by 1654 they were estranged over business matters. See Lowther's out-letter book, 1653–4, Wakefield History Centre, WYW1827/5/5/1/1.

[147] Members of the Hamburg Merchant Adventurers to Company at London, 27 June 1654, Whitelocke Papers XVI, #11, and to Cromwell, 30 June 1654, *Thurloe State Papers* II, pp. 406–7.

Perhaps in the knowledge that Samuel Avery, the London governor, was likely to take Bradshaw's side, Townley offered to resign his post after just one week as deputy.[148] However, when a letter from the London court arrived favouring Bradshaw's re-appointment, Townley refused to go quietly, only conceding the office of deputy after two further meetings, and not before his supporters had produced a remonstrance and petition vindicating themselves to the Protector.[149] Following another admonitory letter from Cromwell on 22 December, the same merchants addressed another justificatory petition, which was met by a riposte from Bradshaw, now restored as annual deputy.[150] In spite of Bradshaw's best preparations (including supportive letters from the London Company and Cromwell), at the next midsummer elections he once again was voted from his place in favour of Townley, this time by two votes. Again Townley resigned the post, with the Hamburg court this time writing to its London counterpart asking that it nominate an acceptable candidate as deputy, which office in the meantime was resumed into the court's hands.[151] Rather than nominate a successor to Bradshaw, the Company court at London referred the matter to the Protector, but in October 1655 the Hamburg brethren took matters into their own hands by selecting the London Merchant Adventurer Alexander Baron, though he turned down the place.[152] Only in midsummer 1656 did Hamburg elect a deputy, again for the period of a single mart, a decision approved by the London court.[153]

Throughout this dispute, Bradshaw was emphatic that opposition to him was politically motivated, although the ranks of the malignants had been swelled thanks to their willingness to cultivate support amongst a class of youths merely seeking licence for their unruly behaviour; Townley himself was represented as an unprincipled opportunist. As with the 1650 non-engagers, it does appear that the opponents of Richard Bradshaw were generally of a younger generation than his supporters. Of the twenty-seven who signed letters defending his de-selection, Townley had been resident far longer than any of the others (see the appendix to this chapter). Only four are known to have been married by that date.[154] This contrasts with the sixteen Merchant Adventurers who wrote in defence of

---

[148] Members of the Hamburg Merchant Adventurers to Governor Avery, 4 July 1654, Whitelocke Papers XVI, #15; Governor Avery and Merchant Adventurers at London to Richard Bradshaw, 19 July 1654, ibid., #23.

[149] These documents have not been traced, but they are mentioned in a signed letter to Bulstrode Lord Whitelock, 25 July 1654, Whitelocke Papers XVI, #29. It was answered by ten of Bradshaw's supporters in another petition to Cromwell, Bodl. Lib., Rawlinson A22, #22.

[150] Petition of certain Hamburg Merchant Adventurers to Cromwell, 1655, *Thurloe State Papers* III, pp. 118–21; Petition of Richard Bradshaw to Cromwell, 1655, *Thurloe State Papers* II, pp. 407–10.

[151] Bradshaw–Cromwell and the Company at London, 3 July 1655, *Thurloe State Papers* III, pp. 605–8.

[152] Bradshaw–Thurloe, 23 Oct. 1655, *Thurloe State Papers* IV, pp. 103–4; Baron–Hamburg Merchant Adventurers, 30 Nov. 1655, ibid., p. 267; 14 Mar. 1656, ibid., pp. 612–13.

[153] Merchant Adventurers at London to Deputy George Watson and Company at Hamburg, 19 Dec. 1656, *Thurloe State Papers* V, pp. 718–19.

[154] Namely Townley, Leonard Scott, Thomas Ruggells, and William Wolfenden.

Bradshaw in 1654, which included six known married men, and five of at least a decade's residence in Hamburg.[155] Only five had been amongst the covenanters in 1645, however, suggesting significant turnover within the merchant community since then. Of the twenty-seven enemies of Bradshaw, three had been amongst the covenanters (notably Townley), and four amongst the twenty 1650 non-engagers. Bradshaw's emphasis on the 'malignancy' of his opponents was perhaps exaggerated, then.

In fact, Bradshaw's supporters within the Company tended not to portray their opponents in such terms, although they did describe them as the 'disaffected party'.[156] The overriding theme of their addresses was Townley's demagoguery, and his subversion of corporate norms. Although there was a precedent for it in the Company's regulations, for instance, the position of martly deputy was represented as an affront to the dignity of the office, it being impossible to expect any man of honour to 'every quarter Subject himselfe to the discontented humor of every young man amongst us'.[157] Faced with the need to cultivate support amongst the membership, the deputy would be unable to administer discipline out of fear of making enemies. Furthermore, Bradshaw's supporters argued that even annual elections should not be contested: no person of substance would be willing to leave their business at home to serve in the mart towns only to be 'yeerly subject to the affronts of the lose partie'.[158] Perhaps aware that many of their number had been complicit in Joseph Avery's recent de-selection, they qualified this maxim by adding that in cases of 'some great & hainous Crime' a deputy might be displaced. But for all their protestations of moderation, Bradshaw's supporters were themselves open to the charge of faction. Indeed, they had to concede that they were in a minority, outnumbered by 'the worst & lowest partie in the Company, who are allwaies the most in the yearly elecons', another reason to oppose open contests.[159]

Statements like this provided Townley and his supporters with ample opportunity to pose as the real defenders of Company freedoms. Although initially the expedient of a martly deputy was justified on grounds of cost, later on it was presented as a means 'to prevent presumptious irregularities, which they found to be incroaching upon them, striking at the very root and foundation of their government'.[160] Bradshaw had been manipulated by a faction who had 'an overruling interest' in the resident becoming 'a perpetual, rather than an elective

[155] The married men were Robert Palmer, David Hechstetter, John Gilbert, Isaac Blackwell, Gabriel Whitley, and William Strange.

[156] Certain Hamburg Merchant Adventurers to Cromwell, 30 June 1654, *Thurloe State Papers* II, p. 406.

[157] Members of the Hamburg Merchant Adventurers to Company at London, 27 June 1654, Whitelocke Papers XVI, #11.

[158] Reasons of 'divers well affected Members' at Hamburg for dissenting from Townley's election, Bodl. Lib., Rawlinson A22, #22.

[159] Ibid.

[160] Petition of certain Hamburg Merchant Adventurers to Cromwell, 1655, *Thurloe State Papers* III, p. 119.

deputy'. This was a subversion of the traditional powers of the court, something that the revival of the role of martly deputy was intended to correct, in the hope that Bradshaw would then 'goe along with the Company according to the orders & practise of the Fellowship, in those things which by Majority of Votes (the ancient & only Rule to measure out the Companies actions) should be Judged & concluded to be for the generall good & peace of the Fellowship'.[161] Those members who had boycotted elections once Bradshaw had refused this office were guilty of a 'Separcion', which was 'contrary to the Orders & their obligacions to the Fellowship'.[162] Once Bradshaw had been restored as annual deputy their designs were made clear, as they sought revenge against their critics. Thus it again became necessary to turn Bradshaw out of office in June 1655, although Townley's party emphasized that they had sought the resident's advice on how best to secure 'the peace of the Companie'.[163]

Although the rhetoric of peace and tradition deployed by both sides could be interpreted as masking more partisan political ends, it is notable that Townley's party repeatedly denied any allegations of disloyalty to the Commonwealth or Protectorate. We should not underestimate the value that members may have placed on upholding the customs and privileges of the Company, as well as the integrity of the court as a forum for collective decision making, things which were deeply embedded into their communal as well as business lives. This was certainly the stance that Townley claimed to hold, although he remains something of an enigma. The criticisms which he levelled at Bradshaw for seeking a perpetual authority could conceivably be read as a veiled republican critique of the Protectorate, a conclusion strengthened by Bradshaw's assertion that Townley's 'cheefe confident and abetter' in London was Slingsby Bethel, a future critic of the Protector. However, it is unclear whether Bethel was by this point openly hostile to Cromwell, and in fact Townley apparently saw Bethel as an intermediary to approach government circles.[164] Because the political situation in England was in flux throughout this dispute, allegiances were in any case subject to change. The Protector's concern with healing and settling, and the increasingly conservative drift of his rule, could allow former opponents of the regime to reach accommodation: the protestations of loyalty by Townley's supporters were not necessarily empty ones. In the Company at London, this shift is captured by the succession of the position of governor from the old Puritan Samuel Avery (whose estate had failed early in 1656), to Sir Christopher Packe, perhaps the archetypal Cromwellian loyalist, best known for presenting the pseudo-royalist Humble Petition and Advice in Parliament in February 1657.[165]

---

[161]   Merchant Adventurers at Hamburg to Cromwell, 17 July 1655, Bodl. Lib., Rawlinson A22, pp. 573–4.
[162]   Ibid., p. 573.   [163]   Ibid., p. 574.
[164]   Bradshaw–Thurloe, 22 Apr. 1656, *Thurloe State Papers*, p. 722.
[165]   James Wainwright–Bradshaw, 23 Mar. 1656, *Bradshaw Letters*, p. 440.

Interpreting political developments in England from the distance of the mart town was not easy, but if anything, Townley was more adroit at capitalizing on these changes at home than his antagonist Bradshaw, who felt increasingly abandoned by the regime. When Cromwell's ambassador to Sweden, Edward Rolt, arrived in Hamburg, Townley and his party saw this as a chance to ingratiate themselves with a potential supporter, leading to a rather farcical incident on 29 March 1656 on Rolt's departure.[166] Rolt had been escorted by a retinue that included both Bradshaw and Townley, as well as Jeremiah Elborough, the Company treasurer George Watson, and secretary, Samuel Missenden (son of the former Delft deputy).[167] But it descended into a squabble over whether Missenden had the right to confer privately with Rolt before his departure, which Bradshaw denied, and Townley, predictably, asserted. Tempers raised, Townley directed a number of insults at the resident, including the revealing charge (recounted by Bradshaw) 'that a merchant adventurer was better than a Bilboa merchant, and that he was a merchant adventurer and no Bilboa blade, as I was'.[168] The two men nearly fell into fisticuffs. When summoned to London to answer for his conduct, however, Townley appears to have won some support amongst his Company.[169] By November he was heading back to Hamburg, which Bradshaw considered would be 'to the exposeing of me unto the scorne and derision of the whole citty and country'.[170] As it happened, Townley had not obtained licence to leave England and so was ordered to return, but still he boasted 'much of the favour he hath found at Whitehall'.[171]

In his dealings with the Company at Hamburg, Bradshaw increasingly fell back on his credentials as representative of the Protectorate, warning its members that they seemed 'to clash with the Authority of the State that gave you what beinge & proteccion you have as a Company'.[172] The cause of this particular exchange was the decision of the Hamburg court to impose fines on those members who were still refusing to attend or take their martly oath: clearly Bradshaw's supporters had yet to reconcile with the prevailing party, though they were less vocal in his defence than they had been two years previously. Eventually Bradshaw's warnings that the honour of the state was at stake persuaded Cromwell to reprimand the Company at London, who then wrote a reproachful letter to the Hamburg court

---

[166] Bradshaw–Cromwell, 29 Mar. 1656, *Thurloe State Papers* IV, pp. 659–60.
[167] Bradshaw's narrative of his encounter with Francis Townley at Blankenheyes, 29 Mar. 1656, *Thurloe State Papers* IV, pp. 666–8.
[168] Ibid., p. 667.
[169] Bradshaw–Charles Lloyd, London deputy of the Company, 27 May 1656, *Thurloe State Papers* V, pp. 62–3.
[170] Bradshaw–Thurloe, 4 Nov. 1656, *Thurloe State Papers* V, p. 550.
[171] Bradshaw–William Gessop, 9 Dec. 1656, TNA, SP 82/9, fol. 199r.
[172] Bradshaw to the Hamburg Merchant Adventurers, 22 Sept. 1656, Bodl. Lib., Rawlinson A42, pp. 591–3.

asking that they restore Bradshaw in place of the incumbent, George Watson.[173] Watson's offer of resignation was voted down by the Hamburg court by twenty hands to fifteen, however, even in Townley's absence. The court then sent a letter to its London equivalent complaining of the 'unbrotherly and disrespectfull stile' of its request, repeating its claim to merely have been acting to prevent 'encroaching irregularities'.[174] Bradshaw's supporters now broke their silence to condemn the 'impudent confidence' of this letter, calling on the London court to assume the power of election into their hands, at least until 'pease and unity' could be restored at Hamburg. They added a request that the role of assistant at Hamburg be restored to those 'whose interest in the trade of the company, and the antiquity of freedom, might justly plead preheminence to others chosen in their places, that have no trade at all'.[175] The signatories of this letter included such longstanding Hamburg residents as Robert Palmer and David Hechstetter, who doubtless saw themselves as the natural leaders of the community. However, their numbers were somewhat depleted from two years previously, and a handful of relatively new arrivals in the mart town were needed to bring their number up to fourteen (see the appendix to this chapter).

Although it is unclear how these rival letters went down in London, the fact that in April 1657 Bradshaw was directed to Russia on a diplomatic mission suggests that the government had concluded that his presence in Hamburg was itself the problem. Perhaps the London court now saw George Watson as the best candidate to pacify the rival factions: he was a longstanding resident of Hamburg, and although he had been amongst the non-engagers in 1650, he had apparently stayed aloof from the Bradshaw–Townley disputes, although by 1657 Bradshaw considered him as a leading opponent.[176] Watson claimed that Bradshaw's supporters had been 'pretty well callm'd and brought into orderly conjunction with us', before the letter from London ordering his resignation had engendered 'a new spirit of dissention and disturbance' amongst them.[177] Watson's successor, John Gilbert, was the one Merchant Adventurer to be counted amongst the covenanters in 1645, the non-engagers in 1650, and the supporters of Richard Bradshaw in 1654 (though he did not sign the 1657 letter). Given this chequered career, perhaps Gilbert was the ideal figure to pacify the divisions in Hamburg.

Although the forty-nine Merchant Adventurers who between them signed letters for or against Bradshaw probably reflected a majority of the court, there was

---

[173] Merchant Adventurers at London to Hamburg Company, 19 Dec. 1656, *Thurloe State Papers* V, pp. 718–19.

[174] Hamburg Merchant Adventurers to Company at London, 6 Jan. 1657, *Thurloe State Papers* V, p. 763.

[175] Certain members of the Merchant Adventurers at Hamburg to the London Company, 6 Jan. 1657, *Thurloe State Papers* V, p. 767.

[176] Bradshaw–Cromwell, 6 Jan. 1657, *Thurloe State Papers* V, pp. 759–60.

[177] Deputy George Watson–Governor Packe and the Merchant Adventurers at London, 6 Jan. 1657, *Thurloe State Papers* V, p. 762.

clearly a constituency which did not take a side, although identifying its size and composition is difficult. But the case of William Attwood may be instructive. Attwood first took communion in the Hamburg church in 1626, and had five children baptized in Hamburg from 1639 to 1646. His absence from the 1645 covenanters is thus notable, though he may have been out of Hamburg at that time. But he was certainly present in 1650, when as Company treasurer he wrote to thank the Commonwealth for sending Bradshaw as resident to secure justice for 'the inhumane practises of malitious wicked instruments against our persons, estates & priviledges'.[178] He had left Hamburg by 1654, but his correspondents included individuals from all sides of the subsequent contest: enemies of Bradshaw (Edward Halford; William Edlin), allies (William Strange; Cuthbert Jones; Richard Twyford), as well as George Watson. Personal association, business relations, and kinship ties cut across political divisions. As the remainder of the decade apparently generated no major controversies within the Hamburg Company's ranks, it might be that the departure of Bradshaw had restored a level of harmony based on such associations.

Conclusion

The discovery that the Company of Merchant Adventurers was politically divided in this most polarized of eras is not surprising. However, the way that these divisions played out across the Company's different residences reveals much about changing relationships between these branches. The stance of the London court is perhaps the simplest to interpret. Although clearly the membership was divided in its allegiances, it was in the general interests of the Company to align itself with the present rulers of London, particularly after the passing of the 1643 parliamentary ordinance and the king's desertion of the Company. In the mart towns, decades of religious practice according to Presbyterian-style church government and discipline meant that there was a constituency of members inclined to lean to Parliament, particularly those senior residents closely acquainted with the two long-serving ministers, John Forbes and Jeremiah Elborough. These loyalties appear to have been weaker in the younger generation, however, which in Hamburg at least exhibited a greater willingness to openly support the royalist cause, particularly after the regicide (we have less information for Rotterdam, though in 1649 the parliamentary resident complained about the royalism prevalent in the Company, including its deputy, Hugh Jones).[179] This was associated with a drift away from the Company's religious traditions, first in Rotterdam

---

[178] William Attwood, treasurer, and Merchant Adventurers of Hamburg to Council of State, 28 May 1650, TNA, SP 82/7, fol. 190.

[179] Sprunger, *Dutch Puritanism*, pp. 253–4.

under Beaumont in the 1630s, and then in Hamburg in the 1660s, when the Company consented to the crown's demands for religious conformity. Elborough was dismissed in 1665, though by then his base had been weakened by the separation of some congregationalist-leaning members from the Company church.[180] The new Hamburg deputy, Sir William Swann (also an appointee of the state) found certain members 'to be dangerously schismaticall in their principels and the leading men in the compagney to continue their obstinacy against the discipline of the church of England', including two prominent Bradshaw supporters— David Hechstetter and Samuel Richardson.[181] Now they were joined again by none other than Francis Townley, described by Swann as 'a most pestilent phanatique', a sign of how Anglican persecution was capable of healing some of the divisions that had previously opened within the ranks of the godly.[182]

Although the willingness of the Hamburg residency to conform to the Church of England in the 1660s removed one potential source of division with the Company in London, over the following decades the divergence between Hamburg and London only widened. The complaint of the London membership to their Hamburg brethren in 1657 about becoming implicated in the continued opposition to Bradshaw—'you see how you have involved us, as well as yourselves'—is telling of how distanced the two courts had now become from one another.[183] This was not only a consequence of diverging political loyalties, however. Changes in the composition of the merchant community on both sides of the sea now meant that it was becoming harder to identify the common interests that might bind them together, in spite of the London court's request that their Hamburg brethren 'submit your private disgusts and sense to the interest of the whole'. Given these changes, defining the bounds of this merchant community became an increasingly fraught task.

We see this in the contests discussed above, when each of the three controversial deputy governors were represented by their opponents as an outsider, guilty of infringing moral standards expected of the merchant communities in the mart towns. Misselden's portrayal as bankrupt and perjurer marked him as a transgressor of corporate ethics, Avery's violent demeanour contradicted the function of his office in maintaining the Company's peace, and the 'Bilboa blade' Bradshaw was a political appointee, imposed on the Fellowship without respect for its traditions of self-government. Each was presented as an aspiring tyrant, crushing the independence of the Company court and the ability of its members to participate in government and hold authority to account. The deputies and their antagonists interpreted the role of this office in fundamentally different terms, then.

[180] Ibid., p. 260.   [181] Swann–Sir Henry Bennet, 1 July 1664, TNA, SP 82/10, fol. 180.
[182] Swann–Sir Joseph Williamson, 29 Sept. 1665, TNA, SP 82/10, fol. 259.
[183] Merchant Adventurers at London to Hamburg Company, 19 Dec. 1656, *Thurloe State Papers* V, p. 719.

Misselden, Avery, and Bradshaw all emphasized that their power was rooted in the Company's charter. Misselden had a particularly hierarchical conception not just of his own office, but also of relations within the Company and between its branches, advocating rule by the seniority at London, closely watched over by the crown. The opponents of these deputies all emphasized instead how the power of the Company's government flowed upwards from the membership, and argued in favour of upholding the power of the court, its discursive traditions, and the liberties of freemen. This vision was not without its own hierarchical implications, particularly in Delft in the 1630s and Hamburg in the 1640s, when the leaders of opposition presented themselves as the patriarchs of the community—literally, its elders. In the case of the opposition to Bradshaw, however, this claim was harder to sustain, though Townley was described by his supporters as 'an ancient and orderly brother of the fellowship'.[184] But in the face of the evident seniority of their opponents, Townley's party fell back on the rule of the majority as their key legitimizing principle. It was their opponents who appealed to the principle of hierarchy, even going so far as to repeat Misselden's call for rule from London. Their support for Bradshaw also led these merchants, many of whom had earlier opposed Avery's infringements of the liberty of the court, to privilege the Company's charters over the power of its assembled membership. As they explained to the Protector, 'our Charters were given to our Company before they were constituted into Courts, and by Vertue of that Priviledge & power they did, and doe Constitute Courts'.[185]

At stake in these contests was the ability of these merchant communities to regulate themselves as well as their trade: to define the bounds of acceptable conduct and thereby membership. The Company's baroque constitutional structure, with authority dispersed across different locales, was increasingly unsuitable to this role, however, and the role and status of the Company deputy—caught between the Company and the state, as well as London and the mart towns— became the focus for wider uncertainties about where power resided. Conflict was mitigated by appeals to the peace of the community, a peace on which its prosperity depended. But was this a community that encompassed the entire membership of the Company, dispersed as it was, or was the Company an umbrella organization bringing together separate communities of merchants with distinct interests, coordinating between them? This question would continue to animate Company politics as it sought, in the Restoration, to restore its privileges, and repair the breaches that had opened up within Company ranks.

---

[184] Certain Merchant Adventurers of Hamburg, petition to Cromwell, 1655, *Thurloe State Papers* III, p. 119.
[185] Answer and petition of diverse Merchant Adventurers at Hamburg to Cromwell, 1655, Bodl. Lib., Rawlinson A22 #22. Perhaps significantly, this petition was signed by only ten of Bradshaw's supporters, including some of the more senior ones.

Allegiances of Hamburg Merchant Adventurers, 1640s/1650s (listed according to date when first identifiable in Hamburg)

	First present in Hamburg	1645 pro-covenant	17 June letter to Elborough	19 June resolution	1650 anti-engagement	1654 opponent of Richard Bradshaw	Supporter of Richard Bradshaw 1654	Supporter of Richard Bradshaw 1657
John Dogett Sr	1620c		X	X				
William Angell	1620c		X	X				
Isaak Lee	1620c			X (except letter)				
John Wardes	1620cm		X	X				
William Gore	1620c?		X	X				
Henry Taylor	1621nc		X	X			X	X
Robert Palmer	1622nc			X (except letter)				
George Shippe	1622nc			X (except letter)			X	X
Henry Crispe	1625nc			X (except letter)				
John Gilbert	1626nc			X (except letter)	X		X	
Jeremiah Elborough	1629nc		X	X				
John Phippes	1630nc			X (except letter)				
Francis Townley	1632nc			X (except letter)		X		

Name	Date	1	2	3	4	5	6
George Watson	1632nc					X	X
James Baber	1632nc						X
John Dogett Jr	1633nc	X					
Melchior Wolfenden	1634nc		X				
Pearce Starkie	1635nc		X (except letter)				
Jefferie Northelight	1635nc		X (except letter)				
George Franklyn	1638e				X		
Arthur Baron	1640e		X				
Thomas Aldersy	1640e			X	X		
William Edlin	1640e; 1651nc		X				
David Hechsteter	1641e	X	X		X		
Allen Baron	1641e		X		X		
John Metcalfe	1641e			X			
Nathaniel Hearinges	1642e		X				
Leonard Scott	1642e		X (except letter)	X			
George Wakefield	1642e		X	X			
Edmond Bowater	1645f		X	X			
William Lee	1645x		X	X			
Henry Spurway	1645x		X	X			
Renold Wainwright	1645x		X				
John Midlemoore	1645x		X				
George Warcoppe	1645x		X (except letter)				
John Glynne	1645x		X				
Christopher Jones	1645x		X				
Thomas Jenckinson	1645x		X				
Slingsby Bethel	1645x		X			X	
Gabriel Whitley	1645x		X				
Richard Waller	1645x		X				
Thomas Ashwin	1645x		X		X		
Thomas Tites	1645x		X				

Continued

	First present in Hamburg	1645 pro-covenant		1650 anti-engagement	1654 opponent of Richard Bradshaw	Supporter of Richard Bradshaw	
		17 June letter to Elborough	19 June resolution			1654	1657
James Wolfenden	1645x		X	X			
Edward Keelinges	1645x		X				
Edward Knightley	1645x		X (except letter)				
Walter Woolsley	1645x		X (except letter)				
Robert Biddolphe	1645x		X (except letter)				
John Dusy	1646nc			X		X	
John Northleigh	1646nc					X	
Richard Twyford	1646nc						
William Strange	1647nc			X		X	X
Daniel Milward	1647nc			X	X		
Isaac Blackwell	1647nc					X	X
Thomas Lee	1648nc			X		X	
Thomas Walker	1648nc				X		
Samuel Richardson	1648nc					X	X
John Palmer	1648nc					X	
Thomas Scott	1649nc				X		
Thomas Ruggells	1649nc				X		
Henry Wainwright	1649nc				X		
Robert Duke	1649nc						X
Francis Orange	1650nc				X		
Thomas Farrington	1650nc				X		
John Parker	1650x			X	X		
Edmond Starkie	1650x			X	X		
Richard Jenkinson	1650x			X	X		
Thomas Bellingham	1650x			X	X		

Name	Date				
Clement Clarke	1650x	X			
George Wayte	1650x		X		
Thomas Laurence	1650x		X		
George Sharpuls	1650x		X		
William Fownes	1650x; 1651nc		X		
Edward Halford	1651e		X		
William Wolfenden	1651m		X		
Samuel Cooth	1651nc				
Gabriel Whitley	1652m			X	
John Banckes	1652nc			X	
Benjamin Hechstetter	1652nc				X
Thomas Dangerfield	1654nc		X		
Francis Anderson	1654x		X		
Charles Andrews	1654x		X		
Thomas Stanley	1654x		X		
John Pococke	1654x		X		
Thomas Bennet	1654x		X		
Isaac Coote [Cooke?]	1654x		X		
Richard Clotterbook	1654x		X		
Thomas Harrington	1654x		X		
Cuthbert Jones	1654x			X	X
William Mowbray	1654x			X	X
John Gurdon	1655nc				X
Ralph Trevor	1657x				X
Edward Radcliffe	1657x				X

Note. Letters following dates refer to the following events as recorded in the Hamburg church book: c = communicant in 1620 listing; nc = new communicant; m = marriage; f = father (first born only). The Hamburg church book records no new communicants from 1635 to 1645, which may account for the absences here. In addition, information from bills of exchange in George Warner/William Attwood's accounts have been included to provide evidence of presence in Hamburg (denoted by 'e'). x denotes those who do not appear in these sources prior to the event in question. For sources, see references in Chapter 7.

8

'That Trade which their Charter reaches not'

Contesting the Company from the Restoration to the Glorious Revolution

On 23 October 1690, the London membership of the Fellowship of Merchant Adventurers was summoned to attend a meeting of the General Court, or as it was apparently now known, the 'General Committee', to discuss the selection of its secretary. Usually such matters were decided by the head court at Hamburg during the annual midsummer elections, before being confirmed by the Company's other courts. However, the election of the London secretary had become mired in controversy due to the decision at Hamburg to replace the incumbent, John Ince, by one William Twyford, the son of the senior Hamburg Merchant Adventurer, Richard Twyford. Ince, though, had powerful patrons, including the Company's governor, Lawrence Hyde, Earl of Rochester, whose intervention had caused the London residence to delay confirming Twyford's election. Eventually, on 23 October, Ince was confirmed in his post by a majority of the London membership, a rebuff to the electoral pre-eminence of the Hamburg court.

This episode is indicative of tensions between the Company's London and Hamburg residences that were in evidence in the 1650s, when the members at Hamburg demonstrated their willingness to act independently from the traditionally more senior merchants at London. The divergence between Hamburg and London would only grow over subsequent decades, making clashes such as that over the London secretary increasingly likely. What is perhaps more surprising about this episode is the fact that, according to John Ince at least, at the meeting to decide his fate 'there then appeared the greatest number of Members of the Fellowship...that had been in London for one hundred years before'.[1] Even one of Ince's opponents, the London deputy governor Sir William Cranmer, conceded that the numbers attending this meeting were 'very Numerous'.[2]

The passions ignited by this contest, and the numbers who were drawn to participate in it, may be a cause for surprise because, by the closing decades of the century, the Fellowship of Merchant Adventurers is often seen as a spent force, its

---

[1] John Ince vs Company of Merchant Adventurers, bill of complaint, 1692, TNA, C7/191/1.
[2] Cranmer's answer, ibid.

Fellowship and Freedom: The Merchant Adventurers and the Restructuring of English Commerce, 1582–1700.
Thomas Leng, Oxford University Press (2020). © Thomas Leng. DOI: 10.1093/oso/9780198794479.001.0001

loss of privilege after the Glorious Revolution merely confirming the inevitable. To David Ormrod, as the regulation of trade shifted from the royal prerogative to Parliament, monopoly companies reliant on crown support were vulnerable to attack. In the case of the Merchant Adventurers, this was exacerbated by the regulatory shift signalled by the mid-century Navigation Acts and the corresponding opening up of the export trade through such measures as the ending of prohibitive aliens' duties in 1673. These twin legislative trends combined to produce a system intended to protect 'the English entrepôt rather than the nationality and status of the exporter', the antithesis of the political economy that had favoured the Merchant Adventurers ever since the withdrawal of the Hanseatic privileges over a century earlier.[3] After 1688 the Company was finally defeated in its long-term contest with the supporters of free trade and the manufacturing interest.[4] Accordingly, in 1689, 'An Act for the better preventing the Exportation of Woole and Encourageing the Woollen Manufactures of this Kingdom' opened up the export of 'any Cloath Stuffs Stockings or other Manufacture of Wooll' to all comers.

Coming as it did after at least half a century of commercial and political decline, the passage of such an act might appear inevitable. However, in the politically confused aftermath of the Glorious Revolution, it seems to have caught the Merchant Adventurers, as well as the other trading companies, by surprise. According to John Ince, the clause opening up the woollen trade had by 'cuning' been appended to the chief contents of the bill, which concerned the export of wool. This alarmed several overseas trading companies, which interpreted it as 'a meanes to avoyd their priviledges, & to open theire trade to all men, as well unfreemen at home, as forraigners abroad, and therefore they began to stirr to prevent it'.[5] But when finally heard by the House of Lords, the Merchant Adventurers—now known by the appellation that had become increasingly common since the 1660s, the Hamburg Company—were pointedly left out of a proviso introduced to the bill that its measures should not be 'construed prejudicial' to certain other companies (the Levant, Eastland, Russia, and Royal African companies). The membership at Hamburg were reportedly dismayed at 'the surprising news, that the parliament is laying their trade open', whilst the newly arrived royal resident, Sir Paul Rycaut, was at a loss to know how he should now execute his instruction to ensure that the Company's 'Priviledges and immunityes which they have time out of mind, be not violated or encroached upon'.[6]

As well as showing how low the stock of the Merchant Adventurers had fallen in relation to the newer companies, its failure to successfully lobby Parliament

---

[3] Ormrod, *Rise of Commercial Empires*, p. 44.   [4] Ibid., pp. 35–43.
[5] John Ince to the Eastland Company at York, 5 Sept. 1689, printed in Maud Sellers (ed.), *The Acts and Ordinances of the Eastland Company* (London, 1906), p. 127.
[6] Sir Paul Rycaut–Earl of Nottingham, 4 Sept. 1689, printed in *Laws*, pp. 250–1; Instructions issued to Sir Paul Rycaut, 22 June 1689, TNA, SP 104/194, p. 35.

might suggest a Company that was increasingly moribund, unable to muster the support necessary to survive the Glorious Revolution. Certainly commercial changes over the previous century had complicated the Company's regulatory regime, which emerged when most of England's foreign trade was straightforwardly bilateral in form.[7] The growing complexity of overseas trade opened new opportunities, not just to participate in new markets but to fashion new linkages between them, and such multilateral connections cut across the geographical boundaries between different corporate interests. London merchants able to operate in a range of markets, including the largely deregulated Atlantic, might be expected to withdraw their support from institutions such as the Merchant Adventurers, which imposed limitations on their commercial freedom. Other changes, such as the declining level of exports of the Company's staple export of unfinished broadcloth, and its failure to enforce its privileges in the Netherlands in the light of the Anglo-Dutch wars, made membership less attractive. This was particularly the case for merchants of the outports, often reluctant participants in the London-dominated Company, who were handling a growing share of woollen exports to Germany and the Netherlands by the Restoration. Along with exogenous factors such as the shifting political economy of the state, then, the Company's inability to retain the loyalty of its members, or to attract new ones, could serve as an explanation for why it failed to uphold its status after 1688.

All these factors undoubtedly contributed to the Company's eventual loss of privilege. However, this chapter will argue that this was a more contingent process than has usually been appreciated. The storm over John Ince's de-selection was not the only sign that control of the Fellowship of Merchant Adventurers was still seen by many to be a prize worth fighting for. The fact that the 1689 opening up of trade was initially for a three-year period (although it is unclear whether this was specified in the act itself, the full text of which does not survive) meant that the regulation of the cloth trade continued to be contested, along with the textile industry more broadly.[8] The precise implications of the act even appear to have been unclear to members of the government. When Sir Paul Rycaut requested advice about how to respond should the Senate of Hamburg repeal the Company's privileges, which 'were no longer to continue in force, then the companie remained a body corporate', he was assured by the Earl of Nottingham that 'tho' there be a liberty of Trade granted by it to all Merchants that will send their goods to Hamburg yet the Company is not dissolved but subsists still and consequently

---

[7] Ormrod, *Rise of Commercial Empires*, p. 32.
[8] Tim Keirn, 'Parliament, legislation and the regulation of English textile industries, 1689–1714', in Lee Davison, Tim Hitchcock, Tim Keirn and Robert B. Shoemaker (eds), *Stilling the Grumbling Hive: The Response to Social and Economic Problems in England, 1689–1750* (Stroud and New York, 1992), pp. 1–24.

is intiuled to their Ancient immunities at Hambourg'.[9] However, Nottingham added, 'the Merchants that shall trade thither by vertue of this Act ought to be esteemed there as so many new members added to the Company for if the Company could admitt them, an Act of Parliament can much more make them so'. The Company was worth preserving, then, in order to retain its overseas privileges, but these were now open to all of the crown's subjects, potentially under parliamentary oversight, an effective 'nationalization' of the mart-trading system. However, in a subsequent letter Nottingham backtracked on this threat somewhat, writing that 'a bare liberty of trade to Hamburg' did not automatically open up membership of the Company, 'for then all foreigners that shall carry our Cloath thither would become Members of the Company, which I presume was never the intent of Parliament'.[10] The ambiguity surrounding the 1689 act suggests that there was no clear plan for the regulation of the cloth trade, meaning that the Merchant Adventurers continued to have a part to play in contests over the political economy of the post-revolutionary state.

The fact that it continued to be possible to envisage a future for the Merchant Adventurers even after so many decades of decline is indicative of how, as recent scholarship has shown, corporate forms of commercial government continued to be viable long after the Glorious Revolution, which was no straightforward victory for 'free trade'. The divergent fortunes of the East India and Royal African companies are revealing of the strategies available to trading companies navigating the new legislative and commercial context.[11] The East India Company succeeded by demonstrating (to the government at least) its credentials as a genuinely national venture, at the price of accepting greater accessibility and closer state supervision. The Merchant Adventurers pursued a similar strategy throughout the Restoration, emphasizing openness to English merchants as well as the importance of the cloth trade as the nation's staple trade. The eventual failure of this strategy in its case is evidence less of the obsolescence of corporate government than of the fundamental differences between English trade in Europe and the far east. However, this does not mean that the Company's fate was sealed in 1688. In fact, this chapter will argue that this most venerable of trading companies was on the cusp of a potential revival of its fortunes during the 1680s. That it failed to capitalize on this opportunity was due partly to political contingency, but also to the structural changes that had reshaped relationships within the Company and made the coordination of effective action across its branches increasingly difficult to achieve.

---

[9] Rycaut–Nottingham, 6 Sept. 1689, in *Laws*, p. 251; Nottingham–Rycaut, 17 Sept. 1689, TNA, SP 104/194, p. 70.
[10] Nottingham–Rycaut, 24 Sept. 1689, TNA, SP 104/194, p. 73.
[11] William A. Pettigrew and George W. Van Cleve, 'Parting companies: the Glorious Revolution, company power, and imperial mercantilism', *Historical Journal* 57, 3 (2014), pp. 617–38.

'The bare interest of some few merchants':
Defending the Monopoly

In order to maintain their privileged status, trading companies needed to sustain a series of boundaries which defined the geographical extent of their monopolies, the distinction between non-members and members, and the acceptable conduct which members were expected to follow. Defending their monopolies was, to this extent, tied up with the task of defining them. The threat that interlopers posed towards merchant companies was not just one of unwanted competition: as boundary crossers—literally, trespassing into places or pursuits forbidden to them—interlopers could expose as arbitrary the restrictions that merchant companies constructed in order to channel trade to their members' advantages. As discussed in Chapter 4, interlopers might also become a conduit for company members themselves seeking to overcome the limits of their trade, so threatening the behavioural norms expected of them.

Chapter 4 also discussed how the ambiguous nature of the Merchant Adventurers' privileges meant that, in practice, the Company shared its marketplaces with outsiders plying the same trade routes, English and non-English, although the Company's charters could be interpreted in such a way as to suggest that the former still fell under Company jurisdiction. The Company's monopoly was thus defined as much by a commodity as by the region to which its members traded—cloth, and more specifically the unfinished broadcloth which (except in exceptional circumstances) the Company held exclusive rights to export under licence. In many ways, the licensing system was a more effective bulwark of the Company's monopoly than its charters, policed as it was by the licensees and their officers supervising cloth passing through the customs houses. Those variants not subject to this system, the cheaper kerseys and dozens, alongside finished broadcloths, were harder to control. This was also true of the new draperies, which were only specifically included in the Company's monopoly from 1618. By then, significant communities of English merchants had established themselves throughout the United Provinces, which could potentially compete with the Company's mart towns, though this was less the case in Germany following the move to Hamburg in 1612. Company discourse tended to describe these non-members as interlopers whether or not they were actively trading in woollens, just as it described non-Company ships as interloper ships, and certain commodities largely handled by non-members (particularly non-European imports) as interloping goods.[12] The challenge the Company faced was to ensure that these interlopers resident

---

[12] 'Deduction of the Title of the Merchant Adventurers to the Trade of all the draperies of England vented in Germany and the Low Countreys', Nov. 1634, TNA, SP 16/277, fols 224–5. For interloper ships and interloping goods, see Chapter 2.

overseas did not become a means for non-members in England to intrude on its monopoly, or for members to 'straggle' beyond the mart towns.

Given the ambiguous nature of its privileges, the Company had little prospect of successfully prosecuting English-based interlopers through the common law courts, something recognized by Edward Misselden: 'The Lawes of this Realme in such case relieving him against the Company, either by action of wronge Imprisonement, or of Trespasse, notwithstanding the Priviledges of our Charter.'[13] This increased the Company's reliance on royal support, in the form of occasional letters to the customs officers ordering them to enforce the Company's monopoly, or summonses to interlopers by the Privy Council. The Company acquired a more regular means of defence with its 1618 charter, which absorbed the powers that had been granted to the King's Merchant Adventurers during the Cokayne Project to oversee entries of goods in the customs house, and to take bond from shippers to ensure that they delivered to the place entered in the cocket. Customs officials were ordered not to allow shipments of woollens unless the bills of entry were signed by a Company officer. The Company's subsequent complaints to the Privy Council about interlopers, including many former Cokayne projectors, indicates that this was not immediately effective.[14] In November 1620 the Company brought a case in Star Chamber against a number of 'disordered obstinate and contemptuous persons not brought upp in merchandize', who were accused of covertly transporting cloths from London to Dover for export to the Low Countries.[15] The outports thus continued to be a weak link in the Company's enforcement mechanisms, but the case suggests that its powers of inspection in London's customs house at least were having some effect.

The Company, however, had little time to enjoy these powers before the depression of the 1620s led to the opening up of trade in the new draperies and narrow cloths, and (for the outports) dyed and dressed cloth, in 1624.[16] The royal proclamation restoring the Company's monopoly in 1634 confirmed its privileges, at the price of requiring the Company to admit all mere merchants for the cost of £50 (£25 for the outports).[17] In 1639 the Company had to petition the Privy Council to have its officers' seat in the customs house restored, having apparently been denied it for the previous three years.[18] If the 1640 port books for London are to be trusted, this had the desired effect of confining direct exports of both old and new draperies (with the exception of stockings) from London to the mart

---

[13] Misselden, 'Discourse', fol. 31v.

[14] Friis, *Alderman Cockayne's Project*, pp. 366–74; APC 1618–19, pp. 1–2, 86–7, 112–13, 428.

[15] *Attorney General Sir Thomas Coventry v. William Wade, William Ellwood, Robert Weekes, Augustine Phillips, John Kinge, John Matthew*, Nov. 1620, STAC 8/31/8; Merchant Adventurers to Lord Zouch, 31 Aug. 1620, TNA, SP 14/116, fol. 121.

[16] For details, see Chapter 6.

[17] *A Proclamation for the better ordering the Transportation of Clothes, and other Woollen Manufactures into Germany, and the Low-Countreys*, 7 Dec. 1634.

[18] PC 2/50, pp. 170–1.

towns of Hamburg and Rotterdam. Evidence of the Company deploying its customs house powers comes from a 1641 petition by six London merchants, who complained that the Company had procured a stop of their shipment of Spanish cloths, kerseys, perpetuanas, stockings, and caps destined for Flanders or Holland, enforced by a £100 bond.[19] This petition was addressed to the recently summoned parliament, which provided an opportunity for grievances against the Company to be heard, and soon it was facing seven hostile petitions and the scrutiny of a parliamentary committee. As well as familiar attacks from excluded outsiders and resentful cloth producers, the Company also faced criticism from within. One petition represented the Merchants of the Staple, which continued to exist in spite of the loss of Calais and the prohibition of its traditional wool exports. Its members had been persistent interlopers in the Merchant Adventurers' trade, before being granted membership in 1634. Their petition complained, however, that they had been 'enforced...to come into the Company' and pay 'excessive Fines', its members having been previously 'greivously vexed and imprisoned'.[20] Another member who had reluctantly joined following the 1634 proclamation, William Sykes of Hull, petitioned for release from his imprisonment by the Company in Rotterdam for disobeying its rules, probably by continuing to trade to Amsterdam.[21] The Merchant Adventurers of Hull also complained to the London court about being confined to the mart towns and subjected to Company impositions, demanding instead 'that freedome and liberty which wee conceive is due unto free Subjects; and most proper for our Northern Trade'.[22] The restoration of the Company's monopoly in 1634 had thus created its own problems.

Most of these petitions were from rival corporate interests or, in the case of the Staplers and the Merchant Adventurers of Hull, ones which had been imperfectly incorporated within the Company. One petition, presented in the name of 'the Merchantes and traders in Draperies', however, offered a more fundamental critique of the corporate restriction of trade, heralding the increasingly ideological tenor that free trade discourse would assume in the following decade.[23] This petition attacked not only the Company's regulations, including the use of an 'illegall oath' and 'illegall ordinances taxes imposicions' (prominent themes also in Sykes' petition), but the charter in which these regulations were rooted, which was presented as against the law and the 'Subjectes right of free trade'. The petition was signed by fifty-one individuals and headed by several major colonial merchants, including Maurice Thomson, whose main interests certainly were not in the

---

[19] Petition of John Hodgson, Thomas Hincksman and four others, 9 Mar. 1641, Whitelocke Papers VIII, #39.

[20] Petition dated 12 Jan. 1641, Whitelocke Papers VIII, #31.

[21] Petition dated 2 Feb. 1641, Whitelocke Papers VIII, #36. See Thomas Leng, ' "His neighbours land mark": William Sykes and the campaign for "free trade" in civil war England', *Historical Research* 86, 232 (2013), pp. 230–52.

[22] Merchant Adventurers of Hull to those at London, c.Jan. 1641, Whitelocke Papers VIII, #34.

[23] Petition dated 16 Mar. 1641, Whitelocke Papers VIII, #41.

export of draperies, but whose expansive, multilateral trading operations did intrude on the Company's privileged areas, particularly the Low Countries which were a market for tobacco. Several of these 'new merchants' (to deploy Robert Brenner's label) were disqualified from membership of the Merchant Adventurers by virtue of their pursuit of other occupations such as shopkeeper or clothier (as was the case of Thompson's collaborator Richard Shute, another signer), and the petitioners also complained about being unfairly charged with 'the name of Interlopers'.[24] The fact that this diverse group still considered the Merchant Adventurers worthy of attack demonstrates the continued power of the Company, as well as the strategic value of the trade in woollens.

In the event the Company survived these challenges, largely due to Parliament's pressing fiscal needs, which led to an ordinance of 1643 upholding its government and confirming that admission was reserved for mere merchants. However, the extent to which the Company was able to exercise its powers thereafter is questionable. Faced with criticism from radicals such as the Levellers (joined by William Sykes), the Company was perhaps wary about pursuing interlopers too vigorously, and it is possible that its powers in the customs house were in abeyance in this period. The account by the Baptist William Kiffin of his commencement of trade to the Netherlands at around this time gives the impression of an open marketplace.[25] The letters of William Attwood's agents in Rotterdam, Robert Gay and Thomas Bale, in 1655 are full of complaints of the 'vagrant interloopers' spoiling their trade.[26] However, they also pointed the finger at 'refractory Brethren of our Company'.[27] Even if the Company was able to prevent direct shipments of cloth to such ports as Amsterdam, the interlopers there could be supplied via the mart towns, potentially with the collusion of Merchant Adventurers. In the late 1630s and early 1640s, the Rotterdam deputy governors' efforts to prevent this traffic by seizing interlopers' goods were thwarted due to the influence of the Amsterdam cloth-buyers over the States of Holland. These well-organized Dutch merchants also boycotted the purchase of northern cloths in Rotterdam following the Company's 1634 move there, allegedly with the intention to 'disband the Brethren of the Fellowship, that in a loose Trade they might still pursue their advantages upon the Seller, and overthrow the Drapery of this Land'.[28] One of the cloth-buyers' grievances was the clause in the Company's contract with Rotterdam

---

[24] Whitelocke Papers VIII, #42.

[25] William Orme (ed.), *Remarkable Passages in the Life of William Kiffin: Written by Himself, and edited from the Original Manuscript* (London, 1823), pp. 22–3.

[26] Gay and Bale–Attwood, 21 May 1655, C109/19.

[27] Gay and Bale–Attwood, 10 Nov. 1655, C109/19. One Merchant Adventurer singled out by Gay and Bale as underselling his brethren, presumably by trading outside of Rotterdam, was Ralph Bressy (30 Apr. 1655), who was a collaborator of John Sykes, probably the son of the William Sykes discussed above, suggesting a lineage of such 'refractory' behaviour. TNA, SP 44/14, fol. 3.

[28] Complaints of the Merchant Adventurers to the Council of State, 16 July 1651, TNA, SP 46/96, fol. 57v.

requiring English merchants to relocate to the new mart town, a move they successfully mobilized against, probably with the support of the Amsterdam interlopers.[29] If Gay and Bale's complaints are anything to go by, increasing numbers of Merchant Adventurers were being drawn to directly collaborate with the latter by the 1650s.

The outbreak of the first Anglo-Dutch war further disrupted the Company's position in the Netherlands, but the ensuing peace negotiations raised the prospect of having its grievances addressed.[30] However, these hopes proved to be fruitless, and in 1656 the Company instead attempted to revive its flagging fortunes by relocating its mart town to Dordrecht, accompanied by a supportive proclamation by the Protector.[31] This did little to restore the position of the Company in the Netherlands, however, and Gay and Bale warned that 'if our Company continue thus at a constant ebb noe doubt wee shall heere bee suddenly on the sands, wee wonder that our Company there regard us noe more, to bringe us heere & leave us'.[32] The continuation of Anglo-Dutch hostility after the Restoration exacerbated these problems, and in 1669 the States of Holland passed a resolution nullifying the Company's remaining privileges and customs exemptions, supported by all the towns except Dordrecht.[33] The Company warned that unless efforts were taken to restore its position, Dordrecht would not renew its privileges, which were due to expire in 1670.[34] Although the Company continued to maintain a Dutch residence after this date, the crown's ambassador Sir William Temple accurately summed up its plight: 'whatever privileges are allowed your company at *Dort*, will be given by the other towns, either openly or covertly, to all those interlopers, who bring their woollen manufacture directly thither; and in this, the very *States* themselves cannot hinder what each town will do for their own particular advantage'.[35]

Temple's pessimism was also influenced by the crown's failure to support the Company against interlopers, 'which makes it look as if the present interest of your company here were no more than the bare interest of some few merchants habituated at Dort, and their enjoyments of certain exemptions, which are

[29] Te Lintum, *De merchant adventurers in der Nederlanden*, pp. 146–53; Petition of the Merchant Adventurers to the Privy Council, May 1635, TNA, SP 16/289, fol. 180; Petition of Merchant Adventurers to House of Lords, 1640, BL, Stowe 133, fols 289–92.

[30] Petition of Merchant Adventurers to Protector Cromwell, 31 Aug. 1654, TNA, SP 18/75, fol. 116; Protector Cromwell to the States General, States of Holland, and cities of Rotterdam and Dordrecht, 26 Oct. 1654, TNA, SP 84/160, fol. 7.

[31] *A Proclamation concerning the Residence of the Merchants Adventurers of England at the City of Dordrecht* was eventually issued on 29 May, TNA, SP 18/127, fol. 102, following opposition by interlopers. Petition of Merchant Adventurers to Protector Cromwell, 27 May 1656, TNA, SP 18/127, fol. 84.

[32] Robert Gay and Thomas Bale–William Attwood, 6 July 1657, C109/19.

[33] PC 2/61, p. 238.

[34] Petition, Merchant Adventurers to the king, 6 May 1670, TNA, SP 29/275, fol. 103.

[35] Sir William Temple to the Merchant Adventurers, 26 Mar. 1675, in *The Works of Sir William Temple*, IV (London, 1754), pp. 97–8.

considerable, perhaps, to their domestic and personal concernments, but very little so to the woollen trade of the nation, in which they have but a very small share, in proportion to what the interlopers drive'.[36] The flourishing state of the interlopers' trade belied the Company's arguments for the necessity of its government. Rather, the interlopers might now appear to have a comparative advantage, something that the Company had inadvertently conceded in 1634 when complaining of 'there being noe equality that the Marchants Adventurers that have the ancient right and possession of the Trade by Charters and Privyledges should now be bound to the Mart Townes being of small Trade, and not be as free as the Interlopers to goe to Amsterdam, where the Trade is most plentifull and beneficiall'.[37] When this claim was repeated in the 1660s, the interlopers did not miss the opportunity to use it to their favour, arguing that 'if the merchants tyed not up themselves to one Towne but dispersed into places more Comodious for the Buyer, it might have prevented many thousand Clothes & Stuffes making by them' (the Dutch).[38] By then, successful interlopers like William Kiffin were frequently consulted alongside the Company over the state of the cloth trade to the Netherlands, despite Kiffin's religious nonconformity.

Although the Company had its charter and customs house privileges confirmed in 1661, then, the Restoration did not bring respite from criticism. Particularly vocal were the merchants of Exeter, who were enjoying a growing trade to the Low Countries, largely in perpetuanas, which was now threatened by the Company's renewed customs house powers.[39] The subsequent debates about the status of the Company paralleled contemporary discussions about whether the restored national church should seek to incorporate dissenting Protestants through 'comprehension', or else either persecute or tolerate ('indulge') them.[40] In the case of the Merchant Adventurers, the question was whether interlopers into its trade should be granted an indulgence to pursue their trade freely, or should be incorporated into a more accessible and perhaps lightly regulated Company. Kiffin was called on by the Exeter merchants to lobby for the former, which he did successfully before both a committee of the House of Commons and the king and Privy Council, in spite of the Company's best efforts to paint him as a political

---

[36] Ibid., p. 97.

[37] Petition of Merchant Adventurers to Privy Council, c.Nov. 1634, TNA, SP 16/277, fol. 226.

[38] 'The humble Addresse & Petitcion of several Merchants of London desiring a generall liberty for exporting woollen manufactures', c.1666, TNA, SP 29/380, fol. 117.

[39] Stephens, *Seventeenth-Century Exeter*, pp. 85–8. *The Reasons Humbly offered to Consideration, why the Incorporating the whole Trade of the Woollen Manufactures of this Kingdom to the Company called the Merchant-Adventurers of England, is and will prove more and more detrimental as to the Country in general, so especially to the County of Devon, and City of Exon* (1662); *From the City of Exon: A second Remonstrance declaring the continual decay of Trade, occasioned by the power of the Company of Merchant Adventurers* (1662).

[40] For the renewed charter, see TNA, SP 29/27. For the customs house powers, see CTB 1660–67, pp. 140–1.

radical.[41] The result was a 'temporary indulgence' for interlopers trading in woollens from 20 May to 25 December 1662, though Dordrecht and Hamburg were reserved for the Company.[42] When this was formally ended by another proclamation in April 1663, admission to the Company was opened to mere merchants for just £13 6s. 8d., with shopkeepers in the outports also permitted to join.[43] Such sums were clearly intended to be affordable to all English merchants, who were to have access to the Company's privileges in the mart towns at the cost of obeying its regulations.

This was a reform that the Company generally embraced, presenting itself as a national organization whose main task was to keep the cloth trade in English hands. In fact, the competition of non-English merchants had been a source of growing concern to the Company since the early 1660s, when certain citizens of Hamburg with the support of the Senate had begun to assert their right to directly import woollens to the city.[44] The Company's complaints about this yielded a favourable proclamation in May 1665 that specifically prohibited this trade.[45] The Company's hand had been strengthened by the recent outbreak of the second Anglo-Dutch war, following which the government feared that the close links between Hamburg and the Netherlands would be exploited by Dutch ships sailing under Hamburg flags.[46] This conflict also soured relations between the Company and the rulers of Hamburg. When in August 1666 a fleet of six English ships returning from Hamburg was destroyed by the Dutch near to the city, the Company was quick to pin blame on its hosts for failing to offer protection.[47] Richard Twyford, one of those who had suffered losses, commented that 'the Hamburgers have discovered themselves reall Hollanders in theire hearts'.[48]

Unfortunately for the Company, the depressed state of trade during the war, combined with the effects of the plague in London, provided the interlopers (again led by Kiffin) with an opportunity to successfully lobby for another period of free trade, from April 1666 to December 1667.[49] The fact that this was not ended by any proclamation, combined with the uncertain status of the Company's

---

[41] Orme (ed.), *Remarkable Passages in the Life of William Kiffin*, pp. 32–6; CJ, VIII, pp. 399–400; TNA, PC 2/55, pp. 598, 603.

[42] TNA, PC 2/55, p. 620; *A Proclamation for the free Exportation of Woollen Manufactures of this Kingdom* (14 May 1662).

[43] *A Proclamation declaring a former Proclamation of the Fourteenth of May last to be void* (8 Apr. 1663).

[44] Newman, 'Anglo-Hamburg trade', pp. 274–7; C. Brinkmann, 'England and the Hanse under Charles II', *English Historical Review* 23, 92 (1908), pp. 683–708.

[45] *A Proclamation for the better Ordering the Transportation of Clothes*, 10 May 1665, TNA, SP 29/121, fol. 16.

[46] Sir William Swann–Sir Joseph Williamson, 14 Mar. 1665, TNA, SP 82/10, fol. 223.

[47] Brinkmann, 'England and the Hanse', pp. 696–700.

[48] Richard Twyford–William Attwood, 22 Sept. 1666, C190/23.

[49] TNA, PC 2/58, pp. 373, 382, 386, 400; *A Proclamation for the Free Exportation of Woollen Manufactures until the 25th day of December next* (15 Apr. 1666); PC 2/59, pp. 201, 207; *A Proclamation for the Free Exportation of Woollen Manufactures until the 25th day of December next* (29 Mar. 1667).

privileges in the Netherlands, ensured that interloping to the latter continued unabated.[50] The Privy Council now attempted to broker an agreement whereby the interlopers would finally accept Company government, Kiffin again playing a key role in negotiations, though the resistance of the Exeter merchants put paid to this latest attempt at comprehension.[51]

As well as objecting to the regulations that they would be subjected to (particularly the obligation to trade to Dordrecht), interlopers had another reason to resist such attempts at incorporation, namely the debt liability that the Company was burdened with, and which by the Restoration was prompting crisis in its ranks.[52] The Company's increasing need to pay for its privileges in the form of loans to the state since the end of the Cokayne Project meant that by 1664 it had accrued a debt of £75,113 13s. By then it had ceased regular payments to its creditors, who responded with a series of petitions, attempted parliamentary bills, and legal suits. Paradoxically, this made the Company's creditors one of the few parties with a vested interest in its survival, this being the only realistic means whereby they might recover their debts. However, the normal means by which the Company raised money, through impositions on exported cloth, was politically unacceptable in a time of falling exports. The rival solutions of the creditors and the Company took the form of two bills presented to Parliament in 1664, with the Company seeking to raise money through a charge on all imports into England from Germany and the Netherlands, whether by denizens or strangers, and the creditors proposing a tax on the wealth of members proportionate to their total cloth exports since 1634.[53] Only the latter received a second hearing in the Commons, though this was ultimately voted down.[54]

The Company's increasing willingness to admit members for nominal sums in the 1660s should be understood in the context of needing to find new ways to meet its debts, and in both 1668 and 1674 it formally offered to admit all English subjects on the proviso that it was permitted to raise money on imports. Reflecting the challenges that the Company had faced from places like Exeter and Hull, it also promised to allow self-government for each individual residence, with the only requirement being to send goods to the mart towns.[55] These proposals were accompanied by offers to resign its charter, which in any case, the Company argued, its members had been 'weaned from' in the years of free trade.[56]

This, at least, was the position taken by the London residence, whose members were most immediately at risk from the attempts of the Company's creditors to

[50] Petition, Merchant Adventurers to the king, 6 May 1670, TNA, SP 29/275, fol. 103.

[51] Attorney General Finch's report on negotiations, 17 June 1670, TNA, SP 29/276, fol. 183; PC 2/62, pp. 196, 320, 341.

[52] Newman, 'Anglo-Hamburg trade', pp. 248–57.

[53] Attwood–Watson, 25 Apr. 1664, TNA, C109/23 (1663–6 letterbook); HMC 8th report, #310; Draft copy of the Company's bill, TNA, SP 29/106, fol. 106.

[54] CJ, VIII, pp. 535–6; 577–8; 580–1.   [55] HMC 9th report, #186.

[56] Petition, Merchant Adventurers to the king, 19 Nov. 1674, TNA, SP 29/360, fol. 205.

recover their debts from their personal estates.[57] The membership in Hamburg, however, seem to have been rather dismayed about the London residence's lukewarm efforts to uphold their privileges. In 1665 William Attwood's correspondent George Watson expressed his concern about 'our Company affaires so much neglected with you'.[58] When, following the suspension of its privileges in April 1666, the London court proposed that the Hamburg residence should cut costs and 'keepe uppe only a face of government & that each should residence should beare its owne charge', with all Company impositions to be henceforth suspended, Richard Twyford of Hamburg reacted with alarm.[59] He complained to William Attwood that 'this Modell...hath beene layd by some restlesse spirit nowe with you, together with the helpe of some particuler private penns from hence, soe that it beginnes to appeare that nothing will serve some men but the ruine of the Company with the losse of all our priviledges'. Twyford's language reveals how the Company's German residence considered itself to have been abandoned by the London court:

> for I suppose if your Company will not stand by us here I believe they will finde this Company here to preserve the priviledges of the Company by some other meanes...I desire that you would be pleased as a faithfull member to endeavor the support of the Company & not to suffer it to be rent in pieces by some whoe I feare are not soe mindfull of the Oath they tooke at theire admission as they ought to be.

Attwood could only reply that, although he spoke against the proposal in court, 'a parlament man (one of the Company too) a very understanding man tould me not long scince that our Company could never answer it to the parlament, our laying such a Charge upon the Comodities of the kingdome and not paying of any of the debt of the Company'.[60]

The gulf between Hamburg and London that Twyford's letter signalled was an ill omen of the internal contests that would plague the Company throughout the 1680s. However, paradoxically these contests coincided with a revival in the Company's political fortunes that promised to reverse the deterioration it had experienced during the early years of the Restoration. The idea of a national incorporation, embraced in a context of desperation in the 1660s, now became the grounds for what was hoped would be a newly revived Company that would continue to act as custodian of the nation's staple export, and keep it out of the hands of the foreigner.

---

[57] See, for instance, *Merchant Adventurers* v. *Susan Battailhe, John Woodhall, and John Banckes*, 1676, TNA, C8/270/50.
[58] Watson–Attwood, 17 Jan. 1665, TNA, C109/23.
[59] Twyford–Attwood, 12 May 1666, TNA, C109/23.
[60] Attwood–Twyford, 1 June 1666, TNA, C109/23 (1663–6 letterbook).

'Soe Nactionall a Concerne': The 1683 Proclamation and Its Aftermath

The nadir in the Company's fortunes in the first two decades of the Restoration was paralleled by a fall in the number of baptisms in the Company's church at Hamburg, which dropped to an average of 5.6 per year from 1660 to 1679, compared to 9.6 for the previous twenty years.[61] Just one child was baptized in 1670. The Hamburg church book does not record new communicants after 1665, but the average number of new males joining the church per year from 1660 to 1665 fell below four, compared to over twelve in the early 1630s. Only fourteen marriages were registered from 1660 to 1679, compared to twenty-one for the period 1640–59 and forty-one for 1620–39. Together these data suggest a diminishing number of new entrants to the merchant community in Hamburg. However, the early 1680s witnessed something of an upturn of baptismal rates (6.5 per year from 1680 to 1685, compared to 3.5 for the 1670s). Marriage rates also saw a modest rise. Whilst not being pronounced enough to suggest a major influx of new members, these trends might indicate a slight upturn in the number of merchants who considered Hamburg a propitious place to establish their households.

This partial demographic recovery at Hamburg was mirrored by an improvement in the Company's political fortunes, centred on *A Proclamation for the better Ordering and Transportation of Cloths and other Woollen Manufactures into Germany and preventing the Encroachments on the Fellowship of Merchants-Adventurers of England in relation to their Trading in those Commodities*, dated 13 June 1683. Although the title only mentioned Germany, the proclamation itself was clear that its provisos extended to the Netherlands as well. Like the 1665 proclamation, the focus was on foreigners guilty of intruding into the export of woollens, notably those 'to whom We have extended Our Grace and favour of Naturalisation or Endenization'. Once again the principle of liberal admission for all qualified English subjects (i.e. mere merchants) for the nominal entrance fee of £13 6s. 8d. was confirmed. The export of England's national staple was to remain in English hands.

The Company had drawn the attention of the Privy Council to the intrusions of largely foreign-born merchants exporting woollens to Germany, and particularly to Hamburg's rival port of Bremen, in a petition from August 1682.[62] According to the 1677 London port book for old drapery exports, twenty-one denizens exported just under 1,000 notional shortcloths in total to Bremen, compared to 5,654 to Hamburg, damaging competition in the context of the falling

---

[61] Hamburg Register. See also Figures 1.1–1.3 in Chapter 1.
[62] Merchant Adventurers to the king, 20 Aug. 1682, TNA, SP 29/420, fol. 33. See Margrit Schulte Beerbühl, *The Forgotten Majority: German Merchants in London, Naturalization, and Global Trade, 1660–1815*, trans. Cynthia Klohr (New York, 2015), pp. 52–6.

volume of sales.[63] The Company's complaints to the Privy Council singled out five individuals, whose actions were presented as an attack not so much on the Company's monopoly, as on the 'many nationall Priviledges' which it had won overseas. This was also a matter of royal honour: by disobeying the king's proclamations of 1663 and 1665, the royal prerogative had been 'brought into publique Controversy and Question even by Strangers'. Although the Privy Council reprimanded the accused individuals, early in the following year the Company and these interlopers were locked in a legal battle in the Court of King's Bench, wherein, the Company complained, their charters were brought into question 'by a sort of men who are factors for Aliens, and contrive to divert the Trade from English into forreigne hands'.[64] After another hearing before the Privy Council, the matter was referred to the Committee for Trade and Foreign Plantations, which, having failed to persuade the interlopers to join the Company, eventually reported in the Company's favour, adding the suggestion that any future letters of denization should be conditional on the recipients respecting trading company charters.[65] The Company's request to have its rivals banished from the kingdom (which had been the fate of a Hamburger resident in England, Georg Otto, accused of the same thing in 1674) was not successful. However, the proclamation that followed in June still came as a relief to the Company's members at Hamburg, and the number exporting old draperies to Bremen from London in that year fell to five.[66]

The passage of this act represented a political realignment between the Company and the crown after several years of lukewarm relations. Just as the Company had been able to rely on anti-Dutch sentiment in 1665 to win the government's support, so in 1683 the Company could draw on concerns about foreign threats, though this time they were more closely linked to domestic political disturbances. The Exclusion Crisis and Rye House Plot had led to a new wave of English exiles on the continent, whom the crown feared were plotting in collaboration with hostile powers overseas. Embarrassingly for the Company at Hamburg, one of its members, Thomas Shepherd, had been implicated in the Rye House Plot.[67] The fact that the Whig sheriff of London, Slingsby Bethel, was a former member had also not been forgotten.[68] However, this political context also provided the Company with an opportunity to present itself as a bastion of loyalism and its membership as free from foreign contagion, in contrast to those subjects of the crown who had become burghers of Hamburg and other Hanseatic

[63] TNA, E190/67/2.
[64] PC 2/69, p. 669; TNA, SP 44/66, fol. 130; Bevil Skelton–William Blathwayt, 8 Sept. 1682, BL, Add. 37984, fol. 40.
[65] CO 389/11, pp. 339–44; PC 2/70, p. 4.
[66] Skelton–Earl of Sunderland, 27 Apr. 1683, BL, Add. 41824, fol. 70; TNA, E190/141/1.
[67] Skelton–Earl of Sunderland, 7 Aug. 1683, BL, Add. 41824, fol. 97.
[68] Skelton–Blathwayt, 9 Feb. 1682, BL, Add. 37983, fol. 58r.

cities, and who thereby had become 'the bitterest Ennemyys, not onely to the Government, but to all their Countrymen in generall'.[69] The Company paid most attention to the exiled Whig politician Sir William Waller, who had arrived in Bremen with a promise to bring over a number of British exiles skilled in the cloth industry.[70] The Hamburg residence seized on this to emphasize the value of English expatriates being under Company government, a means to uphold English identity as well as loyalty to the crown, preventing the danger of assimilation into a foreign culture. Following James II's accession, the crown's resident in Hamburg, Sir Peter Wyche, made a direct request to the Senate of Hamburg that it cease granting burgher status to any subjects of the crown without notifying him first, which he framed as being made on behalf of 'the considerable Colony of his subjects here, that they might enjoy the Privileges granted them by his Royal Charter'.[71]

Such cordial relations between the royal resident and the Hamburg court were quite a turnaround from the previous decade, when Sir William Swann had faced open contempt from many Hamburg Merchant Adventurers. Swann had arrived as resident in 1664 with instructions to purge the Hamburg court of any remnants of republicanism and nonconformity, including Richard Bradshaw's old antagonist, Francis Townley.[72] Although the majority took the oaths of allegiance and supremacy, as late as 1667 Swann complained of 'some factious persons' whose 'Gangrene' threatened to 'take through the whole body'.[73] In 1675 he described one of his critics, Samuel Free, as 'a person, whom I have spared this twelve yeares, in hopes of reducing him to conformity in our Church'.[74] Nonetheless, the affronts Swann was subjected to in the Company court, such as during the 1672 midsummer elections (discussed in Chapter 4), seem to have been largely prompted by resentment about an outsider occupying the role of deputy governor rather than any deep-seated attachment to the Presbyterian-style church structure that the Company had been forced to abandon in the 1660s. Charles II's inconsistent support for the Company can hardly have endeared its members to him or his resident. One Hamburg Merchant Adventurer was reported to have told Swann during the 1672 elections that 'we are a free companie we have nothinge to doe with a Courtier'.[75] Following Swann's death in 1678, he was replaced as deputy governor by the Hamburg secretary, Samuel Missenden, before a new resident could arrive, the members having allegedly resolved 'never more to be imposed upon by the Court (as they cal'd it) & not make choyce hereafter of any Minister the King should send but choose one of their owne members'.[76] This report was

[69] Bevil Skelton–Earl of Conway, 22 Dec. 1682, BL, Add. 41824, fol. 9.
[70] Bevil Skelton–Earl of Conway, 30 Nov. 1683, BL, Add. 41824, fol. 133; 11 Dec. 1683, fols 143–4.
[71] Sir Peter Wyche–Earl of Middleton, 2 June 1685, BL, Add. 41824, fol. 240v.
[72] Swann–Sir Henry Bennett, 1 Apr. 1664, TNA, SP 82/10, fol. 165.
[73] Swann to ?, 21 June 1667, TNA, SP 82/11, fol. 65.
[74] Swann–Coventry, 13 Sept. 1675, Coventry Papers 39, fol. 142r.
[75] Swann–Lord Arlington, 14 Oct. 1672, TNA, SP 82/11, fol. 211.
[76] Skelton–Blathwayt, 1 Sept. 1682, BL, Add. 37984, fol. 31r.

given by Bevil Skelton, who arrived as resident in 1682 and much resented not holding the post of deputy governor, which he saw as necessary 'That soe the members of the Compagny may have a more imediate dependance upon his Majestie'.[77] According to Skelton, however, the Hamburg residence was resolved 'to rather throwing up theire Charter then to have a Deputie imposed by the King', although he also claimed to have found 'very few that are taynted with Whiggisme'. Overall, he considered the Hamburg court to be in the grip of 'a cabal of 6 or 7 that carry all before them, for in their Court noe man speakes, but votes are given by holding up of hands, without arguing the justice of the case, soe that it often happens that things are carried when some of them whoe lifted up theire hands doe not know for what they voted, following onely the example of some of their ringleaders'.[78] Presiding over them was deputy Missenden, 'he carrying himself as an absolute sovraigne' not just over the Company, but over all subjects of the crown who arrived in Hamburg.[79]

Relations between Skelton and the Hamburg court, and particularly deputy Missenden, may have started badly, but the growing threat posed by Bremen, first as a rival destination to Hamburg for English woollens, and then as a centre of cloth making in its own right, seems to have brought the two parties together. In April 1683 Skelton wrote to the Earl of Sunderland in support of the Company's efforts against the interlopers, 'for besides the Justice of Theire cause, theire Loyalty & Zeale in promoting whatever is for his Majesties honor & service will I presume engage your Lordship to be kinde to them'.[80] Skelton also vigorously opposed the Burgomasters of Bremen's attempts to assert the right of their subjects to export woollens from England.[81] The Company at London went to further lengths to demonstrate its loyalist credentials by sponsoring the erection of a statue of Charles II in the Royal Exchange in 1684, and possibly also the publication of two loyalist sermons preached by its minister, Augustine Freezer, to the dwindling membership at Dordrecht, on the occasions of Charles II's death and the defeat of the Monmouth Rebellion.[82] News of the latter was celebrated in Hamburg, at a reception hosted by Skelton's successor, Wyche, for some fifty Merchant Adventurers, the festivities accompanied by 'by the noice of Trumpets, Kettle Drums, and Instruments very chearfully, the Guns from the English ships in Port keeping time with us'.[83]

---

[77] Skelton–Blathwayt, 26 Sept. 1682, BL, Add. 37984, fol. 55v.
[78] Skelton–Blathwayt, 8 Sept. 1682, BL, Add. 37984, fol. 40.
[79] Skelton–Blathwayt, 1 Sept. 1682, BL, Add. 37984, fol. 31.
[80] Skelton–Earl of Sunderland, 15 Apr. 1683, BL, Add. 41824, fol. 64v.
[81] Skelton to the Burgomasters of Bremen, 14 Mar. 1684, BL, Add. 41824, fol. 180.
[82] *The Divine Original and the Supreme Dignity of Kings, No defensative against Death* (Oxford and Rotterdam, 1685), and *The Wickedness and Punishment of Rebellion* (Rotterdam, 1686), which was dedicated to Skelton in his capacity as envoy to the United Provinces.
[83] Sir Peter Wyche–Earl of Middleton, 17 July 1685, BL, Add. 41824, fol. 270r.

By the mid-1680s, relations between crown and Company were arguably more cordial than at any time since before the Cokayne Project. However, translating this support into effective action against the interlopers was not straightforward. In June 1684 the Company exhibited a bill of complaint in Chancery against forty-five individuals who were accused of continuing to violate its charters in spite of the previous year's proclamation, by which 'all his Majestyes Loving subjects who were bred up in merchandize might come into the said trade & pertake of the benefitt thereof'.[84] Evidently serious efforts had been made to encourage interlopers to take up this option: the proclamation had been widely published, with a committee appointed to meet weekly at Founders Hall in London to admit new members, with equivalents in the outports. In spite of this, the defendants in the case were alleged to have 'privately entred into a Combinacion with severall Forreigne merchants to interrupt & disturb the trade of your orators & to invade the same in Contempt of the said severall Letters Pattents'. The consequence would be to 'carry the said trade into the hands of the said Forreigners & to make them sole masters thereof'.

Other ill effects promised to follow from this foreign usurpation of the nation's staple trade. The abandonment of the mart towns would 'undermine the Foundations & Advantages of Comerce, which your Orators have procured & settled in those parts', which would have the effect of 'destroying soe Nationall a Concerne as the said Trade is for a little present gaine to themselves'. These interlopers had also 'debased the Creditt & suncke the reputacion which the English woollen manufactures exported by your orators had obteyned abroad', to the detriment of the Company's own market. This failure to maintain standards of quality that the Company prided itself upon was partly because of the identity of the forty-five individuals named in the bill. They included a mixture of naturalized aliens (amongst them, several of those whom the Company had accused of trading to Bremen in 1682–3), and English merchants and shipmasters, but also several Englishmen, who, the bill complained, were not 'bred merchants but are tuckers weavers Fullers Packers Dyers & Hatpressers & such like Artificiers employed in the makeing ordering & dressing the said woollen manufactures who merely to gaine the Custome & employment of the said Forreigne shopkeepers & Retaylors doe send them great quantities of the said woollen manufactures'. This direct contact between clothworkers and foreign retailers was a fundamental threat to the position of the Merchant Adventurers, as well as (the Company argued) to the reputation of English cloth: clothworkers could not be trusted to uphold the quality of their own products. Furthermore, the bill alleged, the actions of the interlopers went hand-in-hand with the efforts of Bremen to

[84] TNA, C6/419/110.

promote its own cloth-making industry, using English workers who had been 'drawne from that Duty & allegiance which they owe to their Kinge & Kingdome'.

Many of the tropes that the bill deployed can be found in Company apologia stretching back throughout its history, such as the claim that the Company was responsible for maintaining the reputation of English cloth. But one important difference was that, whereas traditionally interlopers were represented as rather isolated figures whose disorderly manner of trade would ultimately be their undoing, the antithesis of the Company's own ordered commerce, here the Company presented itself as facing a much more organized, and sinister, conspiracy. This extended to the alleged establishment of 'a common purse' to carry out their trade and answer any legal suits. The bill thus requested a full investigation of their affairs over the last two years.

Answers for about half of the defendants survive, and unsurprisingly given that many of the parties were represented by the same legal counsel, they have much in common.[85] Some simply denied any involvement in the export of woollens, such as those of William and Benjamin Palmer (both Thames watermen), Hugbert Dunbaes and Arthur Rowlands (shipmasters trading to the Netherlands), and William How (another shipmaster, of Tiverton).[86] Four shipmasters of the Hodder family of Topsham in Devon admitted to having occasionally transported woollens to Rotterdam, but pleaded ignorance as to whether they belonged to members of the Company or not; Paul Bendix made the same answer regarding his shipments to Hamburg.[87] The merchants John Elwill, Thomas Crispin, Arthur Scolar, John Foxwell, Thomas Townesend, Thomas Heath Jr, and Matthew How could not deny involvement in the export of woollens themselves, and so their joint answer asserted the legality of their trade, arguing that 'any of his Majesties subiects of this his Realme that are Merchants Adventurers or Traders as merchants may as these defendants are advised trade to any place of the world in amity with the Crowne...notwithstanding any the Charters' granted to the Company.[88] The very title 'Merchant Adventurer' could be claimed by any practising English merchant, therefore. Citing legal precedents such as Edward III's statute declaring the freedom of the seas to merchants, and James I's statute of monopolies, the answer asserted that any 'such Restraint is contrary to the auncient & fundamentall Laws of this Realme & tendeth to the establishing a Monopoly in the plaintiffs & is voyd in Law'. Other accusations against them, such

---

[85] Of the defendants for whom answers have not been located, several were naturalized German/ Flemish subjects.

[86] Answer of Hugbert Dunbaes and Arthur Rowlands, TNA, C5/83/49; Answer of William and Benjamin Palmer, TNA, C7/105/50; Answer of William How, TNA, C7/106/8.

[87] Answer of George Hodder the elder, George Hodder the younger, Edward Hodder, and Joseph Hodder, TNA, C7/106/8; Answer of Paul Bendix, TNA, C7/105/50.

[88] TNA, C7/106/8. Crispin and Elwill were leading serge exporters from Exeter in 1676, along with a Thomas Heath, so this group were probably all Exeter merchants. Stephens, *Seventeenth-Century Exeter*, p. 179.

as entering into a combination with strangers or promoting the establishment of woollen manufacturing in Bremen or Emden, were dismissed as a 'perfect fiction'.

Another English merchant, John Rebow of Colchester, provided a very similar answer.[89] The answer of David de Barry and John Martens Elkins, both naturalized foreigners, also followed this template, only adding that their naturalization made them entitled to all privileges of natural born subjects; Elkins also asserted his identity as one 'bred a Merchant Adventurer'.[90] Another naturalized merchant, James Rallyard, who was Swiss born and based in Exeter, departed from this formula somewhat, however.[91] His answer argued that the Company had 'Extended their priviledges beyond what was Intended them by their first Charter...And though they style themselves the Governour Assistants and fellowshipp of Merchant Adventurers of England as if ther were none besides, yet he hath heard they have a narrower Tytle or Appellation and are knowne by the name the Hamborough Company'. Whilst conceding that they might reasonably have a claim to manage the woollen trade there, it would be impossible for any corporation to extend its government over the many towns of the Low Countries. Furthermore, the answer claimed, as it was a regulated rather than a joint stock company, every member 'may Endeavour to Endersell One the other and alsoe to sell worse clothes', giving the lie to their claimed ability to maintain the price of English cloth. Moreover, the Company's charters predated the rise of the new draperies, which had grown in number precisely because of free trade. However, despite these assertions Rallyard claimed to have forgone trade since the 1683 proclamation, preferring not to join the Company because of the risk of becoming liable for its debt.

Whatever the outcome of this particular case, two years later the Company again complained to the Privy Council of the 'secret Practices of Interlopers'.[92] Although the Company singled out one English merchant, William Browne, it focused on naturalized foreigners trading to Bremen, again led by Elkins, who eventually submitted to the Privy Council's demands that he cease trading in November 1686.[93] Old drapery exports to Bremen from London in 1687 were virtually nil.[94] Perhaps buoyed by this success, in February the Company petitioned against the remitting of alien duties on woollens, something it appears to have failed to do when Parliament passed the act in question in 1673.[95] Interloping to the Netherlands proved to be more obdurate than to Bremen, however, and in 1687 the Company launched a suit against John Rebow of Colchester in the Court of King's Bench. This action might have been prompted by the East India Company's successful prosecution of the interloper Thomas Sandys in King's

[89] TNA, C7/105/50.
[90] Answer of David de Barry, John Martens Elkins, James West, TNA, C7/105/50.
[91] TNA, C6/419/110.
[92] TNA, PC 2/71, p. 324.   [93] TNA, PC 2/71, pp. 326, 331, 334.   [94] TNA, E190/141/2.
[95] TNA, PC 2/71, p. 400.

Bench, in 1685. The Company's counsel included the prosecutors of this case, Heneage Finch and Sir John Holt, whilst Rebow employed Sandys' defender Henry Pollexfen, making it something of a sequel.[96] The Company probably hoped to capitalize on the increasingly politicized nature of the contest over monopolies in the 1680s, and the crown's increasing identification with the trading companies.[97] An anonymous manuscript note from the time suggested the production of 'Some lettre to the Judges to recomend the dispatch of the Hamboro Company cause as relating to the Kings prerogative in the consequence thereof, as was done in the East India Companie cause about Interlopers', or failing that a direct intervention by the king with the judges.[98]

The prosecution's strategy against Rebow was to cast the case as hinging on the king's prerogative power to 'restrain his subjects from trading to particular places'.[99] Rather than directly contest this, Pollexfen countered by questioning the point that 'the King can make such a grant excluding all others from trading', drawing on the 1497 statute opening up the Company's marts to all Englishmen, as well as common law precedents against engrossing and monopolizing. In response, the defence argued that 'In our case the liberty of the subject is not taken away, for one that is skilful in the trade, may demand to be made free of a company.' Pollexfen countered that 'The corporation is not compellable to admit all persons; but admitting that, yet tis impossible that all should meet; and so the merchants of London, which is most likely to be the place of meeting, will by consequences govern the estates, &c, of the rest of the company.' In a reversal of his argument in the Sandys case, then, Pollexfen argued that the regulated form of the Company precluded it from being genuinely inclusive, on practical grounds which made it impossible for all members to meet and would invariably favour some members over others.[100] In fact, Pollexfen adroitly exploited the decision against him in the Sandys case, arguing that the victory of the East India Company was based on the king's right to prohibit trade with infidels, 'for they who argued then did admit, that if the grant to that company had restrained the subjects from trading to Christian countries, it had been void'. His strategy seems to have been successful on this occasion, for the case appears not to have come to a judgement.

The failure of this case is indicative of how legal objections could still outweigh political support. The Company's strategy of emphasizing its openness to all

[96] This case has recently been discussed in Edward Cavanagh, 'Infidels in English Legal Thought: Conquest, Commerce and Slavery in the Common Law from Coke to Mansfield, 1603–1793', *Modern Intellectual History* 16 (2019), p. 400.

[97] Steve Pincus, *1688: The First Modern Revolution* (New Haven and London, 2009), pp. 372–81.

[98] BL, Add. 41806, fol. 230r.

[99] Thomas Leach, *Modern Reports, or Select Cases, Adjudged in the Court of King's Bench, Chancery, Common Pleas and Exchequer*, III, fifth edition (London, 1793), case 87.

[100] William A. Pettigrew and Tristan Stein, 'The public rivalry between regulated and joint stock corporations and the development of seventeenth-century corporate constitutions', *Historical Research* 90 (2017), pp. 355–6.

English merchants, as well as its capacity to exclude foreigners from participation in the cloth trade, had won the support of an increasingly embattled crown, which was particularly worried about foreign threats and the allegiances of its subjects overseas. This was not dissimilar to the strategy deployed by the East India Company before and after the Glorious Revolution. However, Pollexfen's astute differentiation of trade to Christian Europe from that of others operating within the territories of 'infidels' exposed the limitations of this strategy. The extent of cooperation between English clothworkers and foreign buyers, exposed by the 1684 Chancery case, demonstrated a reality of cross-national cooperation outside of corporate trading structures, which made it harder to cast foreign merchants, naturalized or otherwise, as a threat. Underlying this was the unresolved ambiguity regarding the Company's monopoly, which provided plentiful legal precedents which interlopers could use in their favour. Perhaps this is why the Company surrendered its charter on the accession of James II, in the hope of receiving a new one which might more clearly define its authority. But the context for this was not only the Company's attempts to reassert its monopoly. The prospect of a new charter also became embroiled in a contest that had divided the Company's ranks for almost two decades, and which now threatened to reverse the political gains made since 1683.

'The strange arbitrary power of the Company's proceedings': The Fellowship Divided

The growing cordiality between the Merchant Adventurers and the crown was cemented in 1684, when it selected a governor with impeccable Tory credentials (although no obvious prior connections to the Company), namely Laurence Hyde, Earl of Rochester, who would soon become James II's Lord Treasurer. The Company appeared well set then to continue the process of political rebuilding under a king who was if anything a more enthusiastic supporter of monopoly companies than his predecessor had been.[101] However, just a month after its members had celebrated the defeat of Monmouth's Rebellion, the Hamburg court under deputy Samuel Missenden wrote a letter to Rochester that revealed the existence of a schism in the Company's ranks that cast a shadow over its recent revival.[102] The issue that brought the division into the open was the decision of the Hamburg court to select as the London deputy governor one Sir Edward Dering, half-brother of the recently deceased governor (also called Sir Edward). Although the choice of London deputy was the prerogative of the Hamburg court,

---

[101] Francis Stratford–[Earl of Middleton?], 12 May 1685, BL, Add. 41824, fol. 231r.
[102] Hamburg Merchant Adventurers to Governor Rochester, 28 Aug. 1685, BL, Add. 15898, fol. 135.

this decision had prompted an angry reaction from many London-based Merchant Adventurers, twenty-seven of whom had written to Hamburg announcing their refusal to accept Dering as their deputy without order from Rochester.[103] This group included several of London's leading old drapery exporters. Heading the signatories was the London treasurer, John Hide, but perhaps more significant in understanding the ramifications of this contest was the second name to appear, that of John Banckes.

As discussed in Chapter 4, Banckes had been a controversial figure in the Company since at least 1672, when he had used the threat of the outbreak of the third Anglo-Dutch war as a pretext to have his packs of stuffs sent to the Leipzig mart. The Hamburg residence responded by prosecuting Banckes' agents, his brothers Charles and James, for violating Company rules against straggling beyond the mart town. This dispute was also instrumental in the Hamburg court's decision in 1675 to deselect its governor, Sir Richard Ford, who along with Sir William Swann was a keen supporter of Banckes' case. Ford had been chosen in 1660, probably due to his royalist credentials during the previous two decades, though it was reported that the Company's preference had been for William Attwood's former partner Walter Pell who, unlike Ford, was a former Hamburg resident with close links within its merchant community.[104] Ford's background, by contrast, was in the Dutch branch of the Company's trade, and in the 1640s he had been amongst those Merchant Adventurers at Rotterdam conspiring on behalf of the crown, although he eventually compounded with the Commonwealth.[105] His chequered career in the interregnum did not prevent Ford from winning the patronage of the Duke of York, and he went on to be a significant figure in the Company of Royal Adventurers Trading to Africa, and the East India Company, as well as an MP and Lord Mayor of London, 'perhaps the single most powerful merchant in Restoration London'.[106] Whilst Ford's political connections made him the ideal figurehead for a Company needing to draw a veil over its previous support for Parliament, his broad commercial interests and lack of familiarity amongst the Hamburg community meant that he was not necessarily the ideal spokesman for the majority of members, who were now focusing their trade on Germany. Ford's background was also potentially problematic: he was the son of an Exeter Merchant Adventurer who had pioneered

---

[103] Ibid., fols 131–2.

[104] Edward Halford–William Attwood, 26 June 1660, TNA, C109/24.

[105] M. W. Helms and Paula Watson, 'FORD, Sir Richard (c.1614–78), of Seething Lane, London, and Baldwins, Dartford, Kent', in B. D. Henning (ed.), *The History of Parliament: The House of Commons 1660–1690* (1983), online edition [https://www.historyofparliamentonline.org/volume/1660-1690/member/ford-sir-richard-1614-78].

[106] Steven C. A. Pincus, *Protestantism and Patriotism: Ideologies and the Making of English Foreign Policy, 1650–1688* (Cambridge, 1996), p. 249.

the direct export of woollens from Exeter to the Netherlands in the 1630s, much to the chagrin of the London court.[107]

The Company's desperate political plight throughout much of the 1660s probably did little to convince sceptical members that Ford was representing the Company effectively. Ford's tendency to put his other commercial interests before that of the Company was shown by his enthusiastic support for launching a second war against the Dutch, who were rivals to the Africa Company, although this conflict caused serious difficulties for the Merchant Adventurers at Hamburg.[108] Some of the latter also held Ford culpable for the handling of the suit against the city of Hamburg following the burning of the Company's fleet by the Dutch in 1666. In 1670, the crown threatened Hamburg with letters of marque due to its refusal to pay reparations.[109] Thomas Scott of Hamburg reported that many of the Company were 'much startled att the proceeding in England against this Towne':

here we heare our Governor has been too much active in driving on the business For the Intresents & if he did what he hath done in the name of the Companie I see not how he Can answer itt. its most Sure if this Towne had that vnreasonable demand our privilidges in Germanie are gone & wee heare none of the Companie with you regard it. but lett the Governor & those intresed in the burnt ships doe what they please and with the companies money drive on the Companies ruine for theire private gaine, and unconscionably force restitution of that which this Towne never tooke from them nor Could hinder those which did itt. if they goe on we shall here not be secure, either our persons or goods. Scarce ever was the like knowne to give letters of mark out against a people in midst of whom we are seated & stil doe Continew to send shiping weekely[110]

Although some of these 'Intresents' were based in Hamburg, including Richard Twyford, most of the claimants were London-based merchants. Amongst them were John Banckes, who had been co-owner of one of the destroyed ships whilst resident in Hamburg, which he had left in 1669. Banckes and Ford had a long history together by then, the former having acted as Ford's Hamburg agent in the purchase of linen in 1653.[111] This connection might have been the reason why Banckes briefly acted as Hamburg agent of the East India Company in 1658.[112]

By the time of the 1675 midsummer elections, the Hamburg merchants had many reasons to believe Ford was 'negligent of the Companyes affaires', but his

---

[107] Stephens, *Seventeenth-Century Exeter*, pp. 31–2.
[108] Pincus, *Protestantism and Patriotism*, pp. 247–50.
[109] Brinkmann, 'England and the Hanse', p. 700.
[110] Scott–Attwood, 27 Aug. 1670, TNA, C109/20.
[111] http://www.marinelives.org/wiki/HCA_13/68_f.246v_Annotate. I thank Colin Greenstreet of Marine Lives for providing access to this resource.
[112] E. B. Sainsbury (ed.), *A Calendar of the Court Minutes etc. of the East India Company 1655–1659* (Oxford, 1916), pp. 233, 237, 257.

support for Banckes was particularly damaging.[113] Hostility to Ford was not confined to the Hamburg membership, however. Several members of the London court heartily endorsed Ford's de-selection, amongst them John Sanford, who urged the Hamburg court to proceed in its own choice of governor, without waiting for a nomination from London (the position having been turned down by Hamburg's initial choice, Rowland Wynne).[114] Anticipating that Banckes and his allies would be lobbying for Ford's restoration, Sanford's party approached statesmen such as Sir Joseph Williamson, presenting the issue in terms of the Company's 'liberty to exercise our privileges in the manidgment of our affaires & government according to his royall charter'.[115] Ford was supported in Hamburg by deputy Swann, and Sanford advised his Hamburg correspondent Francis Stratford that if Swann did 'not act according to his oath & duty I thinck you did not the Company right if you did not displace him'.[116]

By August a suitable alternative candidate as governor had been located, in the form of Sir Edward Dering, a well-connected MP whose half-brother was a member of the Company. When the Hamburg court eventually endorsed this choice, Sanford poured praise on Stratford and his allies: 'you have behaved your selves like brave old Romans & true Englishmen for which you deserve to have your names recorded in Golden letter having defend the truth stood up for the maintenances of our priviledges & made choise of a worthy Person'.[117] Sanford himself led the delegation of thirteen members who visited Dering on 14 September, in order (as Dering described in his autobiography) to 'entreat me to accept of the name of Governor of the Hamburgh companies, I having been unanimously chosen to it by the companie there', a half-truth at best given the attitude of deputy Swann.[118] Dering was clearly surprised at the invitation, 'being utterly a stranger to every one at Hamburgh, and ... very unwilling to ingage in a businesse I understood not, but their importunitie and my good nature prevailed'.[119] He was thus chosen for his very inexperience of the Company's contested politics, making him all the more fitting a figurehead for the now dominant group: as Sanford put it, although he 'be not verst in our affares yet may sooner be informed by the assistance of an able deputy'.[120] Dering continued in the role until his death in 1684, 'though new elected every year at Hamburgh upon Midsumer day'.[121]

Ford's connections with the court and the republican language with which Sanford eulogized the actions of the Hamburg Fellowship, as well as the alleged nonconformity of some of Swann's critics in Hamburg, might suggest that this

---

[113] Swann–Coventry, 13 Sept. 1675, Coventry Papers, 39, fol. 141r.
[114] Sanford–Francis Stratford, 23 July 1675, SRO, DD\SF/7/2/1.
[115] Sanford–Stratford, 30 July 1675, ibid.   [116] Sanford–Stratford, 27 July 1675, ibid.
[117] Sanford–Stratford, 31 Aug. 1675, ibid.
[118] Maurice F. Bond (ed.), *The Diaries and Papers of Sir Edward Dering Second Baronet 1644 to 1684* (London: House of Lords Record Office Occasional Publications No. 1, 1976), p. 113.
[119] Ibid., pp. 113–14.   [120] Sanford–Stratford, 31 Aug. 1675, SRO, DD\SF/7/2/1.
[121] Bond (ed.), *Diaries and Papers of Sir Edward Dering*, p. 147.

contest had become implicated in the increasingly polarized political situation in England over the spectre of 'popery and arbitrary government'. However, the choice of Dering, a supporter of the Earl of Danby, suggests otherwise, whilst Sanford (despite the Presbyterianism of his father-in-law Lucy Knightley) would go on to act as Tory MP for Taunton, and Francis Stratford was later rumoured to be have questioned the legitimacy of the accession of William and Mary.[122] Following Ford's defeat, Sanford took up the position of London treasurer, and the grip of his allies at Hamburg was strengthened when Stratford successfully called for Charles and James Banckes to be ejected as court assistants, on the grounds that the Company's rules barred bankrupts and perjured men from holding office.[123] John Banckes was adamant that this baseless claim was simply revenge for their support of Ford.[124] In London, the Company pursued its vendetta against Banckes at the Court of Chancery, alleging in a bill of complaint that he had combined with some of its creditors to recover their debts from the personal estates of London members.[125] Faced with such opposition and the wavering support of his superiors at Whitehall, Swann now accommodated himself to the dominant faction, endorsing their continued attempts to prosecute Banckes for his earlier violations.[126]

As well as concerns about the integrity of the Company's regulatory regime, it is possible that more pecuniary motives had played a part in Ford's de-selection. Several of the leading London members were at this point preoccupied with sharing the spoils finally gained from the Senate of Hamburg in compensation for the 1666 burnt ships, which amounted to £35,000. The largest claimant was Governor Dering's half-brother Edward, and it was alleged by one of the interested parties (the Whig shipowner Sir John Shorter) that the commissioners engaged to distribute the sums, Dering amongst them, had paid out several inflated gratuities to their supporters, including £250 to Missenden.[127] Banckes, though a commissioner himself, sided with Shorter in the dispute.[128]

Even so, there is evidence that following Ford's defeat the Company did embark on a campaign to tighten up its regulatory regime and improve its finances.

---

[122] Irene Cassidy/Basil Duke Henning, 'SANFORD, John (1640–1711), of Basinghall Street, London and Nynehead Court, Som', in B. D. Henning (ed.), *The History of Parliament: The House of Commons 1660–1690* (1983), online edition [https://www.historyofparliamentonline.org/volume/1660-1690/member/sanford-john-1640-1711]; Sir Paul Rycaut–Sir William Holt, 18 Feb. 1691, BL, Lansdowne 1153 III, fols 57–8.

[123] Swann–Sir Joseph Williamson, 29 Dec. 1675, TNA, SP 82/13, fols 193–4.

[124] 'Banckes case with the Hambro Company at the Counceill board', 7 Apr. 1676, BL, Egerton 3357, fols 9–10.

[125] *Merchant Adventurers v. Susan Battailhe, John Woodhall, and John Banckes*, 1676, TNA, C8/270/50. Oddly, however, some of those members named as the complainants were Banckes' allies, including his brother James.

[126] Swann–Williamson, 28 July 1676, TNA, SP 82/13, fol. 89.

[127] Report on Sir John Shorter's case, 31 May 1676, TNA, SP 29/381, fol. 268.

[128] TNA, CO 389/11, pp. 22–9.

Banckes complained of certain 'by-laws' being passed at Hamburg that were prejudicial to his trade, including the charging of impositions on the import of bullion into England, on goods imported to England from outside the mart town, and on imports to Hamburg from areas outside of the Company's territory.[129] More controversial was the Hamburg court's order against the shipment of goods to or from Bremen, on pain of a fine of 25 per cent of the value of the said goods, passed in June 1679.[130] As discussed in Chapter 4, William Attwood had engaged in the import of linens via Bremen, apparently without repercussions, in the early 1660s. However, with cloth exports continuing to be depressed, the import of linen became increasingly important to the livelihoods of the Hamburg membership, and so they had much to lose by the growth of the Bremen trade.[131] The response to this order amongst the London membership reveals that Banckes's enemies were far from hegemonic within the Company. According to a later account, the persistence of one member continuing to trade via Bremen after the 1679 order, John Marwood, had led the Company at Hamburg to write to its equivalents in London demanding that the trade be kept to its 'antient and propper Course'. However, the failure of the London court to act against this practice allowed it to continue unabated, Marwood being joined by several other 'selfish men'.[132]

This was apparently only one of many occasions after Ford's defeat that the London membership had cause to be 'agrieved' at 'several pressures by the proceedings of the said Residence at Hamburgh'.[133] The continuation of the Bremen trade, however, seems to have been particularly important in causing the divisions that came to a head in the contested election of Sir Edward Dering as London's deputy governor in 1685. The Hamburg court's letter to Governor Rochester complained that their opponents in London had 'of late in an unbrotherly manner authoritatively given free the trade from Bremen', one of several 'unkindnesses' they had received from them.[134] Just as the Company was winning the support of the crown against interloping to Bremen, its own membership were guilty of continuing the trade, which the Hamburg court considered 'would tend to our owne ruine, and hazard the losse of the privileges wee enjoy in this Citty'.

A second practice which the Hamburg court began to crack down on in the early 1680s proved to be similarly divisive, although the evidence we have

---

[129] 'Banckes case', BL, Egerton 3357, fols 9–10; William Swann–Williamson, 28 Sept. 1676, TNA, SP 82/13, fol. 89. The latter was complained of by several merchants trading to Portugal who were sending their goods direct to Hamburg for sale by the Company's factors, and resented this charge. PC 2/65, p. 280.

[130] 'Of the By=laws of the Hambro. Comp', BL, Add. 28079, fol. 63r.

[131] According to the 1677 London port book for old drapery exports, there was virtually no crossover between those exporting to Hamburg and Bremen, so it is likely that these London Merchant Adventurers were more interested in the import of linen. TNA, E190/67/2.

[132] Answer of Company of Merchant Adventurers to complaint of John Ince, 1692, C7/191/1.

[133] Bill of complaint, *John Ince v. Merchant Adventurers*, 1692, ibid.

[134] Hamburg Merchant Adventurers to Governor Rochester, 28 Aug. 1685, BL, Add. 15898, fol. 135r.

suggests that it was the Company's membership at Hull that objected most strongly. The issue was the tendency of members of the Company to disregard its regulations against collaborating with unfreemen when it came to the Netherlands. As the Company's effective monopoly in the Netherlands had broken down in the 1640s and 1650s, there was little incentive for members to continue to send their goods to the shrinking Dordrecht residence. In 1669 the remnants of the Company at its Dutch mart town complained of members in England who were employing unfreemen both to buy and to ship their woollens, as well as buying cloth on commission to supply strangers and interlopers, presumably in places like Amsterdam. As a result, the Hamburg court issued an order restating the prohibition against members collaborating with unfreemen in this way.[135] But it seems that the Company only began seriously to crack down on members' irregular trade to the Low Countries in the early 1680s. Initially, the strategy was to charge such members with Company impositions for any goods exported beyond the Dutch mart town. Matthew Ashton explained to one indignant Leeds merchant that 'the reason the Company acts thus is by reason of some irregular traders & therefore to bring all such persons into order they designe to present all the members & such as canot cleare themselves they will proceede against them.'[136]

The 1683 proclamation only strengthened the determination of the Hamburg court to restore the Company's position in the Netherlands. This led to the introduction of an oath requiring members to swear that they were not collaborating with unfreemen outside of the mart town. This, however, created much resentment amongst Ashton's principals in Leeds and Hull, as demonstrated in a letter Ashton wrote to William Pickering:

> ...such measures as I suppose are not pleaseing unto you therefore you doe not looke upon your Estate to bee at your owne Commaund by the strange arbitrary power of the Company's preceedeings which I am sorry to heare any member of our Company should write & espetially one that hath soe much prudence & veneration for the Company as I hope you have & that they should tax them with preceedinges contrary to the Laws of our nation which I am very confident is not the thing designed, but if men will make a falce construction of theire preceedeings they may call it what they please...[137]

According to Pickering, the Fellowship at Hull and Leeds were 'unanimously against takeing of the oath', and he required that Ashton sell his goods rather than risk their seizure for his non-compliance. But although the policy risked costing

---

[135] Joan Thirsk and J. P. Cooper (eds), *Seventeenth Century Economic Documents* (Oxford, 1972), pp. 528–9.
[136] Ashton–Richard Mann, 16 Aug. 1681, Bodl. Lib., Eng. misc. c563, fol. 12.
[137] Ashton–Pickering, 23 Oct. 1683, Bodl. Lib., Eng. misc. c563, fol. 110r.

him commissions, Ashton continued to defend it, writing that 'what is done by the Company here is for the Advantage of the Company in generall, that some members should not bee strictly tied to performe the orders made by the Company here & others that have not theire Residence here, should bee left to theire libertye to act to the prejudice of the Company in generall'.[138] To another principal he explained that without this measure 'wee shall bee bound that lives here to observe orders & those that live in England will bee free to drive an irregular trade'.[139] The king's 'gracious proclamation' against the interlopers would only succeed 'if wee keepe the same stricktness in prosecuting of our orders which wee have begun and punish such men as doe either buy or cullour unfreemens goods'.[140]

Although the northern merchants seem to have been the most vocal opponents to the Company's attempts to force them to redirect their trade to Dordrecht, it is probable that their objections were shared by others in London. Although in 1677 almost all the London exporters of old draperies to London refrained from exporting to the Netherlands, nine out of twenty were doing so in 1683, largely to places other than Dordrecht.[141] Amongst them was Francis Boynton, London partner of Ashton's principal Godfrey Lawson, who was a vocal critic of the Company's crackdown on Dutch trade at Hull. Boynton had been a prominent supporter of Sir Richard Ford in 1675, and was one of the signatories of the 1685 letter protesting against Dering's election.[142] Also present in this list was one of Ford's other supporters and another former Hamburg resident, John Morrice, as well as George Marwood, probably a relative of the John Marwood accused of trading to Bremen in 1681.[143] Many of this group shared Ford's interest in the slave trade: Boynton, Banckes, and Morrice were all involved in the Royal African Company, the latter two serving as assistants.[144] William Gore was a major colonial merchant involved in the re-export trade to Germany.[145] Another with similar interests was John Lethieullier, who was descended from a distinguished family of Huguenot refugees who had arrived in England via the Spanish Netherlands, and retained their cosmopolitan contacts across the Calvinist diaspora.[146] As well as investing in the East India Company, Lethieullier was heavily involved in exporting textiles to Spain.[147] Lethieullier had prior dealings with John Banckes, who

---

[138] Ashton–Pickering, 1 Jan. 1684, Bodl. Lib., Eng. misc. c563, fol. 126v.

[139] Ashton–Joseph Kitchingman, 6 Nov. 1683, Bodl. Lib., Eng. misc. c563, fol. 113v–114r.

[140] Ashton–Pickering, 28 Aug. 1683, Bodl. Lib., Eng. misc. c563, fol. 98v.

[141] TNA, E190/67/2, E190/141/1.

[142] Ashton–Kitchingman, 12 Feb. 1684, Bodl. Lib., Eng. misc. c563, fols 113r–v. Boynton was a new communicant in the Hamburg church in 1661 and the last trace of him being in Hamburg was in 1671.

[143] Banckes' supporters in 1675 included both John Morrice and his brother Humphrey. The former had first communicated in the Hamburg church in 1659, the latter a year later, both having being bound as apprentices to Jeoffrey Northleigh; Humphrey appears to have remained in Hamburg until 1669.

[144] K. G. Davies, *The Royal African Company* (London, 1957), pp. 71, 378, 385.

[145] Zahedieh, *Capital and the Colonies*, p. 122.

[146] Roseveare (ed.), *Markets and Merchants*, pp. 1–2.   [147] Ibid., p. 91.

could certainly match Lethieullier's expansive commercial operations.[148] Banckes exploited the insatiable thirst of the growing slave trade for cheap fabrics by supplying linen to the Royal African Company on a large scale.[149] During the 1660s, he owned a ship that imported sugar into Hamburg from St Christopher's, in partnership with a Scot, John Beck, and a German, Jacob Delboe.[150] A decade later his brothers were sending tobacco to Stockholm to be received by another who would go on to sign the 1685 letter, the Baltic merchant Urban Hall.[151] Banckes also claimed to have interests in France and Spain.[152]

Banckes' decision to break the Company's rules by sending his stuffs to Leipzig in 1672 was entirely in fitting with these expansive operations. In fact, Banckes had got into similar trouble with the Company in 1666 when he had been charged with 'great mulcts' for trading to Flanders during the second Dutch war.[153] Such behaviour was particularly resented given that Banckes was considered something of an outsider, having been admitted to the Company's ranks despite being 'a stranger', with 'noe clayme unto the freedome either by service or patrimony', a kindness that he was now repaying with 'the pettie selfish Interest of the hopes of a little private lucre'. His complaint about being charged impositions by the Company for trading to places 'which their Charter reaches not' is indicative of how Banckes' activities extended far beyond the bounds of Company regulation. Appropriately enough, his portrait, painted in 1676 by the artist Godfrey Kneller (who lodged with Banckes following his arrival from Hamburg), depicts him as leaning on an oriental carpet on which is laid a letter, written from Amsterdam.[154]

However much Banckes' trade might have outgrown the bounds of his trading Company, it is notable that he and the other 1685 complainants sought to reform the Company, rather than abandon it. This entailed a significant restructuring of the power balance within the Company in favour of the London court, although one which, it was claimed, was consistent with the Company's history:

> For our first incorporacon was on account of our usefullnesse to the nation, & wee have continued a society 400 years upon that & no other consideracon, therefore tis manifest wee were not made a Company to exercise authority over one another, but wee were constituted & call our selvs a Society of Brethren

---

[148] For Banckes' links to Lethieullier, see the Book of Depositions for the burned ships case, TNA, HCA 32/6/1.

[149] Roseveare (ed.), *Markets and Merchants*, pp. 399, 563.

[150] Swann–Arlington, 6 Oct. 1665, TNA, SP 82/10, fol. 263.

[151] Swann–Williamson, 28 Apr. 1676, TNA, SP 82/14, fol. 153. Gore, Boynton, and Marwood all imported goods from the Baltic in 1685, and the former was a significant trader in the region.Sven Erik Åström, *From Cloth to Iron: The Anglo-Baltic Trade in the Late Seventeenth Century. Part 1: The Growth, Structure and Organization of the Trade* (Helsingfors, 1963), pp. 234–7.

[152] 'Banckes case', BL, Egerton 3357, fols 9–10.

[153] Ibid. Banckes' agent at Bruges was his brother James: John and Charles Banckes to Clifford, 31 Aug. 1666, TNA, SP 82/11, fol. 31.

[154] https://www.tate.org.uk/art/artworks/kneller-portrait-of-john-banckes-t05019.

(which is a term of equality) for promoting the publick welfare of the whole body, in such manner as might answer the ends of our constitucion, which is the Honour of the King, the interest of his subjects, and the advancement of trade, which is more promoted by the peace of the Company then the power of it. And your Worships will find more in the charter to encourage & invite us to peace & unity among our selvs, than to enlarge a power & dominion over one another.[155]

The 'absolute authority' that the Hamburg court claimed in Company elections may have been true to the letter of its charters, then, but not their spirit, and 'as the circumstances of things vary, so the regulacion should alter also'. The electoral pre-eminence of the head court overseas was designed at a time when 'most of the eminent members lived abroad...But now, the case is altered, the maine body of the Company reside in England, who are Principalls, & their factors & actuall servants reside abroad.' The Londoners, then, should choose their own officers.

It was the suggestion that they were 'mere Factors and servants to them att London' that most piqued the Hamburg merchants, who emphasized to Rochester that they were 'as considerably concern'd in the exportation of the Woollen Manufacture, as they, and will engage on our owne accompts, to supply the marckett with as much as can be vended, if our brethren att London will leave that trade to us'. Hamburg Merchant Adventurers like Francis Stratford and Samuel Free, veterans of the battle to depose Ford in 1675, had good reason to resent being labelled in this way. The disputed 1685 election was reflective of how the growing number of long-term residents of Hamburg had weakened the traditional ties of deference that connected its members to London. However, although the 1685 election exposed this growing gulf, Dering had his supporters in London as well as Hamburg. Banckes and his allies alleged that Dering's party had been swelled by many who were unqualified to attend court due to being bankrupt, 'unconcerned in trade', or still servants. However they had been 'rak'd together', this group was sufficient to produce a working Company administration loyal to Dering, and for the next eight months 'one part of the said Residence at London was soe at variance with the other that two distinct parties were sett up', each meeting in separate courts under different officers: a schism unparalleled in the Company's recent history.[156] Eventually this was bought to an end in April 1686 when the Hamburg residence consented to select a new deputy governor for London from two individuals nominated by the London court, preferring William Cranmer, the son of the former Rotterdam deputy governor, over Banckes' long-term ally Francis Boynton. Even so, a residual tension between the

---

[155] 27 London Merchant Adventurers to the Company at Hamburg, c.Aug. 1685, BL, Add. 15898, fols 137v–138r.

[156] *John Ince v. Company of Merchant Adventurers*, bill of complaint, 1692, C7/191/1.

two branches is indicated by the Hamburg residence's terse address to the London court in August 1686, at which point Hamburg was threatened by the prospect of an assault by the Danish king: 'we must entreat you, That in case any Brother shall take a Pretence from hence to give order for the removall of Goods from this Place, or otherwise to direct Trade, you will diswade and highly discountenance such irregular Proceeding.'[157] Banckes' misdemeanours fourteen years before still rankled, even more so when the Company at Hamburg received a letter permitting its members to remove their goods to another city if Hamburg was attacked, which was apparently met with 'a generall stupefaction'.[158]

It was in this divided context that the decision was taken to surrender the Company's charter to James II, on 17 October 1686, with an expectation that a new one would be issued. However, this only entrenched divisions, as certain members attempted to enshrine London's electoral independence from Hamburg in the new charter. Apparently fearing such changes, in October 1688 the Hamburg court agreed to strike a deal with the London residency, in the form of a by-law that delivered the latter much of what its members had been asking for: power to choose its own deputy and other officers, a veto over any future laws made in Hamburg as well as authority to revise those laws already in place, and a say over the introduction of any new impositions.[159] This capitulation may have been linked to the death of deputy Missenden earlier that year, following which the London membership apparently acted to ensure that he was not replaced by the royal resident Sir Peter Wyche, who was considered to be under the sway of the Hamburg merchants, threatening to withdraw commissions from their factors in Hamburg if Wyche was chosen.[160] The Hamburg residency had, on the face of it, been restored to a position of subservience to London.

However, even as this deal was sealed, preparations were under way for William of Orange's invasion of England. The collapse of James II's monarchy was capitalized on by the Hamburg court, which soon reasserted its power over elections, the Company having at some point regained possession of its charter. The deselection of John Ince as London secretary by the Hamburg court in July 1690 and the subsequent mass meeting to have him reinstated that October were thus the latest stages in a contest that had stretched back, in one form or another, to Ford's defeat in 1675. Over the ensuing months, it unfolded over a bewildering succession of London meetings, walkouts, recriminatory letters, and disputed votes.[161] Ince's supporters numbered several of Dering's previous opponents, including

---

[157] Merchant Adventurers at Hamburg to those at London, 3 Aug. 1686, BL, Add. 41825, fol. 220v.
[158] Sir Peter Wyche–Earl of Middleton, 14 Sept. 1686, BL, Add. 41825, fol. 265r.
[159] *Laws*, pp. 195–7, 257–60.
[160] Sir Peter Wyche to ?, 17 Aug. 1688, BL, Add. 41827, fol. 72.
[161] Much of our evidence for this comes from Ince's bill of complaint in his Chancery case against the Company, along with the answers of Sir William Cranmer and the Company itself, although unfortunately all are in a very poor condition and unreadable in parts. TNA, C7/191/1.

Lethuilier, John Morrice, George Marwood, and the surviving Banckes brothers. Ince himself had first been elected as London secretary in January 1684, against the wishes of the Hamburg residence, apparently because of his ability to call on powerful patrons like the Tory Chief Justice, George Jeffreys.[162] He had sided with the Banckes faction in the divisions after Dering's electoral defeat, and after 1688 became a figurehead for those asserting the pre-eminence of the London residency over Hamburg. Furthermore, his supporters included the governor, the Earl of Rochester, who very likely had been instrumental in Banckes' supporters winning the initiative in 1688 (perhaps significantly, Rochester had his portrait painted by Godfrey Kneller in 1685). By now, however, the deputy governor Sir William Cranmer had switched sides, and led a party in London that endorsed the actions of the Hamburg court and the legitimacy of the Company's ancient constitution. Deadlock between these sides led to Ince's case being referred to the Lord Chief Justice, in January 1691. This, however, opened the door to other parties with a stake in the continued existence of the Company, meaning that many of the structural tensions that had emerged within the Company now came under debate.

The position of Ince's London supporters was represented via a petition dated 5 February, which was signed by Governor Rochester. This essentially rehearsed the grievances of Dering's opponents in 1685, complaining of the 'several arbitrary powers' claimed by the Hamburg court over the English membership by virtue of the Company's charters, which had been rendered obsolete by 'the Change of times and alteration of Trade'. The petitioners therefore requested a new charter be issued that was fit for the times.[163] The London petition was joined by another from 'the deputy governor and Fellowship of Merchant Adventurers residing in Exon'. These upstart traders to the Netherlands had been a thorn in the Company's side since the 1630s, but apparently had accepted incorporation into the Company in 1683 as a separate residence following the royal proclamation.[164] However, their petition endorsed the complaints of the London membership about the 'several arbitrary powers' claimed by Hamburg, adding that one of their number, Samuel Baron, had been forced out of Hamburg despite having 'purchased his Freedom of the Company in London'. It closed by following the Londoners in requesting a new charter, whereby they may be 'the better enabled to enjoy our libertyes of trade att home and preserve [our] priviledges'.[165] Another regional interest which had apparently complained to the London court in the previous year was the Hull residence, which raised the issue of being charged impositions for exporting woollens on behalf of unfreemen, precisely the

---

[162] Bevil Skelton–Earl of Sunderland, 30 Nov. 1683, BL, Add, 41824, fol. 133.
[163] A copy is included in the Company's answer to Ince's Chancery bill of complaint, C7/191/1 (though in parts it is unreadable).
[164] Ibid.   [165] Ibid.

objection that had riled Ashton's correspondents a decade earlier, now all the harder to swallow given the 1689 Wool Act opening up trade.[166]

At stake in these complaints was the relationship between the constituent parts of the Company, and the power to regulate trade, with the complainants each seeking to throw off key elements of the regulatory system that the Hamburg residence sought to uphold. A further relationship which came into play was that between the Company and the state. The crown had responded to the breakdown in the Company in late 1690 by commanding the Hamburg membership to elect its resident, Sir Paul Rycaut, as deputy governor. However, when presented with this order in January 1691, the Hamburg court reacted to the prospect of once again being governed by a political appointee with barely concealed horror. Its response was to send four members, namely Francis Stratford, the Company husband William Aldersey, Richard Beale, and Thomas Chaire, on a mission to The Hague to solicit King William.[167]

This was clearly a moment of grave political danger for the Company, heightened by the fact that Rycaut was closely connected to Rochester and his supporters in the Company, including Ince, John Morrice, the Lethieulliers, and the future London mayor William Gore.[168] However, despite being highly disgruntled by the Hamburg court's refusal to select him, Rycaut had misgivings about the line of attack that this party was taking. He warned Rochester that any design to issue a new charter would endanger the Company's remaining privileges in Hamburg, which were already under threat due to the 1689 Wool Act, and would do nothing to heal the divisions within the Company.[169] Meanwhile the petitions of the London and Exeter members had been referred to the Attorney General George Treby, who proceeded to summon parties including representatives from Hamburg.[170] Given Treby's role defending Thomas Sandys against the East India Company in 1685, the Company had good cause to be concerned about the consequences of these discussions, but as it happened Treby's report of 16 July 1691 recommended continuing its charter unaltered, partly because (as Rycaut had warned) reopening discussions would only exacerbate its divided state.[171] Cranmer and his allies took this as a signal that they could proceed with the elections for the Company's officers which had been postponed since January. They therefore wrote to the Hamburg court suggesting that, for the positions of both governor and deputy at London, they select one who had been 'bred a merchant, & versed in all the ways, & constitions of their companie: & to save charges, that

[166] Ince's bill of complaint, ibid.
[167] Sir Paul Rycaut–Earl of Rochester, 20 Jan. 1691, BL, Lansdowne 1153 III, fols 19–20.
[168] Sir Paul Rycaut–John Ince, 22 Oct. 1689, BL, Add. 19514, fol. 12.
[169] Rycaut–Rochester, 13 Feb. 1691, BL, Lansdowne 1153 III, fols 57–8.
[170] PC 2/74, pp. 110–11; TNA, SP 44/236, fol. 235; Sir Paul Rycaut–Earl of Nottingham, 3 Mar. 1691, TNA, SP 82/17, fols 352–3.
[171] A copy of the report is included in Company's answer to Ince's Chancery bill of complaint, C7/191/1.

300 FELLOWSHIP AND FREEDOM

both those Officers should be joyned, & united in one'.[172] Although the London court nominated individuals representing both factions, namely Lethieullier and Cranmer, this was clearly with the knowledge that the Hamburg court would select the latter, which was indeed the case. As in 1675, a seating governor had been deposed, and now Cranmer became both the Company's governor and his own deputy.

Treby's report effectively spelled the end to the campaign for a new Company charter, which would rewrite its constitution in favour of English interests, although its supporters did petition against its findings. This led to another round of Privy Council discussions, which stretched into the next year and became embroiled in Ince's continued campaign to have his expenses paid.[173] Complaints now focused on the so-called 'by-laws' passed by the Hamburg court based on its pretended authority, although a copy of these acts produced by a hostile critic at this time included not only recent measures such as the 1679 act against trading to Bremen, but longstanding regulations confining trade to the mart town, enforcing the stint, and so on.[174] Particular ire was reserved for the Company's 'unlawfull & Insnaring Oathes', and the 'unreasonable Fines Imprisonment & Arbitrary Correction & punishments on divers very slender Occasions': sentiments that the free traders of the 1640s would have heartily endorsed, and a sign of how fundamentally some members had turned against the mart-trading system.[175] Now, however, Rycaut advised William Gore that support for this position was withering away.[176] The Privy Council eventually endorsed the legitimacy of these regulations, and advised Ince to pursue his own complaints in the courts.[177]

Why did a campaign which could count on the support not only of several powerful London merchants and politicians like Rochester, but also the secretary of state the Earl of Nottingham (who endorsed Ince as London secretary in July 1690) fizzle out in this manner?[178] One possible reason for Treby's endorsement of the Company's status quo was his hostility, as a committed Whig, to the Tory politics of Rochester and supporters such as Gore. However, there is little evidence for any Whiggism amongst Rochester's enemies, and in fact one of the first voices to be raised in 1690 in favour of London's right to choose its own officers was George Marwood, nephew of Slingsby Bethel.[179] As with the de-selection of Ford as governor in 1675, Company divisions after 1688 do not seem to have followed party-political lines.

---

[172] Sir Paul Rycaut–Earl of Rochester, 30 June 1691, BL, Lansdowne 1153 III, fol. 211v.
[173] PC 2/74, pp. 219, 269.
[174] 'Of the By=laws of the Hambro. Comp', BL, Add. 28079, fols 63–8.   [175] Ibid., fol. 67r.
[176] Rycaut–Gore, 7 Nov. 1691, BL, Lansdowne 1153 IV, fol. 7r.   [177] PC 2/74, pp. 302, 315.
[178] Nottingham–Rycaut, 23 July 1690, TNA, SP 44/98, fol. 238.
[179] John Morrice may also have been a Whig. Gary S. De Krey, *London and the Restoration 1659–1683* (Cambridge, 2005), pp. 131, 408.

Given that the 1689 Wool Act had essentially robbed the Company of its domestic privileges, Treby may have considered it safer to endorse the status quo than recommend the creation of what might have ultimately been a more powerful monopoly headed by individuals linked to the hated Royal African Company. What form this new chartered company might have taken is difficult to know, but probably it would have been designed to accommodate the interests of England-based merchants reluctant to restrict themselves to the limits of the mart towns. The same end could, of course, be achieved by withdrawing the monopoly entirely, but clearly many merchants continued to see the value of retaining corporate organization, if only as a means to access the privileges the Company retained in Hamburg, and exclude foreign rivals. In general, however, this was to be a corporation accommodating to merchants whose interests ranged well beyond the export of cloth to Germany, and whose corporate loyalties were plural. This entailed a rather different kind of corporate affiliation from that which had traditionally been the case for members of the Fellowship of Merchant Adventurers. Rather than defining the boundaries of a merchant's commercial horizons and the stages of their business life, membership of this Company would simply be the means to access a privileged marketplace: to purchase the freedom, in much the same way as one might buy a share in a joint stock trading company. The renaming of the Company's London court meetings as the 'general committee', which had apparently happened by 1690, may be symptomatic of this attitude, evoking as it did the managerial structure of the East India Company. It may also be significant that during Ince's campaign to reverse his de-selection as Company secretary, his supporters were invited to assemble at Jonathan's Coffeehouse, a place associated with the burgeoning stock market, before being conveyed to Whitehall by coaches in order to meet with Rochester (the opposite party also assembled at a coffeehouse, Widow Vernon's).[180] Ince himself had plural corporate loyalties, serving as secretary to the Eastland Company at the same time as the Merchant Adventurers, and in fact his tendency to carelessly mix the records of the two was cited as one reason for his dismissal.[181]

The allegation that the Hamburg court had refused to allow the Exeter merchant Samuel Baron to trade in the city is indicative of how the merchants there continued to hold to an understanding of corporate affiliation in which membership entailed more than market access, and remained a marker of mercantile identity. The hostile summary of the Hamburg by-laws, cited above, referred to a recent act 'forbidding Merchants free of the Company to goe over & settle at Hambro whereby they engross all Trade & Commissions there to themselves', even though it had to

---

[180] For Jonathan's coffeehouse, see Brian Cowan, *The Social Life of Coffee: The Emergence of the British Coffeehouse* (New Haven and London, 2005), p. 132; Anne L. Murphy, *The Origins of English Financial Markets: Investment and Speculation before the South Sea Bubble* (Cambridge, 2009), p. 119.
[181] C7/191/1.

concede that it had no actual copy of this order to corroborate the allegation.[182] Whether this was an informal practice or an actual rule passed in court, it appears that the Hamburg residence responded to the turmoil following the Glorious Revolution and the passage of the Wool Act by closing its ranks.

Conclusion

By the close of the seventeenth century, the branches of the Fellowship of Merchant Adventurers in England and Hamburg had experienced something of an inversion of their accustomed roles. A century earlier, aspiring Merchant Adventurers would arrive in the mart towns hoping to take their first steps towards commercial independence before returning home to join the established merchants who dominated the London court. The mart towns were a gateway into the Company, although entrance was policed by the existing membership. Ironically, as admission to the Company for English-based merchants became easier, beginning in 1634 with the crown's requirement that mere merchants be admitted for a reduced redemption fine (a bar that was lowered in the Restoration), the Hamburg residency became increasingly exclusive. Long-term residents of the mart town with little prospect of returning to England to commence as cloth exporters on their own account became more jealous of defending their local opportunities. By the Restoration, royal residents arriving in Hamburg commonly commentated on the oligarchic character of the Hamburg court, which reached its apogee under Samuel Missenden's reign as deputy governor from 1678 to 1688.

This is not to say that either the London or Hamburg residences were united by shared commercial interests. Business networks cut across geographical divisions: John Banckes continued to be represented in Hamburg by his brothers, who were thereby able to partake in the cosmopolitan opportunities that Banckes enjoyed in London. Even so, the unequal distribution of these opportunities seems to have increased the resentment of those Hamburg merchants who did not enjoy them to the same extent, and for whom Banckes represented a threat to the integrity of the mart-trading system. This position was evidently shared by many members in England, even if some of these (like John Sanford) were actively trading to other parts of the world. The Company's regulatory framework did not necessarily preclude such multilateral enterprises, then, but it might be an obstacle to some like Banckes seeking to explore new opportunities. The divisions between London and Hamburg, not to mention ports like Exeter and Hull, can be accounted for by the varying distribution of opportunities available to Merchant Adventurers, and the ways in which they shaped members' attitudes towards the Company

---

[182] 'Of the By=laws of the Hambro. Comp', BL, Add. 28079, fol. 68r.

(although the opportunities that particular merchants decided to pursue could be influenced by their corporate loyalties, as well as vice versa).

The tendency of the Hamburg residence to turn its back on the London Company is visible as far back as the 1650s, but this became more pronounced following the Glorious Revolution. This may be one reason why the Company ultimately failed to reverse the effects of the Wool Act. Initially the membership in Hamburg were heartened by reports that the Company's monopoly had been fully restored, in March 1693, following the failure of a bill to continue the period of free trade in the Commons.[183] However, a new free trade bill was prepared in January 1694 following a petition from representatives of the northern cloth industry, who complained about 'their Trade being much decreased since the Expiration of the Act for a free Trade to *Flanders, Germany,* and *Holland*'.[184] Further petitions representing Somerset and Gloucester repeated this call, although these were countered by ones from Leeds and Wiltshire which supported the Company's privileges, on the basis that without them 'the Trade of the Wollen Manufactures to those Parts will devolve into the Hands of Foreigners'.[185] The Company itself apparently responded to this challenge by announcing in the *London Gazette* that it was opening up membership to all Englishmen except handicraftsmen for three years, for a nominal entrance fine of 40s. Although the prorogation of Parliament meant that the new free trade bill failed to pass, the fact that the Company's monopoly had yet to be recognized by Parliament probably counted against it. In 1699 Leeds and Halifax petitioned for a bill re-establishing the Company that soon drew support from a variety of cloth-producing regions, as well as opposition. Again, the debate hinged on the issue of the participation of foreign merchants in the cloth trade. Eventually a bill in favour of the Company was presented by its new governor Francis Stratford, recently arrived in London from Hamburg, but this did not go to a second reading. Further efforts to revive the Company persisted into the following century, but a report of the Lords' Commissioners of Trade and Plantations in 1715 observing the increase of trade in the absence of corporate organization effectively marked the end of this campaign.[186] Before then, the repeal of the laws against the export of undressed broadcloth had robbed the Company of its last vestiges of domestic privilege.[187] The Company's attempt to secure parliamentary recognition was thus a casualty of the 'diffusion of regulatory initiative' under the pressure of increasingly sophisticated lobbying efforts that did much to block economic legislation after 1689.[188]

---

[183] Sir Paul Rycaut–Sir William Colt, 4 Mar. 1693, BL, Add. 37663, fol. 108; Newman, 'Anglo-Hamburg trade', p. 282.
[184] CJ, 11, p. 69.   [185] Ibid., pp. 80–1.   [186] Newman, 'Anglo-Hamburg trade', pp. 283–6.
[187] Keirn, 'Parliament, legislation and the regulation of English textile industries', p. 12.
[188] William A. Pettigrew, 'Constitutional change in England and the diffusion of regulatory initiative, 1660–1714', *History* 39 (2014), pp. 839–63.

The long-term effects of this change on the structure of the cloth trade are largely beyond the scope of this study, but it seems that the Company's warnings about foreign penetration of the cloth trade did come to pass, with Bremen now establishing itself as a serious competitor to Hamburg, particularly as a source for linen imports.[189] It is not surprising, then, that the Hamburg residency seems to have become increasingly reluctant to admit new members into its ranks, even as the Company at home was throwing open its doors to all comers.[190] Some members, such as Francis Stratford (whom Sir Peter Wyche considered to have been the ultimate winner of the contests between London and Hamburg), were able to thrive on the opportunities opened up by the increasingly spendthrift fiscal-military state.[191] Most of the remaining members at Hamburg, however, seem to have settled into their particular niche in the Anglo-European textile trade, exchanging cloth for linen on commission, their Company effectively transformed from a transnational organization incorporating a major trade route, to a local merchant guild. Over a century after the Company had left Antwerp, the cloth trade had finally departed from its 'ancient Channel'.[192]

---

[189] Newman, 'Anglo-Hamburg trade', pp. 286–8.

[190] Ibid., pp. 289–90; Jones, *War and Economy*, pp. 253–8.

[191] Rycaut–John Ince, 30 June 1691, BL, Lansdowne 1153 III, fol. 218; Eveline Cruikshanks, 'STRATFORD, Francis (1645–1704), of Acton, Mdx.', in D. Hayton, E. Cruickshanks, and S. Handley (eds), *The History of Parliament: The House of Commons 1690–1715* (2002), online edition [https://www.historyofparliamentonline.org/volume/1690-1715/member/stratford-francis-1645-1704]. Jacob M. Price, 'The tobacco adventure to Russia: enterprise, politics, and diplomacy in the quest for a northern market for English colonial tobacco, 1676–1722', *Transactions of the American Philosophical Society*, New Series, 51, 1 (1961), pp. 1–120. Stratford was succeeded by a former John Hide supporter, the Tory merchant Sir William Gore, suggesting that the earlier contests may by then have been overshadowed by the Company's worsening political position. 'Journal, May 1708: Journal Book M', in *Journals of the Board of Trade and Plantations: Volume 1, April 1704–January 1709*, ed. K. H. Ledward (London, 1920), pp. 487–97. *British History Online* http://www.british-history.ac.uk/jrnl-trade-plantations/vol1/pp487-497 [accessed 30 November 2018].

[192] *Reasons Humbly Offered, for Excepting the Rivers of Elbe, Weser, and Eyder, out of the Bill for a General Liberty of Exporting the Woollen Manufactures of this Kingdome*, TNA, SP 32/13, fol. 170.

Conclusion

Merchant Adventurers in an
Age of Commercial Revolution

The whole world almost is now aptly cantoniz'd amongst several Societies of our Merchants, whilst some trade East, some West, some neerer, some further off; and were it not for this apt partition, it would unavoidably fall out, that some Mart Towns would prove over-pester'd, or like a Common of Pasture over-layd, whilest others in the mean time would be left utterly unfrequented. And sure if the world were not spatious enough for all out Traders, some pretence might be framed, why all men ought to be licenced in all places: but since the contrary is most true, and no man is so straited for want of roome, but that He may trade in some places to his owne advantage, though he be bounded that he may not trade in all places to another mens disadvantage: nothing but an emulous desire to interfere with others, and to incumber trade could provoke men to be opposite to our regular distributions.

Henry Parker, Of a Free Trade (London, 1648), pp. 1–14

Henry Parker's defence of the governed trade of the Merchant Adventurers appeared at a time when, even though the Company was facing unparalleled pressure, it was still possible to envisage a commercial world neatly partitioned between different merchant societies. The civil war had energized civic discourse and drew on the cultural resources of citizenship, although ultimately the spectre of expanded state power epitomized by Hobbes' *Leviathan* threatened to over-shadow England's 'corporate commonwealths'.[1] Parker's book was published, however, with another threat to corporate privilege in mind, namely the free trade discourse voiced most prominently by the Levellers, in which civic values were turned against restrictive trading companies alongside oligarchic urban corporations. For the Levellers, trading companies were an example of the monopolistic denial of English birthrights, which included the right to travel freely and

---

[1] Withington, *Politics of Commonwealth*, pp. 75–84.

Fellowship and Freedom: The Merchant Adventurers and the Restructuring of English Commerce, 1582–1700.
Thomas Leng, Oxford University Press (2020). © Thomas Leng. DOI: 10.1093/oso/9780198794479.001.0001

expansively in search of new markets, something that William Walwyn predicted would be a consequence of free trade:

> For as to Merchants increasing (as increase they must in few yeares) they will not continue plodding to one or two townes in a Nation or Province, Trading in a stately manner uppon set Dayes, with Grossiers, in great quantityes, making up their gaines in the grosse; but will be dispersed in every Haven and Towne, furnishing (not Grossiers that gain great estates out of our Native Comodities, and soe render them deare to the last user) but the last sellers, and so will be able to give at home the better Rates, which in conclusion redounds to workemen of all sorts, to Farmers, Owners & Land.[2]

Walwyn's vision was a threat not only to the privileged market access enjoyed by Merchant Adventurers. Also at stake was the social system which had developed around the mart-trading system, and the relationships which comprised it. In its defence, the Company turned to Parker, the most effective defender of parliamentary sovereignty within a mixed monarchy. His strategy was to yoke the Leveller concern with individual liberty to an ideal of restraint, partially internalized: 'He injoyes the purest and most refined freedome in his own breast, which has the least furious passions to serve, and the least impetuous appetite to master.'[3] As in politics, order in commerce came through balance, each individual merchant acting within their legal bounds.[4] Indeed, for Parker the chief role of merchant companies was to maintain such boundaries, equated to the enclosure of land which was thereby made more profitable and able to support more people. The division of overseas trade between companies, however, was also an appropriate reflection of the knowledge and skills required to trade into each region, expertise which justified the privileged status of the trained merchant:

> For unto a Merchant not onely a breeding, but a particular breeding in such or such a place, in such or such a Trade is requisite. He that is experienced to trade in *Russia* is not thereby inabled to trade in *Spaine*, and he that can deale warily enough with *Indians*, *Turks* and *Barbarians*, is not alwaies prepared enough to cope with the *Jews*, Hans Townes, and *Hollanders*. Questionlesse to license all men to trade without breeding, nay without the particular advertisements, and preparations of such a breeding is to send men naked into battell, and to render them up as prey to vulpine, circumventing neighbours.[5]

---

[2] William Walwyn, 'Conceptions for a free trade', 1652, in Henry C. Clark (ed.), *Commerce, Culture, and Liberty: Readings on Capitalism before Adam Smith* (Indianapolis, 2003), p. 5.
[3] Henry Parker, *Of a Free Trade* (London, 1648), p. 6.
[4] For the ideal of moderation (and its coercive implications), see Ethan Shagan, *The Rule of Moderation: Violence, Religion and the Politics of Restraint in Early Modern England* (Cambridge, 2011).
[5] Parker, *Of a Free Trade*, p. 15.

Regional specialization was inherent to the practice of trade, even more so as commercial horizons widened: markets, like peoples, were distinctive, and the corporate boundaries between them therefore natural.

At the heart of this book has been an attempt to understand how corporate affiliation shaped the practices of individual merchants, or, in Parker's terms, to ask whether merchants 'bred' into a particular trade were thereby socialized to a distinctive culture of commerce. Parker emphasized how differences between markets and customers necessitated specialization, but trading companies could also potentially instil in particular merchants a distinct set of values and sense of identity centred on participation in corporate culture. As we have seen, individual Merchant Adventurers cannot straightforwardly be identified with the values propagated in Company discourse, which always possessed a rhetorical, persuasive function, directed at outsiders and insiders alike. Nonetheless, there were distinctive elements in the trading lives of Merchant Adventurers that were common enough, and widely enough commented upon, to become normative. Participation in a protected and regulated marketplace centred on a particular commodity, and certain mart towns generated a sense of shared identity: the distinction between insiders and outsiders meant something in practice. Merchant Adventurers did not passively follow the conduct outlined in the Company's regulations, but even when transgressing them, they did so with an awareness of the contours of Company discipline, as well as the informal court of opinion that judged the legitimacy of certain actions. Above all, the mart towns were distinctive social as well as commercial environments, which shaped how Merchant Adventurers interacted with their customers and with each other. The association between the mart towns and the training, or 'breeding', of Merchant Adventurers meant that these locations held an important place in the idealized life-cycle of Company members, and this was perhaps the main way by which membership shaped practice. Experience in the mart towns was something of a rite of passage which reinforced group identity, binding together Merchant Adventurers in different locations and at different stages of their careers. Though successful progression through the Company's ranks was far from guaranteed, aspiring Merchant Adventurers in the mart towns were presented with a recognized pathway to achieve commercial independence, in the earlier part of our period at least, and this served to reproduce the Company's trading system. In Greif's terms, the mart-trading system created expectations that thereby influenced and to some extent regularized behaviour: what he would identify as an institution.[6]

Certain elements of the mart-trading system were common to most of England's trading companies, and in some respects premodern mercantile communities in general. Merchant companies commonly sought to channel trade to particular towns, although import-focused companies such as the Levant

---

[6] Greif, *Institutions and the Path to the Modern Economy*, pp. 15–16.

Company usually sustained a broader range of bases than the Merchant Adventurers. Even in the absence of trading companies, resident agents in foreign territories tended to cluster, whether formally or informally, creating distinctive social sites.[7] Nor was the association between experience abroad and training unique to the Merchant Adventurers, and factors overseas in general tended to be at a formative stage in their careers.[8] Aspiring members of the Levant Company in the Ottoman Empire faced similar challenges to Merchant Adventurers in Hamburg or Middelburg, as they attempted to consolidate their reputations and establish the social ties which would enable them to assume commercial independence.[9] Nonetheless, the social structure of these trades, alongside the organizational structures of the respective trading companies, varied. Factors in the Levant were part of generally smaller communities at a greater distance from their principals and the governors of the Company, and thus might enjoy a greater degree of licence than their equivalents in the Merchant Adventurers' mart towns.[10] At the same time, they were more distant from the decision-making process, and less able to participate in Company politics: 'centre–periphery' contests in these two trading companies were thus likely to take a different form. Merchants resident in different societies varied in terms of their age and experience, performed different roles, and had different relationships with their host communities as well as their domestic partners and principals; certain markets encouraged longer-term patterns of residence and a higher degree of assimilation into the host community signified by intermarriage, though the former did not necessarily lead to the latter, as we see with the Merchant Adventurers in Hamburg.[11] In the case of newer trades, the cumulative experience of established members who had spent time overseas was obviously not present in the way that was the case for the Merchant Adventurers; establishing a foothold within a new market demanded different tactics.[12] Further work on patterns of recruitment and training into different trading companies and branches of trade, as well as the career-paths of members, would allow the distinctiveness of the Merchant

---

[7] Donatella Calabi and Derek Keene, 'Merchants' lodgings and cultural exchange', in Donatella Calabi and Stephen Turk Christensen (eds), *Cultural Exchange in Early Modern Europe. Volume 2: Cities and Cultural Exchange in Europe, 1400–1700* (Cambridge and New York, 2007), pp. 315–48.

[8] For examples, see Willan, *Studies in Elizabethan Foreign Trade*, pp. 12–17.

[9] Games, *Web of Empire*, pp. 89–93.

[10] For an evocative account of life in the Ottoman Empire for one young Levant Company merchant, who was actually apprenticed as a Merchant Adventurer, see William Foster (ed.), *The Travels of John Sanderson in the Levant, 1584–1602*, Hakluyt Society, second series, 67 (1930). See also Gerald Maclean and Nabil Matar, *Britain and the Islamic World, 1558–1713* (Oxford, 2011), pp. 90–112.

[11] For instance, English merchants in northern Spain in the seventeenth century seem to have made little effort to assimilate, suggesting that in this trade service overseas was considered as a means to accumulate assets to be realized at home. Regina Grafe, 'Northern Spain between the Iberian and Atlantic worlds: trade and regional specialization, 1550–1650', unpublished Ph.D. thesis, LSE (2001), pp. 218–31.

[12] The distances involved in colonial trades made it more challenging to incorporate experience overseas during apprenticeship; in fact many colonial traders had prior training with European merchants. Zahedieh, *Capital and the Colonies*, pp. 88–90.

Adventurers' trading regime to be assessed more accurately. However, even within the confines of the period studied here it is clear how the social structure of particular trade routes could change. By the time that Henry Parker wrote his defence of the mart-trading system, its principles were under threat by the actions of not just excluded outsiders, but also members themselves.

At the start of our period apprentices in the mart towns like George Lowe could reasonably hope that, by fulfilling the role of dutiful servant, they might one day join the London merchant community and achieve commercial independence. This was an incentive to conform to expectations, to respect normative standards of conduct, even if, in Lowe's case, his master John Quarles was willing to depart from the Company's regulatory regime in significant ways. This in itself shows how the Company's trading regime was not simply in a state of stable equilibrium, even during its heyday before the disruption of the Cokayne Project. Ever since escaping from the gravitational pull of Antwerp, the Company had to contend with centrifugal forces that might draw its members to seek new market opportunities, and the inclination of Merchant Adventurers like Quarles to find ways to 'straggle' into inner Germany was a sign of this. Chapter 5 demonstrated how, following the Company's expulsion from the Holy Roman Empire in 1597, certain members were prepared to sacrifice Company government, and implicitly the monopolistic protection that came with it, in order to retain access to German markets. The victory of this party over those who sought to uphold the principles of the mart-trading system by restraining trade to Middelburg is a sign of how even this most antiquated of trading companies was capable of changing in response to pressure by its members. It is impossible to know how the liberal regime that subsequently emerged in Stade might have developed had this activity not been stymied by the Thirty Years War. However, the extent to which Merchant Adventurers in the first decades of the seventeenth century were prepared to venture beyond Stade, often in collaboration with interlopers, suggests that, ultimately, it would have been difficult to sustain the mart-trading system in its current form, and the Company would have had to accommodate itself to a different set of boundaries, geographical as well as behavioural.

Had this transpired, a reorganization of the social as well as commercial structure of the Company would have become necessary. In this period the organization of markets was not simply a matter of individual actors optimizing profit margins and minimizing transaction costs: in order to uphold the social relationships on which commerce depended, it was necessary to maintain a balance of interests between a range of participants at different stages of their careers, who were often pursuing diverging social, as well as business, goals. This was true at the corporate as well as individual level, and reconciling its members' interests became more challenging for the Company in the context of structural changes to English commerce. This is demonstrated by the responses of Merchant Adventurers to the Cokayne Project. It was the Hamburg factors who most clearly

recognized how the Cokayne Project threatened to dismantle the mart-trading system by upsetting the traditional division of labour between cloth production in England and its finishing overseas, so imperilling their commercial and social prospects. However, their continued loyalty to the Company's commercial regime was a contrast to the enthusiasm of at least some established Merchant Adventurers in England for the promise of opening up new market opportunities, 'to be free of all trade to all places', that the project represented. The Cokayne Project was thus an early example of a factor that had the potential to divide the Company: the widening opportunities represented by the expansion of English trade, and the uneven capacity of individual Merchant Adventurers to access them.

This book has argued that the engagement of Merchant Adventurers in these new commercial horizons was more complicated than suggested by Robert Brenner, for whom the Company's membership was largely left behind by import-drive growth. In fact, many Merchant Adventurers were amongst the leaders of the new trading companies; Company membership could be a stepping stone to participate in a diverse range of markets. However, it has identified structural factors which, to an extent, limited the participation of Merchant Adventurers in these changes. This was not so much because a reliance on privilege limited entrepreneurial or risk-taking behaviour (something belied by the extensive participation of members in the inland German trade early in the period), as because Merchant Adventurers were not always well placed to participate in those networks through which they might access new markets. Entrance depended on commercial intelligence, but also knowledge of the individuals operating within a particular market: relationships of interpersonal trust relied on the communication of information. Inclination to diversify was not enough: opportunities did not fall equally. This book has discussed some examples of Merchant Adventurers partaking in a range of different markets, and incorporating their core markets into others (notably John Banckes in the Restoration), and doubtless there are many more to be found that would further contradict the image of Company members as complacent rent-seekers. However, overall it would appear that such enterprises had the effect of diversifying the experiences of members, at the potential expense of corporate unity. This was particularly the case when overlaid with the divergences that emerged between the membership at home and overseas, particularly in Hamburg, where accessing such opportunities was harder than in London. In general, this period was characterized less by a succession of merchant groups replacing each other as the pace-setters of commercial change, as Brenner presented it, than by a transformation of the merchant community as a whole. In broad terms, however, Brenner was correct to see this process as having significant implications for how trading companies functioned, and how individual merchants interacted with them.

For Merchant Adventurers, the expansion of opportunities in the Mediterranean, the far east, and the Atlantic would only have accentuated the sense that their

own customary trade was in irreversible decline. This book has endorsed the conventional picture that the 1620s depression represented the major turning point in the Company's early modern history: the subsequent contraction of the Company's trade, and membership, clearly made it less able to counter the arguments of those wanting to open up cloth exports. These were not the only effects of the protracted decline in English broadcloth exports, however: the impact on the social structure of the Company's trade was equally profound. Diminishing opportunities at home led to a reconfiguration of the traditional relationship between the Company's membership in England and the mart towns, disrupting the normalized path to commercial independence. The mart towns were decreasingly associated with a stage in the merchant life cycle, as commission agency displaced servitude as the standard agency relationship. Experience overseas continued to be a part of the expected training of Merchant Adventurers, but it would appear that this increasingly happened under the tutelage of established factors or partners, 'standing in packhouse' rather than managing it independently. As a result, the ties that connected Merchant Adventurers in England and overseas were transformed. Long-term residents of the mart towns, particularly Hamburg, had different commercial aspirations than servants or journeymen looking to establish themselves at home. Decreasing numbers of Merchant Adventurers passed through the mart towns on their journey to independence, then; the role of these places in socializing members of the Company, and transmitting its values to new generations, was diminished.

This was accompanied by changes to the Company's admission regime from at least the 1620s which also unsettled the established career-path for members, although their effects are difficult to evaluate due to the absence of Company admission records. From then on, the Company faced continual pressure to absorb as members merchants who had no experience of service in the mart towns, or even of trading to the Netherlands and Germany at all. William Walwyn may have been one such figure, although he appears to have become a member before the 1634 proclamation which restored the Company's suspended privileges over new draperies and coloured cloths, at the price of admitting new members.[13] Walwyn's comments about the burdens of corporate regulation are suggestive of the difficulties of incorporating reluctant participants like him into the Company:

> ...for having the benefit of mutuall Councells one with another, it is knowne that there is not that Union that is pretended, but that strife & contentions & circumventions doe abound amongst them, the greater lying more heavy upon the more moderate Traders, and the less heavily complaining of their manifold

---

[13] Barbara Taft, 'Walwyn, William (bap. 1600, d. 1681), Leveller and medical practitioner', *ODNB*. In 1640, Walwyn and company exported 280 notional shortcloths (mainly dyed and dressed Reading/Kents, and Spanish cloths), to Dunkirk. TNA, E190/43/4.

burthens, by their many unreasonable Orders, Oathes, fines, Censures: soe that however through Custome & Tradition they are wedded ever superstitiously to continue in this way of a perplexed Society, pleasing themselves in spending very much of their time in Courts & meetings about others affaires, doubtlesse their Lives would be much more Comfortable, and their Trades as gainefull upon the score of Generall & equall freedom, had they harts & Courages to prove it...[14]

As Walwyn presented it, rather than acting as a breeding ground for aspiring merchants the mart-trading system was now working to the advantage of the wealthy, those 'borne Rich & adding wealth to wealth by trading in a beaten Rode to wealth'; newcomers required new markets in which to establish themselves.[15] In place of the destructive contention of corporate politics, free trade would enable a virtuous 'strife & emulation' between merchants competing for goods and markets, who would be satisfied with modest returns.[16]

Although we know little of Walwyn's career as a Merchant Adventurer, he seems representative of those incomers to the trade who, in the absence of deep personal acquaintance of the mart towns, would have been dependent on the local market expertise that resident agents could supply. Such 'weak ties', however, were unlikely to generate much loyalty to either the Company or its mart towns: Walwyn prophesied that free trade would leave 'noe good towne in any province, but where English Merchants would be resident'.[17] For merchants like Walwyn dissatisfied with the Company's regime, 'exit' was one option (to borrow Albert O. Hirschman's terminology), which was increasingly taken by those trading to the Netherlands as the Company's capacity to defend its privileges waned.[18] By the 1650s, changes in the structure of the European-wide textile market had fractured the traditional division of labour in the Anglo-Dutch cloth industry, which had long sustained the Company's privileges in the Low Countries. This complex process, involving a realignment of interests within the Netherlands as well as changes in the markets that its merchants previously served, has to some extent been beyond the scope of this book. Clearly, however, there was a collapse in demand for unfinished English broadcloth in the Netherlands in the era of the Anglo-Dutch wars, probably associated with the growth in Dutch cloth production at Leiden as well as broader shifts in the continental market.[19] The mart-trading system was a casualty of this: a broader range of exported textiles, alongside a more diversified traffic overall, escaped the bounds of the mart towns, and the Company's Dutch membership essentially dissipated into the republic's merchant community. Because much of the evidence that this book has drawn

---

[14] Walwyn, 'Conceptions for a free trade', p. 7.   [15] Ibid., pp. 6–7.   [16] Ibid., p. 5.
[17] Ibid.
[18] Albert O. Hirschman, *Exit, Voice, and Loyalty: Responses to Decline in Firms, Organizations, and States* (Cambridge, Mass., 1970).
[19] Ormrod, *Rise of Commercial Empires*, pp. 106–7.

on, notably merchant papers, has been weighted towards the German side of the Company's trade, the story of how this has happened has only partially been told here and would require different sources to be fully explained.[20] However, it seems that as the Company's effective monopoly contracted to Germany, the experiences of its membership became more plural, with some in England continuing to trade to both Germany and the Netherlands under different institutional conditions. Insofar as they were willing to trade outside of the mart towns, and use non-members as agents, Merchant Adventurers trading to the Netherlands were exhibiting 'exit' from fundamental aspects of its trading regime, as indeed some had been willing to do in the 1620s during the period of trade liberalization. Those based in Hamburg, meanwhile, continued to be bound by requirements to accept cloth exports from other members, even if they might have wished to broaden their commissions.[21]

Although the Company's German markets also experienced the declining demand for broadcloth, Hamburg continued to gain enough from the transit trade in textiles into the German interior (as well as the supply of linen for export into England) for its partnership with the Company to continue to be worthwhile. It was in Hamburg, then, that the mart-trading system survived and indeed remained essential to the commercial interests and identities of the merchant community in a way which was decreasingly so for their English-based counterparts. If the Company's decline in the Netherlands was met by its members through the strategy of 'exit', then the contest over the direction of the Company that unfolded over the Restoration, described in Chapter 8, can be seen in terms of the competing responses of 'loyalty' and 'voice'.[22] The latter was embodied by those London Merchant Adventurers who sought to remodel the Company's constitution and its regulatory regime in the 1680s, and thereby redefine its boundaries in such a way that would accommodate those global opportunities that had developed over the century: sourcing linen from Bremen to supply the Atlantic slave trade, for instance. This was a fundamental threat to the mart-trading system, though, and it is unsurprising that the defenders of the status quo were concentrated on Hamburg, if not confined there. In the case of the Hamburg membership, loyalty to the Company's 'ancient constitution' and its markets persisted in a way which was decreasingly the case for those in England, and bridging this divide proved to be increasingly difficult.

[20] Most promisingly, the notarial records that survive for many Dutch cities, some of which are becoming available in digital form: see, for instance, the Rotterdam notarial archive, https://www.stadsarchief.rotterdam.nl/en/collectie/notarial-deeds.

[21] This was the case with Thomas Shephard of Hamburg, who was forced to turn down business from the interloper Thomas Baret of Norwich, in 1673. Baret–Shephard, 6 Aug. 1673, Thomas Baret letterbook, 1672–95, Norfolk Record Office, 6360/6B8.

[22] Although Hirschman identified 'voice' as a response to decline which was associated with greater levels of loyalty than those who turned to exit. *Exit, Voice, and Loyalty.*

The above analysis suggests that we might understand the fortunes of trading companies not only in terms of performance (how efficient they were), or politics (their ability to defend themselves against opponents), but also in terms of the relationship between their constitutional structures and the organization, or social structure, of their core trades.[23] Fashioning a regulatory regime which could meet the needs of members with potentially divergent interests was a perpetual challenge for trading companies. In the case of the Fellowship of Merchant Adventurers in the post-Antwerp era, this challenge grew along with the diversity of members' experiences. The fact that the Company's decline coincided with an increasingly open admission regime tells us that success for such organizations in part rested on their ability to attract members and retain their loyalty. Loyalty in turn was shaped by how membership of the Company was experienced. Merchant Adventurers socialized to the Company's trading regime in the mart towns could rely on strong, multiplex social ties which were a source of security: insider status, and the benefits that came with it, could be a powerful incentive to remain loyal to the Company and its markets. Those who entered the Company by different paths, or whose experiences in the mart towns were fleeting, lacked such ties, and exit therefore came at less of a price. Structural changes in the Company's trade weakened the connections between the mart towns and the membership in England, as well as English society at large: no longer would gentry families see the Company as a propitious destination for younger sons. As ties coalesced in Hamburg, loyalty to the Company's commercial regime strengthened there, at the same time as it weakened amongst an English membership which was presented with opportunities which might actively encourage them to transgress the mart-trading system. Ultimately, the Company failed to reconcile the fellowship implied by corporate belonging with the freedoms that many members were demanding in the management of their trade.

*   *   *

Central to the Company's justification for privilege was the claim that order in the marketplace could only be sustained by its government. This was an order achieved through discipline and restraint, with members putting their collective interests before the desire for short-term gain: competition amongst sellers was a sign of a disorderly marketplace, the consequence of which would be cloth being valued for less than its proper worth. Commerce was a vocation which should be reserved for those with special 'licence', as Parker put it. In this sense, the mart-trading system was rooted in an understanding of the destabilizing nature of the market, and market-driven behaviour, which is often seen as a casualty of the

---

[23] A similar point was made in regards to the Eastland Company by Sven-Erik Åström, who noted that the divergent interests of members trading to different regions of the monopoly undermined the staple-principle, particularly due to the increased importance of imports. *From Cloth to Iron*, pp. 178–200. Something similar could be said in the case of the Merchant Adventurers with regards to the linen import trade.

emergence of capitalism, or at least the intensification of market activity and the expansion of overseas trade. Such changes are often presented as having been accompanied in England by the emergence of a novel political economy outlook which, in Joyce Appleby's worlds, resulted in the 'differentiation of economic relations from the society they served', and ultimately the reconceptualization of the market as a realm which obeyed predictable laws and therefore generated an order of its own.[24] Even those who emphasize the obduracy of a moralized economic worldview still often implicitly represent this as a brake on the rational maximization of profit by *Homo economicus*.[25] But, as Lawrence Fontaine reminds us, 'Although morality and religion permeate behaviour, techniques to escape their severity are always available.'[26] In the case of the Merchant Adventurers, the Company's claims to bring order to the marketplace always sat uneasily alongside the reality of competition amongst brethren, as well as the willingness of 'disorderly brethren' to test the limits of acceptable conduct. Order in merchant communities, as in other parts of early modern society, was negotiated, and Company discipline could be contested on the grounds that it unfairly restrained members' liberties, or disturbed the social peace on which prosperity rested.[27] There was a fine line between accommodating heterogeneous practices and abandoning the Company's claims to sustain order, not to mention fellowship, in favour of the pursuit of profit. As Edward Misselden put it, 'Some quacksalves are soe cunning that they can eate spiders & not be poysoned; and some anglers find good fishing in troubled waters. There is noe course of trade soe out of course; noe estate soe daingerous, but some can make their proffite thereby.'[28]

Nonetheless, Merchant Adventurers profited from the status which this vision of commercial order conferred on them. The role of the trained merchant was to set a proper value on things, and so to maintain a sense of justice and equity in exchange, ensuring that each party received their due.[29] This was central to the

---

[24] Joyce Oldham Appleby, *Economic Thought and Ideology in Seventeenth-Century England* (Princeton, 1980), p. 47. For similar variants of this narrative, see Jean-Christophe Agnew, *Worlds Apart: The Market and the Theater in Anglo-American Thought, 1550–1750* (Cambridge, 1996); Christopher J. Berry, *The Idea of Luxury: A Conceptual and Historical Investigation* (Cambridge, 1994); Andrew McRae, *God Speed the Plough: The Representation of Agrarian England, 1500–1660* (Cambridge, 1996).

[25] Muldrew, *Economy of Obligation*; Andrea Finkelstein, *Harmony and the Balance: An Intellectual History of Seventeenth-Century English Economic Thought* (Ann Arbor, 2000); Brodie Waddell, *God, Duty and Community in English Economic Life 1660–1720* (Woodbridge, 2012). James Davis emphasizes the obduracy of medieval moralized attitudes, whilst questioning whether these precluded the growth of the market. *Medieval Market Morality: Life, Law and Ethics in the English Marketplace, 1200–1500* (Cambridge, 2012), pp. 410–49.

[26] Lawrence Fontaine. *The Moral Economy: Poverty, Credit, and Trust in Early Modern Europe* (Cambridge, 2014), p. 317.

[27] A classic statement of this interpretation of early modern social relations is Keith Wrightson, 'Two concepts of order: justices, constables and jurymen in seventeenth-century England', in John Brewer and John Styles (eds), *An Ungovernable People: The English and Their Law in the Seventeenth and Eighteenth Centuries* (New Brunswick, 1980), pp. 21–46.

[28] Misselden, 'Discourse', fol. 41r.

[29] As such, this sits closely to what Carl Wennerlind has described as 'neo-Aristotelian' political economy, which understood the role of money as maintaining balance and thus the social order.

claim that the 'mere merchant' stood above other participants in the market: as Henry Parker put it, 'there is not onely an Art and Mysterie in the sale of cloth as aforesaid, but also an Art more abtruse, eminent, and exquisite then that is which consists in the Mechanicall way of making and dressing the same'.[30] These sentiments were redolent of a premodern social economy in which such roles mattered: in part, the Company existed to endow status and therefore value onto the vocation of commerce.[31] Status could be translated into a form of social power to be deployed against others, notably producers: merchant expertise acted as a disciplinary force, ensuring that standards were maintained, and so legitimizing the functional differentiation of production and exchange. The Company's trading regime thus imposed boundaries on the commercial world, prescribing those able to participate within it and restraining if not precluding certain forms of economic activity. This was not unchallenged: in a society dominated by the values of land-ownership, commerce continued to lack social prestige, and rival interests could use this to good effect.[32] Over the course of the period, cloth producers were increasingly successful in contesting the Company's control of the export market, eventually to the extent of establishing a foothold in it themselves. Direct contact between English cloth producers and foreign buyers, in growing evidence by the end of the century, threatened to dispense with the merchant middleman, and perhaps presaged a larger shift from mercantile to industrial capitalism.

This would suggest, in the cloth trade at least, a decline in the prestige associated with the art of traffic and the status of the merchant. Taken in isolation this might appear to be the case, but when understood in context of the transformation of the broader mercantile community, the picture is more complex. Retreat from the 'moral economy' of the Merchant Adventurers was the choice of many merchants as well as manufacturers: the loss of 'mere merchant' status, as defined by the Company, and the privileges that it brought, was a price worth paying in return for freedom from the burdens of corporate affiliation.[33] This is suggestive of a wider broadening of the idea of liberty across the period, from being an exclusive privilege often acquired through corporate affiliation, to a birthright which was in some senses the property of the individual. Although this may initially have implied an extension of the corporate ideal, turning subjects into citizens, such a generalization of the idea of freedom can also be understood as

Casualties of Credit: The English Financial Revolution, 1620–1720 (Cambridge, Mass. and London, 2011), p. 20.

[30] Parker, *Of a Free Trade*, p. 30.
[31] See in particular the work of Bert De Munck on Antwerp guilds: 'Skills, trust, and changing consumer preferences: the decline of Antwerp's craft guilds and the perspective of the product market, c.1500–c.1800', *International Review of Social History* 53 (2008), pp. 197–233; 'One counter and your own account: redefining illicit labour in early modern Antwerp', *Urban History* 37, 1 (2010), pp. 26–44.
[32] See, for instance, Fontaine's conception of early modern Europe as occupied by rival systems of exchange, aristocratic and capitalist: *Moral Economy*, especially chapter 8.
[33] See David Harris Sacks, 'Freedom to, freedom from, freedom of: urban life and political participation in early modern England', *Citizenship Studies* 11, 2 (2007), pp. 135–50.

undermining the core values that informed premodern corporate culture. In modern civil society, individuals are said to be freed from the requirement to formally affiliate with certain institutions in order to achieve a particular status, and are thereby liberated from the fraternal obligations that accompany such associations.[34] Freed to enter into the blossoming associational world of the eighteenth century, the allegiances of 'modular man' are always conditional, and prone to shift.[35]

In the case of the Merchant Adventurers, those merchants of the Restoration era whose market, and corporate, loyalties were plural seem to have been embracing just such a transition in the realm of overseas trade. Perhaps here we can identify the emergence of the liberal commercial world of the eighteenth century out of the shackles of the hierarchical mercantile order of the sixteenth: a new form of commercial society in which commission agency was the relationship of choice, and the flexibility of egalitarian networks replaced bonds of servitude and corporate belonging. But even in the sixteenth century, 'fellowship' for Merchant Adventurers entailed not only formal obligations to the collective, but also the informal sociability through which connections were made within this world, and beyond it. There was no simple succession in commercial government from corporate organization to informal networks: the latter had always combined with the former to provide the infrastructure through which commerce was managed and opportunities were distributed within the merchant community. Well-worn narratives of the early modern period as witnessing the rise of individualism and the death of community underestimate the continued power of alternative relationships of 'mutuality and obligation', as Keith Wrightson has put it, which continued to structure society and denote status.[36] Even where trading corporations were absent, the associational character of commercial life continued to encourage merchants to coordinate their actions, increasingly so as structural changes in the state required more sophisticated lobbying efforts.[37] Merchants were enmeshed in multiple and overlapping allegiances and associations in the eighteenth century, much as they were in the sixteenth, and corporations were by no means missing from these. In the case of the Merchant Adventurers, those on the one hand like John Banckes who were prepared to challenge the mart-trading system in the name of their commercial freedom, and on the other his enemies in Hamburg who obdurately insisted on its survival, do not respectively represent the future and the past of English commerce. Rather, both were responding to the same changing environment in ways which reflected their respective positions, commitments, loyalties, and interests.

[34] Bert De Munck, 'Rewinding civil society: conceptual lessons from the early modern guilds', *Social Science History* 41 (2017), pp. 83–102.

[35] Ibid., p. 87 (quoting Ernest Gellner).

[36] Keith Wrightson, 'Mutualities and obligations: changing social relationships in early modern England', *Proceedings of the British Academy* 139 (2005), pp. 157–94.

[37] Gauci, *Politics of Trade*, p. 115.

Even so, the story of the decline of the Merchant Adventurers is suggestive of larger changes in the mercantile social order, as (in certain regions) corporate boundaries weakened and new synergies became possible. One economic consequence of this was to enable a redirection of English merchant capital towards the Atlantic, its place in the 'old-established channels of Anglo-European trade' increasingly occupied by Dutch merchants.[38] Whether this brought about the democratization of access to the overseas market prophesied by Walwyn and other supporters of free trade is questionable, however. After all, colonial trade, long characterized by relatively low barriers to both entrance and exit, nonetheless demonstrated a growing tendency to concentrate in the hands of larger-scale firms over the century, and it was only the largest-scale traders who were able to cut across different regions in the way that Merchant Adventurers like John Banckes had done.[39] Networks were no new thing in commercial organization, but it may be that as trading opportunities became more pluralistic and multilateral, with some of the most lucrative of these existing on the interface between different commercial zones, their importance in enabling success grew. Admission to the Fellowship of Merchant Adventurers had long represented a means to access the most valuable sector of England's foreign trade, and although this always overlapped with network participation, corporate regulations (however much they might be circumvented in practice) mitigated the power of informal networks to dominate the market in cloth. The Company's role in 'making merchants' was its most prized contribution to the commonwealth, and its admission regime and the relationships that were built around it—characterized by apprenticeship, but also the sociability of fellowship—served to reproduce the social order of its trading world across generations. For decades if not centuries, the Company's commercial regime represented a model for how a merchant's career should progress, from recruitment to retirement. But with the contraction of the cloth trade (and especially the export of shortcloth, the ideal commodity for new entrants), success for many Merchant Adventurers arguably became more dependent on finding means to escape the limits of their customary trade, a process that set in well before the Company's ultimate loss of domestic privilege. In the process, what was lost was not only a lucrative trade route, or a venerable organization, but a social system that shaped expectations about what being a merchant entailed. England's commercial revolution not only involved an expansion of commerce and a restructuring of imports, exports, and re-exports; it also had profound implications for the role of merchant, and the mercantile career. Merchant Adventurers had not been passive bystanders to this shift, but their Fellowship was its chief casualty.

[38] Ormrod, *Rise of Commercial Empires*, p. 65.
[39] Jacob M. Price, 'A revolution of scale in overseas trade: British firms in the Chesapeake trade, 1675–1775', *Journal of Economic History* 47, 1 (1987), pp. 1–43; Zahedieh, *Capital and the Colonies*, pp. 57–65. A different picture is given in Cathy Matson, *Merchants and Empire: Trading in Colonial New York* (Baltimore and London, 1998).

Bibliography

Manuscript Sources

Bodleian Library, Oxford
Eng. misc. c563, c602 (Letterbooks of Matthew Ashton)
North A1–2 (Sir Julius Caesar Papers)
Rawlinson A22, A31, A42 (Papers of John Thurloe)
Tanner 74 (Letter from John Wheeler, fol. 5)

British Library, London
Add. 6394 (Sir William Boswell Papers)
Add. 15898 (Lawrence Hyde, Earl of Rochester Papers)
Add. 19514 (Letterbook of Sir Paul Rycaut)
Add. 22919 (Letters to Sir George Downing)
Add. 28079 ('Of the By=laws of the Hambro. Comp', fols 63–8)
Add. 36785 (Account of exports and imports into London, 1663/1669)
Add. 37663 (Letterbook of Sir Paul Rycaut)
Add. 37983–4 (Letters of Bevil Skelton to William Blathwayt)
Add. 41806 (Papers of Charles Earl of Middleton)
Add. 41824–7 (Letters from Bevil Skelton and Sir Peter Wyche)
Add. 48009, 48126 (Robert Beale Papers)
Add. 70005 (Sir Robert Harley Papers, including letters from Jeremiah Elborough, fols 77–9)
Add. 72436 (Papers of Georg Rudolph Weckherlin relating to diplomatic mission to Denmark of Theodore Haak)
Add. 78178 (Robert Dudley, Earl of Leicester Papers)
Cotton Galba D/XIII (Papers concerning England and Germany, 1558–1603)
Cotton Vespasian C/XIV2 (Dispute concerning the Cumberland licence, fol. 123)
Egerton 3357 (Earl of Danby Papers)
Harleian 36 (Discourse in response to 1604 free trade bill, fols 28–38)
Hargraves 321 (Report of commissioners for trade, 1624, fols 54–9)
Lansdowne 86 (Burghley Papers)
Lansdowne 150, 152 (Sir Julius Caesar Papers)
Lansdowne 487 (Papers on the 1604 free trade bill, pp. 288–359)
Lansdowne 1153 (Sir Paul Rycaut Papers)
Sloane 1453 (Edward Misselden, 'A Discourse, shewing the Necessity of the Restoringe of the Marchaunts Aduenturers Priviledges & Government in their Mart Towne in Germany')
Stowe 133 (1640 Company petition, fols 289–92)

Cornwall Record Office, Truro
AD567 (Richard Daniel account book, 1598–9)

Huntington Library, San Marino, California

Ellesmere (Papers of Thomas Egerton, Baron Ellesmere)
Stowe VIII, Temple Special Subject, Miscellaneous documents, box 10 (1645 Hamburg Covenant dispute)

Kent History and Library Centre, Maidstone

U269/1 (Lionel Cranfield papers)

Lambeth Palace, London

MS 3472 (Letter of the King's Merchants Adventurers at Hamburg, fols 163–7)

Lancashire Archives, Preston

DDCA 1/45 (Account Book of agent of Henry Boothby in Germany, 1638)

The National Archives, London

C2, C5–8 (Chancery Pleadings)
C24 (Chancery Depositions)
C78 (Chancery Final Decrees)
C109/19–25 (William Attwood papers)
CO 389/11 (Board of Trade Entry Books)
E134 (Exchequer Depositions)
E101/29/23 (Papers relating to Antwerp trade of Georg Lowe/John Kendrick)
E190 (Port Books)
HCA 32/6/1–2 (Admiralty Prize Papers relating to Hamburg Burnt Ships case)
PC2 (Privy Council Register)
PRO 30/34/2 (Sir John Popham's draft copy of Merchant Adventurers' charter)
PROB 11 (Prerogative Court of Canterbury, Will Registers)
SP 12 (State Papers Domestic, Elizabeth I)
SP 14 (State Papers Domestic, James I)
SP 15 (State Papers Domestic, addenda)
SP 16 (State Papers Domestic, Charles I)
SP 18 (Papers of Council of State)
SP 21 (Committee of Both Kingdoms Books)
SP 25 (Council of State Books and Accounts)
SP 29 (State Papers Domestic, Charles II)
SP 32 (State Papers Domestic, William and Mary)
SP 44 (Secretary of State Entry Books)
SP 46/19, 21, 176 (John Quarles papers)
SP 46/83–5 (George Warner papers)
SP 46/95–6 (State Papers Domestic, Supplementary)
SP 82 (State Papers Foreign, Hamburg)
SP 84 (State Papers Foreign, Holland)
SP 104 (State Papers Foreign, Entry Books)
STAC8 (Star Chamber Proceedings)

National Library of Wales, Aberystwyth

9053-9E (Wynn Papers)

Norfolk Record Office, Norwich

6360/6B8 (Letterbook of Thomas Baret)

Northamptonshire Record Office, Northampton
C (William Cokayne Papers)

Sheffield Archives
BFM/1293 (Matthew Ashton's Account Book)

Somerset Record Office, Taunton
DD/HY/Box12 (Hylton of Ammerdown MS) (Ledger of John Morley for Randall
    Mannynge, 1601–14)
DD\SF/7/2/1 (Letterbook of John Sanford)

Staatsarchiv Hamburg
521–1 (Register book of the Church of the English Court, Hamburg)

Wakefield History Centre
WYW1827/5/5/1/1 (Letterbook of William Lowther)

Wiltshire and Swindon Archives, Swindon
1178/332–7 (William Calley Papers)

Printed Primary Sources

A discourse consisting of motives for the enlargement and freedome of trade (London, 1645).
A Proclamation against the Exportation of Clothes, vndyed and vndressed contrary to Law
    (23 July 1614).
A Proclamation declaring a former Proclamation of the Fourteenth of May last to be void
    (8 Apr. 1663).
A Proclamation for restoring the ancient Merchants Adventurers to their former Trade and
    Priviledges (12 Aug. 1617).
A Proclamation for the better ordering the Transportation of Clothes, and other Woollen
    Manufactures into Germany, and the Low-Countreys (7 Dec. 1634).
A Proclamation for the better Ordering the Transportation of Clothes (10 May 1665).
A Proclamation for the free Exportation of Woollen Manufactures of this Kingdom (14 May
    1662).
A Proclamation for the Free Exportation of Woollen Manufactures until the 25th day of
    December next (15 Apr. 1666).
A Proclamation for the Free Exportation of Woollen Manufactures until the 25th day of
    December next (29 Mar. 1667).
A Proclamation for the Vent of Cloth, and Woollen Manufactures of this Kingdome (9 Apr.
    1644).
A Proclamation prohibiting the Merchant Adventurers Charter from henceforth to be put in
    practise or execution, either within the Kingdom, or beyond the Seas (2 Dec. 1614).
Acts of the Privy Council of England, 46 vols (London, 1890–1946).
An Ordinance of the Lords and Commons in Parliament Assembled, for the upholding the
    Government of the Fellowship of Merchants Adventurers of England (11 Oct. 1643).
Birch, Thomas (ed.), *A Collection of the State Papers of John Thurloe*, 7 vols (London, 1742).
Bond, Maurice F. (ed.), *The Diaries and Papers of Sir Edward Dering Second Baronet*
    1644 to 1684, House of Lords Record Office Occasional Publications No. 1 (London,
    1976).

Clark, Henry C. (ed.), *Commerce, Culture, and Liberty: Readings on Capitalism before Adam Smith* (Indianapolis, 2003).

Coventry Papers from the Archives of the Marquess of Bath at Longleat, microfilm edition (1969).

Dendy, F. W. (ed.), *Extracts from the Records of the Merchant Adventurers of Newcastle-upon-Tyne*. Vol. I, Publications of the Surtees Society, 93 (1895); Vol. II, idem, 101 (1899).

Forbes, John, *Four Sermons* (1635).

Foster, William (ed.), *The Travels of John Sanderson in the Levant, 1584–1602*, Hakluyt Society, second series, 67 (1930).

Freezer, Augustine, *The Divine Original and the Supreme Dignity of Kings, No defensative against Death* (Oxford and Rotterdam, 1685).

Freezer, Augustine, *The Wickedness and Punishment of Rebellion* (Rotterdam, 1686).

From the City of Exon. A second Remonstrance declaring the continual decay of Trade, occasioned by the power of the Company of Merchant Adventurers (1662).

Hainsworth, D. R. (ed.), *Commercial Papers of Sir Christopher Lowther 1611–1644*, Publications of the Surtees Society, 189 (1974).

Historical Manuscripts Commission, *Sixth Report of The Royal Commission on Historical Manuscripts* (London, 1877).

Historical Manuscripts Commission, *Eighth Report of The Royal Commission on Historical Manuscripts* (London, 1881).

Historical Manuscripts Commission, Buccleuch I: *Report on the Manuscripts of the Duke of Buccleuch and Queensbury. K.G., K.T., Preserved at Montagu House, Whitehall*, I (London, 1899).

Historical Manuscripts Commission, Cowper II: *Twelfth Report, Appendix, Part 1. The Manuscripts of the Earl Cowper, K.G., Preserved at Melbourne Hall, Derbyshire*, II (London, 1888).

Historical Manuscripts Commission, De Lisle & Dudley V: *Report on the Manuscripts of Lord de L'Isle and Dudley Preserved at Penshurst Place, V, Sidney Papers, 1611–1626* (London, 1962).

Historical Manuscripts Commission, Downshire II–V: *Report on the Manuscripts of the Marquees of Downshire, preserved at Easthampstead Park, Berkshire*, vols II–IV (London, 1936–40).

Historical Manuscripts Commission, Portland I: *The Manuscripts of His Grace the Duke of Portland, preserved at Welbeck Abbey* I (London, 1891).

Historical Manuscripts Commission, Sackville I: *Calendar of the Manuscripts of Major-General Lord Sackville... Preserved at Knole, Sevenoaks, Kent. Volume I: Cranfield Papers 1551–1612*, ed. A. P. Newton (London, 1942).

Historical Manuscripts Commission, Sackville II: *Calendar of the Manuscripts of The Right Honourable Lord Sackville of Knole, Sevenoaks, Kent. Volume II*: Historical Manuscripts Commission, Salisbury: *Calendar of the Manuscripts of the Marquis of Salisbury: The Cecil Manuscripts*, 24 vols (London, 1883–1976).

Lawne, Christopher, *The Prophane Schisme of the Brownists* (1612).

Leach, Thomas, *Modern Reports, or Select Cases, Adjudged in the Court of King's Bench, Chancery, Common Pleas and Exchequer*, III, fifth edition (London, 1793).

Lingelbach, W. E. (ed.), *The Merchant Adventurers of England: Their Laws and Ordinances with Other Documents* (1902).

Loe, William, *Songs of Sion* (1620).

Malynes, Gerard, *Consuetudo, vel lex mercatoria, or The ancient law-merchant* (London, 1622).

Orme, William (ed.), *Remarkable Passages in the Life of William Kiffin: Written by Himself, and Edited from the Original Manuscript* (London, 1823).

Parker, Henry, *Of a Free Trade* (London, 1648).

Proceedings and Debates of the House of Commons, in 1620 and 1621, I (Oxford, 1766).

Ramsay, G. D. (ed.), *John Isham Mercer and Merchant Adventurer: Two Account Books of a London Merchant in the Reign of Elizabeth I*, Publications of the Northamptonshire Record Society, 21 (1962).

Redington, Joseph (ed.), *Calendar of Treasury Papers*, vol. I (London, 1868).

Roseveare, Henry (ed.), *Markets and Merchants of the Late Seventeenth Century. The Marescoe–David Letters 1668–1680*, Records of Social and Economic History, New Series, XII (Oxford, 1987).

Sainsbury, E. B. (ed.), *A Calendar of the Court Minutes etc. of the East India Company 1655–1659* (Oxford, 1916).

Sellers, Maud (ed.), *The Acts and Ordinances of the Eastland Company* (London, 1906).

Sellers, Maud (ed.), *The York Merchants and Merchant Adventurers 1356–1917*, Publications of the Surtees Society, 129 (1918).

Sutton, A. F., and Visser-Fuchs, L. (eds), *The Book of Privileges of the Merchant Adventurers of England, 1296–1483* (Oxford, 2009).

Temple, Sir William, *The Works of Sir William Temple*, IV (London, 1754).

The Book of Oaths (London, 1715).

The Ferrar Papers: In Magdalene College, Cambridge, 1590–1790, microfilm edition (1992).

The last will and testament of Mr. Iohn Kendricke late citizen and draper of London (London, 1625).

The Reasons Humbly offered to Consideration, why the Incorporating the whole Trade of the Woollen Manufactures of this Kingdom to the Company called the Merchant-Adventurers of England, is and will prove more and more detrimental as to the Country in general, so especially to the County of Devon, and City of Exon (1662).

'The Society's MSS. Chiseldon, &c', *The Wiltshire Magazine* (Dec. 1900).

Thirsk, Joan, and Cooper, J. P. (eds), *Seventeenth Century Economic Documents* (Oxford, 1972).

Wheeler, John, *A Treatise of Commerce* (London, 1601).

Whitelocke Papers from the Archives of the Marquess of Bath at Longleat, microfilm edition (1992).

Digitized Sources

British History Online (http://www.british-history.ac.uk/cal-cecil-papers/vol7/pp16-31).

Cecil Papers Online (https://www.proquest.com/products-services/cecil_papers.html).

Folger Shakespeare Papers Online Collections (https://luna.folger.edu/luna/servlet/FOLGER%7E3%7E3).

Hartlib Papers Online (https://www.dhi.ac.uk/hartlib/).

Marine Lives (http://www.marinelives.org).

Portrait of John Banckes by Godfrey Kneller (https://www.tate.org.uk/art/artworks/kneller-portrait-of-john-banckes-t05019).

Records of London's Livery Companies Online (https://www.londonroll.org/home).

Rotterdam Notarial Archives (https://www.stadsarchief.rotterdam.nl/en/collectie/notarial-deeds).

Manuscript Pamphleteering in Early Stuart England (https://mpese.ac.uk/t/HaibleyBrief DiscourseFreeTrade.html).

Secondary Sources

Agnew, Jean-Christophe, *Worlds Apart: The Market and the Theater in Anglo-American Thought, 1550–1750* (Cambridge, 1996).

Appleby, Joyce Oldham, *Economic Thought and Ideology in Seventeenth-Century England* (Princeton, 1980).

Arblaster, Paul, *Antwerp and the World: Richard Verstegan and the International Culture of the Catholic Reformation* (Leuven, 2004).

Archer, Ian, *The History of the Haberdashers' Company* (Chichester, 1991).

Ashton, Robert, 'The parliamentary agitation for free trade in the opening years of the reign of James I', *Past and Present* 38 (1967), pp. 40–55.

Ashton, Robert, *The City and the Court 1603–1643* (Cambridge, 1979).

Aston, T. H., and Philpin, C. H. E. (eds), *The Brenner Debate: Agrarian Class Structure and Economic Development in Pre-Industrial Europe* (Cambridge, 1985).

Åström, Sven-Erik, *From Cloth to Iron: The Anglo-Baltic Trade in the Late Seventeenth Century. Part 1: The Growth, Structure and Organization of the Trade* (Helsingfors, 1963).

Baumann, W.-R., *The Merchants Adventurers and the Continental Cloth-Trade (1560s–1620s)* (Berlin, 1990).

Beerbühl, Margrit Shulte, *The Forgotten Majority: German Merchants in London, Naturalization, and Global Trade, 1660–1815*, trans. Cynthia Klohr, (New York, 2015).

Benson, Joel D., *Changes and Expansion in the English Cloth Trade in the Seventeenth Century: Alderman Cockayne's Project* (Lewiston, Queenston, and Lampeter, 2002).

Berry, Christopher J., *The Idea of Luxury: A Conceptual and Historical Investigation* (Cambridge, 1994).

Bison, Douglas R., *The Merchant Adventurers of England: The Company and the Crown, 1474–1564* (Newark, 1993).

Boldory, M., 'Socio-economic institutions and transaction costs: merchant guilds and rural trade in eighteenth-century Lower Silesia', *European Review of Economic History* 13 (2009), pp. 173–98.

Braddick, Michael J., *The Nerves of State: Taxation and the Financing of the English State, 1558–1714* (Manchester and New York, 1996).

Braddick, Michael J., *State Formation in Early Modern England c.1550–1700* (Cambridge, 2000).

Brenner, Robert, 'Bourgeois revolution and transition to capitalism', in A. L Beier, David Cannadine, and James M. Rosenheim (eds), *The First Modern Society: Essays in Honour of Lawrence Stone* (Cambridge, 1989), pp. 271–304.

Brenner, Robert, *Merchants and Revolution: Commercial Change, Political Conflict, and London Overseas Traders, 1550–1653* (Cambridge, 1993).

Brinkmann, C., 'England and the Hanse under Charles II', *English Historical Review* 23, 92 (1908), pp. 683–708.

Calabi, Donatella, and Keene, Derek, 'Merchants' lodgings and cultural exchange', in Donatella Calabi and Stephen Turk Christensen (eds), *Cultural Exchange in Early Modern Europe. Volume 2: Cities and Cultural Exchange in Europe, 1400–1700* (Cambridge and New York, 2007), pp. 315–48.

Carlos, A. M., and Nicholas, S., ' "Giants of an earlier capitalism": the chartered trading companies as modern multinationals', *Business History Review*, 62 (1988), pp. 398–419.

Carlos, A. M., and Nicholas, S., 'Agency Problems in Early Chartered Companies: The Case of the Hudson's Bay Company', *Journal of Economic History* 50, 4 (1990), pp. 853–75.

Carlos, A. M., and Nicholas, S., 'Theory and history: seventeenth-century joint-stock chartered trading companies', *Journal of Economic History* 56, 4 (1996), pp. 916–24.

Carus-Wilson, E. M., 'The origins and early development of the Merchant Adventurers' organization in London as shown in their own mediaeval records', *Economic History Review* 4, 2 (1933), pp. 147–76.

Cassidy, Irene/Henning, Basil Duke, 'SANFORD, John (1640–1711), of Basinghall Street, London and Nynehead Court, Som', in B. D. Henning (ed.), *The History of Parliament: the House of Commons 1660–1690* (1983), online edition [https://www.historyofparliamentonline.org/volume/1660–1690/member/sanford-john-1640–1711].

Cavanagh, Edward, 'Infidels in English legal thought: conquest, commerce and slavery in the common law from Coke to Mansfield, 1603–1793', *Modern Intellectual History* 16 (2019), pp. 375–409.

Clay, C. G. A., *Economic Expansion and Social Change: England 1500–1700. II. Industry, Trade and Government* (Cambridge, 1984).

Coates, Ben, *The Impact of the English Civil War on the Economy of London, 1642–50* (Abingdon and New York, 2004).

Cowan, Brian, *The Social Life of Coffee: The Emergence of the British Coffeehouse* (New Haven and London, 2005).

Croft, Pauline, 'Free trade and the House of Commons 1605–6', *Economic History Review* 28 (1975), pp. 17–27.

Cruikshanks, Eveline, 'STRATFORD, Francis (1645–1704), of Acton, Mdx', in D. Hayton, E. Cruickshanks, and S. Handley (eds), *The History of Parliament: The House of Commons 1690–1715* (2002), online edition [https://www.historyofparliamentonline.org/volume/1690–1715/member/stratford-francis-1645–1704].

Davies, K. G., *The Royal African Company* (London, 1957).

Davis, James, *Medieval Market Morality: Life, Law and Ethics in the English Marketplace, 1200–1500* (Cambridge, 2012).

Davis, Ralph, 'English foreign trade, 1660–1700', in W. E. Minchington (ed.), *The Growth Trade in the Seventeenth and Eighteenth Centuries* (London, 1969), pp. 78–98.

De Jung, Chris, 'John Forbes (*c*.1568–1634), Scottish minister and exile in the Netherlands', *Nederlands archief voor kerkgeschiedenis/Dutch Review of Church History* 69, 1 (1989), pp. 17–53.

De Krey, Gary S., *London and the Restoration 1659–1683* (Cambridge, 2005).

De Munck, Bert, 'Skills, trust, and changing consumer preferences: the decline of Antwerp's craft guilds and the perspective of the product market, *c*.1500–*c*.1800', *International Review of Social History* 53 (2008), pp. 197–233.

De Munck, Bert, 'One counter and your own account: redefining illicit labour in early modern Antwerp', *Urban History* 37, 1 (2010), pp. 26–44.

De Munck, Bert, 'Rewinding civil society: conceptual lessons from the early modern guilds', *Social Science History* 41 (2017), pp. 83–102.

de Roover, Raymond, *Gresham on Foreign Exchange: An Essay on Early English Mercantilism with the Text of Sir Thomas Gresham's Memorandum for the Understanding of the Exchange* (London, 1949).

DuPlessis, Robert S., *The Material Atlantic: Clothing the New World, 1650–1800* (Cambridge, 2015).

Ehrenberg, Richard, *Hamburg und England im Zeitalter der Königin Elisabeth* (Jena, 1896).

Epstein, S. R., *Freedom and Growth: The Rise of States and Markets in Europe, 1300–1750* (London and New York, 2000).

Epstein, S. R., and Praak, Maarten (eds), *Guilds, Innovation, and the European Economy, 1400–1800* (Cambridge, 2008).

Erikson, Emily, and Samilia, Sampsa, 'Social networks and port traffic in early modern overseas trade', *Social Science History* 39 (2015), pp. 151–73.

Erikson, Emily, *Between Monopoly and Free Trade: The English East India Company, 1600–1757* (Princeton and Oxford, 2014).

Ewert, Ulf Christian, and Selzer, Stephan, *Institutions of Hanseatic Trade: Studies on the Political Economy of a Medieval Network Organization* (Frankfurt am Main and New York, 2016).

Finkelstein, Andrea, *Harmony and the Balance: An Intellectual History of Seventeenth-Century English Economic Thought* (Ann Arbor, 2000).

Fontaine, Lawrence, *The Moral Economy: Poverty, Credit, and Trust in Early Modern Europe* (Cambridge, 2014).

Friis, Astrid, *Alderman Cockayne's Project and the Cloth Trade: The Commercial Policy of England in Its Main Aspects, 1603–1625* (London and Copenhagen, 1927).

Fusaro, Maria, 'Cooperating mercantile networks in the early modern Mediterranean', *Economic History Review* 65 (2012), pp. 701–18.

Fusaro, Maria, *Political Economies of Empire in the Early Modern Mediterranean: The Decline of Venice and the Rise of England, 1450–1700* (Cambridge, 2015).

Gadd, Ian Anders, and Wallis, Patrick (eds), *Guilds, Society and Economy in London 1450–1800* (London, 2002).

Games, Alison, *The Web of Empire: English Cosmopolitans in an Age of Expansion 1560–1660* (Oxford, 2008).

Gauci, Perry, *The Politics of Trade: The Overseas Merchant in State and Society, 1660–1720* (Oxford, 2001).

Gauci, Perry, *Emporium of the World: The Merchants of London 1660–1800* (London and New York, 2007).

Gelderblom, Oscar, *Cities of Commerce: The Institutional Foundations of International Trade in the Low Countries, 1250–1650* (Princeton and Oxford, 2013).

Gelderblom, Oscar, and Grafe, Regina, 'The rise and fall of the Merchant Guilds: re-thinking the comparative study of commercial institutions in premodern Europe', *Journal of Interdisciplinary History* 40, 4 (2010), pp. 477–511.

Gervais, Pierre, 'In union there was strength: the legal protection of eighteenth-century merchant partnerships in England and France', in Simon Middleton and James E. Shaw (eds), *Markets, Ethics and Practices, c.1300–1850* (Abingdon and New York, 2018), pp. 166–83.

Goldberg, Jessica L., *Trade and Institutions in the Medieval Mediterranean: The Geniza Merchants and their Business World* (Cambridge, 2012).

Granovetter, Mark, 'Economic action and social structure: the problem of embeddedness', *American Journal of Sociology* 91 (1985), pp. 481–510.

Grassby, Richard, 'The rate of profit in seventeenth-century England', *English Historical Review* 84, 333 (1969), pp. 721–51.

Grassby, Richard, 'English merchant capitalism in the late seventeenth century: the composition of business fortunes', *Past and Present* 46 (1970), pp. 87–107.

Grassby, Richard, *The Business Community of Seventeenth-Century England* (Cambridge, 1995).

Grassby, Richard, *Kinship and Capitalism: Marriage, Family, and Business in the English-Speaking World, 1580–1740* (Cambridge, 2001).

Greif, Avner, *Institutions and the Path to the Modern Economy: Lessons from Medieval Trade* (Cambridge, 2006).

Greif, Avner, Milgrom, Paul, and Weingast, B. R., 'Coordination, commitment, and enforcement: the case of the merchant guild', *Journal of Political Economy* 102 (1994), pp. 745–76.

Griffiths, Paul, *Youth and Authority: Formative Experiences in England, 1560–1640* (Oxford, 1996).

Ha, Polly, *English Presbyterianism 1590–1640* (Stanford, 2011).

Hagedorn, Bernhard, *Ostfrieslands Handel und Schiffart vom ausgang des 16. Jahrhunderts bis zum Westfälischen Frieden (1580–1648)* (Berlin, 1912).

Haggerty, Sheryllyne, *'Merely for Money'? Business Culture in the British Atlantic, 1750–1815* (Liverpool, 2012).

Hailwood, Mark, *Alehouses and Good Fellowship in Early Modern England* (Woodbridge, 2014).

Hancock, David, *Citizens of the World: London Merchants and the Integration of the British Atlantic Community, 1735–1785* (Cambridge, 1995).

Hancock, David, 'The trouble with networks: managing the Scots' early-modern Madeira trade', *Business History Review* 79, 3 (2005), pp. 467–91.

Helms, M. W. and Watson, Paula, 'FORD, Sir Richard (*c.*1614–78), of Seething Lane, London, and Baldwins, Dartford, Kent', in B. D. Henning (ed.), *The History of Parliament: The House of Commons 1660–1690* (1983), online edition [https://www.historyofparliamentonline.org/volume/1660–1690/member/ford-sir-richard-1614–78].

Hentschell, Rose, *The Culture of Cloth in Early Modern England* (Aldershot, 2008).

Hinton, R. W. K., *The Eastland Trade and the Common Weal in the Seventeenth Century* (Cambridge, 1959).

Hirschman, Albert O., *Exit, Voice, and Loyalty: Responses to Decline in Firms, Organizations, and States* (Cambridge, Mass., 1970).

Hodsdon, J., 'Hoddesdon, Sir Christopher (1533/4–1611), merchant', *ODNB*.

Hoppitt, Julian, *Risk and Failure in English Business 1700–1800* (Cambridge, 2002).

Jones, D. W., *War and Economy in the Age of William III and Marlborough* (Oxford, 1988).

Kadens, Emily, 'Pre-modern credit networks and the limits of reputation', *Iowa Law Review* 100 (2015), pp. 2429–55.

Keirn, Tim, 'Parliament, legislation and the regulation of English textile industries, 1689–1714', in Lee Davison, Tim Hitchcock, Tim Keirn, and Robert B. Shoemaker (eds), *Stilling the Grumbling Hive: The Response to Social and Economic Problems in England, 1689–1750* (Stroud and New York, 1992), pp. 1–24.

Kerridge, Eric, *Textile Manufactures in Early Modern England* (Manchester, 1985).

Klein, P. W., "Little London': British merchants in Rotterdam during the seventeenth and eighteenth centuries', in D. C. Coleman and Peter Mathias (eds), *Enterprise and History: Essays in Honour of Charles Wilson* (Cambridge, 1984), pp. 116–34.

Leng, Thomas, ' "His neighbours land mark": William Sykes and the campaign for "free trade" in civil war England', *Historical Research* 86, 232 (2013), pp. 230–52.

Leng, Thomas, 'Interlopers and disorderly brethren at the Stade mart: commercial regulations and practices amongst the Merchant Adventurers of England in the late Elizabethan period', *Economic History Review* 69 (2016), pp. 823–43.

Lindberg, Erik, 'Club goods and inefficient institutions: why Danzig and Lübeck failed in the early modern period', *Economic History Review* 62, 3 (2009), pp. 604–28.

Lindberg, Erik, 'Merchant guilds in Hamburg and Konigsberg: a comparative study of urban institutions and economic development in the early-modern period', *Journal of European Economic History* 39, 1 (2010), pp. 33–65.

Lingelbach, William E., 'The internal organisation of the Merchant Adventurers of England', *Transactions of the Royal Historical Society*, new series, 16 (1902), pp. 19–67.

Lingelbach, William E., 'The Merchant Adventurers at Hamburg', *American Historical Review* 9, 2 (1904), pp. 265–87.

Lipson, Ephraim, *The Economic History of England. II. The Age of Mercantilism* (London, 1931).

Lloyd, T. H., *England and the German Hanse, 1157–1611: A Study of Their Trade and Commercial Diplomacy* (Cambridge, 1991).

Maclean, Gerald and Matar, Nabil, *Britain and the Islamic World, 1558–1713* (Oxford, 2011).

Matson, Cathy, *Merchants and Empire: Trading in Colonial New York* (Baltimore and London, 1998).

McCusker, John J., *Money and Exchange in Europe and America, 1600–1775: A Handbook* (Chapel Hill, 1978).

McLean, Paul D., *The Art of the Network: Strategic Interaction and Patronage in Renaissance Florence* (Durham and London, 2007).

McRae, Andrew, *God Speed the Plough: The Representation of Agrarian England, 1500–1660* (Cambridge, 1996).

Mimardière, A. M., 'SALTONSTALL, Richard (d.1601), of London and South Ockendon, Essex', in P. W. Hasler (ed.), *The History of Parliament: The House of Commons 1558–1603* (1981), online edition [https://www.historyofparliamentonline.org/volume/1558–1603/member/saltonstall-richard-1601].

Minns, Chris, and Wallis, Patrick, 'Networks in the premodern economy: the market for London apprenticeships, 1600–1749', *Journal of Economic History* 71, 2 (2011), pp. 413–43.

Mishra, Rupali, 'Diplomacy at the edge: split interests in the Roe embassy to the Mughal Court', *Journal of British Studies* 53 (2014), pp. 5–28.

Muldrew, Craig, *The Economy of Obligation: The Culture of Credit and Social Relations in Early Modern England* (Basingstoke, 1998).

Murphy, Anne L., *The Origins of English Financial Markets: Investment and Speculation before the South Sea Bubble* (Cambridge, 2009).

Ogborn, Miles, *Indian Ink: Script and Print in the Making of the English East India Company* (Chicago and London, 2007).

Ogilvie, Sheilagh, 'Whatever is, is right? Economic institutions in pre-industrial Europe', *Economic History Review* 60, 4 (2007), pp. 649–84.

Ogilvie, Sheilagh, *Institutions and European Trade: Merchant Guilds, 1000–1800* (Cambridge, 2011).

Ormrod, David, *The Rise of Commercial Empires: England and the Netherlands in the Age of Mercantilism, 1650–1770* (Cambridge, 2003).

Parker, L. A., 'The agrarian revolution at Cotesbach, 1501–1612', *Transactions of the Leicestershire Archaeological Association* 24 (1948), pp. 57–71.

Peacey, Jason, 'Order and disorder in Europe: parliamentary agents and royalist thugs 1649–1650', *Historical Journal* 40, 4 (1997), pp. 953–76.

Pennington, Janet, 'Sherley , Sir Thomas (c.1542–1612)', *ODNB*.

Pettigrew, William A., *Freedom's Debt: The Royal African Company and the Politics of the Atlantic Slave Trade, 1672–1752* (Chapel Hill, 2013).

Pettigrew, William A., 'Constitutional change in England and the diffusion of regulatory initiative, 1660–1714', *History* 39 (2014), pp. 839–63.

Pettigrew, William A., 'Corporate constitutionalism and the dialogue between the global and local in seventeenth-century English history', *Itinerario*, 39 (2015), pp. 487–501.

Pettigrew, William A., and Stein, Tristan, 'The public rivalry between regulated and joint stock corporations and the development of seventeenth-century corporate constitutions', *Historical Research* 90 (2017), pp. 341–62.

Pettigrew, William A., and Van Cleve, George W., 'Parting companies: the Glorious Revolution, company power, and imperial mercantilism', *Historical Journal* 57, 3 (2014), pp. 617–38.

Pincus, Steven C. A., *Protestantism and Patriotism: Ideologies and the Making of English Foreign Policy, 1650–1688* (Cambridge, 1996).

Pincus, Steven C. A., *1688: The First Modern Revolution* (New Haven and London, 2009).

Portes, Alejandro, *Economic Sociology: A Systematic Enquiry* (Princeton and Oxford, 2010).

Posthumus, N. M., *De Nationale Organisatie der Lakenkoopers Tijdens de Republiek* (Utrecht, 1927).

Price, Jacob M., 'The tobacco adventure to Russia: enterprise, politics, and diplomacy in the quest for a northern market for English colonial tobacco, 1676–1722', *Transactions of the American Philosophical Society*, new Series, 51, 1 (1961), pp. 1–120.

Price, Jacob M., 'A revolution of scale in overseas trade: British firms in the Chesapeake trade, 1675–1775', *Journal of Economic History* 47, 1 (1987), pp. 1–43.

Quarles van Ufford, H., A Merchant-Adventurer in the Dutch Republic: *John Quarles and His Times 1596–1646/7* (Amsterdam, 1983).

Rabb, T. K., 'Sir Edwin Sandys and the parliament of 1604', *American Historical Review* 69 (1964), pp. 646–70.

Rabb, T. K., *Enterprise and Empire: Merchant and Gentry Investment in the Expansion of England, 1575–1630* (Cambridge, Mass., 1967).

Rabb, T. K., 'Free trade and the gentry in the parliament of 1604', *Past and Present* 40 (1968), pp. 165–73.

Ramsay, G. D., *English Overseas Trade during the Centuries of Emergence* (London, 1957).

Ramsay, G. D., *The Wiltshire Woollen Industry in the Sixteenth and Seventeenth Centuries* (London, 1965).

Ramsay, G. D., *The City of London in International Politics at the Accession of Elizabeth Tudor* (Manchester, 1975).

Ramsay, G. D., 'Industrial discontent in early Elizabethan London: clothworkers and Merchant Adventurers in conflict', *London Journal* 1 (1975), pp. 227–39.

Ramsay, G. D., *The English Woollen Industry, 1500–1750* (London and Basingstoke, 1982).

Ramsay, G. D., *The Queen's Merchants and the Revolt of the Netherlands* (Manchester, 1986).

Rollinson, David, *A Commonwealth of the People: Popular Politics and England's Long Social Revolution, 1066–1649* (Cambridge, 2010).

Sacks, David Harris, *The Widening Gate: Bristol and the Atlantic Economy, 1450–1700* (Berkeley and London, 1993).

Sacks, David Harris, 'Freedom to, freedom from, freedom of: urban life and political participation in early modern England', *Citizenship Studies* 11, 2 (2007), pp. 135–50.

Safley, Thomas Max, 'Business failure and civil scandal in early modern Europe', *Business History Review* 83 (2009), pp. 35–60.

Schanz, Georg, *Englische Handelspolitik gegen Ende des Mittelalters* (Leipzig, 1881).

Shagan, Ethan, *The Rule of Moderation: Violence, Religion and the Politics of Restraint in Early Modern England* (Cambridge, 2011).

Shepard, Alexandra, 'Manhood, credit and patriarchy in early modern England c.1580–1640', *Past and Present* 167, 1 (2000), pp. 75–106.

Smail, John, 'Credit, risk, and honor in eighteenth-century commerce', *Journal of British Studies* 44 (2005), pp. 439–65.

Smith, Edmond, 'The global interests of London's commercial community, 1599–1625: investment in the East India Company', *Economic History Review*, 71, 4 (2018), pp. 1118–46.

Sprunger, Keith L., *Dutch Puritanism: A History of English and Scottish Churches of the Netherlands in the Sixteenth and Seventeenth Centuries* (Leiden, 1982).

Stephens, W. B., *Seventeenth-Century Exeter: A Study of Industrial and Commercial Development, 1625–1688* (Exeter, 1958).

Stern, Philip J., *The Company-State: Corporate Sovereignty and the Early Modern Foundations of the British Empire in India* (Oxford, 2011).

Stout, Felicity, *Exploring Russia in the Elizabethan Commonwealth: The Muscovy Company and Giles Fletcher, the Elder (1546–1611)* (Manchester, 2015).

Supple, Barry, *Commercial Crisis and Change in England, 1600–4: A Study in the Instability of a Mercantile Economy* (Cambridge, 1959).

Sutton, Anne F., 'The Merchant Adventurers of England: their origins and the Mercers' Company of London', *Historical Research* 75, 1 (2002), pp. 25–46.

Sutton, Anne F., *The Mercery of London: Trade, Goods and People, 1130–1578* (Aldershot, 2005).

Taft, Barbara, 'Walwyn, William (bap. 1600, d. 1681), Leveller and medical practitioner', *ODNB*.

Talbott, Siobhan, *Conflict, Commerce and Franco-Scottish Relations, 1560–1713* (London, 2014).

Tawney, R. H., *Business and Politics under James I: Lionel Cranfield as Merchant and Minister* (Cambridge, 1958).

Te Lintum, C., *De merchant adventurers in der Nederlanden* (Den Haag, 1905).

Thrush, Andrew, 'LOWE, George (c.1569/71–1639), of the Poultry, London; later of Lime Street, London', in Andrew Thrush and John P. Ferris (eds), *The History of Parliament: The House of Commons 1604–1629* (2010), online edition [https://www.historyofparliamentonline.org/volume/1604–1629/member/lowe-george-156971-1639].

Thrush, Andrew, 'LOWE, Sir Thomas (c.1546–1623), of Broad Street, London and Putney, Surr', in Andrew Thrush and John P. Ferris (eds), *The History of Parliament: The House of Commons 1604–1629* (2010), online edition [https://www.historyofparliamentonline.org/volume/1604–1629/member/lowe-sir-thomas-1546-1623].

Tittler, Robert, *Architecture and Power: The Town Hall and the English Urban Community c.1500–1640* (Oxford, 1991).

Tittler, Robert, *Townspeople and Nation: English Urban Experiences, 1540–1640* (Stanford, 2001).

Trivellato, Francesca, *The Familiarity of Strangers: The Sephardic Diaspora, Livorno, and Cross-Cultural Trade in the Early Modern Period* (New Haven and London, 2009).

Trivellato, Francesca, 'Introduction: the historical and comparative study of cross-cultural trade', in Francesca Trivellato, Leor Haveli, and Cátia Atunes (eds), *Religion and Trade: Cross-Cultural Exchanges in World History, 1000–1900* (Oxford, 2014), pp. 1–23.

Turvey, R. K., 'NLW, roll 135: a seventeenth-century pedigree roll from Herefordshire', *Cylchgrawn Llyfrgell Genedlaethol Cymru* 30, 4 (1998), pp. 373–404.

Unwin, George, *Studies in Economic History: The Collected Papers of George Unwin*, ed. R. H. Tawney, second edition (London, 1958).

Volckart, Oliver, and Mangels, Antje, 'Are the roots of the modern *Lex Mercatoria* really medieval?', *Southern Economic Journal* 65 (1999), pp. 427–50.

Waddell, Brodie, *God, Duty and Community in English Economic Life 1660–1720* (Woodbridge, 2012).

Wallis, Patrick, 'Apprenticeship and training in premodern England', *Journal of Economic History* 68, 3 (2008), pp. 832–61.

Ward, J. P., *Metropolitan Communities: Trade Guilds, Identity, and Change in Early Modern London* (Stanford, 1997).

Wauchope, P., 'Wheeler, John (d. 1617), secretary of the Company of Merchant Adventurers', *ODNB*.

Wennerlind, Carl, *Casualties of Credit: The English Financial Revolution, 1620–1720* (Cambridge, Mass. and London, 2011).

White, Jason Cameron, 'Royal authority versus corporate sovereignty: the Levant Company and the ambiguities of early Stuart statecraft', *The Seventeenth Century* 31 (2017), pp. 231–55.

Willan, T. S., *Studies in Elizabethan Foreign Trade* (Manchester, 1959).

Wilson, Charles, 'Cloth production and international competition in the seventeenth century', *Economic History Review* 13 (1960), pp. 209–21.

Wilson, Charles, *England's Apprenticeship 1603–1763* (London, 1965).

Wilson, Charles, *Profit and Power: A Study of England and the Dutch wars* (London, 1978).

Withington, Phil, *The Politics of Commonwealth: Citizens and Freemen in Early Modern England* (Cambridge, 2005).

Withington, Phil, 'Company and sociability in early modern England', *Social History* 32 (2007), pp. 291–307.

Withington, Phil, *Society in Early Modern England: The Vernacular Origins of Some Powerful Ideas* (Cambridge, 2010).

Wood, Alfred, *A History of the Levant Company* (Oxford, 1935).

Wood, Ellen Meiksins, 'Capitalism, merchants and bourgeois revolution: reflections on the Brenner debate and its sequel', *International Review of Social History* 41 (1996), pp. 209–32.

Wrightson, Keith, 'Two concepts of order: justices, constables and jurymen in seventeenth-century England', in John Brewer and John Styles (eds), *An Ungovernable People: The English and Their Law in the Seventeenth and Eighteenth Centuries* (New Brunswick, 1980), pp. 21–46.

Wrightson, Keith, 'Mutualities and obligations: changing social relationships in early modern England', *Proceedings of the British Academy* 139 (2005), pp. 157–94.

Wubs-Mrozewicz, Justyna, 'Rules of inclusion, rules of exclusion: the Hanseatic *Kontor* in Bergen in the late Middle Ages and its normative boundaries', *German History* 29 (2011), pp. 1–22.

Wubs-Mrozewicz, Justyna, 'The medieval Hanse: groups and networks of traders. The case of the Bergen *Kontor* (Norway)', in J. A. Solórzano Telechea, M. Bochaca, and A. Aguiar Andrade (eds), *Gentes de Mar en la Cuidad Atlántica Medieval* (Logroño, 2012), pp. 213–33.

Wubs-Mrozewicz, Justyna, 'The Hanse in medieval and early modern Europe: an introduction', in Justyna Wubs-Mrozewicz and Stuart Jenks (eds), *The Hanse in Medieval and Early Modern Europe* (Leiden and Boston, 2013), pp. 1–25.

Zahedieh, Nuala, *The Capital and the Colonies: London and the Atlantic Economy 1660–1700* (Cambridge, 2010).

Zell, Michael, *Industry in the Countryside: Wealden Society in the Sixteenth Century* (Cambridge, 1994).

Zickermann, Kathrin, *Across the German Sea: Early Modern Scottish Connections with the Wider Elbe–Weser Region* (Leiden and Boston, 2013).

Zins, Henryk, *England and the Baltic in the Elizabethan Era* (Manchester, 1972).

Unpublished Doctoral Theses

Grafe, Regina, 'Northern Spain between the Iberian and Atlantic worlds: trade and regional specialization, 1550–1650', unpublished Ph.D. thesis, LSE (2001).

Newman, Elisabeth Karin, 'Anglo-Hamburg trade in the late seventeenth and early eighteenth centuries', unpublished Ph.D. thesis, LSE (1979).

Spence, Richard Turfitt, 'The Cliffords, Earls of Cumberland, 1579–1646: a study of their fortunes based on their household and estate accounts', unpublished D.Phil. thesis (London, 1959).

Name Index

Index of individuals presumed to have been Merchant Adventurers (excludes honorary members, Company employees, for instance, pastors, and office-holders not known to have actively been a member prior to election, for instance governors Sir Edward Dering and Lawrence Hyde, Earl of Rochester)

Note: Tables are indicated by an italic '*t*', respectively, following the page number.

For the benefit of digital users, indexed terms that span two pages (e.g., 52–53) may, on occasion, appear on only one of those pages.

General Index